Legal Issues of Services of General Interest

More information about this series at http://www.springer.com/series/8900

Lei Zhu

Services of General Economic Interest in EU Competition Law

Striking a Balance Between Non-economic Values and Market Competition

ASSER PRESS

Springer

Lei Zhu
Institute of International Law
Wuhan University
Wuhan, China

Legal Issues of Services of General Interest
ISBN 978-94-6265-386-3 ISBN 978-94-6265-387-0 (eBook)
https://doi.org/10.1007/978-94-6265-387-0

Published by T.M.C. ASSER PRESS, The Hague, The Netherlands www.asserpress.nl
Produced and distributed for T.M.C. ASSER PRESS by Springer-Verlag Berlin Heidelberg

This T.M.C. ASSER PRESS imprint is published by the registered company Springer-Verlag GmbH, DE part of Springer Nature.
The registered company address is: Heidelberger Platz 3, 14197 Berlin, Germany

Series Information

Services of general interest have been high on the political agenda in Europe in recent years as a result of EU liberalisation measures and the case law of the European Courts. At the heart of the debate is the question of how to balance market economies with the pursuit of public policy. Of crucial concern are questions on the role of services of general interest and other public policies essential in modern society.

The aim of the series is to sketch the framework for regulating markets and public interests in Europe and to explore the legal issues raised by developments related to services of general interest and other public policies. The series encompasses, inter alia, analyses of EU internal market and competition law, as well as EU legislation impacting particular public policies, international and domestic law, often from a comparative perspective. Sector-specific approaches will be covered as well (for instance, health, social services, energy, education, environment and communication). Furthermore, the present series also addresses the emergence of a European Social Union and will therefore raise issues of fundamental and theoretical interest in Europe and the global economy.

Series Editors

Ulla Neergaard
Faculty of Law
University of Copenhagen
Studiestræde 6
1455 Copenhagen K
Denmark
e-mail: ulla.neergaard@jur.ku.dk

Johan Willem van de Gronden
Faculty of Law
Radboud University
Comeniuslaan 4
6525 HP Nijmegen
The Netherlands
e-mail: j.vandeGronden@jur.ru.nl

Mary Guy
Law School
Lancaster University
Lancaster, LA1 4YD
UK
e-mail: m.guy2@lancaster.ac.uk

Markus Krajewski
Fachbereich Rechtswissenschaft
Universität Erlangen-Nürnberg
Schillerstraße 1
91054 Erlangen
Germany
e-mail: markus.krajewski@fau.de

Foreword

European Union (EU) law and regulation on 'services of general economic interest' (SGEI) has been evolving rapidly since the late 1980s. When the Treaty of Rome was adopted in 1957, there was strong State involvement in SGEI sectors, such as telephony, the postal service, public transportation, energy production and distribution. These areas were traditionally dominated by publicly owned undertakings, granted exclusive production and distribution rights by law, with protection from internal or external competition by State-sanctioned monopoly rights. Unlike normal market activities, these activities were regarded as public services, essential for the welfare and advancement of modern society, and their provision was guaranteed on a universal basis by the State.

This reality was largely respected, by the founders of the EU, but they did have an eye to the future when they drafted the original Article 90 EEC (now Article 106 TFEU): while that Article did provide that the Member States could grant Article 106(1) 'special and exclusive rights', the Member States had to be mindful that such grants did not lead to other rules of the Treaty being breached, such as the competition rules; furthermore, when Member States entrusted an undertaking with the performance of an Article 106(2) SGEI, the Member States still had to respect the rules of the Treaty unless the Treaty's rules would obstruct the provision of the core service whose provision was entrusted to the undertaking.

However, in practice, there was little activity pursuant to Article 106 at the EU level for the first 30 years of the EU's existence: State-created monopolies provided valuable services, on a universal basis, although their cosseted existence did inhibit new innovative competing services from coming into existence. One recalls the ban on importing telephone equipment in *RTT* by anyone except the monopolist; or the ban on providing a competing form of postal service in *Corbeau*; or the restrictive ship unloading practices in *Merci*; or the cross-subsidisation of the monopolist national postal service in *TNT Traco* by its private courier competitors to compensate it for loss of business: one could go on; the point is that while the services were provided by the State-owned monopolist, at a certain level of quality and universality, the objectionable aspects of such regimes were that the laws of the

Member States also gave the incumbent monopolists control over who else, and under what conditions, could compete against the monopolist, even in neighbouring, upstream or downstream markets, if ever.

However, the traditional model of SGEI provision, protected from competition, was not conducive to the fostering, development or promotion of innovation, for the very reason that it generally sought to prevent new services reaching the market. Also, the Member States were anxious to move many thousands of public servants off the State's payroll, so that they would no longer appear as a liability on the States' balance sheets. And, of course, the Internal Market Programme, which commenced with the Single European Act 1986, saw the start of a massive programme of harmonisation of laws to underpin the EU's Single Market Programme in the lead-up to 1992: in this environment, the straws in the wind made it clear that having national markets in SGEI sectors insulated from competition, or tolerating them controlling who else (and how) could compete against them, was past its sell-by date.

Hence, starting with key Commission Directives in the late 1980s requiring the Member States to remove national telephone monopolists' special and exclusive rights in activities outside their core telephony service activity, followed by an emergence of judgements from the European Court of Justice in Luxembourg, these once-protected sectors were sent a clear signal in the late 1980s and early 1990s that they would, quite rapidly, be transformed into competitive activities driven by an EU liberalisation programme that called for obstacles to competition and market entry to be removed in activities that fell outside of a State-entrusted area of core activity (the SGEI). This new approach called for 'greenfield' independent market entry regulators to be established, which were not to be subject to either the control or influence of the State or the SGEI monopolist. This development, with its potential to jeopardise the non-economic public service values that underpinned the traditional universal service model, naturally caused concerns for stakeholders and the Member States themselves. The key question was, how does one reconcile the introduction of market competition into areas where, traditionally, many consumers of the services do not regard the provision of such services as economic activities per se?

Article 106(2) of the TFEU Treaty, which had long lain dormant, now became the focal point in the struggle between innovation, market forces, liberalisation and the need to introduce cross-border competition, while at the same time maintaining vital services provision to all of the population in a universal manner. How does one 'square the circle' of allowing the Member States to create monopoly rights yet requiring other Treaty rules such as competition and free movement of goods and services to be respected? Slowly, but then rapidly, via a series of Court of Justice of the European Union (CJEU) judgements and EU legislation, the EU legislation shrank national monopolies' permissible scope of protected activities to the core activity, catapulting the now liberalised ancillary activities into 'competitive markets'. In this way, the notion of 'controlled liberalisation' came into being: yes, others could supply new and innovative types of telephones; yes, others could sell new types of telephones or supply new types of courier services without needing permission from the monopolist to compete against them, but at the same time the State could still require operators to respect certain public interest objectives, such as the provision of universal services such as landline telephony services, postal delivery services and public transport services.

The current EU regime was developed during this process, largely using a combination of the Internal Market legal base in the Treaty and the legal base of Article 106, with its particular brand of balancing respect for competition while acknowledging that the provision of SGEI was seen as an acceptable reason for permitting a derogation from the application of Competition Law (or indeed other Treaty rules). The focus was to ensure that the provision of SGEIs did not distort market competition in ancillary activities markets. However, in the intervening years, this mindset has already undergone some fundamental change. Access to SGEI has been recognised as a shared value of the EU and as a fundamental right of its citizens. In the new 'constitutional arrangement', maintenance of SGEI provision is arguably placed on an equal footing with competition as a core value of the EU. For this very reason, this area remains fascinating to observe, and the question continually arises: How will this area of law and policy evolve in the future?

Scholars, students, legislators, industry players and policymakers, all seeking an answer to this question, will find this book an authoritative, well-researched study for anyone seeking a deep understanding of how the law and policy in the SGEI area have evolved and how it might evolve in the future. In undertaking a learned and authoritative study of the evolution of Article 106, Dr. Lei Zhu has demonstrated in this study of sectors as diverse as postal liberalisation, the energy sector, transport liberalisation, telephony liberalisation, etc., that what is tolerable from a restriction of competition perspective, in order to maintain the provision of an SGEI, varies from sector to sector. In other words, the author has demonstrated that while there may be consistency of application of EU principles across the different sectors as they liberalise, there is, on the other hand, no uniform consistency of application of those principles to the different sectors, as liberalisation (toleration of a certain measure of competition, accompanied by a corresponding shrinkage of the area to remain protected from competition) varies from one sector to another. The author's industry, background research and clarity of writing bring often obscure arguments to a clearer understanding and help us to understand emerging SGEI trends and where they might be headed in the future. It was a pleasure to read this book, and a particular pleasure to see one's PhD student emerge as a fully fledged scholar with this magnificent contribution to enhancing our understanding of SGEIs. Illustrating how the EU has attempted to maintain a balance between the need to allow competition, on the one hand, thereby energising once-protected languid sectors by allowing citizens to benefit from the innovation that flows from liberalisation and competition, yet at the same time keeping an eye on the need to ensure citizens continue to have available to them essential services on a universal basis, this book demonstrates how such an approach allows the EU citizen to appreciate the value of the role of both the State and the greater EU project, as guarantors of both innovation and high-quality public services in the Europe of the twenty-first century.

All Souls' Day, 1 November 2018

Prof. Dermot Cahill
Chair in European Union Internal Market Law and Procurement Strategy, Institute for Competition and Procurement Studies Bangor University Law School
Wales, UK

Acknowledgements

This book is a revised version of my PhD dissertation at Bangor University in Wales, which was successfully defended in February 2015. I am very grateful to many people who have contributed, in direct or indirect ways, to this research.

My sincere appreciation goes to my lead supervisor, Prof. Dermot Cahill. With his generous and timely support, Prof. Cahill provided me with effective guidance and kept me on track when my research sometimes unknowingly drifted away from my research questions. He read each draft of my thesis and gave me detailed feedback with great care and patience. I have learnt a great deal from him about the qualities of an independent researcher: critical thinking, commitment and attention to details.

I must also express my indebtedness to my second supervisor and friend, Prof. Zhen Jing. She was always there to listen to my anxieties about the research. During our conversations, she often shared her academic experience, providing me with valuable insights. I am also grateful to other colleagues in Bangor Law School, in particular Dr. Alison Mawhinney, Mr. Howard Johnson and Dr. Mark Hyland.

I would also like to thank the external examiner, Prof. Malcolm Ross, former Head of Sussex University Law School. He provided me with critical comments and encouraged me to consider the issue from other perspectives. I also benefited from an interview with Adinda Sinnaeve, the Deputy Head of the State Aid Policy Unit in DG Competition of the European Commission, who offered valuable observations on the topic.

I would also like to mention my friends who gave me great support in various ways, in particular Ms. Elisabeth Jordan, Ms. Xiujia Wang, Dr. Xiao Ma, Dr. Rois Ni Thuama, Dr. Liangfeng Dong and Dr. Ying Yu, who were always patient and encouraging and helped cheer me up on days when inspiration was not forthcoming.

Contents

Chapter 1
Introduction

Contents

Abstract This introductory chapter places service of general economic interest (SGEI) in its broader legal context. It first traces the historical development of SGEI by outlining its increasing importance in EU law. After remaining dormant for 30 years, it began to occupy a pivotal position from the late 1980s as it provides derogation from the application of Article 106(1), justifying the "controlled liberalisation" process in sectors such as electronic communications, postal services, transport, broadcasting and energy. Its significance rose further after the Treaty of Lisbon, which endorsed SGEI as a fundamental right and grants new legislative competence to the EU. It then summarises four main themes in the academic debate concersening SGEI. It introduces the aim of this book, which is to investigate whether the right balance has been struck in the current EU regime on SGEI, and outlines the plan of this book.

Keywords service of general economic interest · market liberalisation · Europeanisation · public services · exclusive rights · state monopoly

L. Zhu, *Services of General Economic Interest in EU Competition Law*,
Legal Issues of Services of General Interest,
https://doi.org/10.1007/978-94-6265-387-0_1

1.1 Service of General Economic Interest: A Rising Star in EU Law

1.1.1 Dormant Period:[1] From the Treaty of Rome 1957 to the Late 1980s

Service of general economic interest (hereafter SGEI) is a unique EU law term that was created in the Treaty of Rome back in 1957.[2] The term itself did not exist in any of the Member States at the time. In the Treaty of Rome, it is hidden in an unnoticed corner of the competition law chapter, in the second paragraph of Article 106 TFEU.[3] It confirms that undertakings entrusted with SGEI tasks are subject to all the Treaty rules. Meanwhile, it grants a limited derogation from its application. It reads as follows:

> Undertakings entrusted with the operation of services of general economic interest or having the character of a revenue-producing monopoly shall be subject to the rules contained in the Treaties, in particular to the rules on competition, in so far as the application of such rules does not obstruct the performance, in law or in fact, of the particular tasks assigned to them. The development of trade must not be affected to such an extent as would be contrary to the interests of the Union.[4]

In the three decades following the Treaty of Rome, SGEI remained dormant and this provision was of little significance in EU law.[5] From the wording itself, it is

[1] van den Bossche and Coppieters point out that "Article 106 remained for a very long time in a genuine state of hibernation and accordingly remained unused for many years": van Den Bossche and Coppieters 1999, p. 228.

[2] Obermann et al. 2005, p. 9.

[3] Consolidated Version of the Treaty on the Functioning of the European Union [2012] OJ C326/47 (hereafter TFEU).

In the EEC Treaty it was contained in Article 90 and was renumbered as Article 86 in the EC Treaty. The text has remained essentially the same, with slight change of wording from its original version in the EEC Treaty which reads as follows:

> Any enterprise charged with the management of service of general economic interest or have the character of a fiscal monopoly shall be subject to the rules contained in this Treaty, in particular to those governing competition, to the extent that the application of such rules does not obstruct the *de jure* or de facto fulfilment of the specific tasks entrusted to such enterprise. The development of trade may not be affected to such a degree as would be contrary to the interests of the Community.

[4] Article 106(2) TFEU.

[5] Kerf explains that there are three reasons for EU's absence of actions on Article 106 during this period. First, Article 106 is extremely difficult to interpret. Second, increasing competition would lead to undesired results in certain cases. Third, the inactivity of the EU was motivated by political considerations, i.e., the resistance from the Member States. Kerf 1993. See also Pappalardo 1991; Gerber 1994; Buendia Sierra 2000.

only of a declaratory nature and does not contain any new substantive obligations for SGEI undertakings.[6] There were very few Judgments from the Court of Justice of the EU (hereafter the Court).[7] This was also reflected in the Commission's practice, which principally applied Article 101 and Article 102 to tackle anti-competitive behaviour conducted by SGEI undertakings.[8]

In addition, the Article 106(2) derogation granted for such undertakings turned out to be extremely difficult to satisfy. In the Commission's Decisions during this period, no undertakings successfully invoked this derogation from the application of competition law.[9]

1.1.2 A Revolution on the Application of Article 106[10]

The fundamental change started in 1985 when the Commission published a White Paper that set an ambitious target—to complete the Internal Market by 1992.[11] As part of its efforts to further market integration, the EU began to tackle widespread

[6] For more discussion on the literal reading of Article 106(2), see Sect. 3.4.1 of Chap. 3.

[7] Case 155/73 *Giuseppe Sacchi* [1974] ECR-409; Case 311/84 *Centre belge d'études de marché—Télémarketing (CBEM) v SA Compagnie luxembourgeoise de télédiffusion (CLT) and Information publicité Benelux (IPB)* [1985] ECR-3261; Case 66/86 *Ahmed Saeed Flugreisen and Silver Line Reisebüro GmbH v Zentrale zur Bekämpfung unlauteren Wettbewerbs e.V.* [1989] ECR-803.

[8] The Commission adopted five Decisions before 1989, including:

(1) 78/823/EEC: Commission Decision of 21 September 1978 relating to a proceeding under Article 85 of the EEC Treaty (IV/28.824—Breeders' rights —maize seed) [1978] OJ L286/23;
(2) 82/371/EEC: Commission Decision of 17 December 1981 relating to a proceeding under Article 85 of the EEC Treaty (IV/29.995—NAVEWA-ANSEAU) [1982] OJ L167/39;
(3) 82/861/EEC: Commission Decision of 10 December 1982 relating to a proceeding under Article 86 of the EEC Treaty (IV/29.877—British Telecommunications) [1982] OJ L360/36;
(4) 89/205/EEC Commission Decision of 21 December 1988 relating to a proceeding under Article 86 of the EEC Treaty (IV/31.851—Magill TV Guide/ITP, BBC and RTE) [1989] OJ L78/43;
(5) 89/536/EEC Commission Decision of 15 September 1989 relating to a proceeding under Article 85 of the EEC Treaty (IV/31.734—Film purchases by German television stations) [1989] OJ L284/36.

[9] This issue was discussed in two of its Decisions:

(1) 89/205/EEC Commission Decision of 21 December 1988 relating to a proceeding under Article 86 of the EEC Treaty (IV/31.851—Magill TV Guide/ITP, BBC and RTE) [1989] OJ L78/43;
(2) 82/861/EEC: Commission Decision of 10 December 1982 relating to a proceeding under Article 86 of the EEC Treaty (IV/29.877—British Telecommunications) [1982] OJ L360/36.

[10] Blum 2000; van der Woude 1991, p. 68; Gardner 1995.

[11] Commission of the European Communities, Completing the Internal Market (White Paper form the Commission to the European Council), COM (85) 310 final, 14.6.1985; Henry 1993, p. 45.

State intervention in the economy in a number of sectors, including telecommunications, postal services, transport, broadcasting and energy.[12]

Though the actual extent and form of State intervention differed across the Member States, common themes could be found in almost all of them.[13] The Member States had been directly involved in the actual production and delivery of these sectors, often through public undertakings under the protection of State monopolies.[14] Although the Treaty is neutral on public ownership,[15] the creation of State monopolies through the grant of exclusive rights caused concern at the EU level.

The grant of exclusive rights contradicts the principle of undistorted competition in the EU.[16] It would wipe out competition altogether, dividing sectors subjected to State-granted exclusivity along national boundaries, which would lead to *market fragmentation* rather than *integration*. Under such a regime, free movement of certain types of economic activities across the Member States would be impossible.[17] The EU intended to break down national monopolies and opened up these protected sectors to competition. The ultimate goal was to establish integrated EU Common Markets.

This created serious tensions.[18] On the one hand, competence allocation between the Member States and the EU was at stake. The organisation of these sectors (e.g., telecommunications, postal services, transport, energy and broadcasting) had been regarded as falling under the sovereign power of the Member States. The Treaty of Rome did not grant express competence to the EU regarding the organisation of these sectors. These sectors had been assumed to be outside the application of EU Internal Market law.[19] The EU's involvement in these sectors would essentially mean that rules would be decided at the EU level. This inevitably would involve competence transfer to the EU and eroded the Member States' power to organise their national economies.[20] The implications were significant: the Member States might lose their control over the organisation of a large part of their national

---

[12] For an overview of EU's market integration programme in these sectors, see Ehlermann 1993; Nomden 1997; Geradin 2006; Héritier 2001.

[13] Camenen 1996.

[14] Blum 2000; Charles et al. 2007.

[15] Article 345 TFEU provides that "the Treaties shall in no way prejudice the rules in Member States governing the system of property ownership".

[16] Article 3(f) of the EEC Treaty provides that "the institution of a system ensuring that competition in the common market is not distorted". In the EC Treaty, the wording was slightly changed, which in Article 3(g) prescribes "a system ensuring that competition in the internal market is not distorted". In the latest Lisbon Treaty, it is contained in Protocol (No 27) on the Internal Market and Competition.

[17] Ehlermann 1993.

[18] Hordijk 1995.

[19] Nomden 1997.

[20] Szyszczak 2001, p. 37.

economies and therefore their ability to pursue their preferred economic and industrial policies in these sectors.

On the other hand, these sectors had been organised based on a public service model, rather than a free competitive market one.[21] They were not regarded as normal market activities. Instead they were regarded as basic and essential services which were often linked to social and economic human rights which the State has the obligation to guarantee a universal access to for everyone in its territory.[22] Traditionally, public undertakings were established, which were owned and controlled by the State. Their activities were largely regarded as part of State functions. Profit making and efficiency were not the priority of their operations. Instead, a uniform and affordable price was charged to ensure universal availability. Introducing market competition would potentially threaten these public service values.[23]

A similar fundamental change could also be found in the Court's case law regarding the application of Article 106 over the same period.[24] Although the Court had held, in the *Sacchi* case in 1974,[25] that the Member States were free (under Article 106(1)) to create national monopolies through the grant of exclusive rights,[26] its interpretation of Article 106(1), however, changed fundamentally in 1991.[27] In that year, it delivered a series of four Judgments, ruling *inter alia* that the grant of exclusive rights by the Member States was in breach of competition law on different bases.[28] Following these Judgments, it became likely that Member State grants of exclusive rights could be susceptible to being held in breach of Article 106 (1) where the State granted exclusive rights to undertakings.[29]

---

[21] Noaksson 2005.

[22] Graham 2010.

[23] Bell 1999, p. 189.

[24] It is criticised as "judicial activism": Bright 1993; Van Der Woude 1991.

[25] Case 155/73 *Giuseppe Sacchi* [1974] ECR-409.

[26] Pescatore 1986; Blum 2000, p. 57; Prosser 1986, p. 149.

[27] Gerber 1994; Gyselen 2010, p. 494.

[28] In 1991, the Court delivered four Judgments on the interpretation of Article 106(1), including:

(1) Case C-41/90 *Klaus Höfner and Fritz Elser v Macrotron GmbH* [1991] ECR I-1979;
(2) Case C-18/88 *Régie des Télégraphes et des Téléphones v GB-Inno-BM SA* [1991] ECR I-5941;
(3) Case C-260/89 *Elliniki Radiophonia Tileorassi AE (Ert) (Panellinia Omospondia Syllogon Prossopikou Ert intervening) v Dimotiki Étairia Pliroforissis (Dep) and Sotirios Kouvelas (Nicolaos Avdellas and Others intervening)* [1991] ECR I-02925;
(4) Case C-179/90 *Merci Convenzionali Porto di Genova SpA v Siderurgica Gabrielli SpA* [1991] ECR I-05889.

[29] In these cases, the concern of the Court was the distortive effects of exclusive rights. The Member States were found in breach of Article 106 even though no actual abusive behaviour had been committed by undertakings. Broberg and Fenger 1995, p. 369; Bacon 1997, p. 285; Blum 2000, p. 65.

In addition, the Court largely expanded the Commission's power under Article 106(3).[30] In the *France v Commission* in 1991, the Court upheld the Commission's power to issue *liberalisation Directives*.[31] These Directives created new obligations for the Member States, and were not confined within its executive functions as (for example) in the Transparency Directive.[32]

The implications of the case law were far-reaching.[33] Potentially the Commission could use its power under Article 106(3) to require the Member States to abolish all exclusive rights in a number of once protected sectors because they would be very easily found in breach of Article 106(1).[34] Allied to technological advances in areas such as telecommunications, this dramatically altered the organisation of national economies, given the fact that State monopolies were still widespread in the Member States then.

It is against these fundamental changes in the interpretation of Article 106(1) and (3) that the Court began to in parallel apply the SGEI derogation to the Member States from the application of competition law. In the famous *Corbeau* case in 1993, the Court ruled that Article 106(2) permits the grant of exclusive rights by the Member States in so far as restrictions on competition, or even the exclusion of all competition, are necessary to ensure the performance of SGEI tasks under economically acceptable conditions.[35]

1.1.3 The Constitutionalisation of SGEI[36]

The fundamental change in the application of Article 106 by the Commission and the Court caused a lot of concern to the Member States and created much controversy. It triggered a wider debate in EU law and also in academic circles.[37] The interpretation and application of Article 106, in particular its second paragraph on SGEI, became the centre of the debate. This was reflected in the rising status of SGEI in the Treaty, from merely a once unremarkable derogation in competition law to one having significant constitutional implications.

---

[30] Gardner 1995, p. 84.

[31] Case C-202/88 *French Republic v Commission of the European Communities* [1991] ECR I-1223.

[32] Gómez-Barroso and Marbán-Flores 2013.

[33] Ehlermann 1993; Van Der Woude 1991; Kerf 1993; Hordijk 1995.

[34] Sauter 1999, p. 154; Scott 2000, p. 310.

[35] Case C-320/91 *Paul Corbeau* [1993] ECR I-2533.

[36] Prechal points out that "Article 16 may be considered as a first step in the process of constitutionisation of the service of general interest". Prechal 2008, p. 67.

[37] Sauter 2008.

As a direct result of this debate,[38] a new Article 16 on SGEI was added to the EC Treaty in 1993. The ambiguity of the wording[39] of this Article shows the very controversy surrounding SGEI:

> Without prejudice to Articles 73, 86, 87, and given the place occupied by services of general economic interest in the *shared values* of the Union as well as their role in promoting *social and territorial cohesion*, the Community and the Member States, *each within their respective powers* and *within the scope of application of this Treaty*, shall take care that such services operate on the basis of principles and conditions which enable them to fulfil their missions.[40]

The real legal significance of Article 16 in practice seems limited.[41] But it gives SGEI a sound position in the EU legal order: SGEI is not merely an exemption clause in EU competition law any more.[42] It has been recognised as a fundamental value and basic principle of the EU,[43] arguably on an equal footing with the notion of undistorted competition in Internal Market.[44]

The rising status of the "constitutional" importance of SGEI did not stop here. In 2000, the EU Charter of Fundamental Human Rights endorsed SGEI as a fundamental human right. Article 36 of the Charter provides that:

> The Union recognises and respects access to services of general economic interest as provided for in national laws and practices, in accordance with the Treaty establishing the European Community, in order to promote the social and territorial cohesion of the Union.[45]

The constitutional significance of SGEI was reinforced by the Treaty of Lisbon, which entered into force in 2009. It incorporated the Charter into the Treaty, making it legally binding upon the EU and its Member States.[46]

An even more significant development in the Treaty of Lisbon was that, for the first time, it granted the EU an explicit competence in the area of SGEI. A new legislative competence was added to the end of Article 16 EC to form the new Article 14 TFEU. It reads as follows:

> The European Parliament and the Council, acting by means of regulations in accordance with the ordinary legislative procedure, shall establish these principles and set these

---

[38] Sauter 2008.

[39] Van De Walle 2008.

[40] Article 16 TFEU.

[41] Krajewski 2008, p. 379; Behrens 2001; Sole 2003, p. 341.

[42] Van Den Bossche and Coppieters 1999.

[43] Ross 2004; Héritier 2001, p. 829.

[44] Kenny 2009; Prosser 2005, p. 553.

[45] Article 36, Charter of Fundamental Human Rights of the European Union [2012] OJ C326/391.

[46] Article 6 (1) TEU provides that "the Union recognises the rights, freedoms and principles set out in the Charter of Fundamental Rights of the European Union of 7 December 2000, as adopted at Strasbourg, on 12 December 2007, which shall have the same legal value as the Treaties": Consolidated Version of the Treaty on European Union [2012] OJ C326/13 (hereafter TEU).

conditions without prejudice to the competence of Member States, in compliance with the Treaties, to provide, to commission and to fund such services.[47]

Equally important was the incorporation of a Protocol on Service of General Interest (hereafter SGI) to the Lisbon Treaty.[48] As an over-arching concept,[49] it covers both SGEI and non-economic service of general interest (hereafter NSGI).[50] The Protocol confirmed that the Member States' sole competence was in the area of NSGI. Meanwhile, it elaborated the "shared values" of SGEI in very vague terms.[51]

After the Treaty of Lisbon, a new important question arose: how to distinguish SGEI from NSGI. This issue was not theoretical. It had very significant constitutional implications: only in the area of SGEI had the Treaty granted the EU a new legislative competence. The EU has not adopted legislation based on Article 14. It remains to be seen how this power will be used in the future. What is certain is that its application would be a very controversial issue in EU law.

1.2 SGEI—An Area Full of Controversy

From the late 1980s, SGEI has begun to attract much attention from scholars.[52] Since then, a considerable amount of literature has been produced.[53] Though commentators have reached agreement on certain issues, it seems that more disagreements still remain. This section surveys the main issues in the discussion of SGEI and provides the very context of this book.

---

[47] Article 14 TFEU.

[48] Protocol (No 26) on Service of General Interest, TEU.

[49] The term "service of general interest" is a late arrival. Before the Lisbon Treaty, it was only used by the Commission in its Communications which have no binding effect at all: Commission of the European Communities, Service of General Interest in Europe (Communication from the Commission) COM (96) 43 final, 11.09.1996; Commission of the European Communities, Service of General Interest in Europe (Communication from the Commission) [2001] OJ C17/04.

[50] Houben 2008, pp. 7–11.

[51] Article 1 of the Protocol lists the shared values of SGEI, which include:

- the essential role and the wide discretion of national, regional and local authorities in providing, commissioning and organising services of general economic interest as closely as possible to the needs of the users;
- the diversity between various services of general economic interest and the differences in the needs and preferences of users that may result from different geographical, social or cultural situations;
- a high level of quality, safety and affordability, equal treatment and the promotion of universal access and of user rights.

Protocol (No 26) on Service of General Interest, TEU.

[52] The earliest commentary on Article 106 was published in 1965: Deringer 1965, p. 129.

[53] The focus of the literature has been evolving with the development of the EU law, in particular the case law of the Court. It seems that three stages could be roughly distinguished.

1.2.1 The Issue of Definitions

Controversy in this area is largely caused by the lack of proper definition in EU law.[54] Though SGEI has been used in EU law since the Treaty of Rome in 1957, it has not been defined anywhere in the Treaty, or in secondary legislation.[55] In the literature, almost every word of the term itself has been subjected to scrutiny and examination.[56]

First, what is of an "economic nature", a "general interest" or a "service"? It seems that agreement has been reached. It is the service, not the interest involved, which is of an "economic nature". Buendia Sierra points out that "it is more appropriate to speak of '*economic* service of general interest' than of 'service of general *economic* interest'".[57] This is confirmed by the fact that the Court frequently refers to "general interest", rather than "general economic interest".[58]

Second, the term "service" is also misleading. In the context of free movement law, it was crucial to make a distinction between goods and services, because they are subject to different sets of rules. However, this distinction does not make much difference in competition law because the same set of rules applies. In the context of

---

(1) Before 1990, the attention of the discussion was not on Article 106, but on the application of Articles 101 and 102 to the Member States. See for example Marenco 1983; Pescatore 1986; Lang 1989.

(2) From 1990, the focus of the scholars began to shift to the application of Article 106. See for example Slot and Hancher 1990; Van Der Woude 1991; Ehlermann 1993; Kerf 1993; Gardner 1995; Hordijk 1995; Broberg and Fenger 1995; Bacon 1997; Bartosch 1999; Blum 2000.

(3) From 2000, SGEI has begun to attract much attention from commentators. See for example Van Den Bossche and Coppieters 1999; Szyszczak 2001; Napolitano 2005; Krajewski 2008; Ross 2009; Karayigit 2009; Fiedziuk 2011.

[54] Houben 2008, p.10; Kronenberger 2001, p. 301; Sauter 2008, p. 174.

[55] Karayigit 2009, p. 576.

[56] This situation is well-summarised by a report requested by the European Parliament, which reads as:

> Semantically, each word of this term of SGEI is difficult to define as such. And the concept as such – or is it the activity that is meant? – poses real linguistic and terminological difficulties, since it can be understood as an organic structure as a whole, as a national prerogative, as a requirement imposed on the service or a means to achieve general interest.

Obermann et al. 2005.

[57] Buendia Sierra 2000, p. 278.

[58] See for example, Case T-289/03 *British United Provident Association Ltd (BUPA), BUPA Insurance Ltd and BUPA Ireland Ltd v Commission of the European Communities* [2008] ECR II-8; Szyszczak 2001, p. 39.

SGEI, the Court did not pay much attention to the service nature of SGEI, instead it has recognised certain non-service activities as SGEI, such as the supply of electricity.[59]

It seems that agreement has stopped here and more crucial questions surrounding the definition remain unsettled. The first one is how to distinguish SGEI of an economic nature, from a non-economic SGI (NSGI). This question has become constitutionally important after the Treaty of Lisbon. In the area of SGEI, the EU has gained new legislative competence. By contrast, in the area of NSGI, the Member States still have exclusive power.[60] Attempts have been made to clarify this issue; however, no satisfying answers have yet emerged.[61]

A more intriguing question is what constitutes a *general interest*, i.e., the content and scope of SGEI.[62] Reference is often made to the case law. Commentators have compiled a list of all tasks that have been recognised by the Court in its Judgments.[63] The problem with this approach is that the Court has never defined SGEI in general terms. Instead, its case law is ad hoc, often made in the preliminary proceeding dealing with a specific national situation. Therefore, they hardly have any general application effect.

In this respect, different approaches have been proposed by scholars. Sauter argues that a market failure should be adopted as the benchmark. He believes that only the existence of market failure justifies the creation of an SGEI task.[64] The problem with this approach is that the notion of market failure is not a settled issue.[65]

A definition is found in the Commission's Communication. It defines SGEIs as "market services which the Member States subject to specific public service obligations by virtue of a general interest criterion".[66] This definition is even more problematic.[67] First, it avoids tackling the essential question: what constitutes a legitimate general interest in EU competition law? Second, its reference to public service obligation (hereafter PSO) creates further questions. PSO has been used in the Common Transport Policy of the Treaty itself[68] and also in secondary

[59] Case C-393/92 *Municipality of Almelo and others v NV Energiebedrijf Ijsselmij* [1994] ECR I-1477; Deringer 1965, p. 129.

[60] Protocol (No 26) on Services of General Interest, TFEU.

[61] See for example Neergaard 2009.

[62] Behrens 2001.

[63] Buendia Sierra 2000, p. 282; Auricchio 2001, p. 67.

[64] He argues that "it is likewise proposed here that only where markets, in the absence of governmental action, would fail, it will be possible to meet the EU law standard of necessity (proportionality) that is required to successfully invoke the EU law concepts of SGEI and universal service". Sauter 2008.

[65] Schwintowski 2003; Walsh 1995, pp. 6–12.

[66] Commission of the European Communities, Service of General Interest in Europe (Communication from the Commission) COM (96) 43 final, 11.09.1996.

[67] Kronenberger 2001, pp. 301, 319.

[68] Article 93 TFEU provides that "aids shall be compatible with this Treaty if they represent reimbursement for the discharges of certain *obligations inherent in the concept of a public service*".

legislation in sectors like transport[69] and energy.[70] By contrast, in the telecommunications[71] and postal services sectors,[72] the term "universal service obligation" (hereafter USO) has been used as its counterpart. Here arises the puzzling question: what is the relationship between these terms?[73] Third, it suggests that it is the Member State that has the freedom and competence to decide what constitutes a SGEI in the first place. In this respect, Buendia Sierra points out that there is a division between the "national approach" and "Community approach": the former is based on the idea that "Member States were totally free to choose those public services which they wished to provide their citizens with", while the latter "insisted on the possibility of the Community institutions having the power to examine the actual legitimacy of the public interest ends pursued by the Member States".[74]

The reality is far from straightforward. There is no clear-cut boundary in terms of *competence allocation* on this issue.[75] The Treaty affirms that SGEI is an area of shared value and shared competence of the EU and the Members.[76] EU law increasingly had more influence in the organisation of SGEI. Notable examples are found in sectors such as the telecommunications, postal services, transport and in the area of state aid law where regulatory frameworks have been established at EU level.[77] Therefore, it is worth carefully examining how much freedom is left to Member States, and how much competence has been transferred to the EU.

---

[69] Regulation (EC) No 1008/2008 of the European Parliament and of the Council of 24 September 2008 on common rules for the operation of air services in the Community [2008] OJ L293/3; Regulation (EC) No 1370/2007 of the European Parliament and of the Council of 23 October 2007 on public passenger transport services by rail and by road and repealing Council Regulations (EEC) Nos 1191/69 and 1107/70 [2007] OJ L315/1; Council Regulation (EEC) No 3577/92 of 7 December 1992 applying the principle of freedom to provide services to maritime transport within Member States (maritime cabotage) [1992] OJ L364/7.

[70] Directive 2009/72/EC of the European Parliament and of the Council of 13 July 2009 concerning common rules for the internal market in electricity and repealing Directive 2003/54/EC [2009] OJ L211/55; Directive 2009/73/EC of the European Parliament and of the Council of 13 July 2009 concerning common rules for the internal market in natural gas and repealing Directive 2003/55/EC [2009] OJ L211/94.

[71] Directive 2002/22/EC of the European Parliament and of the Council of 7 March 2002 on universal service and users' rights relating to electronic communications networks and services [2002] OJ L108/51.

[72] Directive 97/67/EC of the European Parliament and of the Council of 15 December 1997 on common rules for the development of the internal market of Community postal services and the improvement of quality of service [1998] OJ L15/14.

[73] Simmonds points out that "the difference between these two terms—universal service obligations and public service obligations—has proven to be confusing and is often misconceived". Simmonds 2003, p. 2.

[74] Buendia Sierra 2000, p. 280; Ross 2009, p. 127.

[75] Hancher and Larouche point out that "the dividing lines between European and national regulation are no longer clear-cut but where a choice for a more co-operative and multi-layered approach is evident". Hancher and Larouche 2010, p. 43.

[76] Article 14 TFEU.

[77] Cseres 2008.

In response to this chaos and confusion, scholars proposed that the EU should adopt comprehensive legislation to list all SGEIs.[78] However, the Commission is very unlikely to undertake this initiative: it has pointed out this is not a desirable choice because the concept of SGEI is dynamic and evolving.[79] Consequently, the debate on the issue of definition will continue.

1.2.2 The Application of Article 106 and the Proportionality Test

Article 106 has been at the heart of this debate.[80] The reason lies in the fact that most cases on SGEI have been discussed in the context of Article 106. In addition, the complex structure and the ambiguity of the text mean that it is very difficult to apply and interpret.[81] This difficulty had been pointed out by scholars as far back as 1965.[82]

What is worthy of special attention in the first place, is the fact that Article 106(1) is not necessarily linked with SGEI.[83] Article 106(1) deals with a specific type of measure of the Member States—the grant of exclusive rights and special rights, which has anti-competitive effects. Therefore, it forms an important component of the EU competition law system. On this issue, the case law has been criticised as inconsistent.[84] Edward analysed the case law of the Court and argued that four different approaches were used by the Court to decide the compatibility of exclusive rights.[85] He found that the limited sovereign/competition law approaches prevailed

---

[78] For a review of proposals and initiatives, see for example: Krajewski 2008; Rodrigues 2009; De Vries 2008.

[79] Commission of the European Communities, White Paper on Services of General Interest (Communication from the Commission to the European Parliament, the Council, the European Economic and Social Committee and the Committee of the Regions), COM (2004) 374 final, 12.5.2004, p. 11.

[80] Szyszczak 2001, pp. 35–42.

[81] Hordijk 1995, p. 595.

[82] Deringer 1965. See also Slot and Hancher 1990; Marenco 1983; Kerf 1993.

[83] Van Der Woude 1991; Marenco 1983, p. 502.

[84] Szyszczak 2001, p. 45.

[85] These approaches are: absolute sovereignty, absolute competition, limited sovereignty and limited competition. They differ in the extent of freedom that the Member States enjoy in creating exclusive rights. The absolute sovereignty approach is that the Member States have total freedom in this respect. By contrast, the absolute competition approach argues that the principle of undistorted competition shall apply to its full extent and the Member Stats are prohibited from granting exclusive rights. The limited sovereignty/competition approaches are in the middle, which recognise the power of the Member States in this respect is limited by competition law and vice versa. Edward and Hoskins 1995.

and became the norm, which meant that the Member State had limited freedom to grant exclusive rights.[86]

The crucial question is to what extent and in what circumstances this freedom has been limited. It is generally agreed that it is very likely that the grant of exclusive rights by the Member States would be found incompatible with the Treaty.[87] Some scholars even go further to argue that the case law on Article 106(1) means that the grant of exclusive right is illegal per se.[88]

This is when SGEI derogation under Article 106(2) comes into play. In the famous *Corbeau* case, the Court ruled that restriction of competition (even its exclusion) is allowed *if it is necessary for the provision of an SGEI task under economically acceptable conditions*.[89] Its implications are significant: Article 106 (2) is the only derogation in EU competition law that is available to justify the grant of exclusive rights by the Member States.

Scholars agree that this is essentially *a proportionality test*.[90] But its application is not straightforward and turns out to be very controversial.[91] The reason lies in the fact that the Court has not explained how this proportionality test shall be applied. The application of the proportionality test involves two essential issues. First, what constitutes valid SGEI, and how its content and scope are decided (again this goes back to the issue of definition). Second, what level of scrutiny should be applied in this proportionality test? Scholars have pointed out that different versions of the proportionality test are used in EU law.[92] For example, in the *free movement context*, a very strict test has been used, which involves comparing State measures against other alternatives to find the least restrictive one.[93]

In the context of Article 106(1), the proportionality test has been translated to *evaluate the compatibility of exclusive rights*.[94] On this issue, the case law of the Court has not been consistent.[95] In most cases, it would leave its application to national courts in the preliminary ruling.[96] In other cases where the Court did apply this proportionality test, it often reached its conclusion without clarifying what standard was applied. Its ad hoc approach hardly has any general application effect.

---

[86] Ibid.

[87] Sauter 1999, p. 51.

[88] Bacon 1997, p. 285; Gardner 1995, p. 79.

[89] Case C-320/91 *Paul Corbeau* [1993] ECR I-2533.

[90] Blum 2000; Behrens 2001; Auricchio 2001.

[91] Sierra points out that "the interpretation of the principle of proportionality has become the main legal-political battleground in the field of Article 106 and one of the most controversial areas of Community law". Buendia Sierra 2000, p. 300. See also Nomden 1997; Schwintowski 2003.

[92] Kenny 2009; Kronenberger 2001, p. 320.

[93] Lang 1989, p. 125; Soriano 2003.

[94] Auricchio 2001, p. 73.

[95] Szyszczak 2001; Prosser 1986, p. 132.

[96] See for example Case C-393/92 *Municipality of Almelo and others v NV Energiebedrijf Ijsselmij* [1994] ECR I-1477, para 50; Scott 2000.

1.2.3 Public Services, Liberalisation and Europeanisation

The EU's competence in the area of SGEI was only granted in the Treaty of Lisbon, which has not been used until now. However, this does not mean that the EU has no involvement on this issue. On the contrary, rules have been developed, not based on the EU's explicit competence, but in the market liberalisation and integration process from late 1980s in sectors like telecommunications, postal services, transport, broadcasting and energy.[97]

These sectors had been organised based on a public service model in the Member States, rather than as competitive markets.[98] Here lies the very historical root of SGEI and Article 106. It is generally agreed that SGEI corresponds to the notion of public service,[99] which can be found in the traditions of almost all Member States.[100]

More precisely, Damjanovic and De Witte link SGI[101] with a broad notion of welfare services.[102] They make a crucial distinction between, on the one hand, core welfare services such as public health, public education and social assistance and on the other hand, services provided by public utilities such as public broadcasting, basic telecommunications services, basic postal services, electricity and gas, public transport, waste disposal, water and sanitation, etc. The latter, which constitutes the outer ring of the welfare services, was exactly what SGEI in the original Treaty of Rome in 1957 referred to.

---

[97] Nomden 1997; Rodrigues 2009; Houben 2008.

[98] Camenen 1996; Keune et al. 2008; Walsh 1995, Chap. 1; Van Den Bossche and Coppieters 1999.

[99] Freedland and Sciarra 1998; Szyszczak 2001, p. 55; Louri 2002, p. 168; Scott 2000; Kociubiński 2011.

[100] The notion of public service is particularly strong in France. Bell points out that "public service is a central concept in French public law". Bell 1999, p. 189.

The same argument is also made by Dreyfus. He submits that "the notion of *service public* is old and firmly enshrined in the French legal order". Dreyfus 2009.

By contrast, the idea of public service is much weaker and defined in a loose manner in Britain. Prosser 1986, 2000, 2005.

Van de Walle argues that "in a country such as France, the concept of *service public* has served as the basic framework for discussing the provision of services. No such concept exists in common law, but the concept of 'common callings' shows some similarities". Van De Walle 2008, p. 261.

[101] The concept of SGI (service of general interest) is a relatively new arrival in the Treaty. It was first used by the Commission in its Communications. The concept was adopted by the Lisbon Treaty in its 26th Protocol. As an over-arching concept, it covers SGEI and NSGI. However, it is not clearly defined anywhere in the Treaty or in secondary legislation. See Sect. 2 of Chap. 2

[102] Damjanovic and De Witte 2009. See also Boeger 2010; Sole 2003.

In this respect, in 1996 the European Parliament published a report titled "Public Undertakings and Public Service Activities in the European Union".[103] It surveyed the organisation of these sectors and showed how operations in these sectors were determined and controlled by public authorities in the Member States for the public interest.[104] It demonstrated how the State intervened in these sectors and organised them based on a public service model. The establishment of public undertakings and the grant of exclusive rights[105] was widely used as a means to protect these public service values.[106] This explains why seemingly unrelated concepts, i.e., public undertakings, exclusive rights and SGEI, are contained in one Article: they are inextricably linked.

Since the late 1980s, State intervention in the economy and the public service model began to lose favour across the Member States.[107] The organisation of these sectors was transformed through profound reforms, which were usually labelled as *privatisation, liberalisation/deregulation and commercialisation.*[108] This process has been widely discussed by commentators in economics,[109] politics[110] and law.[111]

---

[103] Camenen 1996.

[104] See also Winter 1951.

[105] Geradin identifies three reasons for the existence of state monopoly in network industries, including:

> (1) There was a belief that such industries were natural monopolies; [...] (2) Monopolies were often granted in return of the monopolist to provide universal service, also often referred to as public services of services of general economic interest; [...] and (3) Because of the importance of these industries from several viewpoints governments believed it was important to consolidate them in one firm, which they controlled.

Geradin 2006.

[106] Bell 1999.

[107] Broberg and Fenger 1995, p. 370; Ehlermann 1993, pp. 67–68; Kenny 2009; Geradin 2006, p. 2.

[108] Jacobi and Kowalsky identified three driving forces for this fundamental change, including:

(1) The understanding of the State has changed right across the political spectrum to the effect that the core business of the State is the provision of sovereign services; (2) Private companies are increasingly thronging to the market for SGI, which is regarded as a lucrative one; and (3) By means of the Single Market the market for SGI has also been Europeanised and so made subject to the general competition regulations of the EU. Jacobi and Kowalsky 2002. See also Keune et al. 2008; Sauter 1999, p. 143.

[109] See for example Tanzi 1997; Stewart and Walsh 1992; Walsh 1995; Henry 1993; Defeuilley 1999; Millward 2011.

[110] See for example Majone 1997; Héritier 2001; Campbell 2002; Charles et al. 2007.

[111] See for example Szyszczak 2001; Simmonds 2003.

The EU's market liberalisation and integration efforts from the late 1980s contributed to this process.[112] While EU law is neutral on the question of public ownership,[113] *the grant* of exclusive rights is in conflict with the fundamental value of the EU—an Internal Market where economic activities can move across borders freely, and where competition is not distorted. From late 1980s, EU legislation began to require the Member States to abolish these exclusive rights.

This is generally regarded as liberalisation. The term "liberalisation" itself is somewhat misleading because liberalisation does not mean the market is totally liberal without any restriction or regulation.[114] In this context, *liberalisation* refers to *the abolishing of sectoral exclusive rights* and *the opening up of these sectors to competition*.[115] This is followed by sector specific rules which set up new regulatory frameworks for the organisation and regulation of these sectors.[116] In this respect, Vogel rightly argues "freer market, more rules".[117]

This process has been described as a process of Europeanisation, under which rules are increasingly made at EU level.[118] It is through this process that EU law began to lay down rules on SGEI, through the notion of PSO or USO.[119] EU sector specific regimes on universal telecommunication services,[120] universal postal

[112] Slot and Skudder 2001.

[113] Article 345 TFEU.

[114] Brooks 2009; Geradin 2006, p. 14.

[115] Martin et al. 2005, p. 6; Van Den Bossche and Coppieters 1999, p. 229.

[116] Behrens 2001; Rott 2005.

[117] Vogel 1998.

[118] Ross 2004; Szyszczak 2001; Jacobi and Kowalsky 2002, p. 186; Napolitano 2005.

[119] Nagy argues that "universal service is central to the European thinking on markets and public services and is an inevitable element of market liberalisation and sectoral competition rules". Nagy 2013, p. 1731.

Napolitano points out that "the growing Europeanisation of the public utilities legal order is becoming manifest in the way in which the new law harmonises service and shapes the nature, power and procedures of the national regulatory authorities". He also argues that "the process is nevertheless still incomplete; […] The European legal order is only partially capable of maintaining and reinforcing the fragile construction of a new regime for public utilities within national regulations". Napolitano 2005, p. 567.

[120] Article 3(1) of Directive 2002/22 provides that "Member States shall ensure that the services set out in this Chapter are made available at the quality specified to all end-users in their territory, independently of geographical location, and, in the light of specific national conditions, at an affordable price": Directive 2002/22/EC of the European Parliament and of the Council of 7 March 2002 on universal service and users' rights relating to electronic communications networks and services [2002] OJ L108/51.

services,[121] public transport services,[122] have been the subject of intense discussion.[123] The focus has been on their definition, scope and funding mechanisms.[124]

Commentators also point out that this is essentially a *political process*, where conflicting interests are balanced.[125] The first is surrounded with *competence allocation*, i.e., the Member States' power to decide how to organise their national economies and the EU's competence to promote its values and principles (market competition and market integration).[126] The second is that the EU is concerned with values, i.e., economic values through market competition, and *non-economic* values embedded in the notion of public services and citizenship.[127]

SGEIs has been at the centre of this balancing exercise because: (1) the SGEI concept allows the Member States to such a derogation from the ongoing liberalisation process;[128] and (2) SGEI also justifies the restriction of competition where non-economic values are being promoted.[129] Therefore, Prosser argues that SGEI reflects the notion of citizenship, which has been incorporated as an equally important value (efficiency) in EU competition law.[130] Some even go further, associating SGEI with basic and fundamental human rights.[131]

---

[121] Article 3(1) of Directive 97/67 provides that "Member States shall ensure that users enjoy the right to a universal service involving the permanent provision of a postal service of specified quality at all points in their territory at affordable prices for all users": Directive 97/67/EC of the European Parliament and of the Council of 15 December 1997 on common rules for the development of the internal market of Community postal services and the improvement of quality of service [1998] OJ L15/14.

[122] In the transport sector, SGEI is defined through the notion of PSO. For example, in the maritime transport sector, PSO is defined as "obligations which the Community ship owner in question, if he were considering his own commercial interest, would not assume or would not assume to the same extent or under the same conditions": Regulation (EEC) No 3577/92 of 7 December 1992 applying the principle of freedom to provide services to maritime transport within Member States [1992] OJ L364/7.

[123] For an overview of SGEIS in different sectors, see Cseres 2008; Noaksson 2005; Simmonds 2003; Hall 2001.

[124] Graham 2010; Rott 2005; Sole 2003.

[125] Ross points out that the principle of solidarity has a key role to play on two fundamental questions: (1) the relationship between social and market values, and (2) competence allocation between the EU and Member States. Ross 2010.

[126] Krajewski 2008.

[127] Ross 2004; Houben 2008; Behrens 2001; Auricchio 2001; Simmonds 2003; Jacobi and Kowalsky 2002, p. 191; Scott 2000, p. 312; Héritier 2001, p. 826; Bruijn and Dicke 2006; Gyselen 2010.

[128] Szyszczak 2001, p. 77.

[129] Nomden 1997; Kenny 2009, p. 25; Houben 2008; Soriano 2003.

[130] Prosser 2005.

[131] Graham 2010, p. 157; Prechal 2008.

1.2.4 SGEI Funding and the Application of EU State Aid Rules

The application of EU state aid rules to SGEI funding came to the attention of EU law only from the late 1990s. This issue often arose because the legality of such measures was challenged before national courts (which then referred such cases to the Court) or the Commission became involved. At the beginning of the twenty-first century, this became a hotly debated issue in the Court, with different approaches being proposed.[132] Since then, the case law of the Court and the Commission's practice have been the subject of much discussion by commentators.

The root of the controversy lies in the fact that the Treaty itself contains no explicit rules on how SGEI funding will be treated under EU state aid regime. The first pressing issue is *the issue of definition*, i.e., whether SGEI funding constitutes state aid in the first place. The stakes are high: if it is categorised as state aid, the Member States have the obligation to notify such measures to the Commission, and to standstill until the Commission has made decision on its compatibility.

On this issue, scholars point out that the Court's case law had been divided between the so-called *state aid approach/compensation approach*.[133] The issue was settled in its landmark *Altmark* Judgment.[134] The Court ruled that SGEI funding does not constitute state aid if it satisfies four conditions.[135] This was the so-called *Altmark* criteria. It was welcomed by scholars because it clarified this very controversial issue. However, the *Altmark* criteria, in particular its fourth condition, has also been criticised by commentators, because its application creates various uncertainties.[136]

Another important issue was how the compatibility of SGEI funding should be evaluated under EU state aid law. This is when the SGEI derogation under Article

[132] Case C-53/00 *Ferring SA v Agence centrale des organismes de sécurité sociale (ACOSS)* [2001] ECR I-09067; Case C-126/01 *Ministère de l'Économie, des Finances et de l'Industrie v GEMO SA* [2003] ECR I-13769.

[133] The key question is whether funding for SGEI constitutes state aid. If it is regarded as state aid, it falls within the scope of EU state aid law and the Member States have the obligation to notify and standstill. On the other hand, if it does not constitute state aid, it is outside the scope of EU state aid control regime. Sinnaeve 2003.

[134] The central issue in the case was whether subsidy granted by local authority in Germany for the provision of public bus service constituted state aid: Case C-280/00 *Altmark Trans GmbH and Regierungspräsidium Magdeburg v Nahverkehrsgesellschaft Altmark GmbH, and Oberbundesanwalt beim Bundesverwaltungsgericht* [2003] ECR I-7747.

[135] These conditions are: (1) there must be clearly defined public service obligations; (2) the parameters for compensation must be established in advance in an objective and transparent manner; (3) compensation cannot exceed what is necessary to cover all or part of the costs incurred in the discharge of public service obligations, taking into account the relevant receipts and a reasonable profit for discharging those obligations; and (4) compensation shall be determined through a public procurement procedure or on the basis of the costs of a typical and well run undertaking: Ibid.

[136] Travers 2003, p. 387; Bartosch 2003.

106(2) comes into play.[137] This has triggered more problems, because Article 106 (2) overlaps with the first three conditions of the *Altmark* criteria. Their relationship has generated much controversy.[138]

Equally important is the Commission's practice. The Commission has developed its rules for the application of state aid rule to SGEI funding, notably the *Monti* package in 2005,[139] which has been replaced by the *Almunia* package in 2012.[140] It has also adopted specific sets of rules for sectors such as maritime transport,[141]

---

[137] The Court has long established that for the SGEI derogation to apply, three conditions must be met: (1) there must be a clearly defined SGEI task; (2) the SGEI task must have been entrusted by public authorities; and (3) a proportionality test must be satisfied: Case C-320/91 *Paul Corbeau* [1993] ECR I-2533. In the context of state aid law, the issue was first discussed by the Court in the *FFSA* case: Case T-106/95 *Federation Française des Societes d'Assurances (Ffsa) and Others v E.C. Commission* [1997] ECR II-229.

[138] Ross 2004; Nicolaides 2003; Klasse 2013.

[139] It is named after the Commissioner who was responsible for competition. The "Monti Package" includes:

(1) Commission Decision of 28 November 2005 on the application of Article 86(2) of the EC Treaty to state aid in the form of public service compensation granted to certain undertakings entrusted with the operation of services of general economic interest [2005] OJ L312/67;
(2) Community framework for state aid in the form of public service compensation [2005] OJ C297/4;
(3) Commission Directive 2005/81/EC amending Directive 80/73EEC on the transparency of financial relations between Member States and their public undertakings as well as on financial transparency within certain undertakings [2005] OJ L312/47.

[140] It is named after the Commissioner who was responsible for competition. The "Almunia package" contains:

(1) Communication from the Commission on the application of the European Union state aid rules to compensation granted for the provision of services of general economic interest [2012] OJ C8/4;
(2) Commission Decision of 20 December 2011 on the application of Article 106(2) of the Treaty on the Functioning of the European Union to state aid in the form of public service compensation granted to certain undertakings entrusted with the operation of services of general economic interest [2012] OJ L7/3;
(3) Communication from the Commission, European Union framework for state aid in the form of public service compensation [2012] OJ C8/15;
(4) Commission Regulation (EU) No 360/2012 of 25 April 2012 on the application of Articles 107 and 108 of the Treaty on the Functioning of the European Union to *de minimis* aid granted to undertakings providing services of general economic interest [2012] OJ L114/8.

[141] The Commission first adopted Guidelines in 1997. After the *Altmark* case, the Commission updated its Guidelines, and also adopted a Communication interpreting the application of Regulation 3577/92 which also contains rules on the application of state aid rules on SGEI funding:

(1) Community guidelines on state aid to maritime transport [1997] OJ C205/5;
(2) Community guidelines on state aid to maritime transport [2004] OJ C13/3;
(3) Commission of the European Communities, Communication on the interpretation of Council Regulation (EEC) No 3577/92 applying the principle of freedom to provide services to maritime transport within Member States, COM (2003) 595 final, 22.12.2003.

public service broadcasting[142] and broadband.[143] Meanwhile, it has adopted significant number of Decisions applying these rules to SGEI funding.[144] The Commission's practice has attracted much attention from commentators.[145] The focus has been on the Commission's approach on two key issues in the application of state aid rules to SGEI funding: (1) the application of the *Altmark* criteria to examine whether SGEI funding *constitutes* state aid; and (2) the application of the SGEI derogation under Article 106(2) to decide whether SGEI funding is *compatible* with the Treaty.

1.3 Research Question and Chapter Plan

The concept of SGEI lies at the intersection between the state and the market. It concerns some basic and essential services that the state has the obligation to guarantee universal access, thus closely associated with citizenship rights and political identity. It is the state that defines, organises and funds the provision of SGEIs in pursuit of non-economic general interest. On the other hand, SGEIs are provided on the market, thus economic in nature. State intervention into the market for the purpose of SGEI may have adverse impact on market competition. This book contributes to the debate by examining whether the right balance has been struck in EU law between the non-economic values of SGEI embedded in the concept of citizenship and the economic values underlying the principle of undistorted market competition.

The book contains eight chapters. This chapter is the introduction. Chapter 2 addresses the issue of definitions. It traces the very historical root of SGEI and SGI. It argues that the concept of SGI corresponds to the notion of state functions, i.e., what functions the state undertakes. This question lies at the heart of sovereignty, which explains the very controversial nature of this issue. It then focuses on the non-economic and economic distinction of SGI in EU competition law. The Court has adopted a functional approach by looking at whether the exercise of public

[142] The Communication was first adopted in 2001 and then updated in 2009:

(1) Commission of the European Communities, Communication from the Commission on the application of state aid rules to public service broadcasting [2001] OJ C320/5;
(2) Commission of the European Communities, Communication from the Commission on the application of state aid rules to public service broadcasting [2009] OJ C257/1.

[143] The Commission Guidelines were first adopted in 2009 and then updated in 2013:

(1) Commission of the European Communities, Community Guidelines for the application of state aid rules in relation to rapid deployment of broadband networks [2009] OJ C235/7;
(2) Commission of the European Communities, EU Guidelines for the application of state aid rules in relation to the rapid deployment of broadband networks [2013] OJ C25/1.

[144] The Commission's Decisions are examined in Sects. 4.3 and 4.4 of Chap. 4.

[145] Sauter 2012; Sauter and Van de Gronden 2011; Bovis 2005; Lynskey 2007.

power is involved. In the area of social insurance, it referred to the principle of solidarity as the benchmark for such distinction. By identifying certain activities as non-economic, NSGIs are excluded from the scope of EU competition law. This essentially isolates them from the market liberation effect and the economic logic of EU competition rules, which will safeguard the non-economic values of NSGI provision.

Chapter 3 deals with the grant of exclusive right under Article 106. The provision of SGEI was often organised under a monopolistic structure through the grant of exclusive right by the Member States. Such measure is inherently anti-competitive because it eliminates market competition, which would naturally cause concern from the EU. The compatibility of exclusive right is covered by Article 106. This research reveals the fundamental change in the interpretation of Article 106 at the beginning of the 1990s. The Court developed doctrines, which ruled that in certain circumstances, the grant of exclusive rights by the Member States was incompatible with Article 106(1). It also largely expanded the Commission's power under Article 106(3). As a result, the grant of exclusive right increasingly comes under the scrutiny of competition law. Against this background, the Court held that restriction or even the exclusion of competition is allowed if it is necessary for the provision of SGEI under economically acceptable conditions.

The application of state aid rules to SGEI funding is discussed in Chap. 4. The provision of SGEI is often not commercially viable under normal market conditions and requires financial support from the state. This chapter examines the interplay between EU state aid rules and SGEI. The essence is still a balancing exercise. On the one hand, rules need to be developed at the EU level to ensure that funding does not distort market competition by exceeding what is strictly necessary for the provision of SGEI. On the other hand, the application of EU state aid rules should not obstruct or disrupt the provision of SGEIs.

The following three chapters (Chaps. 5–7) examine how a balance has been struck at the EU level in three sectors, i.e., telecommunications, postal services and transport. During liberalisation, SGEI derogation allows the maintenance of certain exclusive rights by the Member States (this is the notion of controlled/gradual liberalisation). This research finds that the pace of liberalisation varied across sectors, which essentially meant that the proportionality test has been applied differently across the sectors. Following market liberalisation, SGEI provision justifies State intervention for the provision of SGEI, in order to accommodate *non-economic values in competitive markets*. Chapter 8 sets out the conclusions of this book.

References

Auricchio V (2001) Services of general economic interest and the application of EC competition law. World Competition 24(1):65–91

Bacon K (1997) State regulation of the market and EC competition rules: Articles 85 and 86 compared. European Competition Law Review 18(5):283–291

Bartosch A (1999) EC Telecommunications Law: what aid does Article 90(2) of the EC Treaty offer to the former monopolists. Computer and Telecommunications Law Review 5(1):12–15
Bartosch A (2003) Clarification or confusion? How to reconcile the ECJ's rulings in Altmark and Chronopost? European State Aid Law Quarterly 2(3): 375–386
Behrens P (2001) Public services and the internal market – an analysis of the Commission's communication on services of general interest in Europe. European Business Organisation Law Review 2(4):469–492
Bell J (1999) France: the concept of public service under threat from Europe? An illustration from energy law. European Public Law 5(2):189–198
Blum F (2000) The recent case law of the European Court of Justice on state monopolies and its implication for network industries. Journal of Network Industries 1(1):55–87
Boeger N (2010) Public service, autonomy and community law. In: Nickel R (ed) Conflict of laws and laws of conflict in Europe and beyond: patterns of supranational and transnational juridification. Intersentia Publishing, Antwerp
Bovis CH (2005) Public service obligations in the transport sector: the demarcation between state aids and services of general interest under EU Law. European Business Law Review 16 (6):1329–1347
Bright C (1993) Article 90, Economic policy and the duties of member states. European Competition Law Review 14(6): 263–272
Broberg MP, Fenger N (1995) National organisation of regulatory powers and community competition law. European Competition Law Review 16(6):364–375
Brooks MR (2009) Liberalization in maritime transport. www.internationaltransportforum.org/2009/.../ws1-Brooks.pdf
Bruijn HD, Dicke W (2006) Strategies for safeguarding public values in liberalized utility sectors. Public Administration 84(3):717–735
Buendia Sierra JL (2000) Exclusive rights and state monopolies under EC Law: Article 86 (formerly Article 90) of the EC Treaty, Oxford University Press, Oxford
Camenen FX (1996) Public undertakings and public service activities in the European Union. (European Parliament, Directorate General for Research, Working document, Economic Affairs Series, W - 21) http://www.europarl.europa.eu/workingpapers/econ/pdf/w21_en.pdf
Campbell RM (2002) The politics of postal transformation: modernizing postal systems in the electronic and global world. McGill Queens University Press, Montreal
Charles MB, Dicke W, Koppenjan J, Ryan N (2007) Public values and safeguarding mechanisms in infrastructure policies: a conceptual and theoretical exploration. http://eprints.qut.edu.au/9283/1/PT_Infrastructure_Charles%2520Dicke%2520Koppenjan%2520Ryan.pdf
Cseres KJ (2008) What has competition done for consumers in liberalised markets? The Competition Law Review 4(2):77–121
Damjanovic D, De Witte B (2009) Welfare integration through EU Law: the overall picture in the light of the Lisbon Treaty. In: Neergaard UB et al (eds) Integrating welfare functions into EU Law: From Rome to Lisbon. DJØF Publishing, Copenhagen
De Vries SA (2008) Harmonization of services of general economic interest: where there's a will there's a way! In: Van de Gronden J (ed) The EU and WTO law on services: limits to the realization of general interest policies within the services markets? Kluwer Law International, Alphen aan den Rijn
Defeuilley C (1999) Competition and public service obligations: regulatory rules and industries games. Annals of Public and Cooperative Economics 70(1):25–48
Deringer A (1965) The interpretation of Article 90 (2) of the E.E.C. Treaty. Common Market Law Review 2(2):129–138
Dreyfus M (2009) France. In: Krajewski M, Neergaard U (eds) The changing legal framework for services of general interest in Europe: between competition and solidarity. T.M.C. Asser Press, The Hague
Edward D, Hoskins M (1995) Article 90: Deregulation and EC Law. Reflections arising from the XVI FIDE conference. Common Market Law Review 32(1):157–186

Ehlermann CD (1993) Managing monopolies: the role of the state in controlling market dominance in the European Community. European Competition Law Review 14(2):61–69

Fiedziuk N (2011) Services of general economic interest and the Treaty of Lisbon: opening doors to a whole new approach or maintaining the 'status quo'. European Law Review 36(2):226–242

Freedland M, Sciarra S (eds) (1998) Public services and citizenship in European law: public and labour law perspectives. Oxford University Press, Oxford

Gardner A (1995) The Velvet Revolution: Article 90 and the triumph of the free market in Europe's regulated sectors. European Competition Law Review 16(2):78–86

Geradin D (2006) Twenty years of liberalization of network industries in the European Union: where do we go now? http://papers.ssrn.com/sol3/papers.cfm?abstract_id=946796

Gerber DJ (1994) The transformation of European Community Law? Harvard International Law Journal 35(1):97–138

Gómez-Barroso JL, Marbán-Flores R (2013) Basic financial services: a new service of general economic interest? Journal of European Social Policy 23(3):332–339

Graham C (2010) Social-economic rights and essential services: a new challenge for the regulatory state. In: Oliver D, Prosser T, Rawlings R (eds) The regulatory state: constitutional implications. Oxford University Press, Oxford

Gyselen L (2010) Services of general economic interest and competition under European Law – a delicate balance. Journal of European Competition Law & Practice 1(6):491–499

Hall D (2001) EU competition policies and public services. http://www.psiru.org/sites/default/files/DHepsuConfFinal.doc

Hancher L, Larouche P (2010) The coming age of EU regulation of network industries and services of general economic interest. (Tilburg Law and Economics Center Law and Economics Discussion Paper No. 2010–024). http://papers.ssrn.com/sol3/papers.cfm?abstract_id=1628573

Henry C (1993) Public service and competition in the European community approach to communications networks. Oxford Review of Economic Policy 9(1):45–66

Héritier A (2001) Market integration and social cohesion: the politics of public services in European regulation. Journal of European Public Policy 8(5):825–852

Hordijk EP (1995) EC law versus legal monopolies: a tense relationship. International Business Law Journal 11 (5):595–614

Houben I (2008) Public service obligations: moral counterbalance of technical liberalization legislation? European Review of Private Law 16(1):7–27

Jacobi O, Kowalsky W (2002) Regulated and controlled liberalisation: a means to reconcile market efficiency and social cohesion? Transfer: European Review of Labour and Research 8(2):185–197

Karayigit MT (2009) The notion of service of general economic interest revisited. European Public Law 15(4):575–595

Kenny M (2009) Freezing the state out of the market: the three degrees of state incapacity in Europe. http://www.jura.uni-bremen.de/lib/download.php?file=0abf581818.pdf&filename=wp7_2009.pdf.

Kerf M (1993) The policy of the Commission of the E.E.C. toward national monopolies – an analysis of the measures adopted on the basis of Article 90 § 3 of the E.E.C. Treaty. World Competition 17(1):73–111

Keune M, Leschke J, Watt A (2008) Privatisation and liberalisation of public services in Europe: an analysis of economic and labour market impacts. European Trade Union Institute

Klasse M (2013) The impact of Altmark: the European Commission case law responses. In: Szyszczak E, Van de Gronden JW (eds) Financing services of general economic interest: reform and modernization. T.M.C. Asser Press, The Hague

Kociubiński J (2011) Services of general economic interest – towards a European concept of public services. Wroclaw Review of Law, Administration and Economics 1(2):49–64

Krajewski M (2008) Providing legal clarity and securing policy space for public services through a legal framework for services of general economic interest: squaring the circle? European Public Law 14(3):377–398

Kronenberger V (2001) A model of the transformation process of statutory monopolies in European Community law: from practice to theory. European Business Organization Law Review 2(2):301–338

Lang JT (1989) European Community competition law and member state action. Northwestern Journal of International Law & Business 10(1):114–132

Louri V (2002) "Undertaking" as a jurisdictional element for the application of EC competition rules. Legal Issues of Economic Integration 29(2):143–176

Lynskey O (2007) The application of article 86(2) EC to measures which do not fulfil the Altmark criteria; institutionalising incoherence in the legal framework governing state compensation of public service obligations. World Competition 30(1):153–168

Majone G (1997) From the positive to the regulatory state: causes and consequences of changes in the mode of governance. Journal of Public Policy 17(2):139–167

Marenco G (1983) Public sector and community law. Common Market Law Review 20(3):495–527

Martin R, Roma M, Vansteenkiste I (2005) Regulatory reforms in selected EU network industries. Occasional Paper Series No. 28 https://www.ecb.europa.eu/pub/pdf/scpops/ecbocp28.pdf

Millward R (2011) Public enterprise in the modern western world: an historical analysis. Annals of Public and Cooperative Economics 82(4):375–398

Nagy CI (2013) The metamorphoses of universal service in the European telecommunications and energy sector: a trans-sectoral perspective. German Law Journal 147(9):1731–1756

Napolitano G (2005) Towards a European legal order for services of general economic interest. European Public Law 11(4):565–581

Neergaard U (2009) Services of general economic interest: the nature of the beast. In: Krajewski M, Neergaard U, Van de Gronden J (eds) The changing legal framework for services of general interest in Europe: between competition and solidarity. T.M.C. Asser Press, The Hague

Nicolaides P (2003) Compensation for public service obligations: the floodgates of state aid? European Competition Law Review 24(11):561–573

Noaksson N (2005) Taking stock of the liberalization of public utilities: can structural reforms bring the Lisbon Strategy back on track? European Trade Union Institute for Research, Education, Safety and Health, November 2005. http://www.epsu.org/IMG/pdf/EPSU_Network_Industries_final_version_Nov05.pdf

Nomden K (1997) Reconciling liberalisation and public service obligations. EIPASCOPE, 1997 (1): 1–6.

Obermann G, Hall D, Sak B (2005) Services of general interest in the internal market. http://www.pedz.uni-mannheim.de/daten/edz-ma/ep/05/pe358.357-en.pdf

Pappalardo A (1991) State measures and public undertakings: Article 90 of the EEC Treaty Revisited. European Competition Law Review 12(1):29–39

Pescatore P (1986) Public and private aspects of European Community Competition Law. Fordham International Law Journal 10(3):373–419

Prechal S (2008) Fundamental rights as limits to the liberalisation of service markets. In: Van de Gronden J (ed) The EU and WTO Law on services: limits to the realization of general interest policies within the services markets? Kluwer Law International, Alphen aan den Rijn

Prosser T (1986) Nationalised industries and public control. Basil Blackwell, Oxford/New York

Prosser T (2000) Public service law: privatization's unexpected offspring. Law and Contemporary Problems 63(4):63–82

Prosser T (2005) Competition law and public services: from single market to citizenship rights. European Public Law 11(4):543–563

Rodrigues S (2009) Towards a general framework instrument related to SGEI? Political considerations and legal constraints. In: Krajewski M, Neergaard U (eds) The changing legal framework for services of general interest in Europe: between competition and solidarity. T.M. C. Asser Press, The Hague

Ross M (2004) The Europeanization of public services supervision: harnessing competition and citizenship? Yearbook of European Law 23(1):303–319

Ross M (2009) A healthy approach to services of general economic interest? The BUPA judgment of the court of first instance. European Law Review 34(1):127–140

Ross M (2010) Solidarity – a new constitutional paradigm for the EU? In: Ross M, Borgmann-Prebil Y (eds) Promoting solidarity in the European Union. Oxford University Press, Oxford

Rott P (2005) A new social contract law for public services? – consequences from regulation of services of general economic interest in the EC. European Review of Contract Law 1(3):323–345

Sauter W (1999) Competition law and industrial policy in the EU. Clarendon Press, Oxford

Sauter W (2008) Services of general economic interest and universal service in EU Law. European Law Review 33(2):167–202

Sauter W (2012) The Altmark Package Mark II: new rules for state aid and the compensation of services of general economic interest. European Competition Law Review 33(7):307–313

Sauter W, Van de Gronden J (2011) State aid, services of general economic interest and universal service in healthcare. European Competition Law Review 32(12):615–620

Schwintowski HP (2003) The common good, public subsistence and the functions of public undertakings in the European internal market. European Business Organisation Law Review 4 (3):353-382

Scott C (2000) Services of general interest in EC Law: matching values to regulatory technique in the public and privatised sectors. European Law Journal 6(4):310–325

Simmonds G (2003) Universal and public service obligations in Europe. Consumer Representation in Europe Policy and Practice for Utilities And Network Industries, Research Report 15. http://www.bath.ac.uk/management/cri/pubpdf/Research_Reports/15_Simmonds.pdf

Sinnaeve A (2003) State financing of public services: the court's dilemma in the Altmark case. European State Aid Law Quarterly 2(3):351–364

Slot PJ, Skudder A (2001) Common features of community law regulation in the network-bound sectors. Common Market Law Review 38(1):87–129

Slot VP, Hancher L (1990) Article 90. European Competition Law Review 11(1):35–39

Sole D (2003) Services of general economic interest in the EU: a 50-year-battle between liberalization, deregulation and subsidiarity. European Journal of Law Reform 5(3–4):335-341

Soriano LM (2003) How proportionate should anti-competitive state intervention be? European Law Review 28(1):112–123

Stewart J, Walsh K (1992) Change in the management of public services. Public Administration 70 (4):499–518

Szyszczak E (2001) Public service provision in competitive markets. Yearbook of European Law 20(1): 35–77

Tanzi V (1997) The changing role of the state in the economy: a historical perspective. www.imf.org/external/pubs/ft/wp/wp97114.pdf

Travers N (2003) Public service obligations and state aid: is all really clear after Altmark? European State Aid Law Quarterly 2(3):387–393

Van De Walle S (2008) What services are public? What aspects of performance are to be ranked? The case of "service of general interest". International Public Management Journal 11(3):256–274

Van Den Bossche AM, Coppieters S (1999) Service of general interest: a challenge for European economic integration. In: Meeusen W (ed) Economic policy in the European Union: current perspectives. Edward Elgar Publishing Ltd, Cheltenham

Van Der Woude M (1991) State intervention: Article 90: competing for competence. European Law Review Supp (Competition Law Checklist):60–80
Vogel S (1998) Freer markets, more rules: regulatory reform in advanced industrial countries. Cornell University Press, New York
Walsh K (1995) Public services and market mechanisms: competition, contracting and the new public management. Palgrave Macmillan, London
Winter C (1951) Parliamentary, ministerial, and judicial control of nationalized Industries in Great Britain. Law and Contemporary Problems 16(4):670–701

Chapter 2
SGI: An EU Expression of State Functions

Contents

Abstract This chapter probes into the different terms associated with service of general economic interest (SGEI), including service of general interest (SGI) and non-economic service of general interest (NSGI). It argues that SGI corresponds to the notion of state functions in the national context, i.e. what functions the state undertakes. It lies at the heart of national sovereignty, which explains the controversial nature of the issue. This chapter focuses, secondly, on the distinction between economic and non-economic service of SGI. This is a prerequisite for competition law to apply. It takes a closer look at the case law and finds that the Court has not adopted the potentiality test as a criterion for the demarcation, as argued by some scholars. Instead, the Court has followed the functional approach by looking at whether the exercise of public power is involved. By identifying certain activities as non-economic, NSGIs are excluded from the scope of EU competition law. This essentially isolates them from the market liberation effect and the economic logic of EU competition rules, which will safeguard the non-economic values of NSGI provision.

L. Zhu, *Services of General Economic Interest in EU Competition Law*,
Legal Issues of Services of General Interest,
https://doi.org/10.1007/978-94-6265-387-0_2

Keywords service of general interest · non-economic service of general interest · economic and non-economic distinction · welfare services · functional approach · potentiality test · solidarity

2.1 Introduction

This chapter examines different concepts in the debate, including SGI, SGEI and NSGI. Although these concepts have been used in the Treaty, they are not defined therein or in secondary legislation. The concept of SGEI has been in the Treaty since the adoption of the Treaty of Rome in 1957. By contrast, the concept of SGI is a relatively new arrival. It was incorporated into the Treaty after the Lisbon Treaty. As an overarching concept, SGI covers both SGEI (which is economic in nature) and NSGI (which is non-economic in nature).

The economic and non-economic distinction is of crucial importance. First, it decides whether or not EU competition law is applicable. In other words, it is the precondition for EU competition law to apply. While SGEIs are subject to EU competition law, NSGIs falls outside its scope because of its non-economic nature. Second, it dictates whether the EU has legislative competence. After the Lisbon Treaty, the EU has been granted a new legislative competence in the area of SGEI.[1] Meanwhile, regarding NSGI, the Member States still retain exclusive competence.[2]

The first part of this chapter argues that the concept of SGI refers to the notion of state functions. Traditionally, it is the Member State that has the absolute power to decide what constitutes general interest (or public interest in national contexts) and how to achieve them. This is the very idea of national sovereignty.[3] The key issue is how a particular society is organised. At the heart of the issue is what functions are performed by the State. This is essentially a political question, the answer to which depends on a wide range of economic, political, cultural and even ideological factors.[4] Even within one State, it also evolves over time. This diversity is reflected

---

[1]Article 14 TFEU provides that:

> Without prejudice to Articles 73, 86, 87, and given the place occupied by services of general economic interest in the shared values of the Union as well as their role in promoting social and territorial cohesion, the Community and the Member States, each within their respective powers and within the scope of application of this Treaty, shall take care that such services operate on the basis of principles and conditions which enable them to fulfil their missions.

[2]Article 2 of the Protocol (No 26) on Service of General Interest, TEU, provides that "the provisions of the Treaties do not affect in any way the competence of Member States to provide, commission and organise non-economic services of general interest".

[3]Ferrera 2005.

[4]Schweitzer 2011.

in different traditions and models for the provision of public services and welfare services in the Member States.

This research adopts a historical research method and finds that the historical roots of these concepts lie in the great expansion of State functions in Europe during the years after World War II. It shows how the State organised these functions based on very different models from that of a competitive market. On the one hand, States across Europe began to directly intervene in the economy by controlling and managing certain sectors. This had been the case in the telecommunications, postal services, transport, broadcasting and energy sectors. They had been organised based on a public service model, rather than as market activities. Public undertakings were established under the ownership and control of the State. They were used by the State to pursue a wide range of public interests. Private competition was impossible in the face of the grant of statutory monopoly and the lack of commercial freedoms.[5] This reality was reflected in Article 106 and the concept of SGEI.

On the other hand was the development of the welfare State, i.e. the provision of certain welfare services by the State to its citizens, including public health, public education and different forms of social assistance. They were not regarded as normal market activities but as social goods,[6] associated with basic human rights. Therefore, the State had the responsibility to guarantee their provision to everyone in society.[7] This is the ideal of universal service, which lies at the heart of public services and welfare provision. This research uses the organisation of public health systems as an example to show how NSGI is based on a very different model from that of a competitive market.[8]

The second part of this chapter focuses on the economic and non-economic distinction of SGI. This research finds that there has been a strong *assumption* of the economic nature of SGEI in the Treaty and in the case law. The Court often assumed the economic nature of SGEI without paying attention to the distinct national arrangements. This approach is found in the telecommunications,[9] postal services,[10] transport,[11] and broadcasting sectors.[12] This approach paved the way for

---

[5]EU market integration programme has transformed these sectors into competitive markets.

[6]Saltman and Figueras 1997; Sauter 2013; The High Level Committee on Health (2001) The internal market and health services. http://ec.europa.eu/health/ph_overview/Documents/key06_en.pdf.

[7]Hervey 2011a.

[8]Sauter 2011.

[9]Case C-18/88 *Régie des Télégraphes et des Téléphones v GB-Inno-BM SA* [1991] ECR I-5941.

[10]Case C-320/91 *Paul Corbeau* [1993] ECR I-2533.

[11]Joined Cases 209 to 213/84 *Criminal proceedings against Lucas Asjes and others, Andrew Gray and others, Andrew Gray and others, Jacques Maillot and others and Léo Ludwig and others* [1986] ECR 1425.

[12]Case C-260/89 *Elliniki Radiophonia Tileorassi AE (Ert) (Panellinia Omospondia Syllogon Prossopikou Ert intervening) v Dimotiki Étairia Pliroforissis (Dep) and Sotirios Kouvelas (Nicolaos Avdellas and Others intervening)* [1991] ECR I-02925.

the application of EU competition law to SGEIs, which has had far-reaching implications for the organisation of SGEIs.

By contrast, regarding *the welfare functions* of the State, the Court has been more cautious. The research found that the Court has not adopted the so-called *potentiality test*. Instead, it used *the principle of solidarity* to exclude the organisation of public healthcare systems from EU competition law. In this way, the EU respects national political choices regarding the organisation of national public healthcare systems and excludes them from the application of competition law.

2.2 The Historical Root and Complexities of SGI

2.2.1 The Essence of SGI

The term SGI is a relatively new arrival in the Treaty; it was incorporated into the primary EU law by the Lisbon Treaty in its Protocol (No 26) on Service of General Interest. The wording of the Protocol merely suggests that as an overarching concept, which covers both SGEI and NSGI.[13] However, the term SGI itself has not been defined anywhere in the Treaties, or in secondary legislation.

In fact, the term SGI was largely a creation by the Commission. It was first used by a Commission Communication in 1996;[14] since then it has been used in different Communications by the Commission.[15] The Commission defines it by reference to its subject matter—the pursuit of general interest—and covers all activities for such aims, both economic and non-economic in nature. While the former refers to SGEI in EU law, non-economic SGI activities cover two categories of State activities. The Commission has not given a precise definition but only some examples:

(1) prerogatives of the State, 'such as ensuring internal and external security, the administration of justice, the conduct of foreign relations and other exercise of official authority';
(2) services such as national education and compulsory basic social security schemes.[16]

Such a definition is not satisfactory. It avoids the essential question: why are these activities are of general interest? An even more important issue in the EU law context is, who has the competence to decide what constitutes general interests in the first place, the Member States or the EU?

[13]Craig 2010, p. 303; Neergaard 2009, p. 21.

[14]Commission of the European Communities, Service of General Interest in Europe (Communication from the Commission), COM (96) 43 final, 11.09.1996; Hatzopoulos 2009.

[15]Fiedziuk 2011.

[16]Commission of the European Communities, Service of General Interest in Europe (Communication from the Commission) [2001] OJ C17/04, paras 27–29.

It is submitted that the term SGI corresponds to the notion of State functions, in other words, what functions the State undertakes.[17] This is an ancient question that each society needs to answer. The solution varies across the Member States, which is essentially a political question decided in a political process. It involves value judgments and the balance of different interests at stake. In modern Member States, it is reached through a democratic process, which offers a platform for public debate and compromise. The results largely depend on the national context, where economic, political and cultural factors all play a role. Therefore, the actual extent and organisation often vary across the Member States.

In this respect, a clear pattern could be observed across all Member States. Traditionally, State functions were at a minimum level. They were largely confined within the area of external and internal security,[18] or, in the Commission's words, 'prerogatives of the State'. This lies at the core of State functions. However, the years after World War II witnessed a great expansion of State functions in two respects. First, the provision of welfare services, under which the State had the responsibility to provide certain welfare services for all citizens, such as public education, public health services and social assistance.[19] They began to be incorporated as part of State functions, organised by public authorities and funded through State revenue. Second, the State stepped into the economy through direct control and management of key areas of national economy, such as the telecommunications, postal service, transport and energy sectors. These are the idea and realities of mixed economy, which are reflected in Article 106.

The organisation and delivery of state function is not static, but evolves over time. Such a process is largely influenced by dominant ideologies and political economic theories and thinking of the time, and equally constrained by fiscal and financial considerations. For example, the 1990s marked the beginning of the retreat by the Member States from the direct management of some areas of the economy and their transformation into competitive markets under the broad theme of liberalisation and deregulation. Also, many countries introduced reforms into their public service sectors to improve efficiency and quality under the approach of new public management.[20]

To decide what functions the State undertakes is at the core of national sovereignty. In this respect, it is the Member States that have dominant influence over how these activities are organised. The Member States have adopted different models and logics from that of the market, which will be the focus of the following two sections. The EU's involvement in SGEI would inevitably erode the power and autonomy of the Member States. Meanwhile, applying EU Internal Market law,

---

[17]Damjanovic and De Witte 2009.

[18]External security mainly concerns territorial defence. Internal security relates to the maintenance of order and law enforcement. Borre and Goldsmith 1995.

[19]Though welfare service began to emerge from the end of 19th century, it was only after World War II that a welfare system with extensive coverage took shape.

[20]Hammerschmid et al. 2019.

which is based on the principle of free market and undistorted competition, would potentially challenge and disrupt the operation of SGEI. This is the very reason why the application of competition law to SGI creates serious tensions and conflicts.

2.2.2 SGEI: State Intervention in Economies

The term 'SGEI' was first adopted in the Treaty of Rome in 1957. However, while the term itself had not existed in any Member State, it reflected the economic realities across Member States of that time: a mixed economy where the State undertook a positive role in providing certain products and services.[21] Facing the devastation of World War II, governments across Europe expanded their activities through strong and direct involvement in the economy.[22] This often happened in sectors that were regarded as the commanding heights or as being of strategic importance to national economies, such as energy, railways, electricity and air transport. This had become the consensus after World War II right until the late 1970s.

While the actual extent, justification and organisation structure varied across Member States, some common themes were widespread across Member States.[23] The first was the establishment of public undertakings where the State had a dominant influence over their operations. The second was the creation of monopolies through national legislation in a number of sectors, such as telecommunications, postal services and broadcasting.[24] Third, Member States used these public undertakings to pursue a wide range of objectives not necessarily linked to efficiency and profit making.[25] This explains why seemingly unrelated concepts, such as public undertakings, exclusive rights and undertakings, entrusted with SGEIs are contained in the same Article 106.

It is in this context that the term SGEI was created by the drafters of the Rome Treaty. It did not use traditional national concepts such as public service or public utilities in order to avoid confusion. But the term itself has generated much confusion because it is poorly constructed without a proper definition.

---

[21] Allum 1995, Chapter 1.

[22] Several factors contribute to the development of the realities of mixed economy. The first is the impact of World War II, which ruined the economies of Europe. Facing the lack of private capital and fearing the advance of communism, the State also had no other choice but to organise the reconstruction. The second element lies in the shadow of the Great Depression, which had resulted in the disbelief of market mechanism itself. Thirdly, the planned economy model in the Soviet with impressive development seemed an attractive alternative. Yergin and Stanislaw 1998, Chapter 1.

[23] Majone 1997.

[24] Millward 2008, p. 172.

[25] Allum divides national economies into three sectors: competitive sector, monopoly sector, and State sector. Allum 1995, p. 32.

First, by using 'general economic interest', it has created the impression that there are two groups of general interests, economic and non-economic. However, this is not the case from either a theoretical or a practical perspective. European States intervened in the economy on a wide range of objectives, including economic and non-economic ones, at the same time.[26] It is often difficult, and even impossible, to detect and to distinguish one from another.

This is the very case in the organisation of the telecommunications and postal service sectors. They were organised under a different model from that of a market. Public operators in these sectors did generate a considerable amount of profit. However, profit making and efficiency had never been their top priority. Instead, national governments had been using them to promote a wide range of industrial and economic objectives, including infrastructure development, promotion of employment innovation and research.

What is purely non-economic was the ideal of universal service. Basic telecommunications and postal services were associated with basic human rights, and the State had the responsibility to guarantee its provision for everyone in its society. In order to promote universal access, prices were set by public authorities at an affordable level and at a uniform rate. This was contrary to market principles.

It has been suggested that this term is better framed as 'economic service of general interest'.[27] This implies the economic nature of the organisation of these sectors because they are 'typically provided in some kind of market with payment at point of use'. However, what is also worthy of attention is that the essential features of market mechanisms were absent under state intervention in a mixed economy: (1) state control and restraints often led to the lack of commercial freedom; (2) the grant of exclusive right effectively eliminated competition from other operators, and also the possibility of consumer choice; (3) pricing was often decided by public authorities and did not necessarily reflect the costs of providing such services.

It is submitted, therefore, that the concept of SGEI was closely linked to the expansion of State functions into direct control and management of the national economies after World War II. Essentially, it was a political choice decided in a national political process, regarding the structure and organisation of their economies.[28]

---

[26]Cruz 2005.

[27]Buendia Sierra 2000, p. 278; Office of Fair Trading (2004) Services of general economic interest exclusion. Competition Law Guideline, December. http://www.oft.gov.uk/shared_oft/business_leaflets/ca98_guidelines/oft421.pdf, p. 10.

[28]Borre and Viegas 1995.

2.2.3 *Public Healthcare Systems in the Member States*

In the late 19th century European States had already begun to take measures to look after the welfare of citizens, which marked the very beginning of the welfare State. However, it was only after World War II that modern comprehensive welfare systems took shape. The actual extent and organisation of welfare provision differs across the Member States. It is not within the scope of this study to undertake a comprehensive and detailed survey, so this section provides an overview of the public healthcare systems in the Member States and shows how welfare provision is organised based on a model completely different from that of a competitive market.

The key rationale behind the organisation of public health systems is the sharing of both financial and health risks among individuals within a particular society.[29] This is reflected in the principles of *solidarity, equal access and universal coverage* in the organisation of the public healthcare system.[30] It is based on the connecting factors between individuals and a particular State, including employment, residence or citizenship. Once such elements are established, individuals are required to contribute to the financing of the healthcare system through taxation or social insurance contribution.[31] In return, individuals are entitled to receive free healthcare service or reimbursement of healthcare costs. Essentially, it is a triangular relationship involving healthcare financing and provision, which are the key components of public healthcare systems.[32] The structure is illustrated in Fig. 2.1.

Roughly speaking, Member States have developed three distinct models for the organisation of public health systems, combining different mechanisms for healthcare funding and provision.[33] The first model is the so-called *Beveridge* system,[34] notably in the UK. Under this system, major funding for healthcare services is raised though general taxation, which is then allocated to the managing body, NHS trusts. Healthcare services are then provided free of charge to residents by hospitals that are directly owned and managed by NHS trusts. Or in the case of primary care, services are also provided free of charge by general practitioners under contracts with the State.

In the second model, major funding is raised through compulsory contribution to social insurance funds, which would then provide reimbursement for individuals of

[29]Thomson S, Foubister T, Mossialos E (2009) Financing health care in the European Union: challenges and policy responses. Observatory Studies Series No 17, European Observatory on Health Systems and Policies. http://www.euro.who.int/__data/assets/pdf_file/0009/98307/E92469.pdf.

[30]Szyszczak 2009.

[31]Hervey 2011a.

[32]The High Level Committee on Health (2001) The internal market and health services. http://ec.europa.eu/health/ph_overview/Documents/key06_en.pdf; Mossialos and Dixon (2002).

[33]Szyszczak 2009; Hervey 2011b.

[34]Sauter 2013.

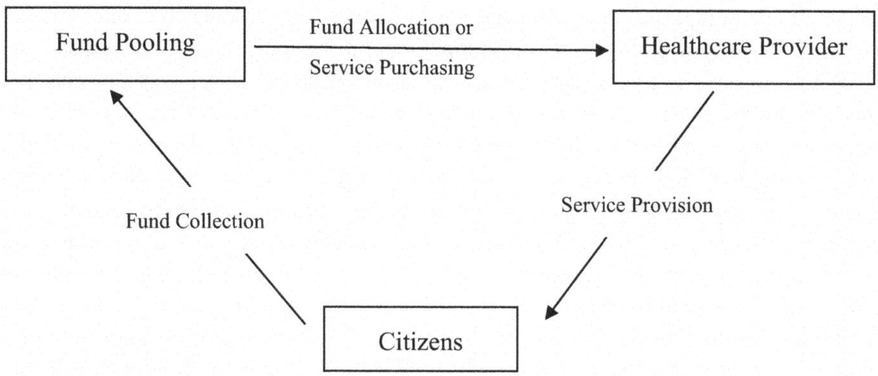

Fig. 2.1 Key components of public healthcare systems. *Source* The author

their healthcare costs.[35] Healthcare providers operate independently on markets, and patients have to pay consideration for medical treatments from these providers in the first place. Under such a model, there is no direct financial arrangement between the social insurance scheme and the healthcare provider.

A third model is found in the Netherlands.[36] Similarly to the second model, individuals are required by national law to pay contributions to social insurance schemes, which forms the major funding collection mechanism. However, it differs from the second model in that the statutory insurance schemes then enter into agreements with healthcare providers. Based on the agreement, healthcare providers provide free healthcare services to members of the insurance scheme, and then those healthcare costs will be paid by the insurance scheme to the service provider some time afterwards.

What should be borne in mind in the first place is that the above description covers only the main structure of public healthcare systems, which reflects the major funding source and the healthcare provision arrangements for the majority of the population. In reality, a mixture of different mechanisms is used across Member States: taxation, social insurance and out of pocket.[37]

In addition, from the late 1970s onwards, national government across Europe began to reform their public healthcare systems. The main aim was to improve efficiency and reduce costs. This often involved the introduction of market mechanisms into the system by granting patients the right to choose service suppliers and

[35]The so-called insurance-based Bismarck system, adopted by countries such as France, Luxembourg and Belgium. Hervey 2011a, fn 27; Sauter 2013.

[36]Also in countries such as Austria and Germany. Hervey 2011a, fn 28.

[37]Thomson S, Foubister T, Mossialos E (2009) Financing health care in the European Union: challenges and policy responses. Observatory Studies Series No 17, European Observatory on Health Systems and Policies. http://www.euro.who.int/__data/assets/pdf_file/0009/98307/E92469.pdf.

to encourage competition between service providers. This essentially meant that the organisation of public healthcare systems began to contain market elements.

What blurred the boundary between State and market further was the fact that markets for both healthcare financing and healthcare provision coexist with the operation of the public healthcare system.[38] On the financing side, a private health insurance market has developed across Member States. It is a risk-sharing mechanism, whereby individuals pay premiums to an insurance company and receive compensation in case of health problems. However, it operates on a voluntary and commercial basis, where premiums are linked to the health risks and benefits are determined by premiums paid.

Regarding healthcare provision, there are specialised clinics and hospitals operating on a market basis. Even within the public healthcare system, healthcare providers are often independent market entities; this is true regarding healthcare providers under the Bismarck models and also primary care providers under the UK NHS model. The only exception is found in the case of the healthcare providers directly owned and managed by NHS trusts, which do not operate on a market basis.[39]

This creates a delicate question in relation to the application of competition law in this sector: where is the boundary between the State and the market in this sector? Will the organisation of public healthcare systems always be excluded from EU competition law? In other words, under what circumstances are the market elements strong enough to make public healthcare provision become part of the market? These issues will be addressed in Sect. 2.3.3.

2.2.4 SGEI, Citizenship and Fundamental Rights

The organisation and provision of service of general interest in the Member States is closely linked with the notion of citizenship, which has strong egalitarian implications. Although the actual extent and organisation vary significantly across Member States, it is a notion common to all the Member States.[40] The underlying principle is that the State assumes the responsibility to ensure all its citizens have access to basic and essential service.[41] Based on the seminal work by T. Marshall, the provision of welfare service by the State to its citizens, including public education, public health, social security and various social assistances, are concrete examples of social citizenship.[42] It reflects the social aspect of society: all citizens

[38] Mossialos and Dixon 2002.

[39] Free health care service is only available for UK residents. NHS hospitals charges oversea visitors for health care provision.

[40] Huffschmid 2005.

[41] Kaufmann 2012.

[42] Marshall 1950.

are treated equally in the market, which might lead to inequality because the material conditions of individuals vary; therefore, welfare provision is necessary to correct this inequality to achieve material equality.[43]

This notion of social citizenship is also reflected in the organisation of the public utilities sector.[44] One of the public interest objectives pursued by these undertakings is universal service, i.e. to ensure that the basic utility services such as telephone, postal services and water supply are made available throughout the country.[45] Therefore, they fall within the broad umbrella of welfare services and citizenship.[46]

When the Treaty of Rome was adopted in 1957, the EU was predominately concerned with the economic aspect, i.e. the creation of the internal market and its proper functioning.[47] The presumption is that the EU was about economic welfare, to provide economic freedom and prosperity through the internal market; the social welfare dimension is guaranteed at the national level. Therefore, the EU did not have competence in the area of welfare provision, and public sector economy was essentially outside the reach of the EU for almost three decades.

The imbalance of social and economic dimension of EU integration has generated much debate since the 1980s. The attribution of constitutional importance to SGEI may be seen as an example of EU's effort to deal with this imbalance. In 1993, Article 16 (now the first part of Article 14 TFEU) was added to the Treaty, which, as a general principle of the EU, recognises SGEI as a shared value of the EU. Its position is reinforced by the Lisbon Treaty in 2009, which incorporated the Charter on Fundamental Rights into the Treaty, where access to SGEI is endorsed as a fundamental right.

Access to SGEI as a social and economic right still remains thin and weak.[48] Unlike political rights, it does not create directly enforceable rights before the court,[49] nor does a uniform level of benefits exist across the Member States.[50] In this respect, Article 36 of the Charter subjects access to SGEI to a very important limit, i.e. 'as provided for in national laws and practices, in accordance with the Treaty establishing the European Community'. In other words, access to SGEI is subject to implementing measures adopted by the Member States and the EU.

---

[43]Picard 1998.

[44]Prosser 2005; Sauter 1998.

[45]Tanzi 1997; Huffschmid 2005.

[46]Universal service is not protected as an enforceable legal right, but through voluntary and political means. Damjanovic and De Witte 2009.

[47]Craig 2010, p. 289.

[48]Ferrera, p. 37.

[49]Ewing 2001, p. 321; Menéndez 2003.

[50]EU action in this area is limited by the principle of subsidiarity. This is also reflected in the Protocol on SGI in the Lisbon Treaty, which in Article 1 recognises "the essential role and the wide discretion of national, regional and local authorities in providing, commissioning and organising services of general economic interest as closely as possible to the needs of the users".

However, the underlying principle is still the notion of citizenship. This is also confirmed by the Protocol on Service of General Interest, which elaborates the shared values as including 'a high level of quality, safety and affordability, *equal treatment* and the promotion of *universal service* and of user rights.' Equally important, if SGEI is regarded as a fundamental right, its access must be guaranteed for every citizen. In this respect, Article 14 provides that the Community and the Member States '*shall* take care that such services operate on the basis of principles and conditions which enable them to fulfil their missions'. Reading together, these Treaty provisions provide the mandate and guiding inspiration for the Member States and the EU to put into place measures and mechanisms to guarantee the provision of SGEI. In other words, when they take measures involving SGEI they must give proper care and attention to its provision.[51]

Therefore, the EU current regime on SGEI does not adopt the rigid EU citizenship right model,[52] but focuses on the organisation and delivery of SGEI.[53] This study finds that the market liberalisation and integration programme transformed the traditional model of SGEI provision into a competitive market. In this new setting, a new paradigm has emerged in EU law regarding the provision of SGEI, which is essentially a triangular relationship: while the Member States have the ultimate responsibility for the organisation and delivery of SGEI, such tasks are often entrusted to market undertakings through regulatory arrangements or public service contract.[54] Under this model, SGEI undertakings are the actual providers of SGEI, subject to terms and conditions defined by sector legislation, which are often translated as explicit consumer rights. Therefore, it is essentially a web of complex regulatory arrangements through which responsibilities regarding SGEI provision are allocated (see Fig. 2.2).[55]

---

[51]Ross 2000.

[52]Maas makes a distinction between citizenship as a right and citizenship as a policy. He points out that rights are fundamental and unalienable, while policies are freely altered. Such distinction is also crucial in the discussion of SGEI: while it is a policy consideration for the EU to guarantee access to SGEI, it is not an enforceable legal rights. Maas 2007, p. 4.

[53]Prosser 2005, p. 34; Ross 2000.

[54]Prosser 2005, Chapter 8.

[55]Three different sets of rules can be identified in this triangle arrangement:

(1) Access to SGEI is a fundamental right and is closely linked with the notion of citizenship and social welfare. The Member States and the EU have a joint responsibility to guarantee its provision for all EU citizens. This issue has strong constitutional implications.
See for example O'Leary 2005; Ross 2009.

(2) The relationship between the Member States and SGEI undertakings is dealt with by EU competition law. The main concern is to ensure measures adopted by the Member States for the provision of SGEI do not distort market competition.
See for example Prosser 2005; Szyszczak 2007.

(3) After market liberalisation, SGEI providers are undertakings on the market. Their relationship with consumers (citizens) are governed by contract law and consumer law. Universal access and affordability is often seen as part of the consumer protection package.
See for example Rott 2005, 2007.

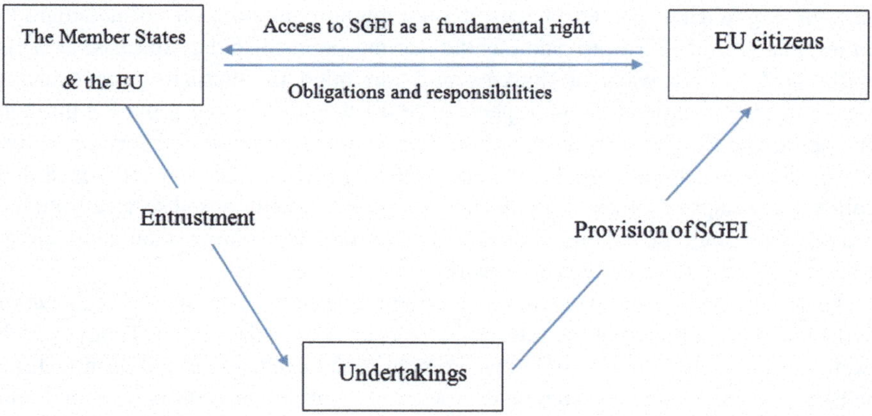

Fig. 2.2 SGEI provision in competitive markets—a triangle relationship. *Source* The author

Equally important, it might be just a matter of time before the Court expands the scope of citizenship rights to cover access to SGEI.[56] This would have far-reaching and potentially transformative implications for the current regime on SGEI. First, on the issue of competence allocation, currently there is minimal and limited harmonisation on SGEI provision at the EU level, and many aspects of the SGEI provision of SGEI are left to the Member States to decide. In practice, this often lead to variations, and sometimes poor implementation, in the actual level of SGEI provision across the Member States. This is the very case concerning the affordability of SGEI, which is left to the Member States to implement. In the energy sector, the lack of affordability has caused concerns in the Member States.[57] This is not satisfactory from the EU citizenship point of view because unaffordable SGEI essentially means access denied. Recognising SGEI as enforceable citizenship rights would require further harmonisation at the EU level.

Second, on the issue of mechanisms for the provision of SGEI, the current regime on SGEI is largely set in the market framework. Competitive market provision has been the preferred choice for the provision of SGEI.[58] Restriction of competition is justified only if it is necessary for the provision of SGEI.[59]

---

[56]Ferrera 2005, p. 37.

[57]Rott 2007.

[58]This is evident from the market liberalisation and integration programme in sectors such as telecommunication, postal service and transport. This way of thinking is also reflected in the *Altmark* criteria where public tendering procedure is used as an important yardstick to exempt Member States from notifying SGEI funding measures to the Commission.

[59]This is the necessity test first established by the Court in the *Corbeau* case. Case C-320/91 *Paul Corbeau* [1993] ECR I-2533. For a detailed discussion, see Sect. 3.4.4 of Chap. 3.

Recognising SGEI as part of citizenship right might require the shift of paradigm to seeing guaranteed SGEI provision as the starting point for policy discussion. This might lead to new ways of thinking and formation of alternative mechanisms outside market solutions. Some aspects of SGEI would be better provided through the welfare and social assistance system. For example, in the postal service sector, universal postal service could be guaranteed through free postal vouchers for certain vulnerable groups of citizens, which can then be used to buy postal service from the market. This might be a more efficient and better targeted solution than maintaining a country-wide extensive postal network.

There are no clear and fixed answers to these questions. The social dimension of SGEI may be reinforced in the future.[60] This is evident in the Lisbon Treaty, which explicitly prescribes that the EU 'shall combat social exclusion and discrimination, and shall promote social justice and protection … promote economic, social and territorial cohesion, and solidarity among Member States'.[61] In this new setting, priorities may be given to SGEI provision and the underlying values of social justice and citizenship. These principles and values might well be the guiding principles and yardstick for future evolution and development of SGEI.[62]

2.3 The Economic and Non-economic Distinction in Competition Law

EU competition law is a binary system. It makes a crucial distinction between economic and non-economic activities. The implications are significant. It decides whether EU competition law applies at all. In other words, it is the precondition for EU law to apply. If an activity is regarded *as economic in nature*, EU competition law will apply.[63] By contrast, *non-economic activity* falls outside the reach of EU competition law. Regarding SGI, while SGEIs are subject to EU competition law, NSGIs are excluded from its application. In addition, after the Lisbon Treaty, the economic/non-economic distinction began to have constitutional implications.

[60] Ferrera 2005, p. 37.

[61] Article 3(3), TEU.

[62] Ross 2010.

[63] EU competition law contains two sets of rules:

(1) rules for undertakings are found in Articles 101 and 102;
(2) rules for the Member States spread at different places in the Treaty: Article 106 and state aid rules.

Article 14 granted the EU a new legislative basis related to SGEI.[64] Meanwhile, the Member States had exclusive competence in the area of NSGIs.[65]

The Treaty has left this crucial question unsolved.[66] Until now, the EU has not adopted new legislation on SGEI based on Article 14. Therefore, the issue of economic and non-economic distinction has not been raised in the context of SGI. Instead, the Court has examined this issue in a general competition law context, i.e. whether a particular entity constitutes an undertaking in competition law. It is through this exercise that the Court has drawn a line between economic and non-economic activities.

Modern states assume a wide range of functions and responsibilities, stretching from the management of infrastructure to the provision of welfare services and maintenance of the national defence system. In different areas, the level and extent of state intervention varies, which is often a matter of spectrum rather than clear-cut black-and-white distinction. Consequently, it is not an easy task to work out exactly where state functions end and the market mechanism begins to operate. The attitude and the criteria adopted will be crucial. In the Treaty of Rome, state intervention in economies found its position in the competition law chapter. Therefore, there was a strong assumption that this part of state functions constituted economic activity. This approach can also be found in the case law. In its judgments, the Court did not pay attention to the fact that these sectors were organised on a very different model and logic from that of a market. It often assumed the economic nature of these sectors without any discussion. This approach is found in the telecommunications,[67] postal services,[68] transport[69] and broadcasting sectors.[70]

What has caused much contention is in the area of welfare services, particularly in the public health services sector.[71] Controversy often arises because the Member States have reformed the organisation and delivery of welfare service by introducing certain elements of market mechanisms. This often leads to a mixed system of state and market, where public authorities and private entities coexist and play

[64]This power is not exclusive but only of a supporting role. It provides that its exercise shall be "without prejudice to the competence of Member States". Damjanovic and De Witte 2009, p. 86.

[65]Article 2 of the Protocol (No 26) on Service of General Interest, TEU, provides that "the provisions of the Treaties do not affect in any way the competence of Member States to provide, commission and organise non-economic services of general interest".

[66]This is another example of the ambiguity of competence allocation between the EU and Member States. Conway 2010; Neergaard 2009, p. 35.

[67]Case C-18/88 *Régie des Télégraphes et des Téléphones v GB-Inno-BM SA* [1991] ECR I-5941.

[68]Case C-320/91 *Paul Corbeau* [1993] ECR I-2533.

[69]Joined Cases 209 to 213/84 *Criminal proceedings against Lucas Asjes and others, Andrew Gray and others, Andrew Gray and others, Jacques Maillot and others and Léo Ludwig and others* [1986] ECR 1425.

[70]Case C-260/89 *Elliniki Radiophonia Tileorassi AE (Ert) (Panellinia Omospondia Syllogon Prossopikou Ert intervening) v Dimotiki Étairia Pliroforissis (Dep) and Sotirios Kouvelas (Nicolaos Avdellas and Others intervening)* [1991] ECR I-02925.

[71]Neergaard 2009; Ross 2009; Lenaerts 2012; Cruz 2005.

different roles subject to complex legislative and regulatory framework and arrangement. This has raised a very intriguing question: are they still non-economic in nature, or have they become economic activity? This research finds that the Court has not adopted the so-called *potentiality test*.[72] Instead, it has developed its jurisprudence under two themes, the exercise of public authority and the principle of solidarity in the public health sector.

2.3.1 The Höfner Case and the Potentiality Test

A generally accepted criterion for the economic/non-economic distinction is the so-called 'potentiality test' formulated by commentators based on the *Höfner* Judgment.[73] According to Holmes, in this case the Court 'appears to formulate a general test for determining what constituted an economic activity'.[74] He argues that 'an activity will be classed as economic whenever the potential exists for it to be performed by economic operators in a market place'.[75] Or in Winterstein's words, 'an activity is of an economic nature if it faces *actual or potential competition* by companies'.[76]

Based on this approach, the scope of the economic activity is extremely wide and might cover areas where Member States have adopted *a non-market model*. The potentiality test 'establishes a strong presumption for the economic character of any activity' and 'it effectively brings all activities, from medicine to education, into the ambit of competition law since they all can be – and indeed are – performed also by private companies'.[77] This would force the Member States to shrink their State functions further and push market competition to new frontiers.

A closer reading of the *Höfner* case[78] casts some doubts about the approach adopted by the Court and its real significance. The case was concerned with the organisation of the public employment services in Germany, which was organised under the broad umbrella of welfare services and public services. The task was undertaken by Bundesanstalt für Arbeit (Federal Office for Employment, hereafter BA), which was an organ of the state. BA provided various job-search assistance services for the unemployed.[79] In addition, a monopoly right was granted to BA in

[72]The potentiality test is proposed by scholars based on the *Höfner* case. They believe that the criterion to decide whether an activity is economic in nature is to see whether it could potentially be provided by the market. See for example Holmes 2004; Odudu 2011.

[73]Case C-41/90 *Klaus Höfner and Fritz Elser v Macrotron GmbH* [1991] ECR I-1979; Odudu 2011, p. 231.

[74]Holmes 2004, p. 159.

[75]Ibid.

[76]Winterstein 1999, p. 324.

[77]Ibid. A similar argument is made by Sauter, see Sauter 2013, p. 466.

[78]Case C-41/90 *Klaus Höfner and Fritz Elser v Macrotron GmbH* [1991] ECR I-1979.

[79]Greer et al. 2017, p. 23.

the sector: German law explicitly prohibited, with a criminal penalty, the provision of employment recruitment by any other entity. It also prescribed that such contracts would be regarded as void.

Despite this prohibition, a separate market for the recruitment of business executives developed to meet growing market demand. In the main proceedings, Macrotron signed a contract with a recruitment consultant, Höfner, to recruit a sales director. When a candidate was presented by Höfner, Macrotron decided not to appoint him and refused to pay the search fees. It argued that the contract was void under German law. It was faced with such a dilemma that the German court referred several questions to the Court.

A crucial distinction could be drawn regarding the German employment procurement sector. On the one hand the public employment service provided by BA is based on a non-market basis. The service was provided free of charge. It was financed by compulsory contributions from employers and workers, which bore no link to benefits. BA carried out such activities to maintain a high level of employment and to improve job distribution rather than to make a profit. The regime was set up by Germany to fulfil its obligations under International Labour Organisation conventions.[80] Therefore, it was essentially a state function based on a model completely different from the market mechanism. It is submitted that this part of its activity shall be regarded as non-economic in nature.

On the other hand was the market provision of business executives by recruitment consultants. The contract between Höfner and Macrotron in the main proceedings formed part of this market. Although the law on paper did not allow the existence of such a market, in practice it had developed into a market of considerable scale: there were more than 700 such firms. Service was provided for consideration under commercial contracts with a purpose of profit making. It operates under a model no different from that of other normal market transactions and thus constitutes economic activity.

The focus of the proceeding has been predominantly on the second group of activities, the recruitment of business executives, which is economic in nature.[81] The first three questions were raised in the context of free movement of services. The German Court asked whether *the provision of business executives* provided by recruitment consultants constituted a service under Article 57 of the Treaty (ex Article 60 TEC) and whether the German rules were compatible with free movement rules. Only the second part of its fourth question was raised in a competition law context, which is still concerned with business executives. It was framed as follows:

[80]Opinion of Advocate General, Case C-41/90 *Klaus Höfner and Fritz Elser v Macrotron GmbH* [1991] ECR I-1979, para 3.

[81]The national courts referred four questions to the Court. All of them were in connection with the recruitment of business of executives.

> Does the establishment of *a monopoly over the provision of business executives* constitute an abuse of dominant position on the market with the meaning of Article 102 of the EEC Treaty?[82] (emphasis added)

In its Judgment, the Court did not embark on any detailed analysis of the criterion of economic and non-economic distinction. Instead, it *assumed* the economic nature of employment procurement by making the following general statement:

> It must be observed, in the context of competition law, first that the concept of an undertaking encompasses every entity engaged in economic activity, regardless of the legal status of the entity and the way in which it is financed, secondly, that *employment procurement is an economic activity*.[83] (emphasis added)

If employment procurement is *assumed* to be economic in nature, consequently any entity carrying out such activity constitutes an undertaking subject to competition law. It was this very assumption that brought the BA within the scope of competition law. Then the Court pointed out that BA's status as a public authority did not alter this conclusion:[84]

> The fact that employment procurement activities are normally entrusted to public agencies cannot affect the economic nature of such activities. Employment procurement *has not always been, and is not necessarily*, carried out by public entities. That finding applies in particular to *executive recruitment*.[85] (emphasis added)

In the reasoning, the Court *did not take into account* the intention and purpose behind the provision of public employment service in Germany and the regulatory and organisational structure of such services. Nor did it consider what implications these factors may have on the issue of economic and non-economic distinction. In fact, this issue did not occupy much of the attention of the Court. The focus in this case was not on the dividing line between economic and non-economic activities. Instead, the real concern was over the monopoly structure created by the German law, which frustrated the development of the business executive recruitment market.[86]

The approach of the Court on this issue has been more refined in cases subsequent to *Höfner*. It has not followed the so-called 'potentiality test'; it does not assume that any activity that could *actually or potentially* be provided by the market constitutes economic activity in nature.[87] Instead, national regime and regulatory

---

[82]Case C-41/90 *Klaus Höfner and Fritz Elser v Macrotron GmbH* [1991] ECR I-1979, para 13.

[83]Ibid., para 21.

[84]Odudu 2011.

[85]Case C-41/90 *Klaus Höfner and Fritz Elser v Macrotron GmbH* [1991] ECR I-1979, para 22.

[86]In its Judgment, the Court held that the monopoly structure created by German law was in breach of Article 106(1), read in conjunction with Article 102. The reason lies in that the BA as the holder of the exclusive right could not meet demands while the German law prohibited other undertakings from providing recruitment services to satisfy unmet demands. See Sect. 3.2.2 of Chap. 3.

[87]Holmes 2004, p. 160.

arrangements regarding the structure and operation of a particular activity do have influence on whether it constitutes economic activity or not. In fact, such national choice is decisive:[88] the Court merely ascertains whether or not a market model has been adopted by the Member States.[89] In its jurisprudence, the Court develops its doctrines under two broad themes, the exercise of public authority and the principle of solidarity in the area of social insurance.

2.3.2 The Exercise of Public Authority

The essence of the economic and non-economic distinction in competition law is to distinguish state functions from market activities. State functions are carried out under completely different principles and models from those of commercial operations and are thus excluded from the application of competition law. The exercise of public authority is inherent in the sovereign and prerogative power of the state and serves as a clear indication of a state function activity. The Court has adopted a *functional approach*,[90] which means that the decisive criterion for the exclusion of an activity from the application of competition law is *the exercise of public power*.[91] Applying this criterion, the Court has held that the following activities are non-economic in nature,

(1) collection of a duty imposed on paper products and redistribution to research activities;[92]
(2) preventive anti-pollution surveillance services in oil ports;[93]
(3) public education service financed mainly by public funds;[94]
(4) operation of e-procurement platform to assist contracting authorities in executing public procurement;[95]
(5) maintenance and making available to the public of company registration information.[96]

---

[88]Cahill 2010.

[89]Boeger 2007.

[90]Odudu 2010, 2011.

[91]Schweitzer 2011.

[92]Case 94/74 *IGAV v ENCC* [1975] ECR-699.

[93]Case C-343/95 *Diego Cali & Figli Sri v. Servizi Ecologici Porto di Genova SpA (SEPG)* [1997] ECR I-1547.

[94]Case C-74/16 *Congregación de Escuelas Pías Provincia Betania v Ayuntamiento de Getafe* (not yet reported). http://curia.europa.eu/juris/liste.jsf?language=en&num=C-74/16.

[95]Case T-138/15 *Aanbestedingskalender BV and Others v European Commission* (not yet reported). http://curia.europa.eu/juris/liste.jsf?language=en&num=T-138/15.

[96]Case C 138/11 *Compass-Datenbank GmbH v Republik Österreich* (not yet reported). https://eur-lex.europa.eu/legal-content/EN/ALL/?uri=CELEX%3A62011CJ0138.

Although the main function of the state is to provide SGI acting outside the market, there is always a potential that the state may participate in commercial activity and thereby become part of the market. The Court has long been aware of the complex nature of state activities and its potential role on the market. The approach of the Court is to draw a distinction between state activities 'exercising public power' (non-economic) and 'economic activities of an industrial and commercial nature'.[97] Meanwhile, the institutional factor, i.e. a separate and independent legal personality from state administration, has been rejected expressly as relevant for the analysis.[98] This attitude was also explicitly mentioned by the Court in the *Höfner* case, where it held that:

> It must be observed that, in the context of competition law, that the concept of an undertaking encompasses every entity engaged in an economic activity, regardless of the legal status of the entity and the way in which it is financed. [...] The fact that employment procurement activities are normally entrusted to public agencies cannot affect the economic nature of such activities.[99]

Consequently, once the State steps outside the arena of public authorities into the space of market, the veil of the State will be lifted, and such *commercial activities* fall within the scope of competition law.[100] Thus, public authorities could not escape from the application of competition law under the guise of public interest. In the case law, the Court has held the following activities as economic in nature:

(1) transmission of television signals;[101]
(2) management of public telecommunications equipment and offering such equipment to consumers on payment of a fee;[102]
(3) production and marketing of manufactured tobacco;[103]
(4) loading, unloading, transhipment, storage and general movement of goods within the port;[104]
(5) provision of airport facilities to airlines in return for a fee;[105]

---

[97]Case 118/85 *Re the Amministrazione Autonoma dei Monopoli di Stato: E.C. Commission v Italy* [1988] ECR-2599.

[98]Ibid., para 11.

[99]Case C-41/90 *Klaus Höfner and Fritz Elser v Macrotron GmbH* [1991] ECR I-1979, para 21.

[100]Odudu 2010, p. 826.

[101]Case 155/73 *Giuseppe Sacchi* [1974] ECR-409.

[102]Case 41/83 *Italian Republic v Commission of the European Communities* [1985] ECR-873.

[103]Case 118/85 *Re the Amministrazione Autonoma dei Monopoli di Stato: E.C. Commission v Italy* [1988] ECR-2599.

[104]Case C-179/90 *Merci Convenzionali Porto di Genova SpA v Siderurgica Gabrielli SpA* [1991] ECR I-05889.

[105]Case C-82/01 P Aéroports de Paris v Commission of the European Communities [2002] I-9297, para 78.

(6) the operation of the airport, including construction of runways;[106]
(7) provision of necessary technical and administrative services to public schools.[107]

In most cases, distinguishing non-economic activities from market activities does not pose any difficulties.[108] It becomes problematic when the dividing line is blurred when an entity carries out a mixture of both state functions and market activities.[109] In the case law, the Court considers these activities separately to determine the nature of each specific activity; thus a *separation method.*[110] Although such an entity may not form part of the state administration, it has been granted to exercise public power, and this part of its activities will be *excluded* from the application of competition law. On the other hand, it could also be active on the market, conducting commercial activities. This part of activity will be subject to competition law.

The exercise may become tricky, in particular when a particular activity is in the grey area. The Court has not formulated a general criterion that would be applicable in all situations. This is understandable because of the range and diversities in regard to what functions the state undertakes and how they are organised across the Member States. Instead, the Court has adopted a case-by-case approach by taking into account 'the aim, the nature and the rules to which it is subject'[111] to examine whether the activity in question is directly related and indispensable for the exercise of public authority.[112]

This approach is clearly illustrated in cases concerning Eurocontrol,[113] which was an entity set up by several European States to manage their air navigation services. In its judgments, four areas of its activities were analysed separately, and different conclusions about their natures were reached. In the *SAT* case, the activity in question was the collection of route charges.[114] The Court examined several factors and concluded Eurocontrol was merely an agent on behalf of the State. First, charges were fixed by the State, and Eurocontrol did not have any freedom or

[106]C-288/11 P *Mitteldeutsche Flughafen and Flughafen Leipzig-Halle v Commission* (not yet reported). http://curia.europa.eu/juris/liste.jsf?num=C-288/11&language=EN, para 49.

[107]C-108/10 *Ivana Scattolon v Ministero dell'Istruzione, dell'Università e della Ricerca* [2011] ECR I-7491, para 47.

[108]As pointed out by the Commission, in most cases, there is no difficulty in demarcating the line between the State and the market: Commission of the European Communities, Service of General Interest in Europe (Report to the Laeken European Council), COM (2001) 598 final, 17.10.2001.

[109]Odudu 2010, p. 826.

[110]Odudu 2011.

[111]Case C-343/95 D*iego Cali & Figli Sri v. Servizi Ecologici Porto di Genova SpA (SEPG)* [1997] ECR I-1547, para 23.

[112]T-138/15 *Aanbestedingskalender and Others v Commission* (not yet reported) (not yet reported). http://curia.europa.eu/juris/liste.jsf?language=en&num=T-138/15.

[113]Case C-364/92 *SAT Fluggesellschaft mbH v Eurocontrol* [1994] ECR I-43; Case T-155/04 *Selex Sistemi Integrati SpA v Commission of the European Communities* [2006] ECR II-4803.

[114]Case C-364/92 *SAT Fluggesellschaft mbH v Eurocontrol* [1994] ECR I-43.

influence over it. Second, its activities were financed by contributions from the contracting States. Therefore, the activity of charge collection was in the exercise of public power and so was excluded from the application of competition law.[115]

Besides charge collection, Eurocontrol also carried out other activities, including technical standardisation, research and development and assistance to national governments, which has been the dispute in the *Selex* case.[116] In its judgment, the Court examined whether a particular activity could be separate from its exercise of public power. In other words, if a particular activity is an *indispensable or integral part* of its public mission, it is regarded as non-economic in nature and so is excluded from the scope of competition law.[117] By contrast, if a particular activity is in pursuit of other aims/interests, and its link to its public mission is indirect and weak, this part of activity will be regarded as economic in nature and subject to competition rules.

In *Selex*, the Court found that the activities of technical standardisation and research and development could not be separate from its public mission, i.e. the development of a uniform air traffic management system. Thus, these were non-economic in nature. On the other hand, assistance to national administrations was only contributing to such tasks in an indirect way and was 'not indispensable to ensuring the safety of air navigation'.[118]

This line of reasoning is also evident in the *Congregación de Escuelas Pías Provincia Betania v Ayuntamiento de Getafe case* delivered by the Court in June 2017. In the case, CEPPB was a religious organisation of the Catholic Church in Spain. Based on a treaty between the Spanish State and the Holy See, such entities are exempted from property taxes. It carried out some renovation and extension to one of its school buildings. Its claim for a tax refund for such work was denied by the authority, which was of the opinion that the building was used for economic activities and tax refund for such activity would constitute incompatible state aid. The case was referred to the Court with the specific query as to whether the tax exemption regime is compatible with EU state aid rules. One of the issues the Court had to address was whether CEPPB carries out economic activities and thus constitutes undertakings.

[115]Ibid.

[116]Case T-155/04 *Selex Sistemi Integrati SpA v Commission of the European Communities* [2006] ECR II-4803.

[117]Case 343/95 *Diego CalÃ & Figli Srl v Servizi Ecologici Porto di Genova SpA (SEPG)* [1997] ECR I-1547, para 24; Case C-364/92 *SAT Fluggesellschaft mbH v Eurocontrol* [1994] ECR I-43, para 28; Joined cases C-264/01, C-306/01, C-354/01 & C-355/01 *AOK Bundesverband, Bundesverband der Betriebskrankenkassen (BKK), Bundesverband der Innungskrankenkassen, Bundesverband der landwirtschaftlichen Krankenkassen, Verband der Angestelltenkrankenkassen eV, Verband der Arbeiter-Ersatzkassen, Bundesknappschaft and See-Krankenkasse v Ichthyol-Gesellschaft Cordes, Hermani & Co* [2004] ECR I-2493, para 58.

[118]Case T-155/04 *Selex Sistemi Integrati SpA v Commission of the European Communities* [ECR] II-4803, para 87.

The Court applied its separation method and made a very important distinction regarding two categories of its education services. On the one hand, based on an agreement between CEPPB and local authority, it provided education service that was integrated into the state public compulsory education system and was financed entirely from public funds. Such activity is non-economic in nature because 'the state is not seeking to engage in gainful activity, but is fulfilling its social, cultural and education obligations towards its population'.[119]

On the other hand, it also undertook non-compulsory education service, including early-years teaching, extracurricular activities and post-compulsory education. Organised by CEPPB itself, it was offered for remuneration, which constitutes consideration for the service provided and financed by private funds (from students and their parents). Therefore, it was based on a model completely different from that of public education service and constitutes economic activity.

The judgment clarifies an important issue in EU competition law, namely whether education constitutes economic activity. Educational service could potentially be and is actually provided by the market. In this case the Court did not adopt an abstract potentiality test that would bring public education service (as part of SGI state functions) within the scope of competition law. Instead, the decisive factor lies in the organisational structure and model set up by the Member State, thus a concrete test. In this way it offers some certainty that public education service organised and funded by the state as part of its SGI functions are outside the reach and scrutiny of EU competition law.

The essence of the Court's approach was to examine whether a particular activity involved the exercise of public power. This is the key aspect of the State functions that make it distinct from market activities. This functional approach enables the Court to draw a line between market and non-market activities. In this way, it does not intervene in the proper functioning of State activities[120] and meanwhile brings all economic activities under the scope of competition law.

2.3.3 *The Principle of Solidarity in Social Insurance*

Social insurance is a collective risk-sharing mechanism under which funding is pooled together to pay for the costs in case the insured event happens. Providing a source of funding for healthcare, it forms an essential part of the public health system of the Member States, thus falling under the broad umbrella of SGI. The Court has been using the principle of solidarity as the criterion to decide whether a

[119] Case C-74/16 *Congregación de Escuelas Pías Provincia Betania v Ayuntamiento de Getafe* (not yet reported). http://curia.europa.eu/juris/liste.jsf?language=en&num=C-74/16, para 50.
[120] Boeger 2007.

particular social insurance scheme could be classified as economic activity in nature.[121] It was first adopted by the Court in 1993 in the *Christian Poucet* case.[122] The issue in question was whether the managing body of a Dutch sickness and maternity insurance was an undertaking in competition law. In the Judgment, the Court examined four factors to reach its conclusion that the insurance fund in question was not an undertaking in competition law,[123] including:

(1) the pursuit of social objectives and its non-profit-making nature;
(2) the principle of solidarity (it acknowledged that solidarity could be embodied in different forms. The basic requirement is the redistribution of wealth within a group of people or between groups. In its conclusion part, it emphasised that benefits bore no relation to the amount of the contributions.);
(3) compulsory contribution (which 'is indispensable for application of the principle of solidarity and the financial equilibrium of the schemes');[124]
(4) the control of the state (the managing body had no influence on the decision of the amount of contributions and benefits).[125]

Although such listing of different factors enabled the Court to reach a conclusion in this case that the management of the insurance schemes was not tantamount to the carrying out of an economic activity, more issues remain unsolved.[126] First, which factors are decisive in finding that a particular activity is of non-economic nature?[127] This question is particularly important because the Member States organise their social insurance schemes in different ways and are experimenting new ways of operating.[128] That means that in practice certain elements could be missing in a particular scheme.

Second, it is clear from this case that solidarity was not the sole standard to decide the nature of a particular social insurance scheme, but only one of the parameters for such an exercise. Although the basic idea is redistribution of income, its very definition remains unfixed. Also, the operation of the solidarity principle is a matter of scale.[129] It remains unclear what level of solidarity is overwhelming enough to exclude a particular activity from the application of competition law.

This problem has attracted much attention from commentators, and the jurisprudence of the Court has been criticised as lacking certainty and

---

[121] Haffner 2005.

[122] Joined cases C-159/91 & C-160/91 *Christian Poucet v Assurances Générales de France and Caisse Mutuelle Régionale du Languedoc-Roussillon* [1993] ECR I-637.

[123] Cahill 2010; Krajewski 2006.

[124] Joined cases C-159/91 & C-160/91 *Christian Poucet v Assurances Générales de France and Caisse Mutuelle Régionale du Languedoc-Roussillon* [1993] ECR I-637, para 13.

[125] Ibid., paras 8–15.

[126] Holmes 2004; Schweitzer 2011.

[127] Szyszczak 2009.

[128] Giaimo 2014; Freeman 1998.

[129] Ross 2007.

consistency.[130] The reason lies in the nature of the concept of solidarity itself, which is a very broad and vague one.[131] As argued by Alexander Winterstein, even though it could be confined as meaning 'transfer of wealth', it could still exist on different occasions at different levels.[132] In this respect, Malcolm Ross provided a complete survey of the operation of the principle of solidarity and rightly concluded that solidarity worked as a moral consideration and value choice.[133]

Among these factors, *the social aim* and *the non-profit-making nature* of a particular insurance fund are *relevant* for the economic and non-economic distinction, but they are not decisive in drawing the dividing line. This approach is well reflected in its reasoning in the *Kattner Stahlbau* case.[134] In this case, German law established a compulsory insurance scheme for workers against accidents at work and occupational diseases. The operation of this scheme was entrusted to Maschinenbau- und Metall-Berufsgenossenschaft (employers' liability insurance association in the mechanical engineering and metal sector, hereafter 'MMB'). In the main proceedings, Kattner Stahlbau, as a private company, was active in steel construction. It refused to contribute to the scheme, preferring to purchase private insurance on the market instead. It argued that the German law on compulsory affiliation was in breach of Article 106 in EU competition law.

In its Judgment, the Court explicitly rejected the plea that the social aim and non-profit-making status was sufficient to exclude it from the scope of economic activity.[135] The Court went further to examine whether the operation of such social insurance was based on a market model. It held:

> [T]he social aim of an insurance scheme is not in itself sufficient to preclude the activity in question from being classified as an economic activity. It remains to be examined, in particular, whether that scheme can be regarded as applying *the principle of solidarity* and to what extent it is subject to *supervision by the State*, given that these factors that are *likely* to preclude a given activity from being regarded as economic.[136] (emphasis added)

---

[130]Cygan 2008, p. 535; Lasok 2004, p. 383; Ross 2007, 2009; Neergaard 2009, p. 39; Hatzopoulos 2005, p. 157.

[131]Somek 2007; Ferrera 2005.

[132]Winterstein 1999; Holmes 2004.

[133]Ross 2007, 2009.

[134]Case C-350/07 *Kattner Stahlbau GmbH v Maschinenbau- und Metall-Berufsgenossenschaft* [2009] ECR I-1513, paras 42–43.

[135]The same approach is adopted in the *INAIL* case, where the Court dealt with essentially the same issue regarding similar social insurance scheme in Italy: Case C-218/00, *Cisal di Battistello Venanzio & Co. Sas v Istituto Nazionale Per L'Assicurazione Contro Gli Infortuni Sul Lavoro (INAIL)* [2002] ECR I-691. In his opinion, Advocate General even went further to regard social aim and non-profit-making status as *irrelevant factors*. Opinion of Advocate General, Case C-218/00, *Cisal di Battistello Venanzio & Co. Sas v Istituto Nazionale Per L'Assicurazione Contro Gli Infortuni Sul Lavoro (INAIL)* [2002] ECR I-691, para 46.

[136]Case C-350/07 *Kattner Stahlbau GmbH v Maschinenbau- und Metall-Berufsgenossenschaft* [2009] ECR I-1513, paras 42–43.

The essential elements of social insurance are the amount of contributions and the amount of benefits.[137] In this case, two features of the social insurance scheme led the Court to conclude that it was non-economic in nature.[138] First, benefits were not strictly proportionate to contributions, and there was *no direct link* between contributions and benefits.[139] Second, the amount of contribution and the amount of benefits were subject to state control. This essentially meant that the social insurance scheme was not an independent entity with autonomy, but merely carried out a function designated by the state.[140] These two factors suggest that the social insurance scheme was operating under a model that was completely different from its counterpart on the market (private health insurance). It is these two essential features that led the Court to conclude that the management of such social insurance schemes was not economic in nature.

By contrast, when such crucial elements are absent in the organisation of a social insurance scheme, the Court would regard it as economic activity subject to competition law. The *FFSA* case offers a very good example.[141] This case was concerned with a French regime on supplementary old-age insurance schemes for self-employed farmers. The French law entrusted the management task exclusively to Caisse Nationale d' Assurance Vieillesse Mutuelle Agricole (CNAVMA).

In this case, the Court explicitly rejected the plea that non-profit making in itself is enough to exclude the contested activity from the scope of economic activity. Instead, it focused on the following two factors: (1) membership was optional; and (2) benefits depended on the amount of contributions and the financial results of the investments made by the organisation.[142] These features meant that the insurance scheme in question operated on a market model different from that in the *Kattner Stahlbau* case. Therefore, the Court concluded that the management of the insurance scheme was an economic activity in nature. Similar reasoning can also be found in the Judgment of the Court in the *Albany* case.[143]

However, drawing a line between economic and non-economic is far from straightforward because the Member States introduced reform measures to their social insurance sector, often following a gradual and piecemeal approach.

---

[137]Ibid., para 65.

[138]In the *INAIL* case, the Court also mentioned another factor: the rate of contribution is proportionate to the insured person's income rather than its risks. This element is not obvious in this case because contribution is calculated by reference to funding requirements, the salaries of the insured persons and the categories of risk.

[139]Case C-350/07 *Kattner Stahlbau GmbH v Maschinenbau- und Metall-Berufsgenossenschaft* [2009] ECR I-1513, para 59.

[140]Ibid., para 62.

[141]Case C-244/94 *Fédération Française des Sociétés d'Assurance, Société Paternelle-Vie, Union des Assurances de Paris-Vie and Caisse d'Assurance et de Prévoyance Mutuelle des Agriculteurs v Ministère de l'Agriculture et de la Pêche* [1995] ECR I-4013.

[142]Ibid., para 17.

[143]Case C-67/96 *Albany International BV v Stichting Bedrijfspensioenfonds Textielindustrie* [1999] ECR I-5751.

Although the speed and extent of such reforms varied significantly across the Member States, the common theme is to combine elements from both ends of the spectrums (the principle of solidarity and the market mechanism). As a result, the organisation structure of the social insurance sector is not based on a pure solidarity or market model but often a mixture of both. Consequently, the demarcation line between the state and the market has become very blurred. This has created tensions and controversy as EU competition law is a binary system based on the distinction between economic and non-economic activities.

The case law of the Court suggests that some elements of solidarity do not render a particular social insurance programme non-economic in nature. Instead, the Court would take into account the regulatory framework and arrangements put in place by the Member States in organising their social insurance sector. If it is based on a model that is predominantly market, the operation of such a programme would constitute economic activity in nature.

First, solidarity-based health insurance could be purchased from the market, as in the *AG2R* case.[144] The case is concerning a French supplementary insurance scheme for the bakery sector. It contains a high degree of solidarity and clearly serves a social purpose. Contribution is a fixed uniform flat rate for all members irrespective of the health risks of each individual and thus not proportionate to the risk insured. Benefits are predetermined and has no direct link with contribution paid. Membership was made mandatory for the whole sector by ministerial decree.

These elements of solidarity persist among the members who pooled their risks together to form a risk group or a portfolio of risks. Then a group insurance is purchased from the market through collective bargaining and agreement. The state played no role in designating AG2R as the managing body of the insurance scheme. It was the result of free choice made by representatives of the employers and employees of the bakery sector. Such choice will be re-examined every five years with the possibility of choosing a new insurer. Therefore, AG2R competed on the market with other insurers to win the contract, although it was non-profit-making. These elements suggest that the insurance scheme was organised under a market mechanism. The state has a minimal role to play in the process. It set up the framework for collective bargaining and recognised the binding effect of the collective agreement. Therefore, the Court rightly concluded that the management of the insurance scheme constitutes economic activity subject to competition law.

Second, the private insurance market could be regulated to achieve solidarity purpose. This is well illustrated in the BUPA case concerning the Irish private health insurance market.[145] In this case, solidarity related obligations are imposed upon all the insurers on the market. Open enrolment is put in place to increase the level of coverage. Community rating was introduced which required the insurer to charge the same amount of rate for the same level of benefits regardless of the

[144]Case C-437/09 *AG2R Prévoyance v Beaudout Père et Fils SARL* [2011] I-973.

[145]Case T-289/03 *British United Provident Association Ltd (BUPA), BUPA Insurance Ltd and BUPA Ireland Ltd v Commission of the European Communities* [2008] ECR II-8.

health risks of the insured, which essentially means contribution is not proportionate the health risks of the insured. A minimum level of benefits is also prescribed by the law.

These elements suggest a significant level of solidarity, but do not change the fundamental nature of private insurance as a market activity. Insurance is purchased through the free choice of consumers. And insurance companies operate under normal market principles and compete with each other to attract customers. Therefore, the Court has no problem in classifying it as economic activity. Meanwhile, the solidarity elements qualify was in pursuit of general interest, thus constitute a SGEI task justifies a derogation from the application of competition law.

Thirdly, as the recent DZP/UZP case demonstrates,[146] public social insurance could be structured and organised under a market model. The case concerns the organisation of the public health insurance in Slovakia. As an important component of the state welfare system, it was set up to fulfil the constitutional obligation of the state towards its citizens. It is characterised with a high degree of solidarity. Participation in the public insurance scheme is compulsory by law to achieve universal coverage. Contribution is fixed by law proportional to the income of the insured, rather than the health risks. Benefits are the same for all members, not linked to the contribution paid.

Meanwhile, market mechanisms were introduced to organise and manage the public health insurance. The sector is open to competition and private investors are allowed to enter into the market. All insurers are stock companies with identical status and on equal footing, including the traditional state insurer. Slovak residents have the freedom of choice to contract with any of the insurers and could switch providers. Though the basic benefits are the same fixed by the law, insurers compete with each other by offering additional benefits. They enjoy management autonomy and are fully responsible for their financial deficits. Profit making is allowed and insurers do make a profit.

The Commission and the Court of First Instance were divided on whether the Slovak insurance scheme could be classified as economic or non-economic. It seems that Commission was strongly influenced by the fact that insurance scheme in question constitutes Slovak public social insurance. It focused on the "predominant social, solidarity and regulatory feature" and argued that elements of the market was put in place to serves the solidarity objective of the system.[147] Another factor played a significant role in its reasoning is the fact competition was limited to quality and price competition was eliminated because contribution is fixed by the law.

---

[146]Case T-216/15 *Dôvera zdravotná poist'ovňa, a.s. v European Commission* (not yet reported). http://curia.europa.eu/juris/liste.jsf?language=en&num=T-216/15.

[147]Commission Decision (EU) 2015/248 of 15 October 2014 on the measures SA.23008 (2013/C) (ex 2013/NN) implemented by Slovak Republic for Spoločná zdravotná poisťovňa, a. s. (SZP) and Všeobecná zdravotná poisťovňa, a. s. (VZP) [2015] OJ L41/25.

The approach of the Commission is not well founded. The pursuit of the solidarity purpose does not necessarily preclude the existence of the market mechanism. The framework under which Slovak insurance companies operates bears significant level of resemblance with the system in Ireland as in the BUPA case. In both cases, price competition was eliminated by the state for solidarity purpose. Instead, the insurers compete with each other through value for money on the basis of quality of service (the benefits provided), as pointed out by the Court of First Instance.[148] And in both countries similar risk adjustment scheme have been set up to mitigate the difference of risk portfolios undertook by insurers as a result of regulation imposed by the State. Such measure may constitute a SGEI task and justifies derogation from competition law, rather than qualifying it as non-economic in nature and thus an exclusion. Therefore, the Court of First Instance was right to hold that the insurance programme was economic in nature. The case is in the process of appeal and it remains to be seen what approach the CJEU (Court of Justice of the European Union) will adopt on this important issue.

The common thread underlying these cases is that national regime regarding how health insurance is organised and structured determines whether an activity is economic or not. The social purpose of solidarity could be achieved through different means and mechanisms. If a social insurance programme operates as part of the state function, the Court will exclude the activity from the application of competition law. By contrast, if the Member State has adopted a market model, it will constitute economic activity and thus fall within the scope of competition law. In this way, the Court respects the national political choices regarding the organisation of its social insurance sector in the Member States.[149]

2.4 Conclusion

This chapter traces the historical root of different concepts in the debate of SGEI. It argues that the concept of SGI refers to State functions. This is essentially a political question, inherent in the idea of national sovereignty. Different nations have offered varied answers to this question: what functions shall be allocated to the State? It also evolves over time. In the Member States, traditional State functions were confined within certain core areas—the prerogatives of the State, such as security, law enforcement and foreign relations. This part of State functions is closely connected with the exercise of public power.

After World War II, State functions expanded greatly in two respects. First, the Member States intervened in their economies directly, by controlling and managing certain sectors including: telecommunications, postal services, transport,

[148]Case T-216/15 *Dôvera zdravotná poist'ovňa, a.s. v European Commission* (not yet reported). http://curia.europa.eu/juris/liste.jsf?language=en&num=T-216/15.

[149]Boeger 2007; Schweitzer 2011; Cahill 2010.

broadcasting and energy. These sectors were organised based on a public service model rather than on a competitive market. Public undertakings were established and were controlled by national governments in order to pursue a wide range of economic and non-economic values. They did not have commercial freedom: important decisions were made by public authorities. Competition was impossible because exclusive rights were often granted by the Member States to these undertakings.

The second respect of expansion of State functions was in the area of welfare services. The idea was that the State assumes responsibilities towards its citizens to look after their welfare. Based on this principle, modern comprehensive welfare systems began to take shape in the Member States covering health, education and other forms of social assistance.

The organisation of public health systems well illustrates how the organisation of welfare systems is based on logic different from that of the market. Funding is pooled together through taxation or compulsory contribution. Benefits are provided based on individual needs, and often free of charge. Coverage is universal, meaning everyone in the society is entitled to receive welfare service, in spite of the actual amount of his contribution. This is well reflected in the principle of *solidarity*.

The application of EU competition law in the area of SGI creates serious tensions and much controversy for two reasons. On the one hand, the EU's involvement in this area would inevitably erode the sovereign power of the Member States. In other words, making rules at EU level would mean competence transfer from the Member States to the EU. On the other hand, free movement of economic activities and undistorted competition lie at the foundation of the EU Internal Market. Applying EU rules on competition and free movement to SGEIs would potentially challenge the structure and values underpinning the organisation of SGI.

The precondition for EU competition law to apply is that the activity in question must be economic in nature. Regarding the prerogatives and welfare functions of the State, they are regarded as non-economic, and consequently outside the reach of competition law. The essential question is where to draw the line between economic and non-economic activities. The demarcation line is not straightforward, because the Member States increasingly undertake reforms in discharging its functions that were formerly solid State functions, which often means the introduction of market elements and competition incentives.

This research finds that the Court has adopted *a functional approach*. The essential criterion is whether the exercise of public power is involved. Only if a particular activity forms an indispensable part of its public function, will it be regarded as *non-economic in nature* and therefore be excluded from the application of EU competition law. In the social insurance sector, the Court referred to *the principle of solidarity* as the benchmark to distinguish non-economic from economic activities. This research finds that the key criteria for excluding social insurance from the scope of competition law have been: (1) the lack of link between contributions and benefits; and (2) State control over the amount of contributions and benefits.

By contrast, the fate of SGEI is very different. Though they were not organised based on a competitive market model, there has been a strong assumption that they are economic in nature. This is reflected in the fact that the drafters of the Treaty of Rome placed rules for SGEI (Article 106) in the competition law chapter of the Treaty. This approach is also reflected in the case law of the Court, which often assumes SGEI's economic nature without any in-depth discussion, therefore subjecting SGEIs to the application of EU competition law. As will be seen in the next chapter, the interpretation and application of Article 106 has changed fundamentally, starting in the beginning of 1990s, which ultimately transformed the landscape of SGEIs across the Member States.

References

Allum P (1995) State and society in Western Europe. Polity Press, Cambridge

Boeger N (2007) Solidarity and EC competition law. European Law Review 32(3):319–340

Borre O, Goldsmith M (1995) The scope of government. In: Borre O, Scarbrough E (eds) The scope of government. Oxford University Press, Oxford

Borre O, Viegas JM (1995) Government intervention in the economy. In: Borre O, Scarbrough E (eds) The scope of government. Oxford University Press, Oxford

Buendia Sierra JL (2000) Exclusive rights and state monopolies under EC Law: Article 86 (former Article 90) of the EC Treaty. Oxford University Press, Oxford

Cahill D (2010) The ebb and flow, the doldrums and the raging tide: single market law's ebb and flow over services of general economic interest, the legal doldrums over services of general interest, and the raging tide of Article 106(2) (ex Art 86(2)) over state aid & public procurement. European Business Law Review 21(5):629–662

Conway G (2010) Conflicts of competence norms in EU law and the legal reasoning of the ECJ. German Law Journal 11(9):966–1005

Craig P (2010) The Lisbon Treaty: law, politics, and treaty reform. Oxford University Press, Oxford

Cruz JB (2005) Beyond competition: services of general interest and European community law. In: De Búrca G (ed) EU law and the welfare state: in search of solidarity. Oxford University Press, Oxford, pp 169–212

Cygan A (2008) Public healthcare in the European Union: still a service of general interest? International and Comparative Law Quarterly 57(3):529–560

Damjanovic D, De Witte B (2009) Welfare integration through EU law: the overall picture in the light of the Lisbon Treaty. In: Neergaard UB, et al (eds) Integrating welfare functions into EU law: from Rome to Lisbon. DJØF Publishing, Copenhagen

Ewing KD (2001) Constitutional reform and human rights: unfinished business? Edinburgh Law Review 5(3):297–324

Ferrera M (2005) Towards an 'open' social citizenship? the new boundaries of welfare in the European Union. In: De Búrca G (ed) EU Law and the welfare state: in search of solidarity. Oxford University Press, Oxford, pp 11–38

Fiedziuk N (2011) Services of general economic interest and the Treaty of Lisbon: opening doors to a whole new approach or maintaining the 'status quo'. European Law Review 36(2):226–242

Freeman R (1998) Competition in context: the politics of health care reform in Europe. International Journal for Quality in Health Care 10(5):395–401

Giaimo S (2014) Cost containment vs. solidarity in the welfare state: the case of German and American health care reform. American Institute for Contemporary German Studies: Policy Papers No. 6, 1998. http://webdoc.sub.gwdg.de/ebook/lf/2003/aicgs/publications/PDF/giaimo.pdf

Greer I, Breidahl NK, Knuth M, Larsen F (2017), The Marketization of employment services: the dilemmas of Europe's work-first welfare state. Oxford University Press, Oxford
Haffner A (2005) United States Postal Service v Flamingo Industries (USA) Ltd: does the USA have the answer to the 'undertaking problem' in Europe? European Competition Law Review 26(7):397–402
Hammerschmid G, Van de Walle S, Andrews R, Mostafa A (2019) New Public Management reforms in Europe and their effects: findings from a 20-country top executive survey. International Review of Administrative Sciences 85(3):399–418
Hatzopoulos V (2005) Health law and policy: the impact of the EU. In: De Búrca G (ed) EU Law and the welfare state: in search of solidarity. Oxford University Press, Oxford, pp 111–168
Hatzopoulos V (2009) Service of general interest in healthcare: an exercise in deconstruction. In: Neergaard U, Nielsen R (eds) Integrating welfare functions into EU law: from Rome to Lisbon. DJØF Publishing, Copenhagen
Hervey TK (2011a) If only it were so simple: public health services and EU law. In: Cremona M (ed) Market integration and public services in the European Union. Oxford University Press, Oxford, pp 179–310
Hervey TK (2011b) The impacts of European Union law on the health care sector: institutional overview. Eurohealth, 16(4):5–7
Holmes J (2004) Fixing the limits of EC competition law: state action and the accommodation of the public services. Competition Law and Policy 57(1):149–174
Huffschmid J (ed) (2005) Economic policy for a social Europe a critique of neo-liberalism and proposals for alternatives. Palgrave, Macmillan
Kaufmann FX, Veit-Wilson J (Trans) (2012) European foundations of the welfare state. Berghahn Books, New York & Oxford
Krajewski M (2006) Background paper on a legal framework for services of general (economic) interest. https://www.epsu.org/sites/default/files/article/files/Paper%20legal%20framework%20SGI_M_Krajewski_2006.pdf
Lasok KPE (2004) When is an undertaking not an undertaking? European Competition Law Review 25(7):383–385
Lenaerts K (2012) Defining the concept of 'services of general interest' in light of the 'checks and balances' set out in the EU treaties. Jurisprudence 19(4):1247–1267
Maas W (2007) Creating European citizens. Rowman & Littlefield, Washington DC
Majone G (1997) From the positive to the regulatory state: causes and consequences of changes in the mode of governance. Journal of Public Policy 17(2):139–167
Marshall TH (1950) Citizenship and social class, and other essays. Cambridge University Press, Cambridge
Menéndez AJ (2003) The rights' foundations of solidarity: social and economic rights in the Charter of Fundamental Rights of the European Union. Working Papers 03/1, Advanced Research on the Europeanisation of the Nation-State, University of Oslo
Millward R (2008) Private and public enterprise in Europe: energy, telecommunications and transport 1830–1990. Cambridge University Press, Cambridge
Mossialos E, Dixon A (2002) Funding health care: an introduction. In: Mossialos E, Dixon A, Figueras J, Kutzin J (eds) Funding health care: options for Europe. European Observatory on Health Care Systems, 2002. http://www.euro.who.int/document/e74485.pdf?ua=1
Neergaard U (2009) Services of general economic interest: the nature of the beast. In: Krajewski M, Neergaard U, Van de Gronden J (eds) The changing legal framework for services of general interest in Europe: between competition and solidarity. T.M.C. Asser Press, The Hague, pp 17–50
O'Leary S (2005) Solidarity and citizenship rights in the charter of fundamental rights of the European Union. In: De Búrca G (ed) EU Law and the welfare state: in search of solidarity. Oxford University Press, Oxford, pp 39–87
Odudu O (2010) The public/private distinction in EU Internal Market Law. Revue trimestrielle de droit europeen 46(4):826–841

Odudu O (2011) Are state-owned health-care providers undertakings subject to competition law? European Competition Law Review 32(5):231–241

Picard F (1998) Citizenship, fundamental rights, and public services. In: Freedland M, Sciarra S (eds) Public services and citizenship in European Law: public and labour law perspectives. Oxford University Press, Oxford

Prosser T (2005) The limits of competition law: markets and public services. Oxford University Press, Oxford

Ross M (2000) Article 16 EC and service of general interest: from derogation to obligation. European Law Review 25(1):22–38

Ross M (2007) Promoting solidarity: from public services to a European model of competition? Common Market Law Review 44(4):1057–1080

Ross M (2009) The value of solidarity in European public services law. In: Krajewski M, van de Gronden J, Neergaard U (eds) The changing legal framework for services of general interest in Europe: between competition and solidarity. T.M.C. Asser Press, The Hague, pp 81–99

Ross M (2010) Solidarity—a new constitutional paradigm for the EU? In: Ross M, Borgmann-Prebil Y (eds) Promoting solidarity in the European Union. Oxford University Press, Oxford, pp 23–45

Rott P (2005) A new social contract law for public services?—Consequences from regulation of services of general economic interest in the EC. European Review of Contract Law 1(3):323–345

Rott P (2007) Consumer and Services of General Interest: is EC Consumer Law the Future. Journal of Consumer Policy 30(1):49–60

Saltman RB, Figueras J (eds) (1997) European health care reform: analysis of current strategies. WHO Regional Publications, European Series, No. 72

Sauter W (1998) Universal service obligations and the emergence of citizens' rights in European telecommunications liberalization. In: Freedland M, Sciarra S (eds) Public services and citizenship in European law: public and labour law perspectives. Oxford University Press, Oxford, pp 117–143

Sauter W (2011) Harmonisation in healthcare: the EU patients' rights directive. TILEC Discussion Paper No. 2011–030

Sauter W (2013) The impact of EU competition law on national healthcare systems. European Law Review 38(4):457–478

Schweitzer H (2011) Services of general economic interest: European Law's impact on the role of markets and of member states. In: Cremona M (ed) Market integration and public services in the European Union. Oxford University Press, Oxford, pp 11–62

Somek A (2007) Solidarity decomposed: being and time in European citizenship. European Law Review 32(6):787–818

Szyszczak E (2007) The regulation of the state in competitive markets in the EU. Hart Publishing, Oxford

Szyszczak E (2009) Modernising healthcare: pilgrimage for the Holy Grail? In: Krajewski M, Neergaard U, Van de Gronden J (eds) The changing legal framework for services of general interest in Europe: between competition and solidarity. T.M.C. Asser Press, The Hague, pp 191–213

Tanzi V (1997) The changing role of the state in the economy: a historical perspective. IMF Working Paper, WP/97/114. www.imf.org/external/pubs/ft/wp/wp97114.pdf

Winterstein A (1999) Nailing the jellyfish: social security and competition law. European Competition Law Review 20(6):324–333

Yergin D, Stanislaw J (1998) The commanding heights: the battle between government and the marketplace that is remaking the modern world. Simon & Schuster Ltd, New York

Chapter 3
The Grant of Exclusive Rights Under Article 106

Contents

Abstract The provision of services of general economic interest (SGEIs) was often organised under a monopolistic structure through the grant of exclusive right by the Member States. Such a measure is inherently anti-competitive because it eliminates market competition, which would naturally cause the EU concern. Exclusive right is covered by Article 106, which will be the focus of this chapter. Article 106 has been at the heart of this debate, and it has a 'notorious' reputation as being very difficult to interpret and apply. When the Treaty of Rome was adopted in 1957, State monopolies were widespread across the Member States in sectors such as electronic communications, postal services, public transport and broadcasting. This

L. Zhu, *Services of General Economic Interest in EU Competition Law*, Legal Issues of Services of General Interest,
https://doi.org/10.1007/978-94-6265-387-0_3

reality was largely taken for granted and remained outside the reach of EU competition law until the late 1980s. There was a fundamental change in the case law of the Court in early 1990s, which transformed the landscape of SGEI. The grant of exclusive rights is increasingly regulated and limited by EU competition law unless it is necessary for the provision of SGEIs under economically acceptable conditions.

Keywords service of general economic interest · exclusive right · necessity test · Article 106 TFEU · limitation of supply · equal opportunity · extension of monopoly

3.1 Introduction

Article 106 has been at the heart of the debate surrounding services of general economic interest (SGEIs) and has attracted a lot of discussion from scholars.[1] It is not surprising because for decades Article 106 had been the only Treaty provision that mentions SGEI. Until now, all important cases of the Court on SGEI have been made under this Article. Although other Articles were added into the Treaty, the real effects of these new provisions are doubted owing to their general and ambivalent nature.[2]

Article 106 has a 'notorious' reputation as being very difficult to interpret and apply with certainty.[3] The case law has been criticised as being inconsistent and even contradictory. Regarding the compatibility of exclusive rights under Article 106(1), four possible approaches have been formulated by commentators, including the absolute/limited sovereignty approach and absolute/limited competition approach.[4] This issue is complicated by the SGEI derogation provided for in Article 106(2):[5] the restriction of competition is justified if it is necessary for the provision of SGEIs under economically acceptable conditions.[6] However, it is unclear what standard should be applied under this necessity test.

This chapter will reveal the evolving nature of the application and interpretation of Article 106. It finds that it was not the intention of the drafters of the Treaty of Rome to challenge the organisation of SGEIs by Member States. When the Treaty

---

[1]Blum and Logue 1998; Buendia Sierra 2000; Szyszczak 2007; Pappalardo 1991; Lang 2005; Sauter 2008; Zevgolis 2012; Davies 2009.

[2]Blum and Logue 1998, p. 21; Buendia Sierra 2000, p. 34; Sauter 2008.

[3]Pappalardo 1991; Edward and Hoskins 1995; Davies 2009; Szyszczak 2007.

[4]Hancher 1999; Edward and Hoskins 1995.

[5]Hancher 1999.

[6]Case C-320/91 *Paul Corbeau* [1993] ECR I-2533.

of Rome was drafted, the founders must have been aware of the realities of mixed economy in Member States.[7] They largely took state intervention in the economy for granted and respected the Member States' sovereign power in this respect.[8] This approach was followed by the Court in its early case law on Article 106(1). In the *Sacchi* Judgment in 1974, the Court ruled explicitly that Article 106(1) permitted the Member States to grant or extend exclusive rights.[9]

From the late 1980s onwards the EU's political agenda changed dramatically: it aimed to further market integration and to complete its Internal Market programme by 1992.[10] As part of its efforts, the Commission began to invoke Article 106 to challenge national monopoly rights in the telecommunications[11] and postal services[12] sectors. It was not a mere coincidence that in roughly the same period serious doubts about the compatibility of exclusive rights were raised by national courts and several cases were referred to the Court. In this context, the Court's interpretation of Article 106 became critical to the ongoing liberalisation process.

In 1991, the Court fundamentally changed its original approach in the *Sacchi* case. Its rulings rendered direct support to the Commission's liberalisation efforts in the telecommunications and postal services sectors. On the one hand, it delivered

---

[7] Allum divides national economies into three sectors: competitive sector, monopoly sector and state sector. Allum 1995, p. 32.

[8] This approach is generally adopted by the Treaty of Rome as a whole, which on several occasions made special arrangements for state intervention in the economy:

(1) Article 37 did not abolish state monopolies but merely required the Member States to progressively adjust their behaviour to be in line with rules on free movement;
(2) Article 48(4) grants a derogation for employment in the public service from the application of rules on free movement of workers;
(3) Article 77 grants a derogation for PSO compensations from the application of state aid rules;
(4) Article 222 expressly confirms that the EU is neutral to public property ownership.

[9] Case 155/73 *Giuseppe Sacchi* [1974] ECR-409.

[10] Commission of the European Communities, White Paper from the Commission to the European Council: Completing the Internal Market, COM (85) 310 final, 14.06.1985; Single European Act 1986.

[11] In 1988, the Commission issued a Directive to liberalise the telecommunication terminal equipment market based on its power under Article 106(3): Commission Directive 88/301/EEC of 16 May 1988 on competition in the markets in telecommunications terminal equipment [1988] OJ L131/73.

[12] In 1989, the Commission made two Decisions under Article 106(3), concluding that the Netherlands and Spain were in breach of Article 106(1) in conjunction with Article 102 by reserving express mail service for its postal monopolist:

(1) 90/16/EEC: Commission Decision of 20 December 1989 concerning the provision in the Netherlands of express delivery services [1990] OJ L10/ 47;
(2) 90/456/EEC: Commission Decision of 1 August 1990 concerning the provision in Spain of international express courier services [1990] OJ L233/19.

four Judgments in 1991 on the interpretation of Article 106(1) read in conjunction with Article 102—*Höfner* in April,[13] *ERT* in June,[14] *GB Inno*[15] and *Porto di Genova* in December.[16] In these cases, the Court ruled that grant of exclusive rights was incompatible with Article 106(1) (read in conjunction with Article 102). Given the fact that exclusive rights were still widespread in many areas across the Member States, the implications of the ruling were significant. The Court's interpretation of Article 106(1) will be the focus of Sect. 3.2.

Meanwhile, in the *France v Commission* Judgment in March 1991,[17] the Court recognised the Commission's power under Article 106(3) to act alone, without the involvement of the Council or the Parliament, to issue Directives to Member States directing them to break down national monopoly structures. This will be discussed in Sect. 3.3.

The last section of this chapter focuses on Article 106(2). It shows that a literal reading of Article 106(2) suggests that its original function was only to bring SGEI *undertakings* under the jurisdiction of competition law and to grant a limited derogation for such undertakings. However, a dramatic change happened in the *Corbeau* case in 1993,[18] when the Court applied the derogation to *Member States*. It is in this case that *the necessity test* was established by the Court.

3.2 The Application of Article 106(1) to Member States

3.2.1 The Original Reading—Absolute Sovereignty Approach

Article 106(1) is a 'reference rule':[19] it does not lay down any substantive obligations for Member States, but instead simply refers them to the whole range of the rules in the Treaty.[20] The text of the provision reads as follows:

[13] Case C-41/90 *Klaus Höfner and Fritz Elser v Macrotron GmbH* [1991] ECR I-1979.

[14] Case C-260/89 *Elliniki Radiophonia Tileorassi AE (Ert) (Panellinia Omospondia Syllogon Prossopikou Ert intervening) v Dimotiki Étairia Pliroforissis (Dep) and Sotirios Kouvelas (Nicolaos Avdellas and Others intervening)* [1991] ECR I-02925.

[15] Case C-18/88 *Régie des Télégraphes et des Téléphones v GB-Inno-BM SA* [1991] ECR I-5941.

[16] Case C-179/90 *Merci Convenzionali Porto di Genova SpA v Siderurgica Gabrielli SpA* [1991] ECR I-05889.

[17] Case C-202/88 *French Republic v Commission of the European Communities* [1991] ECR I-1223.

[18] Case C-320/91 *Paul Corbeau* [1993] ECR I-2533.

[19] Pappalardo points out Article 106(1) is superfluous because Member States are subject to Treaty provisions without its reference. Pappalardo 1991.

[20] Bright 1993.

> In the case of public undertakings and undertakings to which Member States grant special or exclusive rights, Member States shall neither enact nor maintain in force any measure contrary to the rules contained in the Treaties, in particular to those rules provided for in Article 18 and Articles 101 to 109.

A literal reading of this provision suggests that the drafters of the Treaty of Rome in 1957 had not intended to prescribe that the grant of exclusive rights was to be illegal under this Article. This approach is confirmed in the early case law of the Court in the *Sacchi* case.[21]

The *Sacchi* case was referred to the Court by an Italian court concerning the compatibility of exclusive rights in the broadcasting sector. Sacchi refused to pay the licence fee on the ground that his reception was confined exclusively to cable television, which was outside the scope of the monopoly of the public broadcaster RAI (Radio Audizione Italiana). In the preliminary procedure, the Court was asked specifically:

> Whether exclusive rights *granted by a Member State* to a limited company in relation to television broadcasts, and the *exercise of such rights*, are compatible with the competition rules of the Treaty?[22] (emphasis added)

This was the first time that the Court had the chance to deal with the question of the compatibility of State-granted exclusive rights under EU competition law. The stakes were high because the organisation of the broadcasting sector in Italy was in question. Italian law reserved all activities of television broadcasting to the State, and granted an exclusive right to its public undertaking RAI[23] for the transmission of programmes. All television signal receivers were required to pay licence fee.

This is a good example regarding how the Member States organised the broadcasting sector. Under the notion of public service broadcasting, the State established public undertakings to pursue the public interest. In this case, from the very beginning, RAI's mission was set out as to education, information and entertainment, rather than profit making.[24] In return, the Italian State granted a statutory monopoly right to RAI over the whole television broadcasting sector in Italy.

Under this model, there is overlap between different concepts referred to in Article 106: broadcasting was regarded as an activity in the public interest—the notion of public service broadcasting in Member States; the whole sector was reserved for a *public undertaking* through *exclusive rights* granted under national law. Consequently, public undertakings, undertakings with exclusive rights and

---

[21] Case 155/73 *Giuseppe Sacchi* [1974] ECR-409.

[22] Ibid., para 12.

[23] RAI's status as a public undertaking was not mentioned in the Judgment of the Court or in the Opinion of Advocate General. This fact can be found on its official website. The company was established in 1954, and the Ministry of Economy and Finance owns 99.56% of its shares. RAI Official Website, 'RAI Group Reports and Financial Statements 2010' http://www.rai.it/dl/bilancio2010/eng/dwl/pdf/RAI_Financial2010_ENG.pdf.

[24] Ibid., p. 14.

SGEI undertakings refer to one entity in practice. This is the very position of RAI in this case.

In its ruling, the Court applied Article 106(1) to Member States and Article 106 (2) to undertakings. As to the State measure granting exclusive rights, it is Article 106 (1) that applies. The Court ruled expressly that:

> Article 106(1) *permits* Member States inter alia *to grant special or exclusive rights to undertaking.* [...] It is therefore the same as regards *an extension* of exclusive rights following a new intervention by this State.[25] (emphasis added)

This is a clear statement of the so-called '*absolute sovereignty approach*' formulated by scholars,[26] based on which Member States have complete sovereignty in relation to the creation of monopoly.[27] As the Advocate General explained in his Opinion: Article 102 'does not prohibit *dominant positions in themselves*; it is certainly not, therefore, the dissolution of every kind of *monopoly structure* that can be demanded under Article 102'.[28]

In other words, competition law prohibits only the *abusive behaviour* of a dominant position, rather than the *monopoly structure* itself. Therefore, at this stage, national law, which created a monopoly through exclusive rights, was permitted under EU competition law.[29] Such state measures were compatible with the competition rules of the Treaty, even though the outcome was the total elimination of competition altogether.[30]

In its Judgment, it is implied that Member States also had absolute sovereignty to define SGEIs and their scope. Indeed a whole sector could be regarded as SGEI and be covered by statutory monopoly. This approach is shown clearly in the Court's observation that:

> Member States could treat undertakings entrusted with the operation of television, even as regards their *commercial activities*, in particular *advertising*, as undertakings entrusted with the *service of general economic interest*.[31] (emphasis added)

So at this stage of Article 106 jurisprudence's development, while Member States were left *free to create exclusive rights and to define SGEIs*, the key function of Article 106 was to subject SGEI undertakings to the application of competition law. Following this approach, the only concern of competition law with respect to SGEIs was whether SGEIs perpetuated *anti-competitive behaviour*.

---

[25] Case 155/73 *Giuseppe Sacchi* [1974] ECR-409, para 14.

[26] Schweitzer 2011.

[27] Edward and Hoskins 1995.

[28] Opinion of Advocate General, Case 155/73 *Giuseppe Sacchi* [1974] ECR-409, 196.

[29] Szyszczak 2007, p. 112.

[30] This approach was substantively changed in later case law, where the structure of exclusive rights was regarded as incompatible with the Treaty without any commitment of abusive behaviour by undertakings in 1991. This issue will be dealt with in the next section.

[31] Case 155/73 *Giuseppe Sacchi* [1974] ECR-409, para 15.

However, the Court's attitude changed fundamentally in 1991: the Member States were found in breach of Article 106(1), read in conjunction with Article 102 in four Judgments delivered at around the same time—*Höfner* in April,[32] *ERT* in June,[33] *GB Inno*[34] and *Porto di Genova* in December.[35]

The difficulties lie in that Article 102 prohibits only the abusive behaviour of a dominant position, not the creation of the monopoly structure itself. In order to hold Member States accountable under Articles 106 and 102, two conditions must be met.[36] First, it must be established that abusive behaviour under Article 102 has actually been committed by the holder of the exclusive right. Second, a causal link between the Member State's grant of the exclusive right and the abusive behaviour by the undertaking must be established. In other words, it must be established that it was the Member State's conditions set for the SGEI's operation that have caused the undertaking to abuse its State-conferred dominant position. Otherwise, if the abuse is an independent behaviour of the undertaking, it is the undertaking itself, not Member State that would be held responsible under Article 102.

In fact, what the Court did was to loosen the standards in the application of these two conditions. As will be shown in the following sections, more often than not, the Court did not find that abusive behaviour had actually been committed by the holder of an exclusive right, but rather that the conditions set by the State for its operations put it in a position whereby abusive conduct became inevitable. Accordingly, the causal link between *the grant* of exclusive rights and *their abuse* became very easy to establish.[37] As a result, *the creation of exclusive rights* in the first place came more easily to be found incompatible with the Treaty.[38]

The implications of these Judgments were very significant for the ongoing liberalisation process, where, at this very time, the Commission was using Article 106 (1) to challenge statutory monopolies in the telecommunications and postal services sectors.

---

[32] Case C-41/90 *Klaus Höfner and Fritz Elser v Macrotron GmbH* [1991] ECR I-1979.

[33] Case C-260/89 *Elliniki Radiophonia Tileorassi AE (Ert) (Panellinia Omospondia Syllogon Prossopikou Ert intervening) v Dimotiki Étairia Pliroforissis (Dep) and Sotirios Kouvelas (Nicolaos Avdellas and Others intervening)* [1991] ECR I-02925.

[34] Case C-18/88 *Régie des Télégraphes et des Téléphones v GB-Inno-BM SA* [1991] ECR I-5941.

[35] Case C-179/90 *Merci Convenzionali Porto di Genova SpA v Siderurgica Gabrielli SpA* [1991] ECR I-05889.

[36] Bright 1993; Edward and Hoskins 1995.

On this issue scholars are divided into two camps: the behaviour doctrine versus the effects doctrine. Buendia Sierra 2000.

[37] The link was so weak in the *ERT* and *Porto de Genova* cases that former Judge Edward argued that the Court adopted a complete competition approach. Edward and Hoskins 1995.

[38] Gyselen 1993; Bright 1993; Zevgolis 2012; Davies 2009.

3.2.2 The Höfner Case—Prohibition of Service Provision

The *Höfner* case[39] has attracted much discussion from commentators and also produced a lot of controversy.[40] A brief account of its factual background is highly necessary. The case was concerned with a German regime on employment procurement, which involved the establishment of a public undertaking and also the grant of exclusive rights. In order to maintain a high level of employment, the Act for the Promotion of Employment in 1969[41] entrusted the task of employment procurement to *Bundesanstalt* (the Federal Office for Employment), which is a *public administration body*. Its activities were funded by *compulsory contribution* from employers and employees. In return, the service was provided *free of charge*. Meanwhile, the law also reserved the whole sector of employment procurement to *Bundesanstalt* and prohibited others from such activities. The law also prescribed penalties for offenders of such exclusive rights.

Certain features of the organisation of the German system on employment procurement are noteworthy. The first is the dominant influence of the State in the provision of the activities in question. In this case, the influence of the State is even stronger than that in the case of a public undertaking—the body was part of the public administration, carrying out its activities in the public interest, rather than to make a profit. Second, the whole sector was reserved for the *Bundesanstalt* by statutory monopoly rights. The law defined its activities in a general and abstract way, rather than in specific and detailed terms. Therefore, when new services emerged as a response to new demands in the market, the scope of the monopoly and its compatibility became the focus of attention.

Despite the general prohibition on one engaging in the employment procurement activity, a market for recruitment service for business executives had developed in Germany. In the main proceedings, the defendant Macrotron refused to pay for such services, even though it had entered into a contract with a recruitment agency Klaus Höfner and Fritz Elser, and it sought a declaration that the contract was void since it was in breach of German law. Several questions were referred to the Court, including one question regarding the compatibility of such exclusive rights under EU competition law.

In its Judgment, the Court divorced from its complete sovereignty approach established in its earlier *Sacchi* case and began to challenge the existence of exclusive rights under Article 106(1).[42] This essentially meant that the model of SGEI organisation was under attack. In this case, the Court applied two sets of competition rules to the Member States and to undertakings separately. Regarding

---

[39] Case C-41/90 *Klaus Höfner and Fritz Elser v Macrotron GmbH* [1991] ECR I-1979.

[40] Hancher 1999; Lang 2005.

[41] –, 'Short Chronicle of the Federal Employment Agency (Bundesagentur für Arbeit)' http://www.arbeitsagentur.de/nn_426292/EN/Navigation/zentral/BA/Geschichte/Geschichte-Nav.html.

[42] Szyszczak 2007.

rules applicable to undertakings, Articles 101 and 102 were applicable. On the other hand, as to rules for the Member States, it was Article 106(1) that was of relevance.

In its Judgment, the Court ruled that 'the Treaty requires the Member States not to take or maintain in force measures which could destroy the effectiveness of that provision [note: Article 102]'.[43] The legal basis for the obligation of the Member States lies in Article 106(1), which was interpreted by the Court as:

> The simple fact of creating a dominant position of that kind by granting an exclusive right within the meaning of Article 106(1) is not as such incompatible with Article 102 of the Treaty. A Member State is in breach of the prohibition contained in those two provisions *only if* the undertaking in question, merely by exercising the exclusive right granted to it, *cannot avoid abusing* its dominant position.[44] (emphasis added)

The wording 'cannot avoid abusing' suggests that a causal link is established between *the grant of monopoly* by German law and *abusive behaviour* by the undertaking in question simply by virtue of the conditions set by the State for the SGEI itself. In other words, the reason for finding state responsibility (for the infringement of Article 102 by the public undertaking) lies in the *causal link* between State measures and the *abusive behaviour* of the undertaking being established in the eyes of the Court. However, a closer investigation of the case reveals that neither condition could be supported by the facts of the case.

Regarding the abusive behaviour of the undertaking, the alleged abuse was the limitation of services, i.e. the law prohibited anyone else providing the service where clearly there was unmet demand for the service. However, the case suggests something opposite.[45] *Bundesanstalt* had been trying to *increase the provision* of the employment procurement in two ways. First, it established a special agency for business executive recruitment to meet the demand. Second, it had openly tolerated the presence of independent employment procurement activities in the market, which eroded its exclusive rights. This was also the finding of the Advocate General in his Opinion, which read as follows:

> It may seem *harsh* to describe the Bundesanstalt's conduct as abusive. There is *nothing* in the file to suggest that it has not endeavoured to the best of its ability *to satisfy the demand* for assistance in the recruitment of executives. Moreover, it has voluntarily relaxed its monopoly by expressing its willingness to tolerate competition from private operators.[46] (emphasis added)

The real concern of the Court was German law itself because it 'creates a situation in which the provision of a service is limited',[47] when: (1) the holder of the exclusive rights is *manifestly incapable of satisfying market* demand; and (2) the effective pursuit of such activities by others was *prohibited by law*. It is clear that if

---

[43] Case C-41/90 *Klaus Höfner and Fritz Elser v Macrotron GmbH* [1991] ECR I-1979, para 26.

[44] Ibid., para 29.

[45] Gyselen 1993.

[46] Opinion of Advocate General, Case C-41/90 *Klaus Höfner and Fritz Elser v Macrotron GmbH* [1991] ECR I-1979, para 45.

[47] Case C-41/90 *Klaus Höfner and Fritz Elser v Macrotron GmbH* [1991] ECR I-1979, para 31.

the provision of the service had been *actually* limited, it arose from the *effects of German law*, not because of the behaviour of the public undertaking in question: it was the German State that had reserved the whole sector for one entity, and it was German law that prohibited others from providing such service; and so it was that State that was at 'fault' for not allowing others to respond to new market demand.

The *Höfner* case is significant in the sense that the Court essentially departed from its approach in the *Sacchi* case regarding the compatibility of exclusive rights. Henceforth, the application of Article 106(1) began to challenge state measures *granting* exclusive rights; the freedom of the Member States was not absolute any more.[48] However, the wording of the Judgment seems to be modest. A literal reading of it suggests that it does not require the abolishment of exclusive rights altogether. Such state measures are still allowed to be maintained as long as the holder of the exclusive rights could meet the demand of the market, or such rights could be relaxed to allow other providers to step in to meet unmet demand for services.

3.2.3 *The* ERT *Case—The Doctrine of Equal Opportunity*

The principle of equal opportunity was first mentioned by the Court in the *France v Commission* case in March 1991.[49] In that case, the Court condemned the grant of *market regulation* power to the undertaking *which was also active on the same market*. It might seem obvious that this situation will inevitably lead to a *conflict of interest*, as suggested by the wording of the Court:

> It should be observed that a system of undistorted competition, as laid down in the Treaty, can be guaranteed only if *equality of opportunity* is secured as between the various economic operators. To entrust an undertaking with markets terminal equipment with the task of drawing up the specifications for such equipment, monitoring their application and granting type-approval in respect thereof is tantamount to conferring upon it the power to

[48] Hancher 1999.

[49] As part of the Commission's liberalisation efforts in the telecommunications sector, it adopted its Terminal Equipment Directive 88/301, which required the Member States to withdraw exclusive rights over terminal equipment. The legality of the Directive was challenged by France before the Court. The main argument put forward by France was that the Commission did not have the power to issue Directives of general application under Article 106(3). The case is discussed in more detail in Sect. 3.3.3. Article 6 of Directive 88/301 also required the Member States to ensure that the responsibility for drawing up specifications, monitoring their application and granting type-approval is entrusted to a body independent of undertakings on the market. It was in dealing with the validity of this Article that the Court made the observation on the principle of conflict of interests: Case C-202/88 *French Republic v Commission of the European Communities* [1991] ECR I-1223.

> determine at will which terminal equipment may be connected to the public network, and thereby placing that undertaking at an *obvious advantage over competitors*.[50] (emphasis added)

The Court did not state exactly what the legal basis is. It seems that such doctrine is inherent in the principle of fair competition, rather than in any substantive rules in competition law. What is clear is that this prohibition has nothing to do with abusive behaviour by the undertaking. It merely concerns state measures that grant the (quasi)-regulation power to undertakings active on the market and create the seedbed for conflict of interests to inevitably arise.

Under the doctrine of equal opportunity, there was another significant Judgment: the *ERT* case,[51] delivered in June 1991 only three months after the *France v Commission* case. The case was concerned with the organisation of the broadcasting sector in Greece, where the State had direct control over radio and television broadcasting. The Greek State established a public undertaking ERT (Elliniki Radiophonia Tileorassi AE) for radio and television broadcasting. It was under the control and supervision of the State and carried out broadcasting activities to contribute to the information, culture and entertainment of the people, rather than profit making. Meanwhile, the State granted ERT an exclusive right, covering all activities related to radio and television broadcasting, and prohibited any other entity from engaging in broadcasting.

In the main proceedings, DEP was a television station company that broadcast programmes in Greece. It was accused of breaching the statutory monopoly held by ERT under Greek law. The national court raised several questions about the compatibility of the exclusive rights under Treaty rules on free movement and competition.

It was quite clear that the case was 'concerned not with any *specific conduct of the undertaking'*, but with the *structure of the monopoly*.[52] In other words, what was in question was *the model of organisation of the broadcasting sector*, with the dominance of the public undertaking under the protection of the statutory monopoly covering all activities of the sector. The compatibility of such exclusive rights was not a new issue. If the Court had followed the approach in the *Sacchi* case, the monopoly structure would be perfectly compatible with the Treaty. Even under the *Höfner* doctrine, the exclusive right held by ERT could hardly be regarded as in breach of competition law because there was nothing in the case to suggest that ERT could not meet market demand.

---

[50] Ibid., para 51.

[51] Case C-260/89 *Elliniki Radiophonia Tileorassi AE (Ert) (Panellinia Omospondia Syllogon Prossopikou Ert intervening) v Dimotiki Étairia Pliroforissis (Dep) and Sotirios Kouvelas (Nicolaos Avdellas and Others intervening)* [1991] ECR I-02925.

[52] Opinion of Advocate General, Case C-260/89 *Elliniki Radiophonia Tileorassi AE (Ert) (Panellinia Omospondia Syllogon Prossopikou Ert intervening) v Dimotiki Étairia Pliroforissis (Dep) and Sotirios Kouvelas (Nicolaos Avdellas and Others intervening)* [1991] ECR I-02925, para 36.

However, the Court essentially departed from both the *Sacchi* and the *Höfner* case law. It attacked the statutory monopoly under *the doctrine of equal opportunity*. But its reasoning was far from consistent. It did not follow its approach in the *France v Commission* Judgment, which only prohibited Member States from granting an undertaking *the power to regulate the market* (in which it itself was also a participant).[53] Quite surprisingly, the Court conveniently borrowed the concept from the context of free movement and applied it in the competition law context.

In its Judgment, the Court first discussed the issues in the free movement context. The precondition for its application is the presence of a cross-border element. Notwithstanding that both undertakings in question were both Greece based, the Court broke down the statutory monopoly structure by focusing on its cross-border element, i.e. the *retransmission* of television programmes in Greece that were *produced in other Member States*. In this respect, the Court found that the Greek legislation granted a *dual monopoly* to a single undertaking. This structure led to the monopoly concentration of *transmission of its own programmes* on the one hand and, on the other hand, *retransmission of programmes* produced in other Member States. The Court found that such structure of exclusive right leads to *potential discrimination against foreign undertakings*. Consequently, the Court found that the state legislation that conferred such a monopoly was in breach of free movement rules, without any mention of the actual behaviour of the undertaking.

The Court went on further to examine the compatibility of the exclusive rights under Article 106(1) in conjunction with Article 102. Surprisingly, it essentially borrowed the above reasoning regarding the potential discriminatory nature of monopoly and ruled that the grant of such a monopoly structure was incompatible with Article 106(1) in conjunction with 102. Its Judgment reads as follows:

> The reply to the national court must therefore be that Article 106(1) of the Treaty prohibits the granting of *an exclusive right to transmit* and *an exclusive right to retransmit* television broadcasts to a single undertaking, where those rights are *liable to create a situation* in which that undertaking *is led to infringe Article 102* by virtue of *a discriminatory broadcasting policy* which favours its own programmes, unless the application of Article 102 obstructs the performance of the particular tasks entrusted to it.[54] (emphasis added)

By using the phrase ‘led to infringe’, it seems that the Court was to establish a causal link between *the grant of exclusive right by State measures* and *the infringement of 102 by the undertaking*. However, in this case the actual existence of infringement of Article 102 by the undertaking could hardly be established. Indeed, the Court did not make any factual assessment as to such abusive behaviour at all.[55]

---

[53] This doctrine could hardly be applied in this case, which was not concerned with such power. Following this approach, the exclusive right was perfectly legal under competition law.

[54] Case C-260/89 *Elliniki Radiophonia Tileorassi AE* (*Ert*) (*Panellinia Omospondia Syllogon Prossopikou Ert intervening*) *v Dimotiki Étairia Pliroforissis* (*Dep*) *and Sotirios Kouvelas* (*Nicolaos Avdellas and Others intervening*) [1991] ECR I-02925, para 37.

[55] Gyselen 1993.

In this case, what is at issue is the structure of exclusive rights that covers both *transmission and retransmission,* which place the holder of the exclusive rights in a position of an almost inevitable path towards a *conflict of interest.*[56] In other words, the Court was using Article 106(1) (read in conjunction with Article 102) to *attack the structure of the exclusive rights* and consequently to challenge the very existence of statutory monopoly itself.[57]

This could only lead to confusion because Article 106(1) is a reference rule that does not contain any substantive obligations for the Member States. In order to challenge exclusive rights, the substantive legal basis is found in Article 102. The difficulty is that Article 102 is not designed to challenge the very existence of the exclusive rights. On the contrary, Article 102 permits *the existence of monopoly structure* but prohibits only *abusive behaviour* of undertakings in a dominant position. In other words, the target of Article 102 is the *abusive behaviour of dominant undertakings in the market* rather than *the structure of monopoly itself.*

In this case, without finding actual abusive behaviour by the undertaking, the Court largely expanded the scope of Article 102 to cover the *potentiality/danger* of such abuse. In this regard, the opinion of the Advocate General is illuminating:

> In the light of that case-law one may in fact, as the Commission has done, express reservations regarding the fact that the applicant has been granted a *comprehensive monopoly* in areas with *divergent interests* (note: the broadcasting of its own programmes and the retransmission of foreign broadcasts). [...] Inherent therein is the *danger* of discrimination against foreign products and because this – as it must be *assumed* that the undertaking favours its own products – must be regarded as a kind of limitation of production contrary to Article 102(b).[58] (emphasis added)

In this way, the Court aggressively uses Article 102, which prohibits only abusive behaviour rather than the presence of monopoly itself, to challenge the very existence of exclusive rights. What is significant about the *ERT* case is that it established a new principle under Article 106(1) (read in conjunction with Article 102), i.e., the principle of *equality of opportunity.* State measures that place a market undertaking in a position of *conflict of interest* would be condemned as incompatible with competition law.[59]

---

[56] Szyszczak 2007, p. 124.

[57] Bekkedal argues that this principle 'does not share much in common with competition law in its true and original sense. The doctrine is not really about efficiency or freedom to compete'. Bekkedal 2011, p. 87.

[58] Opinion of Advocate General, Case C-260/89 *Elliniki Radiophonia Tileorassi AE (Ert) (Panellinia Omospondia Syllogon Prossopikou Ert intervening) v Dimotiki Étairia Pliroforissis (Dep) and Sotirios Kouvelas (Nicolaos Avdellas and Others intervening)* [1991] ECR I-02925, para 40.

[59] Later case law and the Commission practice show that the implications of this principle are far-reaching. In this respect, the establishment of a breach of the Article 106(1) in conjunction with Article 102 by Member States does not require any actual commission of abusive behaviour by undertakings any more. The target of the Court is the very structure of the exclusive right itself. This approach of the Court could be clearly observed in the *Decoster* case in 1993, where an

3.2.4 The GB Inno *Case—Prohibition of Monopoly Extension*

Another development in the Article 106 case law regarding the incompatibility of the grant of exclusive rights came about in the *GB Inno* case delivered by the Court in December 1991.[60] The case was concerned with the organisation of the telecommunications sector in Belgium. A 1930 law established a *public undertaking,* RTT (Régie des Télégraphes et des Téléphones), to operate telegraph and telephone service in Belgium. The company was owned and managed by the State for the *public interest*. Meanwhile, the law granted RTT an *exclusive right* over the telecommunications network.[61] The key issue in this case was concerned with RTT's power to grant type-approval to telephone equipment connected to the network. This power derived from a Ministerial Order of 1978, which provided that equipment connected to the network must be supplied or approved by RTT.

The facts of the case in the main proceeding were quite straightforward. A private Company GB Inno sold telephones that were not approved by RTT. In the preliminary ruling procedure, the Belgian court asked specifically about the compatibility of such a regime with the rules on free movement and competition.

In the competition law context, the exclusive right in question was attacked by the Court from two aspects. First, it challenged RTT's regulatory power relating to type-approval, holding that it breached the *principle of equal opportunity* principle as established in the *ERT* case and that consequently such power should be withdrawn.

---

exclusive right was found incompatible with the Treaty because it granted a *market regulation* power to an undertaking that was also active on the same market.

This case was concerned with the organisation of the telecommunications sector in France. French telecommunications law granted the task of operation of public telecommunication network to the Directorate General of Telecommunication in the Ministry of Posts and Telecommunications. In order to safeguard the functioning of the network and user safety, the law also prescribed that any terminal equipment connected to the network must submit a type-approval certificate issued by the CNET (Centre National d'études des Télécommunications), which was also part of the Ministry of Posts and Telecommunications. In the main proceedings, Mrs Gillon sold telecommunication terminal equipment without obtaining any type approval, which was a criminal offence under the French law. She argued that the CNET was not independent.

The very issue in question was the structure of the telecommunications sector in France: the Ministry of Posts and Telecommunications was responsible for the management of telecommunication network, the grant of type approval and the marketing of terminal equipment. The Court found its legal basis in the *ERT* case and ruled that such a structure was incompatible with Article 106(1).

Case C-69/91 *Criminal proceedings against Francine Gillon, née Decoster* [1993] ECR I-5335.

[60] Case C-18/88 *Régie des Télégraphes et des Téléphones v GB-Inno-BM SA* [1991] ECR I-5941.

[61] Ibid., para 2.

More significantly, the Court went further to challenge RTT's exclusive rights over the telephone equipment market,[62] establishing a new prohibition under Article 106 jurisprudence, namely the prohibition of *extension of monopoly rights* from the telecommunications network to equipment marketing.[63] Indeed, the Court had to make such intervention because the exclusive right in question could hardly be caught by previous case law under the *Sacchi* case, the *Höfner* case or the *ERT* case.[64]

The reasoning of the Court is worthy of attention. In order to establish an extension under competition law, there must be two related, but separate, markets. The approach of the Court was to break down the comprehensive structure of the national monopoly into two parts. First, it defined 'the establishment and operation of the public telecommunications network' as one market.[65] There is no doubt that RTT enjoyed a dominant position on this market, because the Belgian law had granted RTT an exclusive right. Second, it stated that telecommunications equipment is an ancillary, but separate, market from the telecommunications network market.[66]

Based on such separation of markets, the Court applied competition law to undertakings and the Member States separately. As to the application of competition law to undertakings, it ruled that Article 102 prohibited undertakings in a dominant position from reserving to itself neighbouring but separate markets unless there was an objective justification.

For Member States, it was Article 106(1) that was applicable: if the extension of the dominant position is *a consequence of a State measure*, the State is thereby in breach of Article 106(1), read in conjunction with Article 102.[67] The Court held as follows:

---

[62]The actual existence of such monopoly right over the telephone equipment market is still in doubt. As pointed out by Advocate General in his Opinion, RTT did not have such rights. Its exclusive rights over telephone equipment only covered first telephones connected to the network. As to the second telephones connected to the network, it did not have exclusive rights but competed with other private providers. Meanwhile, it had the right to lay down technical specifications and type-approval. This dual role as competitors and regulators leads to a conflict of interest and goes against the principle of equal opportunity.

[63]This principle has long been established under Article 102, which prohibited private undertakings in a dominant position from reserving a downstream or ancillary market for itself. See Joined Cases 6 & 7–73 *Istituto Chemioterapico Italiano S.p.A. and Commercial Solvents Corporation v Commission of the European Communities* [1974] ECR-223; 88/518/EEC: Commission Decision of 18 July 1988 relating to a proceeding under Article 86 of the EEC Treaty (Case No IV/30.178 Napier Brown—British Sugar) [1988] OJ L284/41.

[64]Under the *Sacchi* case, Member States are permitted to grant and to extend exclusive rights. Based on the *Höfner* case, exclusive rights are incompatible with competition law only when the holder of exclusive right was manifestly incapable of meeting market demand. In this case, there were no facts to suggest that RTT could not meet market demand. Furthermore, the principle of equal opportunity in the *ERT* case is unlikely to apply in this case because the concentration of two pure market activities, namely operation of telecommunication network and equipment marketing, does not lead to a conflict of interest situation.

[65]Case C-18/88 *Régie des Télégraphes et des Téléphones v GB-Inno-BM SA* [1991] ECR I-5941, para 15.

[66]Ibid., para 19.

[67]Lang 2005.

Accordingly, where *the extension of the dominant position* of a public undertaking or undertaking to which the State has granted special or exclusive rights *results from* a state measure, such a measure constitutes an infringement of Article 106 in conjunction with Article 102 of the Treaty.[68] (emphasis added)

It is clear that the case was not concerned with any *abusive behaviour of the undertaking* in question. The target of the Court was the very structure of the exclusive right itself. It essentially applied Article 102 directly to state measures.[69] It condemned the state measure, because it led to an extension of monopoly, which is prohibited by Article 102.[70]

What is also interesting in the case is that the monopoly structure *extending* to the telecommunications equipment market was not created by newly adopted legislation but derived from a *comprehensive monopoly structure* granted by law in 1930. From the very beginning, the domestic statutory monopoly rights had been covering both network operation and telecommunication terminal equipment. So the principles established in this case rendered direct support to the ongoing liberalisation process in the telecommunications and postal services sectors.[71] A *direct consequence* of the *GB Inno* Judgment (that the exclusive rights over the telephone equipment market were in breach of competition law and must be withdrawn) meant that the Judgment had a far-reaching liberalising effect, at least in the telecommunications sector: in *GB Inno*, the exclusive rights over telephone equipment were regarded as an incompatible extension (with competition law and free movement rights) of monopoly from the network market to the equipment market. Following this logic, other areas of the telecommunications sector, such as telecommunications services, satellite communications and mobile services, could

[68] Case C-18/88 *Régie des Télégraphes et des Téléphones v GB-Inno-BM SA* [1991] ECR I-5941, para 21.

[69] This approach is different from its previous Judgment in the *ERT* case and in the *Höfner* case, where the Court was struggling to find the actual commission of abusive behaviour of the undertaking and to establish its direct link with the State.

[70] Buendia Sierra 2000, p. 171.

[71] In the postal service sector, the Commission adopted a Decision in December 1989 that prohibited the reservation of express mail service for the incumbent monopolist. The Decision was then challenged in the Court and was still pending when the *GB-Inno* Judgment was given. This issue will be covered in Sect. 3.3.3.

90/16/EEC: Commission Decision of 20 December 1989 concerning the provision in the Netherlands of express delivery services [1990] OJ L10/ 47.

Joined cases C-48/90 & C-66/90 *Kingdom of the Netherlands, Koninklijke PTT Nederland NV and PTT Post BV v Commission of the European Communities* [1992] ECR I-565.

Very recently, the Commission has adopted similar Decisions to liberalise the postal service market in Member States, including:

(1) 2001/176/EC: Commission Decision of 21 December 2000 concerning proceedings pursuant to Article 86 of the EC Treaty in relation to the provision of certain new postal services with a guaranteed day-or time-certain delivery in Italy [2001] OJ L63/59;
(2) COMP/F-1/39.562: Commission Decision of 7 October 2008 on the Slovakian law on hybrid mail services [2008] OJ C322/10.

also be regarded as ancillary, but separate, markets from the network market. Therefore, exclusive rights over these markets could also be condemned as an incompatible extension of monopoly of network operations under competition law and so must be withdrawn.

3.2.5 The Porto di Genova *Case—A Loosened Standard of Attribution*

The year 1991 also witnessed another case that made state measures granting exclusive rights vulnerable under EU law. In the *Porto di Genova* case,[72] the Court held that the State was responsible for the abusive behaviour of undertakings holding a statutory monopoly. Distinct from the above three cases, this case was not concerned with *the structure of the exclusive rights* in question: rather it dealt with the *actual occurrence of abusive practice*, which could be *attributed to the Member State-conferred monopoly*.

The case was concerned with an Italian law regarding the operation of loading and unloading of goods in Italian ports. Italian law granted the dock work companies an *exclusive right* to organise dock work for loading and unloading goods in Italian ports. The national legislation also prohibited others from undertaking such activities. In the Port of Genoa, such monopoly rights were held by Merci Covenzionali Porto di Genova Spa (hereafter Merci Covenzionali), which was also a *public undertaking* under the control of the port authorities. It held a concession to organise dock workers in the Port of Genoa. Meanwhile, *the scale of charges* and other *conditions of operations* were laid down by the port authority.

In the main proceedings, a company, Siderurgica, applied to Merci Covenzionali to unload its ship's steel cargo in the Port of Genoa. Owing to a workers' strike, Merci Covenzionali failed to perform the task, which led to delays and also financial loss to Siderurgica. In the preliminary proceedings, the Italian court referred to the Court questions concerning the compatibility of the Italian regime with the Treaty rules.

In its Judgment, the Court applied a two-step approach to hold the Italian State accountable for anti-competitive behaviour: first, the existence of such behaviour under Article 102 and, secondly, its causal link with state measure granting the exclusive rights. The wording of the Advocate General in his opinion suggested this approach expressly:

For this purpose two points must be considered: first, whether Merci or Compagnia or both *committed acts* which, irrespective of any action by the authorities, represent *the abuse of a dominant position* […] and, secondly, whether

[72] Case C-179/90 *Merci Convenzionali Porto di Genova SpA v Siderurgica Gabrielli SpA* [1991] ECR I-05889.

the national legislation in question *facilitates* such abuse or makes it *compulsory or inevitable*.[73] (emphasis added)

As to the existence of abusive behaviour by the undertaking in question, the Court suggested several types of conduct constituted abuses of a dominant position in light of Article 102. These included: (a) imposing unfair purchase prices or other unfair trading conditions; (b) limiting technical development; and (c) application of dissimilar conditions to equivalent transactions. However, the Court did not conduct a serious economic assessment to reach such a conclusion.[74]

A more significant question was how the abusive conduct of the undertaking could be *attributed to the State*. In other words, in what circumstances is the link between the State, which conferred a monopoly, and the abusive behaviour of the undertaking strong enough to hold a State responsible under Article 106(1)? In its Judgment, the Court devoted only one short paragraph to confirm the link between *the grant* of exclusive rights and the *aforementioned abusive behaviour*. It held as follows:

In that respect it appears that [...] the undertakings in question enjoying exclusive rights in accordance with the procedures laid down by the national rules in question *are, as a result, induced* either to demand payment for services which have not been requested, to charge disproportionate prices, *to refuse to have recourse to modern technology* [...] or to grant price reduction to certain consumers and at the same time to offset such reductions by any increase in the charges to other consumers.[75] (emphasis added)

Its reasoning is far from convincing. Indeed, in this case the Court did not require a *causal link*, i.e. that the abusive behaviour was a *direct consequence* of the state measure.[76] In fact, the Court had largely lowered the standard when assessing the link between the grant of exclusive rights by the States and the abusive behaviour by the undertakings: even if the grant of exclusive rights only *facilitates* the abuse or *potentially* leads to inefficiency, then the State will be held in breach of Article 106(1) read in conjunction with Article 102. This could be observed from the careful choice of wording in the Opinion of the Advocate General:

In fact, the scale of charges and other, *presumably unfair*, contractual conditions applied by Merci and Compagnia are *made possible*, if *not inevitable*, by the national legislation applicable and are *facilitated*, if *not made compulsory*, by the port authorities under the powers conferred on them by national legislation.[77] (emphasis added)

---

[73] Ibid., para 16.

[74] Nevertheless, it would not lead to much of a problem in practice because it is the national courts that are responsible for such factual issues in the application of Article 102.

[75] Case C-179/90 *Merci Convenzionali Porto di Genova SpA v Siderurgica Gabrielli SpA* [1991] ECR I-05889, para 19.

[76] Buendia Sierra 2000, p. 167.

[77] Case C-179/90 *Merci Convenzionali Porto di Genova SpA v Siderurgica Gabrielli SpA* [1991] ECR I-05889, paras 22–23.

In this case, if there was certain link between the grant of the exclusive rights and the abusive practices, it was the inherent *potential effect* of the exclusive rights. The grant of exclusive rights through national legislation essentially wipes out competition from the market. This might, but not necessarily, lead to a less efficient provision of the service in question, such as where the monopolist had no incentive to innovate.

The implications are significant. Following this loosening of the standard for the establishment of state responsibility under Article 106(1), the grant of exclusive rights by Member States tends to be more easily found to be in breach of the Treaty. Later EU practice shows this is particularly true if the state measures under examination are concerned with the *pricing policy* of the undertaking in question.[78]

3.3 The Controversial Power Under Article 106(3)

The significance of Article 106 also lies in the enforcement power under its third paragraph. Article 106(3) grants the Commission the power to issue Directives without the involvement of Council or the Parliament, and to make Decisions addressed to Member States in question. This conferral of sole legislative competence is most unusual under the Treaty. It reads as follows:

> The Commission shall ensure the application of the provisions of this Article and shall, where necessary, address appropriate Directives or Decisions to Member States.

These powers, especially the power to issue Directives, have turned out to be very controversial and have become a battlefield between the Commission and the Member States.[79] It lies in the structure of competence allocation between different institutions at the EU level: the Commission is generally regarded as the executive branch of the Union, not the legislative power. If such power can go beyond what is necessary for its executive function, it would undermine the constitutional structure of the EU institutions. More importantly, the Commission could use this competence to bypass national governments to frequently challenge and, by force of law, dismantle national monopolies.[80] As pointed out by the Advocate General in his Opinion, the interpretation of Article 106(1) and (3) is of 'definite importance', but the wording of the provisions is of 'manifest obscurity'.[81]

---

[78] 95/364/EC: Commission Decision of 28 June 1995 relating to a proceeding pursuant to Article 90 (3) of the Treaty [1995] OJ L216/8; 97/745/EC: Commission Decision of 21 October 1997 relating to a proceeding pursuant to Article 90 (3) of the EC Treaty regarding the tariffs for piloting in the Port of Genoa [1997] OJ L301/27; Case C-242/95 *GT-Link A/S v De Danske Statsbaner (DSB)* [1997] ECR I-4449; Joined Cases C-147/97 & C-148/97 *Deutsche Post AG v Gesellschaft für Zahlungssysteme mbH (GZS) (C-147/97) and Citicorp Kartenservice GmbH (C-148/97)* [2000] ECR I-825; Case C-340/99 *TNT Traco SpA v Poste Italiane SpA and Others* [2001] ECR I-4109.

[79] Pappalardo 1991.

[80] Szyszczak 2007, p. 131.

[81] Opinion of Advocate General, Case C-202/88 *French Republic v Commission of the European Communities* [1991] ECR I-1223, para 1.

In its early case law, this power was confined to what was necessary for the Commission's executive function. However, in the late 1980s, the Commission began to adopt liberalisation Directives to challenge state monopolies in the telecommunications sector. When such power was challenged before the Court, the Court confirmed that the Commission has such general legislative power, which rendered direct support to the market integration process.

3.3.1 The Commission's Power to Make Decisions

The effect of a Commission's Decision is confined only to the Member States in question.[82] Therefore, its significance is less far-reaching than that of Directives. Before 1990, the Commission used this power to investigate anti-competitive behaviour by undertakings[83] and discriminatory state measures.[84] In the late 1980s, its focus shifted towards the grant of exclusive rights itself, and it adopted two Decisions challenging national postal monopolies in the Netherlands and Spain.[85]

---

[82] Blum and Logue 1998, p. 43.

[83] The Commission adopted five Decisions against undertakings before 1990, which will be dealt with in Sect. 3.4.3.

(1) 78/823/EEC: Commission Decision of 21 September 1978 relating to a proceeding under Article 85 of the EEC Treaty (IV/28.824—Breeders' rights—maize seed) [1978] OJ L286/23;
(2) 82/861/EEC: Commission Decision of 10 December 1982 relating to a proceeding under Article 86 of the EEC Treaty (IV/29.877—British Telecommunications) [1982] OJ L360/36;
(3) 82/371/EEC: Commission Decision of 17 December 1981 relating to a proceeding under Article 85 of the EEC Treaty (IV/29.995—NAVEWA-ANSEAU) [1982] OJ L167/39;
(4) 89/205/EEC Commission Decision of 21 December 1988 relating to a proceeding under Article 86 of the EEC Treaty (IV/31.851—Magill TV Guide/ITP, BBC and RTE) [1989] OJ L78/43;
(5) 89/536/EEC Commission Decision of 15 September 1989 relating to a proceeding under Article 85 of the EEC Treaty (IV/31.734—Film purchases by German television stations) [1989] OJ L284/36.

[84] Before 1990s the Commission adopted two Decisions based on Article 106(3) against Member States. They are not concerned with the compatibility of exclusive rights itself. These Decisions are:

(1) 85/276/EEC: Commission Decision of 24 April 1985 concerning the insurance in Greece of public property and loans granted by Greek State-owned banks [1985] OJ L152/25;
(2) 87/359/EEC: Commission Decision of 22 June 1987 concerning reductions in air and sea transport fares available only to Spanish nationals resident in the Canary Islands and the Balearic Islands [1987] OJ L194/28.

[85] The facts and legal reasoning of these two Decisions are similar. This section focuses only on the Decision concerning Dutch postal monopoly: (1) 90/16/EEC: Commission Decision of 20 December 1989 concerning the provision in the Netherlands of express delivery services [1990] OJ L10/ 47; (2) 90/456/EEC: Commission Decision of 1 August 1990 concerning the provision in Spain of international express courier services [1990] OJ L233/19.

Its Decision in December 1989 concerning the Dutch postal monopoly offers a very good example. Dutch law reserved the express mail service for its former monopolist and prohibited all other undertakings from conducting such business. The Commission's Decision was tricky in the sense that it dealt only with this new enactment, i.e. the extension of the statutory rights, rather than the postal monopoly as a whole, which had been established over the postal network and all postal services since 1954.[86]

The Decision still created much controversy and was challenged in the Court. The tension could be easily observed from the Court proceeding. On the one hand was the liberalisation force led by the Commission and supported by the beneficiary undertakings, i.e. the express mail carriers that were often new entrants to the market. On the other hand was the Member State, which was struggling to maintain its control over the organisation of the national economy, supported by the State-appointed monopolist that was the holder of exclusive rights. The attitude of the Court is decisive in this battle between these driving forces heading in opposite directions. The Court was in support of the Commission and upheld its power to make Decisions using Article 106(3) as a legal base:

> If the power to adopt Decisions, conferred on the Commission by Article 106(3), is not to be deprived of all practical effect, the Commission must be empowered *to determine* that a given State measure is incompatible with the rules of the Treaty and *to indicate what measures* the State to which the Decision is addressed must adopt in order to comply with its *obligations under Community law*.[87] (emphasis added)

In its Judgment, the Court maintained that such power is 'essential and indispensable' for the Commission to discharge its duty to ensure a system of undistorted competition.[88] It stated that without the power to take actions directly against Member States on the basis of Article 106(3) 'it would be impossible for the Commission to discharge its duty completely'.[89]

3.3.2 The Original Scope of the Commission's Directive-Making Power

The first use of this power by the Commission dated back to 1980, when it issued a Directive on the Transparency of Financial Relations between Member States and Public Undertakings.[90] The focus of the Directive was that the complex financial

---

[86] Postal monopolies were also widespread in other Member States. Camenen 1996.

[87] Joined cases C-48/90 & C-66/90 *Kingdom of the Netherlands, Koninklijke PTT Nederland NV and PTT Post BV v Commission of the European Communities* [1992] ECR I-565, para 28.

[88] Ibid., paras 29–30.

[89] Ibid., para 30.

[90] Commission Directive 80/723/EEC of 25 June 1980 on the transparency of financial relations between Member States and public undertakings [1980] OJ L195/35.

relations between Member States and its public undertakings impeded the application of the state aid rules.[91] Therefore, it required Member States to *provide to the Commission such information* regarding public funds allocated to public undertakings and their use. Although its scope was remarkably limited,[92] its validity was challenged by France, Italy and the UK.[93] The major argument put forward by these Member States was the Commission's *lack of competence* to issue Directives of general application.

In its Judgment in 1982, the Court confirmed the Commission has competence to issue Directives in accordance with the provisions of Article 106(3) as long as the use of the power was limited within the ambit of the Commission's *executive functions*. In its Judgment it held that:

> The power conferred on the Commission by Article 106(3) is *limited to* the Directives and Decisions which are *necessary* to perform effectively *the duty of surveillance* imposed upon it by that paragraph.[94] (emphasis added)

The Court further explained that the Commission's power depends on 'the needs inherent in its duty of surveillance'.[95] Virtually the same wording could be found in the opinion of the Advocate General, which points out that the issue of Directive must be 'indispensable for the effective exercise of its functions'.[96]

It is clear from this case that, under Article 106(3) the power of the Commission is confined within its executive functions.[97] The Commission has the competence

[91] Pappalardo 1991.

[92] Commission Directive 80/723/EEC of 25 June 1980 on the transparency of financial relations between Member States and public undertakings [1980] OJ L195/35, Article 4. The scope of its application was largely expanded through later amendments, including Commission Directive 85/413/EEC, Commission Directive 2000/52/EC and Commission Directive 2005/81/EC.

The codified version of the Directive is Commission Directive 2006/111/EC of 16 November 2006 on the transparency of financial relations between Member States and public undertakings as well as on financial transparency within certain undertakings [2006] OJ L318/17.

[93] Joined cases 188 to 190/80 *French Republic, Italian Republic and United Kingdom of Great Britain and Northern Ireland v Commission of the European Communities* [1982] ECR-2545.

[94] Ibid., para 14.

[95] Ibid., para 14.

[96] In this case, the Directive was designed to facilitate the scrutiny of state aids, rather than to lay down new obligations under state aids rules. The Commission has exclusive competence and executive function to examine the compatibility of state aid under the Treaty. However, the complexities of financial relations between the Member States and their public undertakings 'made the Commission's supervisory task considerably more difficult or even impossible'. As pointed out by the Advocate General, the Directive was not concerned with aid itself in the sense that 'the Directive neither provides a definition of aids nor interferes with the procedure for the control of aids or determines its course'. In other words, it 'leaves the substantive provision of Article 107 et seq. of the Treaty unaffected and only creates the technical pre-conditions for it to carry out its obligations': Opinion of Advocate General, Joined cases 188 to 190/80 *French Republic, Italian Republic and United Kingdom of Great Britain and Northern Ireland v Commission of the European Communities* [1982] ECR-2545, 2587, 2591–2592.

[97] Buendia Sierra 2000, p. 409.

only to issue Directives 'of complementary and technical in character in relation to other Treaty provisions'.[98] This suggests that creating new obligations or challenging state measures based on other substantive Treaty provisions is beyond its competence under Article 106(3).

3.3.3 The Expanded Power of the Commission's Directive-Making Power

However, in 1988, the Commission went much further than purely *complementary and technical* issues as in the Transparency Directive; it adopted its first *liberalisation* Directive in the telecommunications sector: Commission Directive 88/301 on competition in Markets in Telecommunication Terminal Equipment (hereafter, the Terminal Equipment Directive).[99] In the Directive, it *challenged the very compatibility of exclusive rights* and *prescribed new obligations for Member States*. It condemned the statutory monopoly over telecommunication terminal equipment as being in breach of competition law and directed Member States to withdraw such exclusive rights.[100]

Given the fact that state monopolies over the whole telecommunications sector were widespread in all Member States, the substantive effect of the Directive itself was modest, since it only abolished the exclusive right over terminal equipment. However, the Commission's power to issue such Directives could have far-reaching implications: if Article 106(3) grants the Commission such power, then other parts of monopolies in the telecommunications sector could be susceptible to being abolished in the same way. This attracted much concern from the Member States: Article 106(3) procedure does not need any consent from Member States (i.e. the Council) and consequently could mean the Member States' *loss of control* over the organisation of major sectors of their national economies.[101]

It is not surprising that the Directive was challenged before the Court by France, and supported by several other Member States[102] on both substantive and procedural issues.[103] As to the Commission's power under Article 106(3), the Court

[98] Opinion of Advocate General, Joined cases 188 to 190/80 *French Republic, Italian Republic and United Kingdom of Great Britain and Northern Ireland v Commission of the European Communities* [1982] ECR-2545, 2589.

[99] Commission Directive 88/301/EEC of 16 May 1988 on competition in the markets in telecommunications terminal equipment [1988] OJ L131/73.

[100] Pappalardo 1991.

[101] This is the very case in the telecommunications sector where the whole sector is opened up to market competition through Commission Directives.

[102] These Member States are Italy, Belgium, Germany and Greece: Case C-202/88 *French Republic v Commission of the European Communities* [1991] ECR I-1223.

[103] The French Government argued, *inter alia*, that the Commission should initiate infringement proceedings under Article 258 TFEU against France, rather than issue a Directive requiring the Member States to withdraw special and exclusive rights. Ibid., para 16.

pointed out the Commission's duty of supervision under Article 106 may be exercised through the adoption of Directives and Decisions addressed to the Member States.[104] This statement was in line with its approach taken in previous case law.[105] Nevertheless, the Court *essentially departed* from its existing jurisprudence regarding the *constraints and boundaries* of the exercise of the Commission power. The wording of the Judgment reads as follows:

> It must be held in the first place that the supervisory power conferred on the Commission includes the possibility of *specifying obligations* arising under the Treaty, pursuant to Article 106(3). The *extent of that power* therefore depends on *the scope of the rules* with which compliance is to be ensured.[106] (emphasis added)

The underlying logic of the Court was that where Treaty provisions do not contain clear obligations for Member States, the Commission has the power under Article 106(3) to elaborate these Treaty rules and specify these obligations.[107] Based on this approach it inevitably involves the *interpretation of Treaty rules* and its *application* to particular situations. Consequently, it is a process of application of Treaty rules and the evaluation of obligations for Member States under Treaty provisions. This leads to the conclusion whether or not Member States are in breach of substantive Treaty rules. This was exactly the finding of the Commission as to the compatibility of the monopoly over telecommunication terminal equipment. It found that such exclusive rights were in breach of Treaty rules and must be withdrawn.

In the Court's ruling, the attention shifted to the application of *substantive rules* of the Treaty,[108] rather than focusing on the *necessity and the needs inherited in the Commission's supervisory functions*. The implications are significant. Following this approach, issues such as whether the Commission had the competence to issue Directives and its constraints were of little importance; what matters is *whether the Commission applied Treaty provisions correctly*. This shift from the issue of *competence* to *substantive* issues is clearly revealed in the Judgment:[109]

> Accordingly, the Commission *rightly regarded* exclusive rights regarding the connection, bringing into service and maintenance of telecommunications terminal equipment as incompatible with Article 30.
>
> It *follows from the foregoing that the Commission was justified* in requiring the withdrawal of exclusive rights regarding the importation, marketing, connection, bringing into service of telecommunications terminal equipment and/or maintenance of such equipment.[110] (emphasis added)

---

[104] Ibid., para 24.

[105] Ibid.

[106] Ibid., para 21.

[107] Buendia Sierra 2000, p. 412

[108] Edward and Hoskins 1995, p. 185.

[109] Similar wording could also be found in the Judgment as to the abolishment of the regulatory powers held by national monopolists: Case C-202/88 *French Republic v Commission of the European Communities* [1991] ECR I-1223, paras 51–52.

[110] Ibid., paras 43–44.

Based on this approach, the Commission's power under Article 106(3) to issue legislative instruments was to be upheld as long as it had applied substantive rules correctly.[111] Only in the case of misapplication would the Court declare the relevant provision as void.[112] In this case, the Court did find that the Commission applied some Treaty provisions requiring the withdrawal of special rights incorrectly, and declared a number of provisions in the Directive void.[113] This 'setback' was not significant, given the fact that the relevant vulnerable provisions could be easily corrected by subsequent amendment.[114]

The argument put forward by the Court is far from convincing. The correct application of Treaty rules to Member States *does not necessarily justify* the Commission's use of power under Article 106(3) to issue Directives. In this respect, the Commission is also granted the power to bring the infringement to an end through judicial proceedings on a case-by-case basis under Article 258. Compared with judicial proceedings, the preferred use of Directives by the Commission is largely due to its '*direct and immediate effect'*.[115] This issue was well observed in the Opinion of the Advocate General, in which he pointed out correctly that:

> Whilst it is already by no means certain whether a Decision adopted under Article 106(3) can constitute a suitable and lawful alternative to proceedings brought under Article 258, the use of a Directive seems *even less appropriate*, since as an instrument it is *inherently unsuited* to bringing an infringement to an end, especially when – as here – it is addressed to the Member States *en bloc*. […] Neither observation seems sufficient to compensate for the lack of an explicit derogation from Article 258 and *the absence of the minimum guarantees of fair hearing* which are to be found in repressive procedures.[116] (emphasis added)

Taking such grounds into consideration, the Advocate General reached the opposite conclusion to that of the Court: 'as *a matter of principle*',[117] the Commission is not entitled to use Directives to challenge exclusive rights, according to the Advocate General.

---

[111]This approach is closely followed in a case shortly afterwards where the Directive of the Commission to liberalise the telecommunication services market was challenged by four Member States on similar grounds: Joined cases C-271/90, C-281/90 & C-289/90 *Kingdom of Spain, Kingdom of Belgium and Italian Republic v Commission of the European Communities* [1992] ECR I-5833.

[112]This does not affect the validity of other provisions of a Commission Directive or the power of the Commission to issue Directives in general. As in this case, the Court only declared certain provisions void.

[113]Case C-202/88 *French Republic v Commission of the European Communities* [1991] ECR I-1223, paras 45–47.

[114]Commission Directive 94/46/EC of 13 October 1994 amending Directive 88/301/EEC and Directive 90/388/EEC in particular with regard to satellite communications [1994] OJ L268/15.

[115]Case C-202/88 *French Republic v Commission of the European Communities* [1991] ECR I-1223, 1250.

[116]Opinion of Advocate General, Case C-202/88 *French Republic v Commission of the European Communities* [1991] ECR I-1223, para 32.

[117]Ibid.

The Court did not follow the approach proposed by the Advocate General and essentially departed from its previous case law. It supported the Commission's use of Directives to tackle widespread national monopolies. Its Judgment itself became part of this political process: it provided the legal basis that conferred competence on the Commission to promote market integration in the telecommunications sector. This accelerated the process of liberalisation of national monopolies and market integration of the telecommunications sector.[118]

What is worthy of special attention is the fact that even though the Court upheld the Commission's sole legislative power to issue Directives against the Member States under Article 106(3), its practical usage by the Commission is very limited. It was only in the telecommunications sector during the market liberalisation process that the Commission actually used this power.[119] By contrast, in other sectors, the Commission did not choose this path to promote market liberalisation and

---

[118] This is the very situation in the telecommunications sector. It took ten years to liberalise the sector fully into market competition through Commission Directives. By contrast, in the postal sector, without the adoption of Commission Directive, it took twice the time to liberalise the sector fully.

[119] This process will be discussed in Chap. 4. The Commission adopted a series of six Directives based on Article 106(3), which broke down national monopolies in the telecommunications sector gradually. These Commission Directives include:

(1) Commission Directive 88/301/EEC of 16 May 1988 on competition in the markets in telecommunications terminal equipment [1988] OJ L131/73;
(2) Commission Directive 90/388/EEC of 28 June 1990 on competition in the markets for telecommunications services [1990] OJ L192/10;
(3) Commission Directive 94/46/EC of 13 October 1994 amending Directive 88/301/EEC and Directive 90/388/EEC in particular with regard to satellite communications [1994] OJ L268/15;
(4) Commission Directive 95/51/EC of 18 October 1995 amending Directive 90/388/EEC with regard to the abolition of the restrictions on the use of cable television networks for the provision of already liberalised telecommunications services [1995] OJ L256/49;
(5) Commission Directive 96/2/EC of 16 January 1996 amending Directive 90/388/EEC with regard to mobile and personal communications [1996] OJ L20/59;
(6) Commission Directive 96/19/EC of 13 March 1996 amending Directive 90/388/EEC with regard to the Implementation of full competition in Telecommunications Markets [1995] OJ L256/49 OJ L74/13.

After the market was liberalised, legislation for a new regulatory framework is usually adopted by the Parliament and the Council. For example:

(1) Directive 95/62/EC of the European Parliament and of the Council of 13 December 1995 on the application of Open Network Provision (ONP) to voice telephony [1995] OJ L321/6;
(2) Directive 98/10/EC of the European Parliament and of the Council of 26 February 1998 on the application of Open Network Provision (ONP) to Voice Telephony and on universal service for telecommunications in a competitive environment [1998]OJ L101/24;
(3) Directive 2002/22/EC of the European Parliament and of the Council of 7 March 2002 on universal service and users' rights relating to electronic communications networks and services [2002] OJ L108/51.

Exceptions are found in early ONP Directives where Council Directives were issued, including:

integration. A good example is the postal sector.[120] The Commission intended to use its Article 106(3) power to liberalise the postal market. However, it was expressly rejected by the Council and the Parliament.[121] At the end, postal legislation was adopted through the harmonisation of legislative procedure (under Article 100), where the Member States (via the Council) could have more influence over the process.

3.4 The Interpretation of Article 106(2)

The first part of Article 106(2) is a reference rule. It does not contain any substantive obligations for undertakings. Instead, it merely confirms that SGEI undertakings are subject to competition law. It reads as follows:

> Undertaking entrusted with the operation of services of general economic interest or having the character of a revenue-producing monopoly shall be subject to the rules contained in the Treaties, in particular to the rules on competition.

In a competition law context, Articles 101 and 102 are addressed to undertakings and are therefore applicable to SGEI undertakings also.[122] The Court has ruled clearly that in the context of Article 106(2), Articles 101 and 102 have direct effect.[123] However, Article 106(2) modulates this basic position in a key respect: the significance of Article 106(2) lies in its second part, *which grants derogation from the application of competition law to SGEIs*. It provides that:

> Undertakings entrusted with the operation of services of general economic interest or having the character of a revenue-producing monopoly shall be subject to the rules contained in the Treaties, in particular to the rules on competition, in so far as the application of such rules does not obstruct the performance, in law or in fact, of the particular tasks assigned to them. The development of trade must not be affected to such an extent as would be contrary to the interests of the Union.

---

(1) Council Directive 92/44/EEC of 5 June 1992 on the application of Open Network Provision to leased lines [1992] OJ L165/27;

(2) Council Directive 90/387/EEC of 28 June 1990 on the establishment of the Internal Market for telecommunications services through the implementation of Open Network Provision [1990] OJ L192/1.

[120] In the telecommunications sector, there had been technological transformation and a political consensus on market liberalisation had been reached among the Member States. By contrast, such technological breakthrough did not occur in the postal sector, and the Member States had doubts about the real benefits about liberalisation in the postal market.

[121] This issue is discussed in more detail in Sect. 5.3.1 of Chap. 5.

[122] Case 94/74 *Industria Gomma Articoli Vari IGAV v Ente nazionale per la cellulosa e per la carta ENCC* [1975] ECR-699.

[123] Case 311/84 *Centre belge d'études de marché - Télémarketing (CBEM) v SA Compagnie luxembourgeoise de télédiffusion (CLT) and Information publicité Benelux (IPB)* [1985] ECR-3261.

A literal reading of the wording suggests that this derogation is applicable only to undertakings. This was also the original approach adopted by the Commission in its Decisions, and by the Court in its Judgments before the late 1980s. During this period (1971–1989), the practice of the Commission was more consistent. It focused on anti-competitive behaviour by SGEI undertakings and applied SGEI derogation to them very stringently.

However, from the late 1980s and early 1990s onwards, a fundamental change occurred in relation to the function of the second part of Article 106(2)—the SGEI derogation. It began to be applied *to state measures as derogation from competition law:* this was established in the *Corbeau* case in 1993.[124] Meanwhile, in the telecommunications liberalisation Directives, the Commission used this derogation to allow Member States to reserve the voice telephony services from the liberalisation process.[125]

3.4.1 A Literal Reading of the First Part of Article 106(2)

At the early stage of the case law, the real function of the first part of Article 106 (2) was to bring SGEI undertakings within the scrutiny of competition rules.[126] This principle was first established in the *Sacchi* case in 1974. In this ruling it applied the Article 106(1) to Member States and Article 106(2) to undertakings respectively. Although state measures creating monopoly structures were held to be compatible with the Treaty, the Court made a distinction between *state measures granting* exclusive rights and the *exercise of such rights by undertakings*. Its attention was focused on the latter, i.e. the behaviour of *the holder* of exclusive rights. In this regard, the Court ruled that:

> The national court has in each case to ascertain the *existence of such abuse* and the Commission has to remedy it within the limits of its powers. Even *within the framework of Article 106, the prohibitions of Article 102 have a direct effect* and confer on interested parties rights which the national Courts must safeguard.[127] (emphasis added)

It is a *declaratory statement* that confirms that all undertakings mentioned in Article 106 are within the scope of competition law.[128] In other words, it confirms that Article 106-type undertakings are all subject to Articles 101 and 102. It does not add new obligations to these undertakings or enlarge the scope of competition law since Articles 101 and 102 *apply to all undertakings on the market.*

---

[124] The case was directly relevant to the ongoing liberalisation process in the postal service and, to some extent, the telecommunications sector. The case was referred to the Court in 1991, concerning Belgium postal monopoly. Case C-320/91 *Paul Corbeau* [1993] ECR I-2533.

[125] SGEI derogation and telecommunications liberalisation will be dealt with in Chap. 5.

[126] Blum and Logue 1998, p. 18.

[127] Case 155/73 *Giuseppe Sacchi* [1974] ECR-409, para 18.

[128] Pappalardo 1991.

At this stage, while Member States were left *free to create exclusive rights and to define SGEIs*, the key function of Article 106 was to subject SGEI undertakings to the application of competition law. Following this approach, the only concern of competition law regarding SGEI was the *anti-competitive behaviour of SGEI undertakings.*[129]

This approach towards Article 106(2) was followed by the Court right until the *Corbeau* Judgment in 1993.[130] The *CBEM* case offers a very good example.[131] The case was concerned with the public service broadcaster in Belgium, RTL.[132] The organisation of the broadcasting sector in Belgium essentially adopted the same model as in the *Sacchi* case. RTL was as an undertaking in charge of the provision of public service broadcasting under the protection of statutory monopoly.[133] Unlike the *Sacchi* case, this case was not concerned with the organisation structure of broadcasting, but with the behaviour of RTL.

In this case, CBEM was a telemarketing company that placed advertisements on television with its telephone number. It is through this telemarketing number that the viewers could obtain further information or respond to the advertisement. RTL imposed one condition for its agreement with CBEM: the telemarketing number contained in the advertisement must be the number of an RTL-related company.[134] This essentially destroyed the commercial model of CBEM because the telephone number directed the customers to its competitor, RTL's subsidiary.

In the preliminary procedure, the Belgium national court did not have doubts regarding the compatibility of state law granting the exclusive rights; the questions raised by it were concerned exclusively with the interpretation of Article 102, i.e. the concept of dominant position and its abuse.[135]

---

[129] Buendia Sierra 2000.

[130] This interpretation of the first part of Article 106(2) was also reiterated in the Judgments of the Court in the *Höfner* case and the *ERT* case. Case C-41/90 *Klaus Höfner and Fritz Elser v Macrotron GmbH* [1991] ECR I-1979, para 24; Case C-260/89 *Elliniki Radiophonia Tileorassi AE* (*Ert*) (*Panellinia Omospondia Syllogon Prossopikou Ert intervening*) *v Dimotiki Étairia Pliroforissis* (*Dep*) *and Sotirios Kouvelas* (*Nicolaos Avdellas and Others intervening*) [1991] ECR I-02925, para 34.

[131] Case 311/84 *Centre belge d'études de marché - Télémarketing* (*CBEM*) *v SA Compagnie luxembourgeoise de télédiffusion* (*CLT*) *and Information publicité Benelux* (*IPB*) [1985] ECR-3261.

[132] Ibid.

[133] RTl's statutory monopoly was abolished in 1987 when the broadcasting sector was opened up to competition in Belgium. Coleman and Rollet 1997, pp. 87–90.

[134] It acted as RTL's exclusive television advertising agent. Opinion of Advocate General, Case 311/84 *Centre belge d'études de marché - Télémarketing* (*CBEM*) *v SA Compagnie luxembourgeoise de télédiffusion* (*CLT*) *and Information publicité Benelux* (*IPB*) [1985] ECR-3261.

[135] Case 311/84 *Centre belge d'études de marché - Télémarketing* (*CBEM*) *v SA Compagnie luxembourgeoise de télédiffusion* (*CLT*) *and Information publicité Benelux* (*IPB*) [1985] ECR-3261.

In this Judgment, the Court did not rule on the compatibility of the exclusive right in question. However, it was aware of the distortional effect of the exclusive rights. In the Opinion of Advocate General, he pointed out that 'in the case of a monopoly, competition is *completely excluded*'.[136] In its Judgment, the Court acknowledged that 'absence of competition [...] is brought about or encouraged by provisions laid down by law'.[137] Although following its reasoning in *Sacchi*, such statutory monopoly was compatible with Treaty rules, in the instant case, the real concern of the Court was about SGEI undertakings. The Court ruled that:

> It is apparent *from the same Article [Article 102]* that such undertakings remain subject to the Treaty rules on competition and in particular those contained in Article 102 [...] *the prohibitions of Article 102* apply, as regards their behaviour within the market, *by reason of Article 106(2)*.[138] (emphasis added)

Furthermore, the Court's focus on undertakings' behaviour could also be observed from the opinion of the Advocate General. He did not challenge the compatibility of statutory monopoly itself, but stated that 'the existence of a *legal monopoly* does not preclude the application of Article 102 but rather is *evidence of a dominant position*'.[139] Following this interpretation, the function of the first part of Article 106(2) is to bring SGEI undertakings within the scope of competition law, which has nothing to do with Member States.

3.4.2 The Application of SGEI Derogation to Undertakings

The second part of Article 106(2) grants a possible derogation to undertakings from the application of competition law.[140] However, the question of how to apply this derogation had not been raised in the *Sacchi* case.[141] In the *CBEM* case, the Court had not been asked what criteria should be applied: it only mentioned this issue by saying 'the prohibitions of Article 102 apply, as regards their behaviour within the market, [...] so long as it is not shown that the said prohibitions are incompatible

---

[136] Opinion of Advocate General, Case 311/84 *Centre belge d'études de marché - Télémarketing (CBEM) v SA Compagnie luxembourgeoise de télédiffusion (CLT) and Information publicité Benelux (IPB)* [1985] ECR-3261, 3267.

[137] Case 311/84 *Centre belge d'études de marché - Télémarketing (CBEM) v SA Compagnie luxembourgeoise de télédiffusion (CLT) and Information publicité Benelux (IPB)* [1985] ECR-3261, para 16.

[138] Ibid., para 17.

[139] Opinion of Advocate General, Case 311/84 *Centre belge d'études de marché - Télémarketing (CBEM) v SA Compagnie luxembourgeoise de télédiffusion (CLT) and Information publicité Benelux (IPB)* [1985] ECR-3261, 3267.

[140] Pappalardo 1991; Buendia Sierra 2000.

[141] Case 155/73 *Giuseppe Sacchi* [1974] ECR-409.

with the performance of their tasks'.[142] Therefore, the question of how to apply the SGEI derogation to undertakings remained unresolved.

In 1989, the Court was asked explicitly to consider this issue in the *Ahmed* case.[143] However, in its Judgment it did not clearly rule what standards would be applied under this test. Instead, it left the assessment of derogation to the national authorities responsible for the application of competition law.

The preliminary question was concerned with the German air tariff system, all of which needed to be approved by the State. Two German agents sold tickets of foreign airlines, which allowed German passengers who boarded the airplane at a German airport when the flight from another country made a stopover in Germany. The price was significantly lower and undercut the tariffs approved by the German authority.[144]

The focus of the Court is the application of Articles 101 and 102 to undertakings. These rules can be applied directly by national courts and competition authorities. Therefore, the examination of possible derogation is part of the process of application of these rules and is the responsibility of national courts and competition authorities. This approach towards Article 106(2) derogation was clearly stated in its Judgment as follows:

> That provision [Article 106(2)] may be applied to carriers who may *be obliged, by the public authorities, to operate on routes which are not commercial[ly] viable but which it is necessary to operate for reasons of the general interest.* However, for it to be possible for the effect of the competition rules to be restricted pursuant to Article 106(2) by needs arising from *performance of a task of general interest*, the national authorities responsible for the approval of tariffs and the courts to which disputes relating thereto are submitted must be able to determine *the exact nature* of the needs in question and *their impact* on the structure of the tariffs applied by the airlines in question.[145] (emphasis added)

The above statement articulates how the derogation would be applied; competition authorities need to establish the SGEI task and its impact on the undertaking. However, in this case the Court did not rule under what conditions the SGEI derogation would be applied: in other words, it did not give guidance on when the negative impacts of the SGEI task would be strong enough to preclude the application of competition law.[146]

---

[142]Case 311/84 *Centre belge d'études de marché - Télémarketing (CBEM) v SA Compagnie luxembourgeoise de télédiffusion (CLT) and Information publicité Benelux (IPB)* [1985] ECR-3261, para 17.

[143]Case 66/86 *Ahmed Saeed Flugreisen and Silver Line Reisebüro GmbH v Zentrale zur Bekämpfung unlauteren Wettbewerbs e.V.* [1989] ECR-803.

[144]The price of air tickets offered by the agent was sometimes 60% cheaper than the tariffs approved by the authorities. Opinion of Advocate General, Case 66/86 *Ahmed Saeed Flugreisen and Silver Line Reisebüro GmbH v Zentrale zur Bekämpfung unlauteren Wettbewerbs e.V.* [1989] ECR-803, 818.

[145]Case 66/86 *Ahmed Saeed Flugreisen and Silver Line Reisebüro GmbH v Zentrale zur Bekämpfung unlauteren Wettbewerbs e.V.* [1989] ECR-803, paras 55–56.

[146]Ibid., para 57.

However, this lack of detailed guidance on the application of SGEI derogation *to undertakings* does not pose much difficulty in practice.[147] The reason lies in the fact that it would be extremely difficult, or even impossible, for the undertaking to prove that its anti-competitive conduct (which are prohibited by Articles 101 and 102) is necessary for an SGEI task. This is well-illustrated in the Commission's Decisions, where no undertaking successfully invoked the SGEI derogation to justify anti-competitive conduct. These Decisions will be examined in the following section.

3.4.3 The Commission's Decision Practice Before 1989

For three decades since the adoption of Article 106, the focus of the Commission had been on anti-competitive behaviour conducted by SGEI undertakings. This was the direct effect of Articles 101 and 102. In this regard, the first part of Article 106 (2) functioned as a reference rule and did not impose new obligations for these undertakings. The SGEI derogation operates only at the end of this process, which examines whether the anti-competitive behaviour in question could be justified by an SGEI task.[148] Before the 1990s, the Commission adopted five Decisions examining their anti-competition behaviour.[149] This section examines two of them

[147] What is also worthy of attention is the fact that, since the 1990s, the focus of the discussion on SGEI has shifted to how it is applied to the *Member States* rather than *to undertakings*. In the *Corbeau* case, the Court ruled that restriction of competition by the Member States is justified if it is necessary for the provision of SGEIs. Since then the application of SGEI derogation to the Member States has generated a lot of controversy and discussion. Case C-320/91 *Paul Corbeau* [1993] ECR I-2533; Blum 2000; Kronenberger 2001.

[148] Buendia Sierra 2000, p. 289.

[149] This section looks at two of them in detail. The other three Decisions include:

(1) 78/823/EEC: Commission Decision of 21 September 1978 relating to a proceeding under Article 85 of the EEC Treaty (IV/28.824—Breeders' rights—maize seed) [1978] OJ L286/23. The Decision was concerned with the National Institute for Agricultural Research (NIAR) in France. NIAR was a state agency responsible for the development of crop productions. Among other missions, it bred maize seeds. In order to exploit these seeds varieties, it signed agreement with German companies and granted them exclusive selling rights of certain seeds in Germany. The Commission found the agreement incompatible with Article 101. Its Decision was later challenged before the Court. Case 258/78 *L.C. Nungesser KG and Kurt Eisele v Commission of the European Communities* [1982] ECR-2015, para 9.

(2) 89/536/EEC Commission Decision of 15 September 1989 relating to a proceeding under Article 85 of the EEC Treaty (IV/31.734—Film purchases by German television stations) [1989] OJ L284/36.
Since 1984, the German broadcasting sector has been opened up to competition; both public and private undertakings are active on the market. The association of public broadcasting undertakings concluded an agreement with an American movie producer, Nefico. Under that agreement, the German public broadcasting undertakings acquired the exclusive rights of broadcasting of all Nefico's films. This essentially excluded German private broadcasting companies from purchasing the same films. This agreement was found to be incompatible with Article 101.

relating to the broadcasting and telecommunications sectors that are of the greatest relevance to this chapter.

3.4.3.1 The *Magill* Decision

The *Magill* Decision was concerned with the television listing licence restraints imposed by public broadcasting companies,[150] RTE (Radio Telefis Eireann Authority) and BBC, which are national public undertakings with monopoly rights over radio and television broadcasting in Ireland and the UK, respectively. ITP (Independent Television Publication) was a British public undertaking for the publication of programmes. They provided daily television programme information free to newspapers.

A publisher, Magill, intended to publish comprehensive weekly listings, which was a separate market from daily television programme listings. Its commercial initiatives were banned owing to the copyright licensing policy of these undertakings. The Commission found such restraints constituted a limitation of production and thus an abuse of dominant position under Article 106(2). After the establishment of abusive behaviour, the issue of SGEI derogation emerged. The issue was dealt with in one very short paragraph by the Commission:

> *Even if* ITP, BBC and / or RTE are under a *public or statutory duty to produce and publish their individual programme listings* in the form of TV guides, the application of the competition rules in this case in no way obstructs the performance of that particular task within the meaning of Article 106(2). Therefore that Article is not applicable in the present case.[151] (emphasis added)

Without any economic analysis, the derogation was simply rejected, and this approach was upheld by the Court on appeal.[152] In its Judgment, this issue did not pose any problems either: the Court merely pointed out that the abuse 'seems to be

(3) 82/371/EEC: Commission Decision of 17 December 1981 relating to a proceeding under Article 85 of the EEC Treaty (IV/29.995—NAVEWA-ANSEAU) [1982] OJ L167/39.
In this Decision, the Belgium water supply companies and electrical appliance supply companies reached an agreement regarding the safety label for washing machines and dishwashers. Under this agreement only manufacturers or sole importers may obtain such conformity labels. It essentially excluded other importers from getting this label, and consequently they were excluded from the market. The Commission found that such agreements were in breach of Article 101.

[150] 89/205/EEC: Commission Decision of 21 December 1988 relating to a proceeding under Article 86 of the EEC Treaty (IV/31.851—Magill TV Guide/ITP, BBC and RTE) [1989] OJ L78/43.

[151] Ibid., para 25.

[152] Case T-69/89 *Radio Telefis Eireann v Commission of the European Communities* [1991] ECRII-485.

justified only on commercial grounds, and therefore in no way contributes to the performance of the *cultural, social and educational tasks* assigned to RTE'.[153]

Furthermore, the case also reveals the model of the SGEI in the broadcasting sector in the UK and Ireland. Both BBC and RTE are statutory companies established by the State to undertake public service broadcasting. They enjoyed a monopoly over the radio and television broadcasting sector. This illustrates the close link between undertakings with exclusive rights in Article 106(1) and SGEI undertakings holding such rights in Article 106(2).

The application of Article 102 to abusive behaviour by these undertakings has little impact on this model. In this case, the status of RTE and BBC as public undertakings was not touched. The compatibility of statutory monopoly rights was not challenged. The *only* target of the Commission was the abusive conduct committed by these SGEI undertakings, which is prohibited under Article 102. In this case, it was the limitation of production of a separate market product (weekly programme listing) that was condemned by the Commission.[154]

3.4.3.2 The *British Telecommunications* Decision

The use of public undertakings and exclusive rights to deliver SGEIs could also be observed from another Commission Decision in 1982 relating to British Telecommunications (BT).[155] The case was concerned with the tariff schemes applied by BT in relation to text retransmission services. Taking advantage of comparatively cheaper telecommunications tariffs in the UK, a market on text retransmission services developed in the UK. Operators received messages by telex sent from foreign countries and relayed these messages on to third countries. This potentially undercut tariffs applied in these foreign counties. In order to fulfil its obligations under the International Telecommunication Convention, BT first prohibited the operation of such message forwarding services in 1971. Later, a tariff scheme was adopted by BT in 1987, which provided that charges should not be such as to enable the originator of the message to send it more cheaply than if he had sent it directly.[156]

---

[153] Ibid., para 83.

[154] The Commission's Decision was later challenged before the Court of First Instance and subsequently before the Court. The validity of the Commission's Decision was upheld by both Courts. Case T-69/89 *Radio Telefis Eireann v Commission of the European Communities* [1991] ECR II-485; Case T-76/89 *Independent Television Publications Ltd v Commission of the European Communities* [1991] ECR II-575; Joined cases C-241/91 P & C-242/91 P *Radio Telefis Eireann (RTE) and Independent Television Publications Ltd (ITP) v Commission of the European Communities* [1995] ECR I-743.

[155] 82/861/EEC: Commission Decision of 10 December 1982 relating to a proceeding under Article 86 of the EEC Treaty (IV/29.877—British Telecommunications) [1982] OJ L360/36.

[156] Ibid.

The Commission found that BT's practice constituted abuse of dominant position in the limitation of the market and application of dissimilar conditions to equivalent transactions.[157] Therefore, BT was found in breach of Article 102. The Commission then dealt with the application of the SGEI derogation. In its Decision, the Commission confirmed the factual existence of SGEI but rejected that the derogation was applicable in its Decision. It pointed out that:

> Under the Post Office Act 1969 and the Telecommunications Act 1981, BT has been entrusted with the operation of services of general economic interest, namely *the provision of telecommunication systems throughout the United Kingdom.* The application of the Treaty rules on competition to BT would not and does not obstruct the performance of its duties in an efficient and economic way. For BT to be exempted from compliance with the rules on competition it is *not sufficient* that such compliance would make performance of its duties *more complicated.*[158] (emphasis added)

This Decision is also a good illustration of the model of SGEI provision developed in the telecommunications sector across the Member State. Public undertakings were established to provide telecommunication services under the protection of monopoly rights, which covered the whole sector.[159] At this stage, the Commission did not deal with the compatibility of state measures that granted exclusive rights to public undertakings. The concern of competition law was with the anti-competitive conduct committed by SGEI undertakings. It focused its attention only on anti-competitive conduct by these undertakings, and, essentially, it allowed, or at least tolerated, the *existence* of such national statutory monopolies. The impact of this approach was very limited on the organisation model of the telecommunications sector in the Member States.

3.4.4 The Corbeau *Case and Later Case Law: SGEI Derogation for the Member States*

In 1993 the Court's interpretation of Article 106(2) underwent a fundamental change in the *Corbeau* case.[160] The case was concerned with the organisation of the postal services sector in Belgium, which was provided by a public undertaking as the sole operator across the whole country, protected by statutory monopoly rights. Mr Corbeau carried out express delivery service in the city of Liège, by collecting mail and delivering it by noon the next day. He was charged with criminal offence

---

[157] Ibid., paras 28–34.

[158] Ibid., para 41.

[159] Camenen 1996.

[160] Case C-320/91 *Paul Corbeau* [1993] ECR I-2533.

because his business was in breach of the national postal monopoly. The concern of the national court was whether such monopoly was compatible with the Treaty and referred this question to the Court, asking specifically:[161]

(1) To what extent is a postal monopoly [...] in conformity [...] with the rule of the Treaty (and in particular with Articles 106, 101 and 102)?
(2) To what extent must such a monopoly be modified in order to comply with the Community obligations imposed on the Member States in this area, in particular with Article 106(1)?[162]

The Court did not rule on the compatibility of the grant of exclusive rights by the Member States *solely* on the basis of Article 106(1); instead, it held that 'Article 106(1) must be read in conjunction with Article 106(2).'[163] In the Judgment, the Court established that the SGEI derogation under Article 106(2) could be used to justify a state monopoly if it was necessary to protect the financial stability of SGEI provision.[164] This is an innovative approach in the sense that the wording of Article 106(2) suggests that it is applicable only to undertakings' anti-competition behaviour,[165] not to Member States' creation of State monopolies. It is in this case (through the interpretation of the Court) that Article 106(2) began to acquire a new function: providing a derogation *for Member States* from the application of competition law.

To apply this derogation, the first issue concerns the definition of a SGEI task. In this case, the Court recognised that the universal postal services, as defined by the national legislation, constituted a valid SGEI task.[166] The issue remains as to what was the boundary of the Member States' power in deciding what constitutes SGEI? Do the Member States have absolute freedom in this respect? Potentially, Member States could enlarge the scope of SGEIs, which would justify potential excessive state intervention in the market.

In this regard, the original Treaty of Rome in 1957 did not contain explicit rules on the competence allocation between the Member States and the EU.[167] This lack of clear boundary has not been solved by subsequent Treaty amendments. The

[161] What is interesting to note is the fact that the national court did not raise the question on the application of Article 106(2): whether the postal monopoly was justified under SGEI derogation. Buendia Sierra 2000, p. 296.

[162] Case C-320/91 *Paul Corbeau* [1993] ECR I-2533, para 5.

[163] Ibid., para 13.

[164] In the *GB Inno* case, the Court suggested that the derogation could be applied for public safety reasons. Case C-18/88 *Régie des Télégraphes et des Téléphones v GB-Inno-BM SA* [1991] ECR I-5941.

[165] Hancher 1999.

[166] Blum and Logue 1998, p. 29.

[167] In the Treaty of Rome, SGEI was only mentioned once in Article 90(2) (now Article 106(2) TFEI). It merely confirms that SGEI *undertakings* are subject to competition rules, with a limited derogation. It did not deal with the issue of competence allocation at all.

Treaty of Maastricht in 1992 provides that the EU and the Member States shall take care of the provision of SGEI, but 'each within their respective power'.[168] This suggests that the EU and the Member States have shared competence in this area but it did not draw a line of demarcation between them. This ambiguous wording remains unchanged in the latest Lisbon Treaty.[169]

On this issue the *BUPA* judgment offered some helpful guidance.[170] In this case, the issue of competence allocation became fiercely contested by the parties, i.e. whether SGEI is a strict and objective Community concept or whether the Member States have absolute freedom to decide. The Court ruled that it is primarily the Member States' competence to decide what constitutes SGEI and they enjoy wide discretion,

> Member States have a *wide discretion* to define what they regard as SGEIs and the definition of such services by a Member State can be questioned by the Commission only in the event of manifest error. The prerogative is confirmed by the absence of any competence specially attributed to the Community and by the absence of a precise and complete definition of the concept of SGEI in Community law.[171] (emphasis added)

This suggests that there is no uniform and universal definition of SGEI at the EU level. In areas without EU harmonisation, the content of SGEI is left to the Member States to decide, i.e. what public interest they would like to pursue under the notion of SGEI and how far they will go. This does not necessarily mean that the Member States have absolute freedom in deciding what constitutes SGEIs. In the *BUPA* judgment, the Court held that the Member State is subject to a manifest error control from EU law and that the SGEI mission must fulfil certain minimum requirements,

---

[168] Article 16 EC Treaty (now Article 14 TFEU).

[169] After the Lisbon Treaty, a new legal basis for EU legislation was added to Article 16 EC to form the new Article 14 TFEU. But this does not mean to give the EU new additional competence in this area. Instead, the competence allocation arrangement remains unchanged in Article 14 TFEU, which provides that the EU and the Member States 'each within their respective powers' shall take care of the provision of SGEI.

[170] The case is concerned with a risk equalisation scheme in the Irish health insurance market. After the market was liberalised, the Irish authorities imposed on all providers public service obligations, including open enrolment and community rates. In order to address the imbalance of health risk profiles among providers, a risk equalisation scheme was introduced that involved the transfer of fund from undertakings with low health risk profiles to undertakings with high health risks profile. The compatibility of this scheme was first the subject of a Commission Decision, which was then appealed before the Court in the *BUPA* case.

State Aid Decision N 46/2003—Ireland risk equalisation scheme in the Irish health insurance market, C (2003) 1322 final, 13.05.2003;

Case T-289/03 *British United Provident Association Ltd (BUPA), BUPA Insurance Ltd and BUPA Ireland Ltd v Commission of the European Communities* [2008] ECR II-8

[171] Case T-289/03 *British United Provident Association Ltd (BUPA), BUPA Insurance Ltd and BUPA Ireland Ltd v Commission of the European Communities* [2008] ECR II-8, paras 166–167.

including: (1) the presence of an entrustment act; (2) indication of the general interests pursued;[172] (3) the compulsory nature of the SGEI.[173]

What is worthy of attention is the fact that the *BUPA* case is raised in the healthcare sector, where there is not much harmonisation at the EU level. By contrast, the issue of competence allocation is very different in sectors such as telecommunications, postal services, transport and energy. In these areas, the EU has adopted sector-specific legislation, which prescribes what constitutes SGEI and how competence is allocated between the EU and the Member States. The Member States must comply with these rules when they organise the provision of SGEI in these sectors. Therefore, the freedom of the Member States is limited to a much greater extent.[174] This will be discussed in detail in Chaps. 5, 6 and 7.

Second, the benchmark for the derogation to apply is even more controversial. The implications are far-reaching. After the case law revolution on the interpretation of Article 106(1), it is increasingly likely that exclusive rights granted by the Member States would be found incompatible with the Treaty. Article 106(2) provides the only derogation to justify the grant of exclusive rights. In the *Corbeau* case, the Court adopted the principle of necessity, under which the compatibility of exclusive right is evaluated. The wording of the judgment reads as follows,

> A restriction on competition or even the exclusion of all competition from other economic operators is *necessary* in order to allow the holder of exclusive right to perform its task of general interest and in particular to have the benefit of *economically acceptable conditions.*[175] (emphasis added)

The stringency of necessity principle depends on the criterion used as the benchmark. In the *Corbeau* ruling, the Court adopted that the 'economically acceptable conditions' test (hereafter, the EAC test), meanwhile rejected the least restrictive means test (hereafter the LRM test) as proposed by the Advocate General. The critical distinction between the two benchmarks lies in whether the appropriateness of exclusive right is subject to scrutiny from EU law. The LRM test requires comparing different measures for the pursuit of a legitimate objective and selecting only the least restrictive one as the means.[176]

This attitude of rejecting the LRM test as applicable is made explicit in the *Commission v the Netherlands* case in 1997.[177] It is concerned with the exclusive

[172] Ibid., para 172.

[173] Ibid., para 188.

[174] The influence of EU law in limiting the discretion of the Member States varies significantly across sectors. In telecom and postal service, EU law set up a minimum level of SGEI requirements that the Member States must guarantee across the EU. By contrast, in the transport sector, the EU has not achieved such harmonisation. Instead, it is up to the Member States to decide how far they would like to go in providing public transport services. There is no uniform solution across sectors.

[175] Case C-320/91 *Paul Corbeau* [1993] ECR I-2533, para 16

[176] Sauter 2013.

[177] Case C-157/94 *Commission of the European Communities v Kingdom of the Netherlands* [1997] ECR I-5699.

right to import electricity granted by the Netherlands to its national electricity operator SEP. The issue is whether or not such right is compatible with the Treaty. The Commission argued that the exclusive right could not be justified because alternative means could also guarantee the SGEI mission, i.e. an LRM test. In the judgment, the Court rejected this strict approach by making the following statement:

> While it is true that it is incumbent upon a Member State which invokes Article 106(2) to demonstrate that the conditions laid down by that provision are met, that burden of proof cannot be so *extensive* as to require the Member State … to go even further and prove, *positively*, that *no other conceivable measure*, which by definition would be *hypothetical*, could enable those tasks to be performed under the same conditions. (emphasis added)

Under the LRM test, the grant of exclusive right for the provision of SGEI is extremely difficult to justify. The reason for this is that the grant of exclusive right is arguably the most restrictive means for the provision of SGEI because it eliminates market competition altogether. It is very likely that there are alternative less restrictive means for the objective it is intended to serve.

For example, in the *Corbeau* case, the exclusive right was put in place to enable cross-subsidisation and to prevent cherry-picking for the provision of universal postal service.[178] This objective could equally be achieved by setting a minimum price threshold for express delivery service, as pointed out by the Advocate General. Also, as later liberalisation reform in the postal sector has demonstrated, universal postal service could be maintained without exclusive right, but through alternative funding mechanisms such as sectoral fund or fund through general taxation by the State. These means are far less restrictive than the grant of exclusive right. Applying an LRM test would require the withdrawal of exclusive right, which may alter the organisation structure of SGEIs and potentially disrupt its provision.

By contrast, the EAC criterion is far less stringent than the LRM test because it does not require the Member States to compare exclusive right with other means and to choose the least restrictive one. The appropriateness of exclusive right is not called into question. The benchmark has become whether or not the grant of exclusive right is necessary to main the economic equilibrium of SGEI provision.

As a funding mechanism, exclusive right is closely related to a distorted pricing mechanism that SGEI operation was subject to. Instead of charging a price that corresponds to the actual cost of each individual service, an average uniform price is charged to achieve social objectives. This is the common theme in the judgments of court concerning SGEI operations in areas such as postal service, health insurance and ambulance.

In the *Corbeau* case, universal postal service is provided at a uniform tariff and on similar quality conditions throughout the country, irrespective of the specific situations or the degree of economic profitability of each individual operation.[179]

[178] Case C-320/91 *Paul Corbeau* [1993] ECR I-2533.

[179] Case C-320/91 *Paul Corbeau* [1993] ECR I-2533.

Similar arrangement is also found in the health insurance area. Under the principle of solidarity, contribution is not proportionate to the risk profiles of the insured, but is proportionate to the income.[180] Also, in the *Ambulanz* case, a permanent standby ambulance service is provided at a uniform rate and on similar quality conditions, without regard to the particular situations or to the degree of economic profitability of each individual operation.[181] Such a regulatory framework is intended to ensure universal coverage, availability and affordability of essential public services, in particular for people in a disadvantageous position, for whom the cost of such services would be prohibitively high under normal market conditions.[182]

The grant of exclusive right by the State to the SGEI undertaking is a necessary precondition of this funding model. It enables the SGEI provider to keep the profitable areas of the sector, which essentially secure the source of revenue for the unprofitable areas. Financial balance is achieved through a flow of cross-subsidisation to offset loss generated in unprofitable areas with revenues from profitable areas. Meanwhile, it prevents potential cherry-picking from other undertakings on the market. Abolishing exclusive right would open the sector to other undertakings that would then target the profitable areas by offering a more advantageous price and leave the loss-making areas to the SGEI operator. Without revenue from the profitable areas to compensate the loss generated in the unprofitable areas, the SGEI operation will not be financially sustainable in the long term.

This potential problem of cherry-picking is well reflected in the case law. In the *Corbeau* case, Mr Corbeau focused on the express mail service (next day delivery) in the city of Liège.[183] Also, in the *Ambulanz* case a private undertaking attempted to offer non-emergency patient transport service.[184] Similarly, in the health insurance-related SGEI regime, individuals with lower risk profiles may opt out of the solidarity-based regime and obtain better deals on the market. These are all the profitable areas of the sectors.

Without the protection of exclusive right, the process of cherry-picking may be gradual and progressive until it reaches a critical point where the SGEI operation begins to run into deficit, threatening the financial viability of the SGEI provision

[180]For example, Joined cases C-159/91 & C-160/91 *Christian Poucet v Assurances Générales de France and Caisse Mutuelle Régionale du Languedoc-Roussillon* [1993] ECR I-637; Case C-437/09 *AG2R Prévoyance v Beaudout Père et Fils SARL* [2011] I-973.

[181]Case C-475/99 *Firma Ambulanz Glöckner v Landkreis Südwestpfalz* [2001] ECR I-8089.

[182]This would be the case for the provision of postal service to people living in remote and sparsely populated areas, the provision of health insurance to people with high health risks and the provision of ambulance service to people requiring urgent and intensive medical care.

[183]Case C-320/91 *Paul Corbeau* [1993] ECR I-2533.

[184]Case C-475/99 *Firma Ambulanz Glöckner v Landkreis Südwestpfalz* [2001] ECR I-8089.

and undermining the integrity of the system as a whole. Such a danger has been well acknowledged by the Court in the case law. It held that the removal of exclusive right might make it impossible to perform the task under economically acceptable conditions and threaten its financial equilibrium.[185]

The crucial question remains as to what conditions are regarded as economically acceptable. The Court referred to concepts such as financial equilibrium and economic viability. It is not entirely clear how they should be applied. A pure equilibrium theory would suggest that the revenue generated by the profitable area equalise with the loss made by the unprofitable areas. On the other hand, an economic viability test would allow a margin of extra surplus to be maintained by the SGEI operator.

Both approaches would involve a significant amount of economic analysis such as identification of the unprofitable areas, calculation and assessment of the loss generated by such areas, the areas needed to generate sufficient revenue and the potential impact of liberalisation. For example, in the *Corbeau* case, a general monopoly covering the whole postal sector for the entire Belgian territory was granted to the SGEI operator. However, the postal market is diverse and dynamic, covering a wide range of services catering to diverse needs of the market. Certain areas of the sector may be the potential candidate for market liberalisation without severe adverse impact on the financial status of SGEI operation. This may suggest that a general all-inclusive monopoly may be excessive and unnecessary. The Court is not in a good position to carry out such economic analysis, especially in the preliminary ruling procedure. Such assessment is often left to the Member States to undertake.

3.5 Conclusion

Article 106 brings the grant of exclusive right by the Member States for the provision of SGEI under the scrutiny of competition law. The interpretation and application of Article 106 has undergone some fundamental change. For three decades since the adoption of the Treaty of Rome, it remained insignificant. Regarding the compatibility of exclusive rights under Article 106(1), the drafters of the Treaty respected the Member States' power in this respect and did not intend to challenge the widespread State monopolies. This attitude was also reflected in the case law of

---

[185] For example Case C-67/96 *Albany International BV v Stichting Bedrijfspensioenfonds Textielindustrie* [1999] ECR I-575, paras 108–111; Case C-437/09 *AG2R Prévoyance v Beaudout Père et Fils SARL* [2011] ECR I-973, paras 77–78.

This approach is also reflected in the *Ambulanz* case concerning the organisation of ambulance and transport of patients services. Case C-475/99 *Firma Ambulanz Glöckner v Landkreis Südwestpfalz* [2001] ECR I-8089, paras 60–61.

the Court: in the *Sacchi* case, it adopted the so-called absolute sovereignty approach. Meanwhile, on the application of Article 106(3), the Court held that the Commission's power was confined within what is necessary for its executive functions.

During this period, the function of Article 106(2) on SGEI was to bring SGEI undertakings within the scope of competition law rules. The focus of the Commission's practice was on the anti-competitive conduct by such undertakings under Articles 101 and 102. Although Article 106(2) grants a derogation from the application of competition law, in practice no SGEI undertaking had successfully invoked this derogation to justify its anti-competitive conduct.

However, by the early 1990s, the Court fundamentally changed its interpretation of Article 106. Regarding the compatibility of the exclusive rights, the Court departed from its absolute sovereignty approach in the *Sacchi* case and began to rule that it was incompatible with the Treaty in different circumstances. It delivered four Judgments in 1991, in which it developed principles to challenge the grant of exclusive rights by the Member States. As a result, the grant of exclusive rights became more likely to be found in breach of Article 106(1).

What is equally significant was its interpretation of Article 106(3). The Court held that the Commission had power to issue Directives without the involvement of the Council or the Parliament. Therefore, it greatly expanded the Commission's competence under Article 106(3) to include a general legislative power. This empowered the Commission to bypass the Member States and thereby to adopt EU legislation to break down statutory monopolies.

The fundamental change of the case law should be read in the broader context of the political agenda in the late 1980s and 1990s when the Commission began to use Article 106 to tackle state monopolies in the telecommunications and postal services sectors. The fundamental change in the case law rendered direct support in the Commission's liberalisation efforts in the telecommunications sector: the case law on exclusive rights provided the substantive legal basis to challenge widespread state monopolies; and the use of Article 106(3) legislative process by the Commission largely accelerated the liberalisation process.

The case law revolution on Article 106(1) and (3) and the Commission's liberalisation process had created a serious tension between EU competition law and the organisation of national economies in the Member States. It is against this background that the Court began to interpret Article 106(2) in an innovative fashion: in the *Corbeau* case, it applied the Article 106(2) SGEI derogation to the Member States under a necessity test. The Court ruled that restriction (even total exclusion) of competition by the Member States was allowed under EU competition law if it was necessary for the provision of SGEI under economically acceptable conditions.

References

Allum P (1995) State and society in Western Europe. Polity Press, Oxford

Bekkedal T (2011) Article 106 TFEU is dead. long live Article 106 TFEU! In: Szyszczak E, Davies J, Andenæs M, Bekkedal T (eds) Developments in services of general interest. T.M.C. Asser Press, The Hague, pp 61–102

Blum F (2000) The recent case law of the European Court of Justice on state monopolies and its implication for network industries. Journal of Network Industries 1(1):55–87

Blum F, Logue A (1998) State monopolies under EC law. Wiley, New Jersey

Bright C (1993) Article 90, Economic policy and the duties of member states. European Competition Law Review 14(6):263–272

Buendia Sierra JL (2000) Exclusive rights and state monopolies under EC Law: Article 86 (former Article 90) of the EC Treaty. Oxford University Press, Oxford

Camenen FX (1996) Public undertakings and public service activities in the European Union. European Parliament, Directorate General for Research, Working document, Economic Affairs Series, W - 21. http://www.europarl.europa.eu/workingpapers/econ/pdf/w21_en.pdf

Coleman JA, Rollet B (1997) Television in Europe. Intellect Ltd, Bristol

Davies G (2009) What does article 86 actually do? In: Krajewski M, Neergaard U, Van de Gronden J (eds) The changing legal framework for services of general interest in Europe: between competition and solidarity. T.M.C. Asser Press, The Hague

Edward D, Hoskins M (1995) Article 90: Deregulation and EC Law. Reflections arising from the XVI FIDE conference. Common Market Law Review 32(1):157–186

Gyselen L (1993) Anti-competitive state measures under the EC Treaty: towards a substantive legality standard. European Law Review Supp. Competition Law Checklist: 55–89

Hancher L (1999) Community, state and market. In: Craig P, De Búrca G (eds) The evolution of EU Law. Oxford University Press, Oxford

Kronenberger V (2001) A model of the transformation process of statutory monopolies in European Community Law: from practice to theory. European Business Organization Law Review 2(2):301–338

Lang JT (2005) Privatisation of social welfare: European Union competition law rules. In: Spaventa E, Dougan M (eds) Social welfare and EU Law. Hart Publishing, Oxford

Pappalardo A (1991) State measures and public undertakings: Article 90 of the EEC Treaty Revisited. European Competition Law Review 12(1):29–39

Sauter W (2008) Services of general economic interest and universal service in EU Law. European Law Review 33(2):167–202

Sauter W (2013) Proportionality in EU law: a balancing act? Cambridge Yearbook of European Legal Studies 15:439–466

Schweitzer H (2011) Service of general economic interest: European Law's impact on the role of markets and of member states. In: Cremona M (ed) Market integration and public services in the European Union. Oxford University Press, Oxford

Szyszczak E (2007) The regulation of the state in competitive markets in the EU. Hart Publishing, Oxford

Zevgolis NE (2012) Anti-competitive conduct from public or privileged enterprises: towards a *per se* abuse of dominant position? Applicability of the provision of TFEU Article by national competition authorities. European Competition Law Review 33(2):84–90

Chapter 4
Application of State Aid Rules to SGEI Funding

Contents

Abstract The provision of service of general economic interest (SGEI) is often not commercially viable under normal market conditions and requires financial support from the State. This chapter examines the interplay between EU state aid rules and SGEI. Two issues are of particular significance—the issue of definition and the issue of compatibility. This chapter studies the case law of the Court, in particular the landmark *Altmark* ruling, and the Commission practice. It argues that by applying state aid law to SGEI funding, the EU regulates how SGEIs are funded by the Member States. The focus of EU state aid law has been on ensuring SGEI funding is competition neutral.

Keywords SGEI funding · *Altmark* criterion · the efficiency test · market failure · the Monti Package · the Almunia Package

L. Zhu, *Services of General Economic Interest in EU Competition Law*, Legal Issues of Services of General Interest,
https://doi.org/10.1007/978-94-6265-387-0_4

4.1 Introduction

Bringing service of general economic interest (SGEI) funding under state aid control poses new difficult issues for the EU. The first is the issue of definition, i.e. whether or not SGEI funding constitutes state aid at all. The EU has established an ex ante system to manage state aid. If SGEI funding is defined as state aid, Member States have the legal obligation to notify such measures to the Commission and stand still until the Commission has concluded whether it is compatible or not. Failure to comply with this obligation would render the measure unlawful and lead to the obligation to recover the aid.

The second important issue is a substantive one i.e. if SGEI funding constitutes state aid, how will its compatibility be assessed by the Commission under EU state aid law? In regard to this, the EU state aid regime is a supranational system: the Commission has the exclusive competence to decide whether or not state aid is compatible with the Treaty.[1] Only compatible aid can be implemented by Member States.

It is in response to these very challenging questions that the EU has developed its rules on the application of state aid rules to SGEI funding. It is an evolving process. Right until the beginning of the 21st century, there had been no clear rules on how SGEI funding would be treated under EU state aid law. The application of state aid law seemed largely irrelevant for the provision of SGEI. The Commission made a dozen Decisions, declaring that state funding for SGEI did not constitute state aid or that it was compatible with the Treaty.[2]

---

[1]Case 78-76 *Steinike & Weinlig v Federal Republic of Germany* [1977] ECR-595.

[2]

(1) State Aid Decision NN 135/92—France tax arrangements applicable to the French postal administration [1995] OJ C262/11.
(2) 94/666/EC: Commission Decision of 6 July 1994 concerning compensation in respect of the deficit incurred by TAP on the routes to the Autonomous Regions of the Azores and Madeira [1994] OJ L260/27.
(3) State Aid Decision NN 141/95—Portugal financing of the Portuguese public television service [1997] OJ C67/10.
(4) State Aid Decision N 514/2001: United Kingdom 'modernisation of the UK benefit payment system and provision of access to universal banking services through post offices', shortened as 'Universal Banking Services' or UBS, C (2002) 311 final, 13.02.2002.
(5) State Aid Decision N 650/01—Ireland: equity injection to An Post for the purpose of restructuring the counter network, C (2002) 941 final, 12.03.2002.
(6) Statligt Stöd Nr N 749/01—Sverige Posten AB (publ); girobetalningstjänster, nedan grundläggande kassaservice, C (2002) 2402 final, 2.07.2002.
(7) State Aid No 252/2002—United Kingdom reinvention of the urban Post Office network, C (2002) 3341 fin, 18.09.2002.
(8) 2002/782/EC: Commission Decision of 12 March 2002 on the aid granted by Italy to Poste Italiane SpA (formerly Ente Poste Italiane) [2002] OJ L282/29.
(9) State Aid N 784/2002—United Kingdom government rural network support funding, debt payment funding and rolling working capital loan to Post Office Limited, C (2003) 1652 fin, 27.05.2003.

The change started from the mid-1990s, when SGEI funding started to be challenged frequently by third parties in national courts or before the Commission. The issue finally became a hotly debated topic at the beginning of the 21st century in the *Ferring*,[3] *GEMO*[4] and *Altmark*[5] cases, where different approaches were formulated and proposed.[6]

The *Altmark* case provides the opportunity and legal basis for the Commission to bring SGEI funding under the scrutiny and control of the EU's state aid regime. It adopted the so-called 'Monti Package' on the application of state aid to SGEI funding in 2005,[7] which has been further revised by the 'Almunia Package' in 2012.[8] What is also equally noteworthy is the fact that the Commission had been dealing with the issue through the adoption of sector-specific rules even before the

[3]Case C-53/00 *Ferring SA v Agence centrale des organismes de sécurité sociale* (*ACOSS*) [2001] ECR I-09067 (hereafter the *Ferring* case).

[4]Case C-126/01 *Ministère de l'Économie, des Finances et de l'Industrie v GEMO SA* [2003] ECR I-13769 (hereafter the *GEMO* case).

[5]Case C-280/00 *Altmark Trans GmbH and Regierungspräsidium Magdeburg v Nahverkehrsgesellschaft Altmark GmbH, and Oberbundesanwalt beim Bundesverwaltungsgericht* [2003] ECR I-7747 (hereafter the *Altmark* case).

[6]The debate really started when Advocate General Jacobs formulated the so-called state aid approach compensation approach division in 2002.

[7]It is named after the Commissioner who was responsible for competition. The 'Monti Package' includes:

(1) Commission Decision of 28 November 2005 on the application of Article 86(2) of the EC Treaty to state aid in the form of public service compensation granted to certain undertakings entrusted with the operation of services of general economic interest [2005] OJ L312/67;
(2) Community framework for state aid in the form of public service compensation [2005] OJ C297/4;
(3) Commission Directive 2005/81/EC amending Directive 80/73EEC on the transparency of financial relations between Member States and their public undertakings as well as on financial transparency within certain undertakings [2005] OJ L 312/47.

[8]It is named after the Commissioner who was responsible for competition. The 'Almunia Package' contains:

(1) Communication from the Commission on the application of the European Union state aid rules to compensation granted for the provision of services of general economic interest [2012] OJ C8/4;
(2) Commission Decision of 20 December 2011 on the application of Article 106(2) of the Treaty on the Functioning of the European Union to state aid in the form of public service compensation granted to certain undertakings entrusted with the operation of services of general economic interest [2012] OJ L7/3;
(3) Communication from the Commission, European Union framework for state aid in the form of public service compensation [2012] OJ C8/15;
(4) Commission Regulation (EU) No 360/2012 of 25 April 2012 on the application of Articles 107 and 108 of the Treaty on the Functioning of the European Union to *de minimis* aid granted to undertakings providing services of general economic interest [2012] OJ L114/8.

Altmark Judgment. This is the very case in sectors such as maritime transport,[9] broadband[10] and public service broadcasting.[11]

This chapter looks at the application of state aid rules to SGEI funding. The first section of this chapter examines the landmark *Altmark* ruling. It is essentially a balancing exercise. On the one hand, it grants exemption for SGEI funding from the scope of EU state aid law by ruling that certain SGEI funding does not constitute state aid. Therefore, SGEI funding would not be declared illegal simply because the Member State has failed to notify such measures to the Commission. On the other hand, the Court lays down four strict conditions in *Altmark* to ensure that no advantage is granted for the provision of SGEI and that market competition is not distorted.

The next two sections focus on the practice of the Commission after the *Altmark* Judgment. Section 4.2 examines the application of the *Altmark* criteria by the Commission. It focuses on the efficiency test under the fourth condition of the *Altmark* criteria. In this way, it can push the Member States to notify SGEI funding under the EU state aid control regime.

Section 4.3 looks at the compatibility test exercise by the Commission under Article 106(2), which grants a derogation from the prohibition of state aid if three conditions are fulfilled: (1) genuine SGEI tasks; (2) entrustment from public authorities; and (3) a necessity test. The focus of the Commission has been on the first and the third conditions.

---

[9]The Commission first adopted Guidelines in 1997. After the *Altmark* case, the Commission updated its Guidelines and also adopted a Communication interpreting the application of Regulation 3577/92, which also contains rules on the application of state aid rules on SGEI funding:

Community guidelines on state aid to maritime transport [1997] OJ C205/5;

Community guidelines on state aid to maritime transport [2004] OJ C13/3;

Commission of the European Communities, Communication on the interpretation of Council Regulation (EEC) No 3577/92 applying the principle of freedom to provide services to maritime transport within Member States, COM (2003) 595 final, 22.12.2003.

This issue will be dealt with in Sect. 7.4 of Chap. 7.

[10]The Commission Guidelines were first adopted in 2009 and then updated in 2013:

Commission of the European Communities, Community Guidelines for the application of state aid rules in relation to rapid deployment of broadband networks [2009] OJ C235/7 (hereafter 2009 Broadband Guidelines);
Commission of the European Communities, EU Guidelines for the application of state aid rules in relation to the rapid deployment of broadband networks [2013] OJ C25/1 (hereafter 2013 Broadband Guidelines).

[11]The Communication was first adopted in 2001 and then updated in 2009:

Commission of the European Communities, Communication from the Commission on the application of state aid rules to public service broadcasting [2001] OJ C320/5;
Commission of the European Communities, Communication from the Commission on the application of state aid rules to public service broadcasting [2009] OJ C257/1.

4.2 Defining SGEI Funding Under State Aid Law

Bringing SGEI funding under EU state aid control has posed a dilemma for the EU's state aid regime. The issue of definition has significant implications for SGEI funding.[12] On the one hand, categorising SGEI funding as state aid means that Member States have the obligation to notify the measure to the Commission and stand still until the Commission has reached a conclusion on its compatibility. National courts are empowered to review non-notified decisions. If a state measure is regarded as state aid by national courts and the Member State in question has failed to notify it to the Commission, such unnotified state measures would be regarded as unlawful and must be recovered.[13] This is due to the direct effect of the last sentence of Article 108(3).[14] The potential ramifications are huge, given the fact that some SGEI funding measures had been implemented without notification.

On the other hand, if SGEI funding is defined as 'compensation', it does not fall into the definition of state aid, and Member States have no obligation to notify and to stand still. SGEI funding might lead to the distortion of market competition if Member States overcompensate the undertaking in the name of SGEI provision. Such potential always exists if it is left unregulated and unchecked by the Commission. This could undermine the effectiveness of state aid control as an ex ante regime. This is the very approach in the *Ferring* case.[15] It is in this context that the issue of whether SGEI funding can be defined as state aid or not has become crucial.

The *Altmark* case has been heavily discussed by commentators.[16] A short description of the facts is still necessary. The main proceeding was concerned with the scheduled bus transport service in the Landkreis of Stendal, which was subject to authorisation from public authorities in Germany. *Altmark* Trans was granted the licence to operate the service from 1990 until 1994, and it was extended until 2002. Meanwhile, the application of another company, Nahverkehrsgesellschaft, to

[12] Prior to the *Altmark* case, the Jurisprudence of the Court was divided between the 'state aid' approach and the 'compensation' approach. The former regarded SGEI funding as state aid that might be compatible with the Treaty under Article 106(2). The latter regarded SGEI funding as not constituting state aid and therefore that fell outside the scope of EU state aid law. Sinnaeve 2003; Karayigit 2009; Bovis 2003.

[13] Case C-354/90 *Fédération Nationale du Commerce Extérieur des Produits Alimentaires and Syndicat National des Négociants et Transformateurs de Saumon v French Republic* [1991] ECR I-5505.

[14] For further elaboration on the issue of direct effect and the role of national courts, see Commission of the European Communities, Study on the Enforcement of state aid Law at National Level. http://bookshop.europa.eu/en/study-on-the-enforcement-of-state-aid-law-at-national-level-pbKD7506493/ accessed 9 October 2014; Commission of the European Communities, Report on the Application of EC state aid Law by the Member State Courts. http://ec.europa.eu/competition/state_aid/studies_reports/application_ms/section1.pdf accessed 9 October 2014.

[15] Case C-53/00 *Ferring SA v Agence centrale des organismes de sécurité sociale (ACOSS)* [2001] ECR I-09067

[16] See for example Travers 2003; Bartosch 2003.

operate this service was rejected. It then brought a suit against the local authority, arguing that financial support granted to *Altmark* was unlawful under EU state aid rules because it had not been notified to the Commission. It is in this context that the issue of definition of SGEI funding under state aid law was referred to the Court for a preliminary ruling.

In its Judgment, the Court generally followed the compensation approach, drawing its conclusion from the *ADBHU* and *Ferring* cases.[17] However, it refined the compensation approach as established in the *Ferring* case in more detail. The Court established the criteria for exempting SGEI funding from being classified as state aid, and consequently the Member States from the notification and standstill obligation. The following four conditions must be fulfilled:[18]

(1) clearly defined public service obligations;
(2) parameters for compensation must be established in advance in an objective and transparent manner;
(3) compensation cannot exceed what is necessary to cover all or part of the costs incurred in the discharge of public service obligations, taking into account the relevant receipts and a reasonable profit for discharging those obligations; and
(4) compensation shall be determined through a public procurement procedure or on the basis of the costs of a typical and well-run undertaking.

In formulating such conditions, clearly, the application of the SGEI derogation under Article 106(2) played a critical role in the assessment of the existence of advantage.[19] In fact, the first three conditions of the *Altmark* criteria overlap with the conditions for the SGEI derogation under Article 106(2).[20] More importantly, the Court's requirements go further than Article 106(2) in that it added a fourth condition in the *Altmark* criteria, which is essentially an *efficiency test*.[21]

This is essentially a balancing exercise between, on the one hand, the pursuit of non-economic values by Member States in funding SGEI and, on the other hand, the pursuit of state aid control by the Commission. The essence of the *Altmark* ruling is to grant Member Sates derogation from the procedural requirements of

[17]The *Altmark* case, paras 85–86.

[18]The *Altmark* case, paras 88–93.

[19]The Court did not expressly explain the basis for its legal reasoning on how it reached such conditions. It seems that it drew its conclusion from Advocate General's opinion in the *GEMO* case, while rejecting the Opinion of the Advocate General for this case.

[20]This point has been expressly mentioned in three Commission Decisions:

(1) 2009/845/EC: Commission Decision of 26 November 2008 on state aid granted by Austria to the company Postbus in the Lienz district C 16/07 (ex NN 55/06) [2009] OJ L306/26;
(2) State Aid No N 582/2008—Ireland health insurance intergenerational solidarity relief, C (2009) 3572 final, 17.06.2009;
(3) State Aid SA.31006 (2013/N)—Belgium State compensations to Bpost for the delivery of public services over 2013–2015, C (2013) 1909 final, 02.05.2013.

[21]This is the merit and real contribution of the *Altmark* case. Ross 2004.

prior notification in the EU state aid control regime.[22] It lays down detailed rules for national courts to review the legality of unnotified SGEI funding measures. If the *Altmark* criteria can be satisfied, unnotified State funding can still be regarded as lawful by national courts. Therefore, the application of state aid law would not disrupt the provision of SGEI. Meanwhile, the application of these four conditions can ensure no advantage is involved and that market competition is not distorted.

The result of this balancing exercise depends largely on how the *Altmark* criteria are applied. In the Commission's Decisions, the fourth condition is extremely difficult to satisfy.[23] Therefore, in most Decisions the Commission concluded that the *Altmark* exemption is not applicable, and SGEI funding measures still constitute state aid and therefore fall within the scope of state aid control.

4.3 The Commission's Two Packages and Its Application of the *Altmark* Criteria

4.3.1 The Monti Package and the Almunia Package

Two years after the *Altmark* ruling, the Commission adopted a comprehensive set of rules on how SGEI funding will be treated under EU state aid law. It was called the Monti Package after the name of the Commissioner who was responsible for competition.[24] It includes:

(1) Decision 2005/842[25]

It grants a derogation from the notification obligation for state aid measures that are compatible under Article 106(2). It is applied in parallel with the *Altmark* criteria.

(2) Framework[26]

It explains how Article 106(2) will be applied to examine the compatibility of SGEI funding that does not fall within the scope of *Altmark* or Decision.

(3) Transparency Directive[27]

---

[22] Muller 2009.

[23] The application of the *Altmark* criteria by the Commission will be discussed in the next section.

[24] Fratini and Filpo 2006.

[25] Commission Decision of 28 November 2005 on the application of Article 86(2) of the EC Treaty to state aid in the form of public service compensation granted to certain undertakings entrusted with the operation of services of general economic interest [2012] OJ L312/67.

[26] Community framework for state aid in the form of public service compensation [2005] OJ C297/4.

[27] Commission Directive 2005/81/EC amending Directive 80/73EEC on the transparency of financial relations between Member States and their public undertakings as well as on financial transparency within certain undertakings [2005] OJ L 312/47.

It requires a clear separation of accounts between SGEI tasks and commercial activities.

In 2012, the Commission updated its Monti Package by revising the Decision[28] and the Framework[29] and adding two more documents. These form the new Almunia Package for the application of state aid rules to SGEI funding, named after the Commissioner for competition in charge:

(1) Communication[30]

It interprets how the *Altmark* criteria will be applied by the Commission.

(2) *de minimis* Regulation[31]

It establishes a *de minimis* ceiling (500,000 Euros for three years) below which SGEI funding is regarded as not affecting trade between Member States and therefore does not constitute state aid.

On the issue of notification obligation, the *de minimis* Regulation and the Decision are very technical in nature and fairly easy to apply. What is more important and controversial is the application of the *Altmark* criteria. The application of the *Altmark* criteria by the Commission will be dealt with in the following three sections.

4.3.2 Dilemmas Facing the Commission

The *Altmark* criteria were established by the Court to help national courts to review the non-notification decision by public authorities. It is concerned with the notification and standstill obligation under Article 107(1). It specifies rules under which the possibility of over-compensation could be ruled out. It grants a derogation for state funding of SGEIs from the strictness of the procedural requirement of the EU state aid control regime (to notify potential aid).

Meanwhile, the *Altmark* doctrine is also relevant in the Commission's practice because the Commission also has the competence to interpret the issue of definition

---

[28]Commission Decision of 20 December 2011 on the application of Article 106(2) of the Treaty on the Functioning of the European Union to state aid in the form of public service compensation granted to certain undertakings entrusted with the operation of services of general economic interest [2012] OJ L7/3.

[29]Communication from the Commission: European Union framework for state aid in the form of public service compensation [2012] OJ C8/15.

[30]Communication from the Commission on the application of the European Union state aid rules to compensation granted for the provision of services of general economic interest [2012] OJ C/8/4.

[31]Commission Regulation (EU) No 360/2012 of 25 April 2012 on the application of Articles 107 and 108 of the Treaty on the Functioning of the European Union to *de minimis* aid granted to undertakings providing services of general economic interest [2012] OJ L114/8.

(essentially the issue of advantage). In fact, such an exercise is the first step in its evaluation of a state measure under state aid control. If a measure does not confer advantage, the Commission will simply declare it as not state aid, and the measure can be implemented by the Member State. Only if it confers an advantage will the Commission proceed to evaluate whether it is compatible with the Treaty under Article 106(2).

Taking the *Altmark* criteria out of its particular context, i.e. the issue of direct relevance to national courts, and applying it in the Commission's state aid practice poses a new dilemma. The reason lies in the fact that *Altmark* criteria cover all the conditions for its compatibility test under Article 106(2).[32] Applying the *Altmark* criteria in assessing the issue of advantage will deprive the compatibility test under Article 106(2) of any value. If the conditions under *Altmark* criteria are not met, this suggests the existence of advantage (and therefore the existence of over-compensation), and the SGEI funding would not be regarded as compatible under Article 106(2) either. On the one hand, if all the conditions are met, the State measure will be regarded as not constituting state aid and can be implemented by Member States without examining its compatibility under Article 106(2).[33] Therefore, the author submits that this essentially sends the wrong signal to Member States in the state aid control regime: SGEI funding does not constitute state aid, and Member States do not have the obligation to notify such State funding measure to the Commission.

---

[32] In the *Altmark* case, the Court ruled that SGEI funding does not constitutes state aid if it satisfies four conditions: (1) there must be clearly defined public service obligations; (2) parameters for compensation must be established in advance in an objective and transparent manner; (3) compensation cannot exceed what is necessary to cover all or part of the costs incurred in the discharge of public service obligations; and (4) compensation shall be determined through a public procurement procedure or on the basis of the costs of a typical and well-run undertaking.

The compatibility of SGEI with EU state aid law is examined under Article 106(2), which includes the following three conditions: (1) there must be a clearly defined SGEI task; (2) the SGEI task must have been entrusted by public authorities; and (3) a necessity test, i.e. the amount of funding does not exceed the costs of SGEI provision.

[33] Until now there are only five Decisions where the Commission concluded all the four conditions of the *Altmark* criteria have been met. They are:

(1) State Aid N 196/2010—Estonia: establishment of a sustainable infrastructure permitting Estonia-wide broadband internet connection (EstWin project), C (2010) 4943 final, 20.7.2010;
(2) Aide d'Etat N 331/2008—France: compensation de charges pour une Délégation de Service Public (DSP) pour l'établissement et l'exploitation d'un réseau de communications électroniques à très haut débit dans le Département des Hauts-de-Seine, C (2009) 7426 final, 30.09.2009;
(3) Aide d'Etat nº N 382/2004—France: mise en place d'une infrastructure haut débit sur le territoire de la région Limousin (DORSAL), C (2005) 1170 final, 03.05.2004;
(4) Aide d'Etat N 381/2004—France: projet de réseau de télécommunication haut débit des Pyrénées-Atlantiques, C (2004) 4343 final, 16.11.2004;
(5) 2009/554/EC: Commission Decision of 21 October 2008 on a state aid scheme implemented by Italy to remunerate Poste Italiane for distributing postal savings certificates (C 49/06 (ex NN 65/06)), [2009] OJ L189/3 (hereafter Decision 2009/554).

The Commission has solved this problem by interpreting and applying the *Altmark* ruling in a 'reverse' way.[34] In its Decisions, the Commission argues that failure to comply with any of the four conditions would mean that the State measure is a state aid. The 'trick' of the Commission is that it does not give equal weightage to each of the four conditions but applies the four conditions selectively.[35] In particular, the fourth condition has become the Commission's key to solve the problem.

A survey of the Commission's Decisions shows that the fourth condition has become the very focus of the Commission in the application of the *Altmark* criteria.[36] In 15 out of 32 Decisions made by the Commission (from after the *Altmark* case in 24 July 2003 until November 2013),[37] the Commission did not discuss the

---

[34]It is very interesting to note how the Commission interprets the *Altmark* ruling. The Court in the *Altmark* Judgment rules that, if four conditions are all met, the state funding measure is not state aid. By contrast, the Commission interprets it in a 'reverse' way: if any of the conditions is not met, the measure is state aid.

[35]Another less important aspect of the Commission's selective approach lies in its application of the second condition of the *Altmark* criteria. In five of its Decisions, the Commission found that the second and fourth conditions were not fulfilled and that therefore the measures in question were regarded as state aid. These Decisions include:

(1) 2005/217/EC: Commission Decision of 19 May 2004 on measures implemented by Denmark for TV2/Danmark [2006] OJ L85/1;
(2) 2004/838/EC: Commission Decision of 10 December 2003 on state aid implemented by France for France 2 and France 3 [2004] OJ L361/21;
(3) 2004/339/EC: Commission Decision of 15 October 2003 on the measures implemented by Italy for RAI SpA [2004] OJ L119/1;
(4) State Aid SA.33989 (2012/NN)—Italy State compensations for the delivery of the universal service over 2009–2011; State compensations for reduced tariffs offered to publishers, not-for-profit organisations and electoral candidates over 2009–2011, C (2012) 8230 final, 20.11.2012;
(5) 2011/1/EU: Commission Decision of 20 July 2010 on the state aid scheme C 38/09 (ex NN 58/09) which Spain is planning to implement for Corporación de Radio y Televisión Españla (RTVE) [2011] OJ L1/9.

[36]It seems impossible to collect all Commission's Decisions on the application of the *Altmark* criteria. Its state aid Register website is useful but confusing. A search of its database under primary objective as 'SGEI' delivers 88 results on 21 November 2013. Among them, some Decisions are irrelevant, while some SGEI Decisions are not even included in the results. Another difficulty is that not all Decision texts have been translated into English. As a result, 32 Decisions have been analysed by this research.

[37]
(1) State Aid No N 244/2003—United Kingdom credit union provision of access to basic financial services in Scotland, C (2005) 977 final, 06.04.2005;
(2) State Aid N 642/05—Sweden Compensation to Posten AB for providing basic payment and cash facilities services, C (2006) 5481 final, 22.11.2006;
(3) State Aid No SA.32019—Denmark Danish radio channel FM4, C (2011)1376 final, 23.03.2011;
(4) State Aid SA.34515 (2013/NN)—Ireland risk equalisation scheme for 2013, C (2013) 793 final, 20.02.2013;
(5) State Aid SA.31006 (2013/N)—Belgium State compensations to bpost for the delivery of public services over 2013–2015, C (2013) 1909 final, 02.05.2013;

first three conditions of *Altmark* criteria at all: instead, it hastily applied the fourth condition and then concluded that the measure constituted state aid merely because the fourth condition was not satisfied.

On the other hand, in five other Decisions,[38] the Commission concluded that the state measure in question fulfilled the first three conditions of the *Altmark* criteria. However, the Commission still regarded these measures as state aid, because the fourth condition had not been satisfied. The next section examines the application of the fourth condition of the *Altmark* criteria by the Commission.

---

(6) State Aid No E 2/2005 and N 642/2009—The Netherlands existing and special project aid to housing corporations, C (2009) 9963 final,15.12.2009;
(7) State Aid No N 178/2010—Spain public service compensation linked to a preferential dispatch mechanism for indigenous coal power plants, C (2010) 4499, 29.09.2010;
(8) State Aid No N 508/2010—United Kingdom Post Office Limited (POL): continuation of network subsidy payment and working capital facility, C (2011) 1770 final, 23.03.2011;
(9) 2010/815/EU: Commission Decision of 15 December 2009 on state aid C 21/05 (ex PL 45/04) which Poland plans to implement for Poczta Polska as compensation of universal postal service obligations [2010] OJ L347/29;
(10) State Aid NN 24/08—Italy Poste Italiane SpA State compensation for universal postal service obligations 2006–2008, C (2008) 1606 final, 30.04.2008;
(11) State Aid N 388/2007—United Kingdom Post Office Limited (POL) transformation programme, C (2007) 5623 final, 28.11.2007;
(12) State Aid NN 8/2007 (ex N 840/2006)—Spain financing of workforce reduction measures of RTVE, C (2007) 641 final, 07.03.2007;
(13) State Aid N 822/2006—United Kingdom debt payment funding to Post Office Limited (POL) for 2007–2008, C (2007) 653 final, 07.03.2007;
(14) 2007/217/EC: Commission Decision of 22 November 2006 on state aid implemented by France for the Laboratoire national de métrologie et d'essais [2007] OJ L95/25;
(15) 2011/140/EU: Commission Decision of 20 July 2010 on state aid C 27/09 (ex N 34/B/09) Budgetary grant for France Télévisions which the French Republic plans to implement in favour of France Télévisions [2011] OJ L59/44.

[38]These decisions are:

(1) State Aid N 196/2010—Estonia's establishment of a sustainable infrastructure permitting Estonia-wide broadband internet connection (EstWin project), C (2010) 4943 final, 20.7.2010;
(2) State Aid No N 582/2008—Ireland health insurance intergenerational solidarity relief, C (2009) 3572 final, 17.06.2009;
(3) 2009/845/EC: Commission Decision of 26 November 2008 on state aid granted by Austria to the company Postbus in the Lienz district C 16/07 (ex NN 55/06) [2009] OJ L306/26;
(4) 2009/325/EC: Commission Decision of 26 November 2008 on state aid C 3/08 (ex NN 102/05)—Czech Republic concerning public service compensations for Southern Moravia Bus Companies [2009] OJ L97/14;
(5) Commission Decision of 23 February 2011 on state aid No C 58/2006 (ex NN 98/2005) implemented by Germany for Bahnen der Stadt Monheim (BSM) and Rheinische Bahngesellschaft (RBG) in the Verkehrsverbund Rhein-Ruhr, C (2011) 632 final, 23.2.2011.

4.3.3 *Public Tendering Procedure Under* **Altmark** *(4)*

The Court ruled that the fourth condition of *Altmark* criteria could be satisfied by the use of a public tender procedure. A public tendering procedure corresponds to a normal market transaction, which would in general rule out the existence of advantage.[39] However, in practice, public tender is not always the best and the first choice for all SGEI tasks in Member States.[40] Without such tender in place, the Commission would simply declare the first scenario of the fourth condition of the *Altmark* criteria (hereafter *Altmark* (4)) is not applicable. The Commission has adopted such an approach in 16 Decisions after the *Altmark* case.

However, selecting SGEI provider through public tender does not automatically exempt SGEI funding from the scope of state aid. In other words, the use of public tender per se is not sufficient to fulfil the first scenario of *Altmark* (4). The Commission has elucidated this attitude by making the following observation in Decision N 382/2004:

> In this case, the procedure for the award of public service delegation was a specific procedure applicable for the award of a concession contract, which is only partially subject to the procurement guidelines and which the public authorities have kept a substantial margin of appreciation in the final selection of the service. In such a situation it is *not possible to automatically* conclude that the end result is equivalent to the market price.[41] (emphasis added)

To fulfil this criterion, the public tendering procedure must be carried out in compliance with EU procurement rules. This approach is well-reflected in the Commission's Decision concerning a funding measure for the deployment of broadband in Estonia, where it rejected the public tender procedure used by Member States as having met the first scenario of *Altmark* (4).[42] The funding measure in question comprised two stages. The first stage concerned the selection of owners of the network. The whole broadband network was divided into a large number of sub-projects. A public tender procedure was carried out for the actual construction and maintenance of the infrastructure. The Commission argued that the state measure constituted state aid because *Altmark* (4) was not satisfied:

> The selection procedure foreseen by Estonia provides for the possibility to award the compensation on simple application outside a tender procedure. Anyway, when there is a

[39] Tosics and Gaál 2007.

[40] For example, in the PSB sector, it is usually the public service broadcaster that is entrusted with the task through legislation without public tender procedure. For an overview of its Decisions in the PSB sector, see Mortensen 2008.

[41] Decision N382/2004, para 68. Similar wording can also be found in Decision N 331/2008, para 166.

[42] Decision 196/2010.

tender, it is only between non-profit organisations. It is therefore *not a public tender according to EU rules*. Also no other mechanism is in place to assure that the service is provided at the least cost to the community.[43] (emphasis added)

Such wording suggests that the Commission goes much further than a simple requirement of a public tender procedure—a public tender in compliance with EU procurement rules must be carried out at all stages.

This point also arises in its three Decisions concerning the deployment of broadband infrastructure as an SGEI in France:[44] these are the very rare occasions that the Commission has concluded that the first scenario of the *Altmark* (4) has been satisfied by a public tender. In these Decisions, the French authorities first launched an advertising procedure and then published the parameters for the calculation of funding through a consultation programme. The final bidder was chosen on the basis of a quantitative and quality analysis by the awarding authority, which was then followed by an additional verification by an independent expert.

Otherwise, the Commission would examine the state measure on a case-by-case basis, taking into consideration the actual design of a particular state aid measure. The key requirement is to ensure that it is the most efficient undertaking that is chosen for the provision at the least cost to the public. If the possibility of advantage could not be ruled out, the Commission would conclude that *Altmark* (4) is not fulfilled. This would be the case if the selection of the winner of the bidding process depends more on *quality* criteria rather than price elements. Its Decision concerning Danish public service radio channel FM4 is illuminating:[45] in order to introduce competition into public service radio broadcasting, the Danish government intended to select an independent operator to operate FM4 through a public tender procedure. It set detailed programme requirements for the broadcast content for FM4. For the selection of the winner, the quantitative element, i.e. the amount of funding, took only 25% weightage in the evaluation. Qualitative elements played a more significant role: the quality of the business plan (35%) and the programme profile (40%).[46] On the basis of these criteria, the provider chosen for the task was not

---

[43]Ibid., para 12.

[44]
(1) Aide d'Etat N 331/2008—France: compensation de charges pour une Délégation de Service Public (DSP) pour l'établissement et l'exploitation d'un réseau de communications électroniques à très haut débit dans le Département des Hauts-de-Seine, C (2009) 7426 final, 30.09.2009;
(2) Aide d'Etat nº N 382/2004—France: mise en place d'une infrastructure haut débit sur le territoire de la région Limousin (DORSAL), C (2005) 1170 final, 03.05.2004;
(3) Aide d'Etat N 381/2004—France: projet de réseau de télécommunication haut débit des Pyrénées-Atlantiques, C (2004) 4343 final, 16.11.2004.

[45]Decision SA.32019.

[46]Ibid., para 14.

necessarily the one that required the lowest level of funding. In its Decision, the Commission argued that *the possibility of advantage* still existed and that therefore the *Altmark* exemption was not applicable.[47]

In another Decision, the Commission declared that the public tender procedure in question did not fulfil the *Altmark* criteria because of its lack of EU-wide publicity. Decision C 3/08 was concerned with public bus services in the Southern Moravia region of the Czech Republic. Instead of carrying out an EU-wide public tender procedure, the local authority only contracted with bus carriers in the local region and invited them to submit tenders for the provision of the public bus service in question. The Commission regarded such local tender procedures as not meeting the first scenario of *Altmark* (4) because the possibility always exists that a more efficient operator from another Member State could provide the service at a lower cost. It found that:

> The procedure excluded the possibility that operators from other regions or districts were informed about the procedure and had a possibility to submit their tenders. Furthermore, this procedure ran counter to the possibility that carriers from other Member States could be taken into account in choosing the operator providing the services.[48]

In summary, the Commission has applied this criterion in a stringent manner. Adopting public tender procedures per se does not exempt SGEI funding from being defined as state aid; EU public procurement rules must be complied with. Otherwise, the Commission will still need to examine the public tender procedures used by Member States on a case-by-case basis. It has essentially adopted a market economy buyer test.

4.3.4 Typical Well-Run Market Undertaking Under **Altmark** *(4)*

In the fourth condition of the *Altmark* criteria, the Court held that compensation can be determined by a comparison with a typical well-run market undertaking. The Court has not provided any further guidance as to how this condition can be applied. In the Commission's practice, it is the Member State that bears the burden of proof. If the Member State has not provided such information, the Commission will simply conclude that this condition has not been met. This is the main reason

[47] In the Decision, the Commission did not conclude whether all conditions of the *Altmark* criteria were met. It pointed out two reasons: (1) the Danish government did not supply all relevant data on the expected costs of the SGEI task; and (2) the criteria used in the public tender procedure included qualitative elements. Therefore, the Commission argued that it was not in a position to reach a conclusion on whether the measure constituted a state aid or not. Nevertheless, it proceeded to decide if the measure was compatible with the Treaty, which implied that the *Altmark* exemption was not applicable: Ibid., para 54.

[48] Decision C 3/08, para 75.

why the Commission concluded that the *Altmark* criteria have not been satisfied in 15 of its Decisions.

The difficulty of its application lies in the establishment of the efficient market undertaking as a benchmark. Without using an open tendering procedure, this turns out to be an extremely difficult exercise. In its Decisions, the Commission has expressly rejected the following as the basis of an efficient undertaking:

(1) an abstract undertaking that does not exist in reality;[49]
(2) a former monopolist;[50]
(3) average cost based on statistical data;[51]
(4) actual costs for the delivery of SGEI tasks.[52]

Furthermore, even if Member States have conducted such an exercise, the Commission would still carry out another independent economic assessment. This very strict approach is well-illustrated in Decision 2009/554 concerning an Italian measure for the compensation of universal banking services.[53] This is the only

---

[49]Decision NN 24/08 was concerned with funding of universal postal service in Italy. The Commission acknowledged that it was impossible to identify comparable market undertaking for the USO provider, *Poste Italiane.* Alternatively, Italy government proposed an abstract proxy based on certain economic assumptions as the benchmark undertaking. The Commission rejected it as valid for the purpose of the *Altmark* criteria.

[50]This is reflected in the Commission Decision concerning State funding for the delivery SGEI tasks by *Belgian Post.* In the case, no public tender was carried out. The Belgium government compared *Belgian Post* with 10 other major European postal operators and argued that *Belgian Post* was the most efficient one. The Commission pointed out this was not enough to fulfil the fourth condition of the *Altmark* criteria: Decision SA.31006.

[51]Decision C 58/06 was concerned with public bus service in Germany. In order to prove the fourth condition of *Altmark* was met, the authority in question argued that compensation was determined by comparison with average market prices based on statistical data. The Commission declared that the use of statistical data itself was not enough to satisfy this condition. It then examined the quality of the data and argued that it was outdated and did not reflect market price: Decision C 58/06.

[52]This point has been reflected in two of its Decisions. SA.33989 was concerned with SGEI tasks entrusted to Poste Italiane by the Italian government. One of the tasks is the obligation to offer reduced tariffs to publishers, not-for-profit organisations and electoral candidates. In the Decision, the Commission recognised it as a valid SGEI task. Regarding the application of the *Altmark* criteria, the Italian government argued that compensation corresponded only to the difference between the reference tariffs and the reduced tariffs and that it therefore did not confer an advantage on Poste Italian. The Commission pointed out that the measure might cover possible inefficiencies of the operator. It then concluded that the measure constituted state aid: Decision SA.33989.

A similar approach could be found in Decision N 178/2020 concerning a Spanish funding measure for the production of electricity from indigenous coal. The Spanish government argued that compensation covered exactly the difference between actual costs and revenues on an ex poste basis. The Commission pointed out the amount of compensation would depend on the efficiency of each power plant rather than an efficient undertaking: Decision N 178/2020.

[53]Decision 2009/554.

occasion where the Commission expressly found that the second scenario of *Altmark* (4) has been satisfied.

Italian law entrusted the Poste Italiane with the task of distributing postal savings books and certificates through its postal networks. These financial instruments were used for fund-raising purposes by the government, with payment guaranteed by the State. Poste Italiane was chosen for the task, not through a public tendering procedure, but due to the universal coverage of its postal network. In return, the Italian State paid financial remuneration each year based on agreement.

In the Decision, the Commission concluded that the first and second conditions of the *Altmark* criteria had been met without any difficulty.[54] Then the focus turned to whether the level of compensation had been determined on the basis of a typical well- run market undertaking. The result depends largely on the benchmark and methodology adopted for the analysis. First, it needed to find a comparable product on the market. This is a very difficult task because the postal saving product is unique in itself, and it is very difficult to find a similar product on the market. Second, a market price based on a comparable product needs to be established. In this case, without a similar product on the market, the amount has to be estimated.

The Italian government conducted a benchmark study to identify a market price for the SGEI task, which was contested by the complainant. In order to reach a conclusion, the Commission launched a public tender to find an independent expert to undertake a study to verify (in its Decision, the Commission relied heavily on the expert opinion to reach its conclusion on whether the fourth condition of *Altmark* had been satisfied).

In summary, the Commission has applied the fourth condition of the *Altmark* criteria very strictly. The focus of assessment has been to check whether the possibility of advantage could be ruled out. Compliance with EU procurement rules would create an automatic assumption that SGEI funding does not involve state aid. Otherwise, the Commission would apply an economic analysis approach to see if there is a potential of advantage. This has rendered the *Altmark (4)* criterion extremely difficult to satisfy. Failure to satisfy the *Altmark* criteria would lead to the conclusion that SGEI funding constitutes state aid and thus falls within the scope of EU state aid control.

---

[54]And in fact it does not undertake any detailed discussion at all but rubber-stamped it. This can be easily observed from the very short wording in its Decision:

> In the opening decision the Commission established that the recipient, PI, had public service obligations to discharge and that these obligations were clearly defined. The parameters on the basis of which the compensation was calculated had been established in advance in an objective and transparent manner, notably by means of agreements between CDP and PI.

Decision 2009/554, para 136.

4.4 The Commission's Compatibility Evaluation of SGEI Funding After *Altmark*

The *Altmark* doctrine does not change the Commission's practice substantively.[55] In the wake of *Altmark*, the Commission essentially follows a two-step approach in the application of state aid rules to SGEI funding. First, it applies the *Altmark* criteria to examine the issue of definition and to decide whether or not SGEI funding constitutes state aid in the first place. If *Altmark* is not fulfilled, as in most of its Decisions, it will then proceed to discuss the issue of compatibility under Article 106(2) to determine whether it is compatible with the Treaty. This is a welcome development because it makes a crucial distinction between the issue of definition and the issue of compatibility in EU state aid law. Therefore, it brings consistency in the application of state aid rules to SGEI funding.

Article 106(2) lies at the heart of the compatibility evaluation process. The Court has long established that for the SGEI derogation to apply, three conditions must be met: (1) there must be a clearly defined SGEI task; (2) the SGEI task must have been entrusted by public authorities; and (3) a necessity test must be satisfied.[56] The Commission's approach in applying Article 106(2) to examine the compatibility of SGEI funding is reflected in its soft law documents. It has adopted separate sets of rules for different sectors, including the maritime transport,[57] broadband[58] and public service broadcasting.[59] In other areas where no such sector-specific rules

---

[55]Fratini and Filpo 2006.

[56]Case C-320/91 *Paul Corbeau* [1993] ECR I-2533. In the context of state aid law, the issue is first discussed by the Court in the *FFSA* case. Case T-106/95 *Federation Française des Societes d'Assurances (Ffsa) and Others v E.C. Commission* [1997] ECR II-229.

[57]The Commission first adopted the Guidelines in 1997. After the *Altmark* case, the Commission updated its Guidelines and also adopted a Communication interpreting the application of Regulation 3577/92, which also contains rules on the application of state aid rules on SGEI funding.

(1) Community guidelines on state aid to maritime transport [1997] OJ C205/5;
(2) Community guidelines on state aid to maritime transport [2004] OJ C13/3;
(3) Commission of the European Communities, Communication on the interpretation of Council Regulation (EEC) No 3577/92 applying the principle of freedom to provide services to maritime transport within Member States, COM (2003) 595 final, 22.12.2003.

This issue is dealt with in Sect. 7.4 of Chap. 7.

[58]The Commission Guidelines were first adopted in 2009 and then updated in 2013:

(1) Commission of the European Communities, Community Guidelines for the application of state aid rules in relation to rapid deployment of broadband networks [2009] OJ C235/7;
(2) Commission of the European Communities, EU Guidelines for the application of state aid rules in relation to the rapid deployment of broadband networks [2013] OJ C25/1.

[59]The Communication was first adopted in 2001 and then updated in 2009:

(1) Commission of the European Communities, Communication from the Commission on the application of state aid rules to public service broadcasting [2001] OJ C320/5;

exist, it applies the EU Frameworks for state aid in the Form of Public Service Compensation contained in the Monti Package[60] and Almunia Package.[61] In the Commission's practice, there is normally no difficulty fulfilling the second condition. The focus of the Commission's Decisions, in practice, has been on the first and third conditions.

Regarding the first condition, i.e. a clearly defined SGEI task, the Commission has been applying different standards in different sectors. In the broadband sector, the Commission has adopted a very strict market failure test to exclude most broadband measures from being defined as SGEIs. In this way, the Commission can limit State intervention in the market to the minimum level. So the market mechanism can be utilised to a full extent. By contrast, in other areas the influence of the Commission over the definition of SGEI is quite limited. This is well-reflected in its Decisions concerning the public service broadcasting and postal services sectors.[62] The Commission has not adopted a market failure test as in the broadband sector. In most cases, the Commission simply rubber-stamps the definition of a SGEI task by the Member State. Therefore, it does not exercise a meaningful scrutiny over the scope and definition of SGEI as decided by Member States.

---

(2) Commission of the European Communities, Communication from the Commission on the application of state aid rules to public service broadcasting [2009] OJ C257/1.

[60]Community framework for state aid in the form of public service compensation [2005] OJ C297/4.

[61]Communication from the Commission, European Union framework for state aid in the form of public service compensation [2012] OJ C8/15.

[62]In the postal sector, the Commission has made 13 state aid Decisions evaluating the SGEI funding. In the public service broadcasting sector, there are 37 state aid Decisions. These Decisions well illustrate the Commission's approach. For a list and discussion of the Commission's Decisions in the postal services sector, see Sect. 6.4.1 of Chap. 6.

For a list of Decisions in the public service broadcasting sector, see the Commission's website http://ec.europa.eu/competition/sectors/media/decisions_psb.pdf accessed 9 October 2014.

By contrast, in other areas, the Commission had made fewer Decisions:

(1) N 178/2010—security of electricity supply

Spain imposed on certain power plants an obligation to produce predefined volumes of electricity out of indigenous coal.

(2) N 582/2008 & SA. 34515—universal health service

Ireland imposed various obligations on private health insurers, including open enrolment, lifetime cover and minimum benefits.

(3) N 244/2003—promotion of social welfare and social inclusion

Provision of access to basic financial services in Scotland.

(4) E 2/2005 & N642/2009—social housing

Social housing for disadvantaged citizens or socially less advanced groups in the Netherlands.

(5) N 158/2009—pension scheme

Access to low-cost voluntary pension savings in the UK.

(6) C 24/2005

The provision of technical assistance to the public authorities and support services to business in the field of testing and conformity attestation by national metrology laboratory in France.

So far as the third condition (satisfaction of a necessity test) is concerned, the focus of the Commission has been on the competition neutrality of state funding of SGEI; in other words, whether state funding leads to over-compensation. This is the key requirement that can be found in all state aid Decisions concerning SGEI funding. What is also very interesting to note is that the Commission has been using the state aid control mechanism to push the Member States to put the provision of SGEI through public procurement procedures. This is most evident in the maritime sector regarding the provision island public service links.[63] The same development can also be observed in its 2012 Framework, which introduced an efficiency incentive requirement. Its implications for the organisation of SGEI are well-reflected in the Commission's Decisions in the postal sector.[64]

The Commission's approaches in the maritime sector and the postal sector are dealt with in Chaps. 6 and 7.[65] This section will look only at the Commission's Decisions in the broadband and public service broadcasting sectors. The first and second sub-sections will examine the first condition of the compatibility test, i.e. clearly defined SGEI tasks. It will show that the Commission uses very different standards in these two sectors. The third sub-section will use the public service broadcasting sector as an example to illustrate the application of the third condition Article 106(2), i.e. the necessity test.

4.4.1 Defining Broadband Deployment as an SGEI: Stringent Market Failure Test

The USO Directive in telecommunications requires Member States to guarantee a minimum set of basic services to be available to all users at affordable price.[66] It also allows Member States to go further than that, by providing a more advanced/comprehensive service on a universal basis. There has been a vigorous debate at the EU level on whether EU USO package should include more advanced services such as broadband and mobile services.[67]

---

[63]In the air transport sector, Regulation 1008/2008 requires PSO air links to be established via an EU-wide public tender procedure. By contrast, EU legislation in the maritime sector does not impose such obligation on the Member States. The Commission has been using the state aid control mechanism to push the Member States to put island PSO links through public tendering. This issue is discussed in Sect. 7.4.4 of Chap. 7.

[64]See Sect. 6.5.5 of Chap. 6.

[65]In the postal sector, the Commission has not adopted sector-specific rules for the application of state aid rules. Instead, it applies the Monti and Almunia Packages. Its state aid Decisions in the postal sector offer a good example of how rules contained in these two packages are applied in practice.

[66]Directive 2002/22.

[67]For a discussion of the scope and review of USO in the telecommunications sector, see Sect. 5.4.2 of Chap. 5.

The importance of broadband service has been in the spotlight in recent years.[68] The Commission has recognised its social and economic benefits, including for competitiveness, social and territorial cohesion and employment.[69] It also expressly acknowledges the contribution of broadband to the fulfilment of universal service. In the first paragraph of its 2009 Broadband Guidelines, it renders active support for 'the widespread availability of broadband services for all European citizens'.[70] However, until now the provision of broadband service has not been incorporated into the USO package at the EU level. It is still the Member States that have the competence to decide what measures they will take to support the development of broadband in its territory.

At the EU level, it is through state aid control that the Commission can have significant influence over Member States' financial support for the deployment of broadband. Any financial support for the deployment of broadband must be notified to the Commission and is subject to its approval under the state aid regime. The Commission has adopted a case-by-case approach to examine state funding measures for broadband under the state aid regime. The treatment of such funding measures by the Commission is reflected in its Guidelines, which were first adopted in 2009[71] and then updated in 2013.[72]

As a general principle, the 2013 Broadband Guidelines point out that all state aid in this area should target *market failure* and *fulfil the objectives of common European interest*.[73] Broadband SGEI measures are no exception. In the Commission's Decisions, it has applied this test very strictly by looking at three aspects of the market failure.

The first one is geographical: *market failure is defined as market will not invest now or in three years without support from the State*.[74] In other words, state funding is justified only for geographical areas where broadband service does not exist on the market. This is to correct a very fundamental market failure problem, i.e. the non-existence of broadband in a defined geographical area.[75] The Commission has been very clear about this requirement:

---

[68]Koenig and Fechter 2009.

[69]Commission of the European Communities, Community Guidelines for the application of state aid rules in relation to rapid deployment of broadband networks [2009] OJ C235/7.

[70]Ibid., para 1.

[71]2009 Broadband Guidelines.

[72]Commission of the European Communities, EU Guidelines for the application of state aid rules in relation to the rapid deployment of broadband networks [2013] OJ C25/1 (hereafter, the 2013 Broadband Guidelines).

[73]2013 Broadband Guidelines, para 6.

[74]This test is more stringent than that used in the broadcasting sector.

[75]This is a very strict test compared with that adopted in the public service broadcasting sector, where Member States are allowed to intervene in the market to guarantee a service of higher quality than similar market products. In the BBC digital curriculum Decision, there was a very competitive market providing very similar products. The provision of such services by BBC essentially meant competing with private undertakings on the market. The Commission still

> Applying this principle to the broadband sector, the Commission considers that in areas where private investors have already invested in a broadband network infrastructure (or are further expanding the network) and are already providing competitive broadband services with an adequate broadband coverage, setting up a parallel competitive and publicly funded broadband infrastructure *cannot be considered as an SGEI* within the meaning of Article 106(2) TFEU.[76] (emphasis added)

This market failure test can ensure that State funding will only flow to geographic areas where the market fails to provide broadband services. In its practice, the Commission makes a distinction between *white, grey and black areas*. State aid is justified for the deployment of broadband in the white areas to promote territorial cohesion and the economic development objective.[77] This is the very case in four of its Decisions where this condition has been met and the measures in question constitute SGEI.[78]

By contrast, if the state measure does not fulfil this condition, it will not be regarded as an SGEI task and is not compatible with the Treaty. Its significance can be illustrated in the Commission Decision regarding a funding measure in Appingedam in the Netherlands.[79] The local authority planned to build an additional advanced broadband service through glass fibre access. In its Decision, the Commission found that broadband service had been offered on the market through two existing networks. Therefore, it concluded that no market failure problem existed in Appingedam and that the measure did not qualify as a legitimate SGEI task. As a result, the Dutch authority was prohibited from implementing such a measure.[80]

---

accepted that the provision of digital curriculum service by the BBC was a valid SGEI because it was free of charge. Similarly, in the BBC 24-h news channel Decision, a very competitive news broadcasting market existed. The Commission did not challenge the UK's decision to include it in BBC's PSB remit because it is advertisement free. For a discussion of the Commission's approach in the PSB sector, see the next section.

[76]2013 Broadband Guidelines, para 20.

[77]On the other hand, financial support for the black area is prohibited, while grey area needs detailed assessment. Koenig and Fechter 2009.

[78]

(1) State Aid N 196/2010—Estonia: establishment of a sustainable infrastructure permitting Estonia-wide broadband internet connection (EstWin project), C (2010) 4943 final, 20.7.2010;
(2) Aide d'Etat N 331/2008—France: Compensation de charges pour une Délégation de Service Public (DSP) pour l'établissement et l'exploitation d'un réseau de communications électroniques à très haut débit dans le Département des Hauts-de-Seine, C (2009) 7426 final, 30.09.2009;
(3) Aide d'Etat nº N 382/2004—France: mise en place d'une infrastructure haut débit sur le territoire de la région Limousin (DORSAL), C (2005) 1170 final, 03.05.2004;
(4) Aide d'Etat N 381/2004—France: projet de réseau de télécommunication haut débit des Pyrénées-Atlantiques, C (2004) 4343 final, 16.11.2004.

[79]Commission Decision on the measure n° C 35/2005 (ex N 59/2005) that the Netherlands are planning to implement concerning broadband infrastructure in Appingedam, C (2006) 3226 final, 19.07.2006.

[80]Ibid.

The second dimension of the market failure test is to make sure financial support is granted only to sections of the broadband sector where the market fails to provide, i.e. the deployment of broadband network (passive network with/without active network).[81] This involves the establishment of the broadband infrastructure where market failure often occurs. On the other hand, the Commission argues that there is a competitive market regarding the provision of retail broadband connection service to end users. Therefore, it prohibits the inclusion of retail broadband service in the scope of SGEI, and that must be left to the market.

This division between network (passive and active) and retail connection service has been emphasised in all its three Decisions where broadband has been accepted as an SGEI.[82] In its practice, the Commission examines the scope of the State funding. It is only if State funding covers only broadband network (passive network with/without active network) that it can possibly be accepted as a valid SGEI task. Its reasoning in Decision N381/04 is a good example:

> This argument [note: market failure] is valid for investment in networks and not all services related to broadband. Thus, the internet connection service to the end users and the provision of content (media, etc.,) may constitute of very different services that do not necessarily fall under the definition of service of general economic interest. In addition, once the network services are available on favorable terms, operators are normally able to provide other service at competitive conditions.[83]

The third aspect of the market failure test used by the Commission is whether the network operator has the obligation to provide access to the whole population in question.[84] This is closely linked with the network-bound nature of the broadband. State intervention is justified owing to market failure where the market undertaking does not have enough incentive to invest in the infrastructure for less profitable consumers. In the Commission's practice, it requires SGEI broadband measures to

---

[81]The broadband sector comprises three sections/layers of elements that together make the provision of broadband service to final consumers possible. The first layer is the physical infrastructure of the network. It is also called passive network, which involves mainly network construction and ownership. The second layer is to make the network active. It needs a network operator for network management and operation. The third layer is the retail connection service, where operators connect end users to the network. Yábar 2012.

[82]

(1) Aide d'Etat N 331/2008—France: compensation de charges pour une Délégation de Service Public (DSP) pour l'établissement et l'exploitation d'un réseau de communications électroniques à très haut débit dans le Département des Hauts-de-Seine, C (2009) 7426 final, 30.09.2009;

(2) Aide d'Etat n° N 382/2004—France: mise en place d'une infrastructure haut débit sur le territoire de la région Limousin (DORSAL), C (2005) 1170 final, 03.05.2004;

(3) Aide d'Etat N 381/2004—France: projet de réseau de télécommunication haut débit des Pyrénées-Atlantiques, C (2004) 4343 final, 16.11.2004.

[83]Aide d'Etat N 381/2004—France: projet de réseau de télécommunication haut débit des Pyrénées-Atlantiques, C (2004) 4343 final, 16.11.2004, para 61.

[84]Aide d'Etat n° N 382/2004—France: mise en place d'une infrastructure haut débit sur le territoire de la région Limousin (DORSAL), C (2005) 1170 final, 03.05.2004, para 50.

cover all groups of users rather than only targeting profitable ones. If the state measure in question benefited only certain groups of users, it would not be accepted as an SGEI task. This is a particular issue for the deployment of very advanced network.

The requirement is well-illustrated by the Commission's Decision N 284/2005. The Decision was concerned with the deployment of broadband infrastructure in Irish towns. In that Decision, the Commission found that the infrastructure was mainly offered to business and concluded that it did not constitute an SGEI task:

> The wholesale services provided by the MSE[85] are high-bandwidth services, dark fibre or sub-ducts which are targeted not at the general public and citizens, but are offered to operators of electronic communications service to provide, first of all, high speed services to business. This is confirmed by the fact that the only users for which a direct connection via the MANs will be economically viable are large businesses located close to the MANs.[86]

In examining broadband as an SGEI, the Commission has adopted a pro-market approach by applying the market failure test very stringently. State funding is allowed only if the deployment of broadband covers the white area, the network itself and is targeted at the general public. This would significantly limit the scope of state intervention in the broadband sector and utilise the force of competitive market to a greater extent.

4.4.2 Defining Public Service Broadcasting as an SGEI: No Market Failure Test

There has been a strong tradition of state intervention in the broadcasting sector in virtually all Member States in the EU.[87] Broadcasting has not been regarded as a normal market activity, but instead one with profound political, social and cultural implications.[88] This is reflected in the notion of 'public service broadcasting' (hereafter PSB), which began to grow stronger, especially after World War II.[89] Although the actual organisation of PSB varies across Member States, common themes could be found in almost all Member States,[90] including:

---

[85]This is the managing undertaking for the network (active layer), which is a private-sector management service entity (MSE). It is created in the framework of public–private partnership.

[86]State Aid N 284/2005—Ireland regional broadband programme: Metropolitan Area Networks ('MANs'), phases II and III, C (2006) 436, 08.03.2006, para 39.

[87]For a brief introduction, see Tigchelaar 2003.

[88]Commission of the European Communities, The Digital Age: European Audiovisual Policy, Report from the High Level Group on Audiovisual Policy.

http://aei.pitt.edu/1592/1/av_oreja_report.pdf accessed 9 October 2014; Harrison and Woods 2001; Mendel 2013.

[89]For more information on the evolution of broadcasting in Europe, see Humphreys 1996.

[90]The organisation of broadcasting was the issue in the case law of the Court on the Application of Article 106(1). Case 155/73 *Giuseppe Sacchi* [1974] ECR-409; Case C-260/89 *Elliniki*

(1) institution: the establishment of public undertakings as the provider of public service broadcasting (public service broadcaster);[91]
(2) market structure: public service broadcaster was granted a monopoly that covered both radio and television broadcasting. This effectively wiped out market competition and obstructed market integration;[92]
(3) nature of broadcasting: public service rather than normal market commercial activity; and
(4) funding mechanisms: different funding mechanisms have been used, including licence fee, advertising revenue and state budget financing.[93]

Since the late 1980s, the EU has been promoting competition in the broadcasting sector.[94] Through EU Directives,[95] the monopoly market structure has been broken down, allowing the development of commercial broadcasters.[96] On the other hand, EU legislation does not have much influence over other aspects of public service broadcasting. There is no harmonisation over the definition of public service broadcasting.[97] On the contrary, the special position of public service broadcasting is confirmed in the Protocol on the System of Public Broadcasting.[98] It recognises and respects the wide freedom of intervention in PSB by the Member States. They have the competence to confer, define and organise the remit of public service broadcasting and, more importantly, to provide funding for PSB.[99] Meanwhile, it also acknowledges the EU interest in safeguarding market competition. It provides that PSB funding shall not affect trading conditions and competition to the extent that would be contrary to the common interest.[100]

The Commission has been using the state aid control regime to examine and scrutinise State funding of PSB. From 1999 to 2012 the Commission has made 36

Radiophonia Tileorassi AE (Ert) (Panellinia Omospondia Syllogon Prossopikou Ert intervening) v Dimotiki Étairia Pliroforissis (Dep) and Sotirios Kouvelas (Nicolaos Avdellas and Others intervening) [1991] ECR I-02925. These Judgments are dealt with in Sect. 3.2 of Chap. 3.

[91]Hanretty 2012.

[92]Cuilenburg and McQuail 2003.

[93]Llorens-Maluquer 2002; Commission of the European Communities, Television without Frontiers: Green Paper on the Establishment of the Common Market for Broadcasting, especially by Satellite and Cable, COM (84) 300 final, 14.06.1984.

[94]Commission of the European Communities, Television without Frontiers: Green Paper on the Establishment of the Common Market for Broadcasting, especially by Satellite and Cable, COM (84) 300 final, 14.06.1984.

[95]Council Directive 89/552/EEC of 3 October 1989 on the coordination of certain provisions laid down by law, regulation or administrative action in Member States concerning the pursuit of television broadcasting activities [1989] OJ L298/23.

[96]Humphreys 2005; Van Cuilenburg and McQuail 2003.

[97]Iosifidis 2009.

[98]Protocol (No 29) on the System of Public Broadcasting in the Member States, TEU.

[99]Smith 2005.

[100]Harrison and Woods 2001.

state aid Decisions concerning public service broadcasting.[101] Its approach is reflected in its Communications first adopted in 2001[102] and then updated in 2009.[103]

PSB is a good example of how SGEI funding is treated under the state aid regime in areas where the EU does not have much influence over the definition of SGEI. In the Commission practice, it does not apply a strict market failure test and has barely challenged the definition and scope of PSB as defined by the Member States. Instead, it has been focusing on the issue of competition neutrality of Member States' funding measures. It uses a case-by-case approach to investigate whether the actual design and organisation of each individual funding mechanism prevents over-compensation and cross-subsidisation.

Traditionally, the scope of PSB is defined in a very broad way without very detailed specifications. In the monopolised market structure, there was little need for a clear definition. Public service broadcasters were the only entity to provide both television and radio broadcasting services. The fundamental changes to technology and market structures pose new challenges and opportunities to the traditional model of the organisation of public service broadcasting. In response, PSB itself is also evolving.

There has been a debate about the existence, the scope and mission and the funding mechanisms of PSB in the EU and in the Member State. This has become a very controversial issue in EU competition law. The tension is particularly acute where a dual funding model is adopted for PSB provision and where commercial operators and public service broadcasters compete for advertising revenue.

Without detailed EU legislation on the issue, the Commission largely respects Member States' competence to define the mission of PSB and to determine its scope.[104] It expressly recognises the *broad non-economic interests* as pursued by Member States in the provision of PSB, including *respect of pluralism, fulfilling the democratic, social and cultural needs of a particular society.*[105]

---

[101]Commission of the European Communities, Legal Framework Conditions Applicable to State Aid to Public Service Broadcasting, http://ec.europa.eu/competition/sectors/media/decisions_psb.pdf, accessed 9 October 2014.

[102]Commission of the European Communities, Communication from the Commission on the application of state aid rules to public service broadcasting [2001] OJ C320/5.

[103]Commission of the European Communities, Communication from the Commission on the application of state aid rules to public service broadcasting [2009] OJ C257/1.

[104]Llorens-Maluquer 2002.

[105]See for example in the following Decisions:

(1) 2011/140/EU: Commission Decision of 20 July 2010 on state aid C 27/09 (ex N 34/B/09) budgetary grant for France Télévisions, which the French Republic plans to implement in favour of France Télévisions [2011] OJ L59/44;
(2) State Aid No SA.32019—Denmark Danish radio channel FM4, C (2011)1376 final, 23.03.2011;
(3) 2004/838/EC: Commission Decision of 10 December 2003 on state aid implemented by France for France 2 and France 3 [2004] OJ L361/21;

Its Decisions in relation to BBC are a very good example.[106] The BBC, as the public service broadcaster in the UK, upgraded its traditional broadcasting services by launching nine new digital channel services[107] and a 24-h news service channel.[108] It also expanded to provide online digital curriculum service, which is clearly outside the scope of traditional public broadcasting services.[109]

The Commission's Decision on BBC digital curriculum service is illuminating. The UK authorities entrusted the BBC with provision of online interactive learning materials free of charge. The programme would cost 150 million pounds and would be funded by the television licence fee. It should be noted that online learning services were not included as the traditional package of PSB, even in the UK legislation. Its legal basis was as an ancillary service, subject to special Ministerial approval.

In its Decision, the Commission did not apply the market failure test, as it did in the broadband sector. As pointed out by the Commission itself, there has been a 'competitive and dynamic' market providing similar products.[110] Applying the market failure test would mean that it should not be accepted as an SGEI task and that the funding would be incompatible with the Treaty. This could potentially undermine the organisation of PSB in the UK.

On the contrary, it chose not to challenge the British government's decision to include digital curriculum as an SGEI. From its Decision, it is not clear what benchmark has been used by the Commission. It seems that the decisive feature of the state measure is its *educational nature and provision free of charge*. In its Decision, it simply declared that the inclusion of digital curriculum was a valid SGEI without any serious discussion. It pointed out that:

> It is Member States who are *primarily responsible* for defining what they regard as service of general economic interest. This definition can only be subject to an examination and determination by the Commission for manifest error. Given that the service is a *free educational service* for schools and students the Commission considers that the UK government has not made a manifest error by defining the Digital Curriculum service to be of general economic interest.[111] (emphasis added)

---

(4) 2005/217/EC: Commission Decision of 19 May 2004 on measures implemented by Denmark for TV2/Danmark [2006] OJ L85/1.

[106] Another very interesting Decision is N 109/2010 concerning the provision of live subtitling for main evening news for the benefit of persons with a hearing disability. The Commission did not apply a market failure test but recognised it as a valid SGEI because it contributed to social inclusion and access to media and information sources: State Aid No N 109/2010—Belgium Vlaamse Mediamaatschappij - Subsidie live ondertiteling "Het Nieuws"—Project iWATCH, C (2010) 7679 final, 17.11.2010.

[107] State Aid No N 631/2001—United Kingdom BBC licence fee, C (2002) 1886 fin, 22.05.2002.

[108] State Aid No NN 88/98—United Kingdom financing of a 24-h advertising-free news channel out of the licence fee by the BBC, SG (99) D/10201, 14.12.1999.

[109] State Aid No N 37/2003—United Kingdom BBC digital curriculum, C (2003) 3371 fin, 01.10.2003.

[110] Ibid., para 10.

[111] Ibid.

It is submitted that the Commission has not exercised any substantial influence over the definition of PSB. This is very different from the broadband and maritime sectors where the Commission examines whether similar services or products are provided by market undertakings without State funding.

4.4.3 The Competition Neutrality Test in Public Service Broadcasting[112]

In most Decisions concerning PSB, the Commission found that the fourth condition of the *Altmark* was not met and therefore that the State measures constituted state aid. The reason lies in the practice of the Member States: PSB is still entrusted to the former public broadcasters without a public tender procedure. Therefore, in most Commission PSB Decisions, the Commission simply concluded that the fourth condition of the *Altmark* criteria had not been met and that the State measure constituted state aid without discussion of other conditions, in particular the third one.

The absence of a public tender procedure does not necessarily render the state funding incompatible with the EU state aid law. In the PSB sector, the Commission does not push/force Member States to use public tendering to choose the provider and to decide the amount of funding. Instead, the Commission focuses on the issue of advantage under the third condition of Article 106(2)—in other words, whether SGEI funding of PSB exceeds the costs of its provision and, as a result, leads to over-compensation.[113]

If the sole activity of the undertaking in question is to provide PSB, then the assessment of the Commission is quite straightforward: state funding must not exceed the actual costs of the provision of PSB. The Commission's Decision regarding the BBC's 24-h advertising-free news channel is a good illustration. This news channel is funded by the licence fee:

> The financing system defined by the UK for the BBC (only a license fee with no market revenues) ensures that the amount of the funds received by the undertaking for fulfilling its public service obligation is *limited to the net costs* deriving from the provision of such

---

[112]The same competition-neutrality test can also be found in other SGEI Decisions. For example, in the area of basic financial services, the Commission made the following two Decisions:

(1) State Aid N 642/05—Sweden Compensation to Posten AB for providing basic payment and cash facilities services, C (2006) 5481 fin, 22.11.2006;
(2) State Aid No N 244/2003—United Kingdom Credit Union Provision of Access to Basic Financial Services -Scotland, C (2005) 977 fin, 06.04.2005.

[113]Bavasso 2002.

> services. Applying the same reasoning, it can be concluded that the amount of license fee used to finance BBC News 24 is *strictly proportional to the actual costs* incurred for the provision of the service.[114] (emphasis added)

On the other hand, if the undertaking in question carries out both SGEIs and commercial activities, it is essential to have a *clear separation* between these activities.[115] The Transparency Directive requires Member States to maintain separate accounting systems that reflect the costs and the revenues for different activities and the methods for such allocation.[116]

In the Commission's practice, the calculation of the costs and necessary funding for SGEI involves a complex economic exercise. First, if both activities share the same facility for its operation, the cost sharing mechanism must reflect the market price. And the costs related to commercial operations shall not be included in the costs of SGEI provision. Secondly, any profits gained from the commercial activity will be deducted from the calculation of the amount of compensation necessary for the provision of SGEI.

These are the key requirements in the Commission's practice of the necessity test under Article 106(2).[117] The Decision on the BBC digital curriculum is a good example. In that Decision, the Commission found that the SGEI funding granted by the UK was less than its costs. Furthermore, the Commission also noticed the following three aspects of the organisation model of the BBC:

> The non-public service activities are performed by separate commercial subsidiaries of the BBC and the accounts of these subsidiaries are published in accordance with the UK Companies Acts. [….] Moreover, the net profits from any commercialisation linked to or deriving from the public service have to be accounted for in arriving at the net costs of the public service. The Fair Trading Commitment and the Commercial Policy Guideline require that the Commercial subsidiaries have to pay fair charges for inputs they receive from the public service entities of the BBC organisation. These charges should be in line with the external market price for such inputs.[118]

Such mechanisms in place can prevent over-compensation of PSB. Therefore, the Commission concluded that the licence fee as a funding mechanism is compatible with the Treaty.[119]

On the other hand, if the funding granted exceeds the costs of the provision of SGEI, the Commission could conclude that such measure is incompatible with the Treaty. The Commission's Decision concerning Denmark TV2 offers a good

---

[114]State Aid No NN 88/98—United Kingdom financing of a 24-h advertising-free news channel out of the licence fee by the BBC, SG (99) D/10201, 14.12.1999, paras 82–83.

[115]Donders 2009.

[116]Commission Directive 2006/111/EC of 16 November 2006 on the transparency of financial relations between Member States and public undertakings as well as on financial transparency within certain undertakings [2006] OJ L318/17, Article 1(2).

[117]Depypere et al. 2004.

[118]State Aid No N 37/2003—United Kingdom BBC digital curriculum, C (2003) 3371 fin, 01.10.2003, paras 54, 56–57.

[119]The same approach is used in Decision SA.32019.

example.[120] In that Decision, the Commission applied the same benchmark to assess whether the Danish funding for its PSB was compatible with state aid rules. The Commission found that its commercial activity shared the same inputs with the PSB and that there was not meaningful cost allocation between them. In its calculation of the net costs of PSB, it excluded all the costs connected with its commercial activity. For the amount needed for the provision of PSB, it deducted from the net costs of PSB the revenue generated by its commercial activity. It found that the funding granted exceeded the net costs of PSB and that it must be recovered.

Another aspect of the competition neutrality test of the Commission is to examine whether SGEI funding is used to cross-subsidise the commercial activity when the undertaking in question carries out both activities.[121] In several cases, the Commission investigated whether the undertaking has kept its pricing for commercial activity artificially low. This practice would reduce the amount of commercial revenue and, as a result, increase the amount of funding needed. This is the very concern raised in its Decisions concerning PSB broadcasting in France,[122] Italy[123] and Denmark.[124]

Through state aid control, the Commission can have significant influence over the organisation of funding for SGEI in Member States. It scrutinises the actual design of the funding measure to see if there are mechanisms in place to avoid over-compensation. Otherwise, SGEI funding would be found to be incompatible with the Treaty and its implementation is prohibited. In this way, the Commission can ensure that state funding for SGEI is granted in a transparent manner and does not distort competition.

4.5 Conclusion

Bringing SGEI funding under EU state aid control has been the latest effort of the EU to regulate the provision of SGEI under competition law. The first is the issue of definition. The issue was settled in the *Altmark* case, where the Court exempted SGEI funding being categorised as state aid (and therefore exempted the Member States' notification obligations) under four conditions. Such requirements go further than the *Ferring* case because of the introduction of the efficiency test. This is the

[120] 2005/217/EC: Commission Decision of 19 May 2004 on measures implemented by Denmark for TV2/Danmark [2006] OJ L85/1.

[121] Depypere and Tigchelaar 2004.

[122] 2004/838/EC: Commission Decision of 10 December 2003 on state aid implemented by France for France 2 and France 3 [2004] OJ L361/21.

[123] 2004/339/EC: Commission Decision of 15 October 2003 on the measures implemented by Italy for RAI SpA [2004] OJ L119/1.

[124] 2005/217/EC: Commission Decision of 19 May 2004 on measures implemented by Denmark for TV2/Danmark [2006] OJ L85/1.

real contribution of the *Altmark* case. The essence is to strike a balance between SGEI funding and the application of EU state aid law. On the one hand, it granted derogation for SGEI funding from being defined as state aid. As a result, if such conditions are fulfilled, the Member States do not have the obligation to notify such a measure; unnotified SGEI funding measures would still be lawful and therefore SGEI provision would not be disrupted. On the other hand, the conditions contained in the *Altmark* criteria can ensure that no advantage is granted and that SGEI funding does not distort market competition. In its practice, the Commission has focused on the efficiency test under the fourth condition of the *Altmark* criteria and applied it very strictly. As a result, in most Decisions, it found that the *Altmark* exemption did not apply and that SGEI funding constituted state aid.

Failure to satisfy the *Altmark* criteria does not necessarily mean SGEI funding would be prohibited by EU state aid law. Its compatibility will be evaluated by the Commission on the basis of Article 106(2) under three conditions: (1) there must be a clearly defined SGEI task; (2) the SGEI task is entrusted by public authorities; and (3) funding for SGEI does not distort market competition. The Commission's approach is reflected in its soft law documents. It has adopted sector-specific rules for the maritime transport, broadband and public service broadcasting sectors. In other areas, its Frameworks are applicable.

On the application of the first condition, the Commission has adopted different standards in examining what constitutes legitimate SGEIs. In the broadband sector, it has adopted a strict market failure approach to reject many state funding measures as SGEI. By contrast, in other areas the Commission respects the Member State's wide freedom in deciding what non-economic interests they will pursue under SGEIs. In its Decisions, the Commission simply rubber-stamps such SGEI tasks as valid under EU law and does not exercise a meaningful control in this respect. This approach is reflected in its Decisions concerning the postal services and public service broadcasting sectors. Regarding the third condition, the necessity test has been translated as to ensure SGEI funding is competition neutral. This book uses the public service broadcasting sector as an example. It finds that the focus of the Commission has been on whether SGEI funding leads to over-compensation and cross-subsidisation.

References

Bartosch A (2003) Clarification or confusion? How to reconcile the ECJ's rulings in Altmark and Chronopost? European State Aid Law Quarterly 2(3):375–386

Bavasso AF (2002) Public service broadcasting and state aid rules: between a rock and a hard place. European Law Review 27(3):340–350

Bovis C (2003) Public procurement, state aid and public services: between symbiotic correlation and asymmetric geometry. European State Aid Law Quarterly 2(4):553–569

Depypere S, Broche J, Tigchelaar N (2004) State aid and broadcasting: state of play. Competition Policy Newsletter (1):71–73

Depypere S, Tigchelaar N (2004) The commission's state aid policy on activities of public service broadcasters in neighbouring Markets. Competition Policy Newsletter (2):19–22

Donders K (2009) State aid and public service broadcasting: how future-proof is the remit of public broadcasting organisations? http://www.ies.be/files/IES%20Working%20paper%201_2009%20Karen%20Donders.pdf

Fratini A, Filpo F (2006) The new EC framework for state aid to public service and the postal sector: where do we stand now? In: Crew MA, Kleindorfer PR (eds) Progress toward liberalization of the postal and delivery sector. Springer, New York

Hanretty C (2012) Public service broadcasting's continued rude health. http://www.britac.ac.uk/templates/asset-relay.cfm?frmAssetFileID=11221

Harrison J, Woods LM (2001) Defining European public service broadcasting. European Journal of Communication 16(4):477–504

Humphreys P (1996) Mass media and media policy in Western Europe. Manchester University Press, Manchester

Humphreys P (2005) The EU and audiovisual regulation: an agency for de-regulation or re-regulation – a research agenda. http://regulation.upf.edu/ecpr-05-papers/phumphreys.pdf

Iosifidis P (2009) Plurality of public service provision in the UK and beyond. Interactions: Studies in Communication & Culture 1(2):253–267

Karayigit MT (2009) Under the triangle rules of competition, state aid and public procurement: public undertakings entrusted with the operation of services of general economic interest. European Competition Law Review 30(11):542–564

Koenig C, Fechter S (2009) The European Commission's hidden asymmetric regulatory approach in the field of broadband infrastructure funding. European State Aid Law Quarterly 8(4):463–472

Llorens-Maluquer C (2002) The European Union policy, pluralism and public service broadcasting. Paper presented at the RIPE@2002 Conference, Helsinki-Tampere

Mendel T (2013) Public service broadcasting: a comparative legal survey. https://unesdoc.unesco.org/ark:/48223/pf0000192459

Mortensen F (2008) Altmark, Article 106(2) and public service broadcasting. European State Aid Law Quarterly 7(2):239–249

Muller T (2009) Efficiency control in state aid and the power of member states to define SGEIs. European State Aid Law Quarterly 8(1):39–46

Ross M (2004) The Europeanization of public services supervision: harnessing competition and citizenship? Yearbook of European Law 23(1): 303–319

Sinnaeve A (2003) State financing of public services: the Court's dilemma in the *Altmark* case. European State Aid Law Quarterly 2(3):351–363

Smith RC (2005) Public service broadcasting in the European Union: no longer simply a matter of domestic concern. Hong Kong Media Digest 3(9):10–13.

Tigchelaar N (2003) State aid to public broadcasting – Revisited. European State Aid Law Quarterly 2(2):169–182

Tosics N, Gaál N (2007) Public procurement and state aid control — the issue of economic advantage. Competition Policy Newsletter (3):15–18

Travers N (2003) Public service obligations and state aid: is all really clear after Altmark. European State Aid Law Quarterly 2(3):387–392

Van Cuilenburg J, McQuail D (2003) Media policy paradigm shifts: towards a new communications policy paradigm. European Journal of Communication 18(2)181–207

Yábar PC (2012) State aid in broadband infrastructures. Staff Working Paper, Joint Assistance to Support Projects in European Regions. http://www.jaspersnetwork.org/download/attachments/4947983/State%20Aid%20Broadband_Guidelines.pdf?version=1&modificationDate=1366385314000&api=v2

Chapter 5
Universal Service Obligation in Telecommunications

Contents

Abstract The chapter studies service of general economic interest (SGEI) in the telecommunications sector, which has been translated as universal service obligations (USO). The ideal of universal service was deeply rooted in the organisation of the sector under the traditional public service model. The EU liberalisation process transformed this sector from state monopolies to competitive markets. It was in this process that USO provision began to be regulated at the EU level. It finds that SGEI was largely a by-product of the liberalisation process. It was defined very narrowly during the market liberalisation process, limited to physical access to telephony network. It remained largely unchanged until now. It is submitted that USO as defined by EU law has become obsolete and meaningless, as is shown by the steady

L. Zhu, *Services of General Economic Interest in EU Competition Law*,
Legal Issues of Services of General Interest,
https://doi.org/10.1007/978-94-6265-387-0_5

decline in the subscription rate to fixed telephone. Instead, the focus of EU law has been on ensuring that USO funding is competition neutral.

Keywords state monopoly · liberalisation · universal telephony service · USO funding · market failure · competition neutrality · public services

5.1 Introduction

In the telecommunications sector, SGEI has been translated as universal service obligations (USO), that is, guaranteed provision of basic telecommunications services for everyone across the Member States. This ideal is deeply rooted in the organisation of the sector in the Member States.

The telecommunications sector had been organised on the basis of a public service model rather than a competitive market. This was the very case in Europe right until the 1990s. The State was involved in the direct control and provision of telecommunications networks and services based on a broad notion of public service.[1] The operators were an integrated part of the national ministry of communications, or later incorporated into public undertakings owned and controlled by the State.[2] They were not supposed to make profits but had become an instrument of the State to pursue a wide range of public interests or public policies.

One of the public objectives was to provide *affordable* telecommunications services to *everyone* in the country.[3] This is the very ideal of universal service. Basic telecommunications services are associated with economic and social human rights. Therefore, the State has a responsibility to guarantee that they are available to everyone in society.[4] In return, the State granted network operators statutory monopoly rights over the whole telecommunications sector and sometimes provided them with extra financial support.[5]

This model contradicted the EU market integration programme and competition principles. The grant of exclusive rights over the whole sector, including the network and all relevant associated telecommunications services, eliminated the possibility of competition.[6] It also virtually divided the telecommunications sector along national boundaries, which led to fragmented EU telecommunications markets. Furthermore, the traditional public service model in the telecommunications sector was also in conflict with basic market principles: operators did not have

---

[1] Rapp 1996.

[2] Larouche 2000.

[3] Bauer 1999.

[4] Eliassen and From 2009.

[5] Larouche 1999.

[6] Leith 2012.

commercial freedom but undertook public interest activities, prices did not reflect the costs, and consumers had no freedom to choose service providers.

The EU did not take any action against this model until 1987, when the Commission published its Telecommunications Green Paper.[7] Since then, the landscape of the organisation of the telecommunications sector in Europe has been transformed. In about a decade the EU has adopted a series of Directives that broke down national monopolies[8] and transformed the telecommunications sector into a competitive market. After the market was liberalised, re-regulation was necessary for the proper functioning of this new competitive market. Directives have been adopted at the EU level to decide what *general interests* justify *State intervention* in the market, on such issues as market entry, consumer protection, etc.[9]

It is in this market integration process that the EU became involved in the issue of SGEI in the telecommunications sector. The SGEI concept was rooted deeply in the national ideal of universal service and has evolved with the liberalisation and re-regulation process in the telecommunications sector. It is in this sector-specific legislative context that the provision of USOs is prescribed in EU law.

This chapter examines the treatment of SGEI in the telecommunications sector. First, it introduces the traditional organisation model of the telecommunications sector in the Member States, where the very roots of USO lie. It shows that the ideal

---

[7] Commission of European Communities, Towards a Dynamic European Economy: Green Paper on the Development of the Common Market for Telecommunication Services and Equipment, COM (87) 290 final, 30.06.1987 (hereafter 1987 Telecommunications Green Paper).

[8] The EU adopted a piecemeal approach by abolishing monopoly rights gradually. These Directives included:

(1) Commission Directive 88/301/EEC of 16 May 1988 on competition in the markets in telecommunications terminal equipment [1988] OJ L131/73 (hereafter 1988 Terminal Equipment Directive);
(2) Commission Directive 90/388/EEC of 28 June 1990 on competition in the markets for telecommunications services [1990] OJ L192/10 (hereafter 1990 Telecommunications Services Directive);
(3) Commission Directive 94/46/EC of 13 October 1994 amending Directive 88/301/EEC and Directive 90/388/EEC in particular with regard to satellite communications [1994] OJ L268/15 (hereafter 1994 Satellite Communication Directive);
(4) Commission Directive 95/51/EC of 18 October 1995 amending Directive 90/388/EEC with regard to the abolition of the restrictions on the use of cable television networks for the provision of already liberalised telecommunications services [1995] OJ L256/49 (hereafter 1995 Television Cable Directive);
(5) Commission Directive 96/2/EC of 16 January 1996 amending Directive 90/388/EEC with regard to mobile and personal communications [1996] OJ L20/59 (hereafter 1996 Mobile Communications Directive);
(6) Commission Directive 96/19/EC of 13 March 1996 amending Directive 90/388/EEC with regard to the Implementation of full competition in Telecommunications Markets [1996] OJ L74/13 (hereafter 1996 Full Competition Directive).

[9] For a list of these Directive and their latest amendments, see 'Regulatory Framework for Electronic Communications' on the EU's legislation summary website:

http://europa.eu/legislation_summaries/information_society/legislative_framework/l24216a_en.htm accessed 9 October 2014.

of universal service lay at the heart of this model, which included requirements for physical and social access to basic telephony services.[10] It also provided a justification for State intervention in the sector, including the grant of state monopolies by the Member States.[11] However, it had not been a clearly defined legal term but had strong economic, political and even ideological implications.[12]

The chapter also looks at the treatment of USO during market liberalisation. During this process, the necessity test has been translated as controlled liberalisation, where the provision of SGEI justifies exclusive rights over certain areas of the telecommunications sector. Special attention is paid to the application of Article 106 by the Commission, which provides the very legal basis for liberalisation.[13] During this process, USO was largely seen as an unwelcome obstacle because it justified retaining a large area of the telecommunications industry under the protection of state monopoly. Therefore, it had been defined very narrowly, limited to physical access to telephony network.

Section 5.4 examines the provision of USO in the competitive telecommunications market. First, it looks at the content and scope of USO and competence allocation in defining it. The research shows that the current regime was essentially established by the harmonisation Directives in the late 1990s.[14] These Directives were designed to ensure open access to the network.[15] It is submitted that the

---

[10] Rapp 1996.

[11] Blackman 1995, p. 172.

[12] Nenova 2007.

[13] This issue is discussed in Sect. 3.2 of Chap. 3. In 1991, the Court delivered a series of Judgments that ruled that the grant of monopoly rights by the Member State was incompatible with the Treaty. These Judgments include:

(1) Case C-41/90 *Klaus Höfner and Fritz Elser v Macrotron GmbH* [1991] ECR I-1979;
(2) Case C-260/89 *Elliniki Radiophonia Tileorassi AE (Ert) (Panellinia Omospondia Syllogon Prossopikou Ert intervening) v Dimotiki Étairia Pliroforissis (Dep) and Sotirios Kouvelas (Nicolaos Avdellas and Others intervening)* [1991] ECR I-02925;
(3) Case C-18/88 *Régie des Télégraphes et des Téléphones v GB-Inno-BM SA* [1991] ECR I-5941;
(4) Case C-179/90 *Merci Convenzionali Porto di Genova SpA v Siderurgica Gabrielli SpA* [1991] ECR I-05889.

[14] Directive 95/62/EC of the European Parliament and of the Council of 13 December 1995 on the application of Open Network Provision (ONP) to voice telephony [1995] OJ L321/6 (hereafter 1995 Telephony ONP Directive).

[15] These Directives respected the monopoly right over the telephony network; meanwhile, it required the network operators to give access to third parties. They are the so-called ONP (Open Network Provision) Directives, including:

(1) Council Directive 90/387/EEC of 28 June 1990 on the establishment of the Internal Market for telecommunications services through the implementation of Open Network Provision [1990] OJ L192/1;
(2) Council Directive 92/44/EEC of 5 June 1992 on the application of Open Network Provision to leased lines [1992] OJ L165/27;
(3) Directive 95/62/EC of the European Parliament and of the Council of 13 December 1995 on the application of Open Network Provision (ONP) to voice telephony [1995] OJ L321/6.

fulfilment of USO was only a by-product of Open Network Provision (ONP) Directives. That is why the scope has been limited to physical access to the telephony network, which Member States have a legal obligation to guarantee. Meanwhile, the social element (affordability) of universal service has been left to the free will of the Member States. It is submitted that this narrow definition of USO is largely obsolete in the modern digital age.

On the other hand, the Commission has invested considerable efforts in ensuring the competition neutrality of USO funding.[16] The EU has not established a uniform procedural framework for the delivery of USO. Instead, the task to design and implement a USO funding mechanism has been left to the Member States.[17] The Commission has been using the infringement procedure to examine USO funding measures on a case-by-case basis. It has applied the market failure test and competition neutrality test to ensure that USO funding does not distort market competition.

5.2 Traditional Organisational Model of the Telecommunications Sector

5.2.1 The Origin of Universal Service: Interconnection

The telephone was invented at the end of the 19th century. The initiative of the network development was undertaken by private undertakings in the market.[18] The problem with competition in the development of the telecommunications network was a typical market failure. In densely populated areas, mainly in cities, there were

---

[16] The focus of the Commission has been to ensure that USO providers do not gain any financial advantages from the Member States because of the provision of USO.

Directive 2002/22/EC of the European Parliament and of the Council of 7 March 2002 on universal service and users' rights relating to electronic communications networks and services [2002] OJ L108/51, Recital 4. The Directive was amended by Directive 2009/136. Directive 2009/136/EC of the European Parliament and of the Council of 25 November 2009 amending Directive 2002/22/EC on universal service and users' rights relating to electronic communications networks and services, Directive 2002/58/EC concerning the processing of personal data and the protection of privacy in the electronic communications sector and Regulation (EC) No 2006/2004 on cooperation between national authorities responsible for the enforcement of consumer protection laws [2009] OJ L337/11. A consolidated version of Directive 2002/22 can be found on the EU's website:

http://eur-lex.europa.eu/legal-content/EN/TXT/PDF/?uri=CELEX:02002L0022-20091219&from=En accessed 9 October 2014 (hereafter 2002 Universal Service Directive).

[17] European Regulators for Electronic Communications, 'BEREC Report on Universal Service—Reflection for the Future' (June 2010). http://berec.europa.eu/eng/document_register/subject_matter/berec/download/0/187-berec-report-on-universal-service-reflec_0.pdf.

[18] For a brief introduction of the early development of telephone industry, see Verhoest 2000.

several competing undertakings building independent duplicated networks.[19] Consequently, in order to be connected with each other, users had to be within the same network, which essentially meant that they had to subscribe to different providers at the same time. This was the problem of interconnection. In rural and remote areas, the problem was different but equally challenging, because there was not enough incentive for private undertakings to develop a network or the price for a connection would be prohibitively high.

The issue was reflected in the notion of natural monopoly, which was the dominant thinking until the 1980s.[20] The telecommunications network, by nature, should be operated by one monopolist, either by the State directly or by private undertakings regulated by the State.[21] This idea reflects the technological feature of the sector at its early stage of development. Communications technology until the 1970s was still quite simple and straightforward.[22] It was confined to *telegraph and telephony*, which essentially involved 'the transmission, at low running costs, of voice or visual images across *a network of lines* with the information routed by switching exchanges'.[23]

In America, in response to the fragmented network and the problem of interconnection, the dominant corporation AT&T proposed the idea of 'one system, one policy, universal service'.[24] The idea was supported by the Congress of the United States, which granted AT&T a monopoly right over the national telephony network.[25]

This was the first time that the notion of 'universal service' appeared in the telecommunications context.[26] It was closely connected with the problem of market failure and interconnection.[27] AT&T had used it as a 'corporate strategy' and aimed to gain political support for the monopolisation of the telephony network.[28] If there was a certain element of universality, it was associated with the organisation of the network, i.e. one network. What is clear is that the real intention behind it (monopolisation) had nothing to do with any social or political redistributive objectives that later became to be associated with the concept of universal service.[29]

[19] Wu 2007.
[20] Cassidy 1999.
[21] Verhoest 2000.
[22] Millward 2008, p. 546.
[23] Millward 2005, p. 244.
[24] Mueller 1993.
[25] Wu 2007.
[26] Cassidy 1999, p. 138; Nenova 2007.
[27] Jayakar and Sawhney 2003.
[28] Young 2005; Nagy 2013.
[29] Verhoest 2000, p. 596; Nenova 2007.

5.2.2 *Telecommunications as Public Services in Europe*

By contrast, on the other side of the Atlantic, a different model had evolved to deal with the issue of market failure in Europe.[30] Owing to its hugely strategic importance for the control of information flow, and also for its significance of military use, national governments in Europe soon stepped into operate the telecommunications networks directly.[31]

This had become the orthodox form for the organisation of the telecommunications sector in Europe until the 1990s.[32] In most Member States, the organisation of telecommunications had been regarded as a public service and the responsibility of the State.[33] The task was undertaken by the national public administration itself, or later by public undertakings under the control of the State.[34]

This is the traditional model for the organisation of telecommunications in Europe under broader notions of public service and mixed economy. Telecommunications was too important to be left in the hands of private undertakings on the market. Therefore, it was operated in the public interest by entities whose activities were controlled by the State.[35]

State control over all aspects of its operation was regarded as necessary for the pursuit of the public interest.[36] Telecommunications was regarded as being part of public administration, within public budgets at an earlier stage.[37] In some cases, States even granted operators certain regulatory powers. Although they became separate public undertakings later, they did not have commercial freedom. Prices were set by Ministers, and investment priorities were decided by the State. As a result, they had become a tool or a means for the State to pursue certain public interest or public policy objectives.[38]

At the early stage of telecommunications development, the main focus of the telecommunications industry was still dominated by the task of network development.[39] Until 1932, in Denmark, which had the highest teledensity rate in Europe, only less than 10% of the population had a telephone.[40] The telephone was largely

---

[30] Bauer 1999; Reiss 2011.

[31] Millward 2005, Chap. 4.

[32] Bauer 2010.

[33] OECD, 'Universal Service and Rate Restructuring in Telecommunications' (OECD Digital Economy Papers, No. 4, 1991) http://dx.doi.org/10.1787/237454868255; Prosser 2000.

[34] European Parliament, 'Public Undertakings and Public Service Activities in the European Union' (Economic Working Paper Series W-21, May 1996) http://www.europarl.europa.eu/workingpapers/econ/pdf/w21_en.pdf, Sect. VII.

[35] Lando 1994.

[36] Eliassen and From 2009, p. 242; Nenova 2007.

[37] Millward 2008, p. 546.

[38] International Telecommunication Union 2012; Nenova 2007.

[39] Milne 1998.

[40] Millward 2005.

regarded as a luxury, rather than a basic or essential service.[41] Advocates for the idea of 'one telephone for every home' were regarded as advocating an impossible mission.

The modern version of universal service in telecommunications was formed only after World War II, which closely connected with the notion of the Welfare State.[42] Since then, the basic telephony service was advocated as essential and basic to support human rights.[43] It began to incorporate principles such as universality and affordability. The ideal of an 'affordable basic telephone service for everyone' has since become a standard notion, associated with universal service in the telecommunications sector.[44]

Under this model there was no need to define specifically its public service objectives or USOs.[45] The whole of the telecommunications sector was supposed to be carrying out activities in the public interest. Indeed, telecommunications was used to achieve a wide range of public interest objectives, including promotion of employment, stimulation of innovation and investment in infrastructure.[46] This could be observed from early case law on the public service exemption in the context of free movement of workers, where Member States clashed severely with the Commission over its scope.[47]

Provision of universal access was only part of the network operators' public service missions, probably the least important one.[48] It was distinct from the modern version of USO developed at the EU level in two ways: first, universal service was not defined in an explicit manner.[49] Universal service or universal access was defined in very broad and vague terms, rather than in any quantitative detail. The waiting list could be very long, and the quality of services provided by the incumbents had been disappointing.[50] Secondly, it could hardly be regarded as an 'obligation'. Telecommunications service providers represented the State and public interest. Universal access was protected through political mechanisms rather than as a legal requirement.[51] Normal commercial and contract law did not apply to them. From the users' perspective, it was not an enforceable legal right.[52] Its

---

[41] Verhoest 2000.

[42] Economides 2004, p. 9; Sawhney 1994; Verhoest 2000.

[43] Young 2005; Nagy 2013.

[44] Milgrom 1996.

[45] Verhoest 2000; Nenova 2007.

[46] Bauer 1999, p. 332.

[47] The cases are not concerned with the telecommunications sector directly, but with the interpretation of the scope of 'public service' as used in the postal and railway sectors. Case 107/84 *Commission of the European Communities v Federal Republic of Germany* [1985] ECR-2655; Case 149/79 *Commission of the European Communities v Kingdom of Belgium* [1982] ECR-1845.

[48] Nenova 2007.

[49] International Telecommunication Union (2012), Sect. 3.1.1.

[50] Nenova 2007.

[51] Prosser 2000.

[52] Thatcher 1999.

achievement was largely dependent on the *voluntary willingness of the operator*. To a large extent, it was a political rather than a legal concept.

5.2.3 The Ideal of Universal Service, Cross-Subsidisation and State Monopoly

The ideal of universal service lies at the heart of the traditional public service model in the telecommunications sector. It provides the justification for the operational model and the monopoly market structure.[53] In order to solve the problem of market failure and ensure that a telephone was available for everyone, in particular for sparsely populated areas, a system of cross-subsidisation was adopted. The essence of this model is: (1) price distortion, i.e. price does not reflect the cost of the provision of the service; and (2) price discrimination, i.e. for certain services, or customers, price was fixed above its real costs, but for others it was below its real cost. Therefore, superprofits generated in one area could be used to subsidise other loss-making areas.

This method of financing universal service in the European telecommunications industry has been considered by many scholars.[54] However, there was no comprehensive data in Europe on how it really worked and what the implications were. In theory, four flows of subsidisation could be generated through this price mechanism.[55] Tariffs were divided into two parts, charges for network connection and, on the other hand, telephony calls, which differed according to length and distance. For connection charges, business users were charged at a higher price than residential users. For residential users, a uniform average price was charged across the whole country, irrespective of the geographical location. For call rates, international calls were charged at a price well beyond the cost to subsidise local calls (where the price was even below its costs). And for local calls, a uniform flat rate was charged. The subsidisation flow is illustrated in Fig. 5.1.

It is worth noting that this exercise of cross-subsidisation was undertaken in a non-transparent fashion.[56] This is the notion of internal transfer.[57] It was not possible to figure out which provision of service to which area and which customers had generated a loss and how much. Financial gains from profitable areas were

[53] Leith 2012; Nenova 2007; De Minico 2011.

[54] For example, Cassidy 1999.

[55] West 1996; Regan 2008.

[56] Gautier and Wauthy 2012.

[57] The monopoly structure allowed the public operator to finance the provision of universal service out of internal revenue transfer, without it being necessary to define either the precise scope or the cost of such universal service: Commission of the European Communities, Developing Universal Service for Telecommunications in a Competitive Environment (Communication from the Commission to the Council, the European Parliament and the European Economic and Social Committee), COM (93) 543 final, 15.11.1993, 5; Nett 1998.

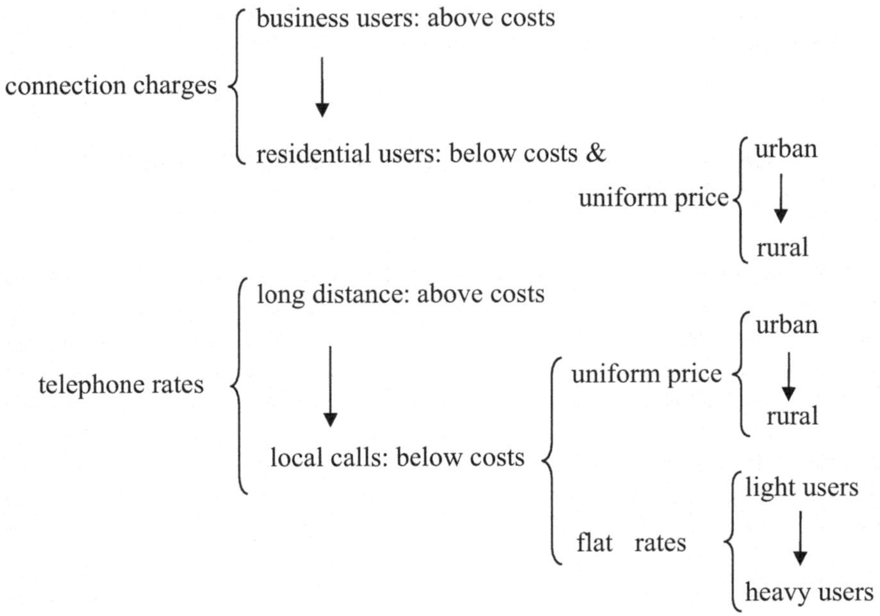

Fig. 5.1 Flows of cross-subsidisation under state monopolies. *Source* The author

pooled together to make up the loss-making practice because of serving certain customers, and probably also for other reasons such as inefficiency.[58] The key issue is to generate enough profits to maintain and develop the network. Indeed, as statistics show, telecommunications operators still made a substantial sum of profit every year during the period 1950–1980.[59]

While it is not within the scope of this book to collect all the data on this issue, the tariff structure for telephony calls in some EU Member States in 1986 could illustrate this funding mechanism very well. It was estimated that the actual cost then was 0.1 ECUs for local calls and 0.3–0.4 ECUs for long-distance calls per 3 min. For local calls, tariffs corresponded roughly to actual cost (as in the case of Denmark, France, Germany and Belgium) or even below it (as in the case of Spain and Netherlands). But for trunk and international calls, tariffs were set four to ten times above actual costs (Table 5.1).

Under the traditional public service model of the telecommunications sector, universal service was also associated with the means that protected the cross-subsidisation flows, statutory monopoly.[60] In order to generate enough

[58] Rapp 1996, p. 392.

[59] An exception was the British telecommunications operator in 1973 and 1974, when it incurred a loss in its operation: Millward 2005, p. 248.

[60] Rapp 1996, p. 392.

Table 5.1 Telephone tariffs in selected member states, 1986. (charges for 3-min calls in ECUs[a])

	UK	Denmark	France	Germany (West)	Italy	Belgium	Netherlands	Spain
Local	0.21	0.10	0.11	0.11	0.20	0.14	0.06	0.03
Trunk up to 100 km	0.56	0.36	0.15	1.00	1.62	0.69	0.26	0.60
Other domestic trunk call	0.56	n.a.	1.59	1.66	1.72	0.69	n.a.	1.07
International	1.94	1.37	1.85	1.67	2.92	2.22	1.75	3.17

[a]European Currency Units, including VAT
Source Millward (2005)

profits, the State granted the operator an exclusive right to provide a telecommunications network and all associated telephony services, prohibiting others from entering into the market.[61] Without this protection in place, it was feared that private undertakings would focus on profitable areas and provide telecommunications services cheaper than the public operator. This could lead to the problem of 'cherry picking' and would undermine the monopolist's tariff structure and its operational model.

Under this model, several features could be identified as reflecting the ideal of telephone service for everyone. On the one hand, there was the physical aspect of universal access. The telephony network had been operated by public undertakings that were owned and controlled by the State. The priority of such operation was to develop a network to cover the whole area of the national territory rather than to make profit. At an early stage of the telecommunications sector, physical access to the network might be a problem for consumers in remote or isolated areas. However, once a network has become mature, with a full coverage of the national territory, physical access to the network is not a big issue any more.[62] In other words, universal physical access is the natural result of network development.

What is more important about the ideal of universal service is its social aspect, i.e. universal and affordable price.[63] For residential users, tariffs for connection and local calls were the same across the country. Tariffs were set by public authorities at an affordable level, after taking into account the particular national social and economic context. Ultimately, it was a *political decision*. The real benefits varied greatly from State to State, from a price even much lower than the real cost (e.g. Spain and the Netherlands) to a price twice that of real cost (e.g. the UK and Italy).[64]

[61]Naftel 1992, p. 451; Cassidy 1999.

[62]This was the very case in Europe by the late 1990s.

[63]Blackman 1995.

[64]Affordability is a vague and subjective concept that is closely associated with the income level of a particular individual. That means that it is practically impossible to decide a price level that could be affordable by everyone in a particular society.

Starting in the mid-1980s, the EU market liberalisation and integration programme transformed the organisation of the telecommunications sector in Europe. As a result, the relationship between the State and the telecommunications market was redefined and reshaped. State monopolies were required to be withdrawn by EU Directives,[65] and the market was opened up to competition. Price was required to be rebalanced to correspond to the costs of the telecommunications products and services. Operators became independent market undertakings competing with other telecommunications providers. In essence, it was a retreat of State intervention from the telecommunications sector and the creation of a fully competitive market. This process undermined the very foundation of the ideal of universal service. The EU had to address the issue of universal service, which had been deeply rooted in the telecommunications sector in Member States.

5.3 Universal Service Obligation During Liberalisation

5.3.1 The Liberalisation Process in the Telecommunications Sector

The traditional model of organisation of the telecommunications sector was clearly in conflict with the basic principle of the Treaty, in particular the principles of competition and the Internal Market programme. Within the Member States the monopoly structure was protected through national legislation, and there was no competition. As a consequence, it hindered the development of the Internal Market programme; the telecommunications sector was divided into different national markets. Free circulation of services, capital and workers seemed impossible to achieve in this context.

This model was largely tolerated, and the EU did not take any wide-ranging measures until 1987,[66] when it adopted its Telecommunications Green Paper.[67] It laid down the foundation and blueprint for the liberalisation process of the telecommunications sector in the EU. It made one crucial distinction regarding 'the reserved service sector and a competitive service sector'.[68] The Commission maintained that due to rapid technology development, it would not be possible to establish a stable natural boundary line between them.[69] Therefore, it opted to define what could be covered by the notion of a 'reserved service'. In the 1987

[65] 1988 Terminal Equipment Directive; 1990 Telecommunications Service Directive; 1994 Satellite Communication Directive; 1995 Television Cable Directive; 1996 Mobile Communications Directive; 1996 Full Competition Directive.

[66] Thatcher 1999.

[67] 1987 Telecommunications Green Paper.

[68] Ibid., part (2), 12.

[69] Ibid., part (2), 12.

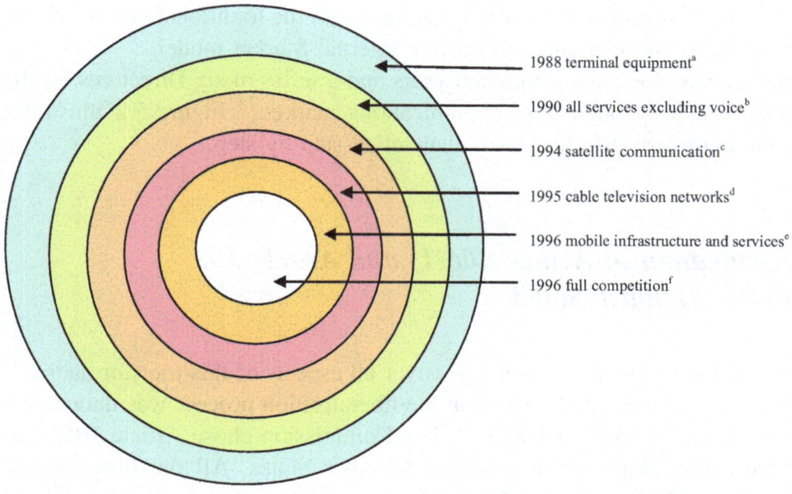

[a]1988 Terminal Equipment Directive; [b]1990 Telecommunications Service Directive; [c]1994 Satellite Communication Directive; [d]1995 Television Cable Directive; [e]1996 Mobile Communications Directive; [f]1996 Full Competition Directive.

Fig. 5.2 The shrinking monopoly in the telecommunications sector. *Source* The author

Telecommunications Green Paper, the Commission identified that 'the only obvious candidate'[70] for reserved/basic service is voice telephony. All other services should fall within the scope of competitive services and be provided on a 'free (unrestricted)'[71] market basis.

Since then, the EU has been very active in the promotion of the Internal Market in the telecommunications sector. Indeed, it has been very successful in this respect.[72] The foremost concern of the EU was the existence of national exclusive rights and its consequent *national monopoly structure*. Through EU Directives, the telecommunications sector was transformed from a closed national monopoly

[70] Ibid., part (2), Figure 3 and part (3), 67.

[71] Ibid., part (2), Figure 3.

[72] The Court's interpretation of Article 106 played a crucial role in this process. This issue is discussed in Chap. 3. On the one hand, in 1991 it began to rule that the grant of state monopolies by the Member States was in breach of Article 106(1). Such Judgments include: Case C-41/90 *Klaus Höfner and Fritz Elser v Macrotron GmbH* [1991] ECR I-1979; Case C-260/89 *Elliniki Radiophonia Tileorassi AE (Ert) (Panellinia Omospondia Syllogon Prossopikou Ert intervening) v Dimotiki Étairia Pliroforissis (Dep) and Sotirios Kouvelas (Nicolaos Avdellas and Others intervening)* [1991] ECR I-02925;Case C-18/88 *Régie des Télégraphes et des Téléphones v GB-Inno-BM SA* [1991] ECR I-5941; Case C-179/90 *Merci Convenzionali Porto di Genova SpA v Siderurgica Gabrielli SpA* [1991] ECR I-05889.

On the other hand, it largely expanded the Commission's power under Article 106(3) in its Judgment: Case C-202/88 *French Republic v Commission of the European Communities* [1991] ECR I-1223.

structure, to a liberalised market: moving rapidly from the traditional public service provision model to an open and competitive Internal Market model.[73]

The process was slow, and it took ten years and a series of six Directives for the achievement of a fully open telecommunications market.[74] Figure 5.2 illustrates how the monopoly structure had been dismantled step by step.

5.3.2 Application of Article 106(1) and Article 102 to the Member States

It is not within the scope of this study to cover all aspects of this transformation.[75] What is of great relevance is the fact that the liberalisation process was undertaken under the legal base of Article 106(3).[76] The Commission chose Article 106(3) as the legal basis for taking actions against Member States. All the liberalisation Directives were adopted in the form of Commission Directives without the involvement of the Parliament and the Council,[77] a competence granted by Article 106(3).[78] This controversial approach was possible because the Court recognised

[73] Thatcher 1999.

[74] Cassidy 1999.

[75] For more discussion on this topic, see Hulsink 1999; Steinfield et al. 1993; Larouche 2000.

[76] Locksley 1994; Carey 1999.

[77] These Directives were designed to break down national monopolies and to open the telecommunications sector to competition, including: (1) 1988 Terminal Equipment Directive; (2) 1990 Telecommunications Service Directive; (3) 1994 Satellite Communication Directive; (4) 1995 Television Cable Directive; (5) 1996 Mobile Communications Directive; and (6) 1996 Full Competition Directive.

After the market was liberalised, legislation for a new regulatory framework was usually adopted by the Parliament and the Council. For example:

(1) Directive 95/62/EC of the European Parliament and of the Council of 13 December 1995 on the application of Open Network Provision (ONP) to voice telephony [1995] OJ L321/6;
(2) Directive 98/10/EC of the European Parliament and of the Council of 26 February 1998 on the application of Open Network Provision (ONP) to Voice Telephony and on universal service for telecommunications in a competitive environment [1998]OJ L101/24;
(3) 2002 Universal Service Directive.

Exceptions are found in early ONP Directives where Council Directives were issued, including:

(1) Council Directive 92/44/EEC of 5 June 1992 on the application of Open Network Provision to leased lines [1992] OJ L165/27;
(2) Council Directive 90/387/EEC of 28 June 1990 on the establishment of the Internal Market for telecommunications services through the implementation of Open Network Provision [1990] OJ L192/1.

[78] Under Article 106(3), the Commission has the power to make Decisions and also to issue Directives. The latter one, i.e. the power to adopt Directives without the involvement of the Parliament and the Council, is regarded as undemocratic and is very controversial. In the early

that the Commission has such power as part of its executive function to make rules in the application of competition law.[79]

Regarding substantive rules, at the beginning with little guidance from the Court the Commission used Article 102 in conjunction with Article 106(1) as the legal basis.[80] In its 1988 Terminal Equipment Directive, it analysed the *effects* of such state measures without any *factual assessment* of the existence of *abusive behaviour*. The wording of the Directive reads as follows:

> The *effect* of the special or exclusive rights granted to such bodies by the State to import and market terminal equipment is to: (1) *restrict users to renting such equipment*; [...] (2) *limit outlets and impede technical progress*. [...] Such conduct is expressly prohibited by Article 102 (d) and (b), and is likely significantly to affect trade between Member States.[81] (emphasis added)

This reasoning was followed by the Commission in its 1990 Telecommunications Service Directive, which provided that the *structure* of the competition within the Common Market was substantially changed owing to the grant of special or exclusive rights.[82] The same approach can also be found in the 1994 Satellite Communication Directive, where the effect of the exclusive rights were condemned as 'limiting access to the market' and 'holding back technical progress'.[83] The essence of this approach was to use Article 102 to attack the very existence of exclusive rights.[84]

The Commission's approach was problematic. The problem lay deep in the nature of Article 102. Article 102 is an *ex pos*t rule in nature and applicable to undertakings only. It is designed to deal with anti-competitive behaviour actually committed by undertakings; it does *allow the existence of monopoly*.[85] Therefore, it is *inappropriate* to use Article 102 as a legal weapon to abolish the very existence of exclusive rights whose structure is *inherently anti-competitive*.[86]

1990s, the Court held that the Commission had the power to issue Directives of general application, which rendered direct support to the ongoing liberalisation process in the telecommunications sector. This issue is discussed in Sect. 3.3.3 of Chap. 3. See also Jauk 2000; De Streel 2003.

[79] This power has been subjected to judicial review of the Court, and the Court upheld the Commission's power to issue Directives under Article 106(3). Case C-202/88 *French Republic v Commission of the European Communities* [1991] ECR I-1223; Joined cases C-271/90, C-281/90 and C-289/90 *Kingdom of Spain, Kingdom of Belgium and Italian Republic v Commission of the European Communities* [1992] ECR I-5833. See Sect. 3.3.3 of Chap. 3.

[80] It also referred to the rules on free movement and argued that state monopolies were in breach of such rules. See, for example, (1) 1988 Terminal Equipment Directive, Recitals 3 & 7; (2) 1990 Telecommunications Service Directive, Recital 6.

[81] 1988 Terminal Equipment Directive, Recital 13.

[82] 1990 Telecommunications Service Directive, Recital 16.

[83] 1994 Satellite Communication Directive, Recital 14.

[84] Buendia Sierra 2000, p. 161.

[85] Szyszczak 2007, p. 142; Lane 2001, p. 31.

[86] Larouche 2000, p. 93.

Probably because the Commission itself also had doubts and felt less confident in its legal reasoning, it used Article 3(f) EEC as an *all-inclusive clause* at the end of its discussion of the incompatibility of exclusive rights.[87] This could be easily observed from the 1988 Terminal Equipment Directive:

> *At all events*, such special or exclusive rights in regard to the terminal equipment market give rise to a situation which *is contrary to the objective of Article 3 (f) of the Treaty*, which provides for *the institution of a system* ensuring that competition in the common market is not distorted, and requires a fortiori that *competition must not be eliminated*. Member States have an obligation under Article 5 of the Treaty to abstain from any measure which could jeopardize the attainment of the objectives of the Treaty, including Article 3 (f).[88] (emphasis added)

In 1991, the Court had the chance to rule on the compatibility of the state monopolies and delivered a series of Judgments.[89] It applied Article 106(1) in conjunction with Article 102 to Member States. It attributed the responsibility for breach of Article 102 to Member States by *establishing a causal link* between the creation of monopoly structures by the Member States and the existence of abusive behaviour by undertakings.[90] The case law rendered direct support to the ongoing liberalisation process in the telecommunications sector. From the 1995 Television Cable Directive, the Commission's argument was more in line with that of the Court. In this Directive the Commission stated the principle established by the Court in the following words:

> The *mere creation of a dominant position* within a given market through the grant of an exclusive right is *not*, as such, incompatible with Article 102. A Member State is, however, not allowed to maintain a legal monopoly where the relevant undertaking is *compelled or induced* to abuse its dominant position in a way that is liable to affect trade between Member States.[91] (emphasis added)

By adopting the words 'compel or induce', it intended to establish a *cause and consequence direct link* between state measures creating a monopoly and the abusive behaviour of the monopolist undertakings. However, the grant of the

---

[87] Article 3 of the EEC Treaty prescribes the activities of the EU. Paragraph (f) of the Article provides that 'the Institution of a system ensuring that competition in the common market is not distorted'. It was renumbered as Article 3(g) in the EC Treaty. After the Lisbon Treaty, it is contained in Protocol (No 27) on the Internal Market and Competition, TFEU.

[88] 1988 Terminal Equipment Directive, Recital 13.

[89] Case C-41/90 *Klaus Höfner and Fritz Elser v Macrotron GmbH* [1991] ECR I-1979; Case C-260/89 *Elliniki Radiophonia Tileorassi AE (Ert) (Panellinia Omospondia Syllogon Prossopikou Ert intervening) v Dimotiki Étairia Pliroforissis (Dep) and Sotirios Kouvelas (Nicolaos Avdellas and Others intervening)* [1991] ECR I-02925; Case C-260/89 *Elliniki Radiophonia Tileorassi AE (Ert) (Panellinia Omospondia Syllogon Prossopikou Ert intervening) v Dimotiki Étairia Pliroforissis (Dep) and Sotirios Kouvelas (Nicolaos Avdellas and Others intervening)* [1991] ECR I-02925; Case C-179/90 *Merci Convenzionali Porto di Genova SpA v Siderurgica Gabrielli SpA* [1991] ECR I-05889. This issue has been discussed in Sect. 3.2 of Chap. 3.

[90] Buendia Sierra 2000.

[91] 1995 Television Cable Directive, Recital 11.

exclusive rights affects only *the structure of the market*, rather than the actual behaviour of the undertakings. Therefore, it is extremely difficult to establish such a direct causal link. This could be illustrated in the Television Cable Directive, in which the Commission argued that:

> The prohibition of the use of other infrastructure, and in particular CATV networks, for the provision of telecommunications services has *encouraged* the telecommunications organisations to charge high prices in comparison with prices in other countries. [...] Those *high prices* in the Community are a *direct consequence* of the restrictions imposed by Member States on the use of infrastructures other than those of the telecommunications organisations, and in particular of those of the cable TV operators, for the provision of telecommunications services.[92] (emphasis added)
>
> It remains far from convincing as to whether simple encouragement could constitute 'compel or induce' in the first place. Furthermore, even though a 10 times higher tariff than that in North America could be deemed to be abusive, its direct link with the grant of exclusive rights is arbitrary. This assumed direct link could also be observed in its later 1996 Full Competition Directive.[93]

The implications were highly significant for the organisation of the telecommunications sector in Member States.[94] What is clear is that the target of the Directives was *the very structure of the exclusive rights*, i.e. exclusive rights over terminal equipment and certain sections of the telecommunications market.[95] The grant of statutory monopoly rights to one undertaking is *necessarily exclusive* and *inherently* has the effect of limiting outlets and consumer choices. The only possible remedy was to abolish such monopoly rights.[96]

The EU did not change the organisation of the telecommunications sector suddenly. Rather, it adopted a piecemeal approach by demanding the withdrawal of exclusive rights gradually.[97] In this respect, Article 106(2) was used as controlling

---

[92] 1995 Television Cable Directive, Recital 12.

[93] It provides that:Exclusive rights granted for the provision of telecommunications services are also incompatible with Article 106(1) of the Treaty, in conjunction with Article 102 of the Treaty, where they are granted to telecommunications organisations which also enjoy exclusive or special rights for the establishment and the provision of telecommunication networks since their grant amounts to the reinforcement or the extension of a dominant position or *necessarily leads to* other abuses of such position.

1996 Full Competition Directive, Recital 3.

[94] Locksley 1994.

[95] Jauk 2000.

[96] Naftel 1992.

[97] Directives were passed that required the withdrawal of monopoly rights in different sections of the telecommunications sector, from terminal equipment, to service provision and finally network operation. These Directives included: (1) 1988 Terminal Equipment Directive; (2) 1990 Telecommunications Service Directive; (3) 1994 Satellite Communication Directive; (4) 1995 Television Cable Directive; (5) 1996 Mobile Communications Directive; and (6) 1996 Full Competition Directive.

See also Larouche 1999, 2000.

mechanism. It was used to justify the reservation of a large portion of the market under monopoly for the pursuit of non-economic values.[98] This is why SGEI had become an unwelcome obstacle to the ongoing liberalisation process.[99]

5.3.3 Application of Article 106(2): Extremely Limited Scope of USO

In the 1987 Telecommunications Green Paper, the Commission allowed the exclusion of voice telephony from the ongoing process of liberalisation. The justification for such exclusion lay in the necessity for the provision of SGEI under Article 106(2). For its application, the Commission first needed to identify what constituted SGEI. With little guidance from the Court, the Commission took national context into account and essentially borrowed the term from its historical backgrounds. In the 1987 Telecommunications Green Paper, the Commission recognised the idea of universal service and essentially adopted the essence of USO for the first time at the EU level:

> Historically, reserved services in the Member States have been *telephone and telex*, which have been regarded generally as *basic services*. Both services are offered on a *universal basis*. This is taken to mean: (1) provided with *general geographical coverage*; (2) provided on demand to all users on reasonably the same terms *regardless of the users' location* within the service providers' territory or franchise area *and the cost of* connection to the network.[100] (emphasis added)

The philosophy of the Commission cannot be more explicit. In the 1987 Telecommunications Green Paper, it emphasised as a conclusion that 'exclusive provision services must be narrowly construed'.[101] It excluded telex services from the scope of the reserved area and narrowed down the scope further at the EU level. Indeed, at this stage of technology development, the core activity in the telecommunications industry was still telegraph and telephony; and only telephony service was a standard telecommunications service for residential consumers.

In the 1987 Telecommunications Green Paper, the Commission pointed out that the *content of universal service* covers *access to network* and *voice telephone service*. Furthermore, the *obligatory requirements* focused only on geographical coverage. It did not deal with the social element of universal service, i.e. affordable price. In this respect, the Commission used a very confusing term—'on reasonably the same terms'—in the 1987 Telecommunications Green Paper.[102]

---

[98] Nagy 2013.

[99] Bauer 1999.

[100] 1987 Telecommunications Green Paper, part (3), 66.

[101] 1987 Telecommunications Green Paper, part (3), 65; Naftel 1992.

[102] 1987 Telecommunications Green Paper, part (3), 66.

However, even this vague social element was missing from later liberalisation Directives. In the liberalisation Directives, the Commission maintained that only the telecommunication network constituted SGEI. Three slightly different wordings have been used in the Directives:

(1) '*the provision of a telecommunications network* for the use of the general public';[103]
(2) 'the *provision and exploitation of a universal network*, i.e. one having general geographical coverage, and being provided to any service provider or user upon request within a reasonable period of time';[104]
(3) 'objectives of general economic interest such as ensuring *geographical coverage*'.[105] (emphasis added)

Without the *affordability* requirement or the guaranteed provision of certain basic services, the scope of the universal service in EU law is confined to the *physical/geographical* coverage of the telecommunication network. This is an extremely narrow approach to the scope of USOs.

5.3.4 Application of Article 106(2): Cross-Subsidisation as the Way of Funding

The reason for the narrow scope of USO is that cross-subsidisation (a means of protecting the exclusive right) was used to fund its provision.[106] Regarding the necessity of the grant of exclusive rights, it did not compare it with other measures to find the least distortive mechanism. In fact, it did not carry out such examination at all but simply assumed its necessity. This approach is reflected in its 1991 Guidelines on the Application of EEC Competition Rules in the Telecommunications Sector:

> This form of *subsidisation* is even *necessary*, as it enables the TOs (note: telecommunications organisations) holders of exclusive rights to perform their obligation to *provide a public service universally and on the same conditions to everybody*. For instance, telephone provision in unprofitable rural areas is subsidised through revenues from telephone provision in profitable urban areas or long distance calls. The same could be said of subsidising the provision of reserved services through revenues generated by activities under competition.[107] (emphasis added)

[103] 1988 Terminal Equipment Directive, Recital 11.

[104] 1990 Telecommunications Service Directive, Recital 18.

[105] 1996 Mobile Communications Directive, Recital 18.

[106] This approach was essentially abandoned by the Commission later when it began to adopt a more stringent test regarding the funding of USO.

[107] Guidelines on the Application of EEC Competition Rules in the Telecommunications Sector [1991] OJ C233/2, para103.

The following key issue is what scope of reserved area could be regarded as legitimate at the EU level? On this issue, the Commission did not carry out any serious economic assessment at all. It did not investigate the costs of the provision of USO, nor did it calculate what scope of exclusive right is necessary to generate enough revenue for a USO. Instead, it excluded the *voice telephony service* from the liberalisation process because it constituted *the main financial resource* for funding the USOs.[108]

In terms of the range of services, it seems that the *scope* of reserved area was quite limited. However, regarding the revenue generated by voice telephony, it was quite a *significant* portion of the telecommunications market at the time.[109] As acknowledged by the Commission itself, in the 1980s it accounted for 85–90% of overall telecommunications revenues.[110] Taking this into account, as pointed out by the Commission:

> Competitive provision of non-voice services, including value-added services, with unrestricted shared use or provision to third parties, *is unlikely* to have *substantial impact* on the revenues of the Telecommunications Administrations and therefore on their ability to carry out the particular tasks assigned to them.[111] (emphasis added)

This attitude towards the funding of USO had been maintained in the liberalisation Directives.[112] Voice telephony services was excluded from the ongoing liberalisation process and preserved as a legitimate monopoly area.[113] Consequently, the 1990 Telecommunications Services Directive made a very important exception; it only liberalised telecommunication services other than voice telephony. In its Recital, it clearly states that:

> The financial resources for the development of the network still derive mainly from the operation of the telephone service. Consequently, the opening-up of voice telephony to competition could threaten the *financial stability* of the telecommunications organisations.[114] (emphasis added)

On the other hand, the Commission was quite strict and did not allow any extension of reserved area beyond voice telephony.[115] Any services or products markets other than voice telephone service must be opened up to competition, though gradually. As in the case of mobile and personal communication, the Commission argued that such services do not fall within the scope of voice

---

[108] 1990 Telecommunications Services Directive.

[109] Lando 1994.

[110] 1987 Telecommunications Green Paper, part (1), 13 and part (3), 66.

[111] Ibid., part (3), 66.

[112] Buendia Sierra 2000, p. 309.

[113] This was not changed until the 1996 Full Liberalisation Directive, where the Commission argued that 'the continuation of the exception granted with respect of voice telephone is no longer justified': 1996 Full Liberalisation Directive, Recital 5.

[114] 1990 Telecommunications Services Directive, Recital 18; 1996 Full Liberalisation Directive, Recital 4.

[115] Bartosch 1999.

telephony after an examination of their definitions.[116] It also rejected the application of the SGEI derogation to satellite communication[117]and television cable network[118] owing to their insignificant contribution to the funding of USO.

It is submitted that the arrangement of the reservation of voice telephone service was a *political compromise* between the Commission and the Member States.[119] For the Commission, the retreat was necessary *to gain support from the Member States*. Even until the mid-1980s, Member States were still reluctant to lose control of their telecommunications sector to the EU liberalisation wave. This attitude was clearly illustrated by a Council Recommendation adopted in November 1984. In that Recommendation, national governments declared that the objectives of the telecommunications development were merely the creation of a harmonised telematic and dynamic community market for telecommunications equipment.[120]

Allowing a monopoly over voice telephony, which represented 85–90% of telecommunications revenue, the impact of the Commission's liberalisation initiatives upon national monopolists was *modest*, at least in the short and middle term. Essentially, it gave national governments and national incumbents enough time to adjust. This adjustment period actually lasted for ten years, from the adoption of the first liberalisation Directive in 1988[121] until the actual achievement of full competition in the telecommunications sector by 1 January 1998.[122]

On the other hand, the Commission had successfully claimed an *exclusive competence* to decide the legitimate scope of exclusive rights at EU law. In its 1987 Telecommunications Green Paper, the Commission stated that the scope of the reserved area would be subject to 'periodic review'.[123] This actually opened a potential gateway to break down national monopolies further and to abolish them completely for the full liberalisation of the telecommunications sector. Therefore, in

---

[116] 1996 Mobile Communications Directive.

[117] 'As regards all services other than voice telephony, no special treatment under Article 106(2) is justified especially in view of the insignificant contribution of such services to the turnover of the telecommunications organisations': 1994 Satellite Communication Directive, Recital 16.

[118] 'Besides the case of voice telephony, no other restrictions for the provision of liberalised services is justified under Article 106(2), particularly if regard is had to the small contribution made to the turnover of the telecommunications organisations by those services, currently provided on their own networks, which could be diverted towards the cable TV networks': 1995 Television Cable Directive, Recital 15.

[119] The Commission intended to promote competition and market integration in the telecommunications sector. This was in conflict with the approach adopted by some Member States that were in favour of State intervention in the economy. This was particularly the case in France, which has a strong tradition of public services: Nenova 2007.

[120] 84/549/EEC: Council Recommendation of 12 November 1984 concerning the implementation of harmonisation in the field of telecommunications [1984] OJ L298/49.

[121] 1988 Terminal Equipment Directive.

[122] 1996 Full Competition Directive.

[123] Telecommunications Green Paper, part (3), 65; Kiessling and Blondeel 1998.

its 1996 Full Competition Directive, the Commission announced that 'the continuation of the exception granted with respect of voice telephony is no longer justified [...] and should be ended'.[124]

5.4 Universal Service Obligations in a Competitive Market

Market liberalisation and integration broke down the traditional model for the provision of universal service. After market liberalisation, the EU faced new issues regarding the provision of USO in this new competitive market environment, such as the scope of USO and the design of new funding mechanisms.[125] Detailed rules are contained in the 2002 USO Directive.[126] This section deals with the provision of USO in telecommunications after liberalisation.

The current scope of USOs can be traced back to the ONP Directives in the early 1990s.[127] The research shows that the scope of USO has not been substantially changed since then. In the EU Directives, a minimum level of service has been defined at the EU level, and the Member States have the legal obligation to guarantee its provision.[128] The research shows that this package of basic telephony service has been virtually achieved by the late 1990s.[129] In the modern digital age, this very limited scope of universal service is less meaningful to consumers because their telecommunications needs are increasingly being met by alternative technologies such as mobile phones and the Internet.[130] On the other hand, EU legislation allows Member States to expand the scope of the USOs.[131] This, however, is not an EU obligation but rather an optional choice for the Member States. Therefore, the real benefits of USO still depend on the political will of individual Member States.

The real focus of the EU is devoted to ensuring USO funding frameworks designed and implemented by Member States are competition neutral. The Commission uses the infringement procedure to scrutinise the USO funding measures in Member States. The main concern has been to ensure that USO provider is not over-compensated and that market competition is not distorted.

---

[124] 1996 Full Competition Directive, Recital 5.

[125] Nenova 2007.

[126] 2002 Universal Service Directive.

[127] Carey 1999.

[128] 2002 Universal Service Directive.

[129] De Streel 2003.

[130] Nenova 2007.

[131] 2002 Universal Service Directive.

5.4.1 USO as a By-product of Harmonisation Legislation

The current scope of USO as defined by the USO Directive dates back to the harmonisation legislation in the 1990s, which goes hand in hand with the liberalisation process.[132] While the gradual opening up of the markets allowed the existence of exclusive rights over the telecommunications network, these measures aimed to guarantee users, in particular potential competitors as new market entrants, to gain 'open and efficient access to and use of the public telecommunications networks' (ONP)'.[133] These Directives were the building pillar for the telecommunications market by facilitating cross-border flow of telecommunication services.[134] On the one hand, it respected certain legally granted exclusive rights and left them untouched. On the other hand, it stipulated the prohibition of discrimination as a basic principle.[135] It provided that access to the network must not be restricted, except for reasons based on expressly listed essential requirements found in the EU Directives, such as security of network, integrity of network, interoperability of services and data protection.

The provision of USO is not the main objective of the harmonisation legislation, but only a by-product.[136] The Telephony ONP Directive only mentions 'the objective of universal service telephone-service accessibility' once.[137] It did not define the term 'universal service' at all,[138] let alone provide a framework for its provision. However, certain elements of universal service obligation could be found in the Telephony ONP Directive. It is these elements that have formed the very foundation of the current framework on universal service obligation in telecommunications.[139]

---

[132] Carey 1999.

[133] Council Directive 90/387/EEC of 28 June 1990 on the establishment of the Internal Market for telecommunications services through the implementation of Open Network Provision [1990] OJ L192/1.

[134] Intra-community voice service represented only a small portion of the revenue (no more than 4–5%) of the telecommunications monopolists. Commission of the European Communities, 1992 Review of the Situation in the Telecommunications Services Sector, (Communication by the Commission), SEC (92) 1048 final, 21.10.1992, Sect. 4.3.1.

[135] Council Directive 92/44/EEC of 5 June 1992 on the application of Open Network Provision to leased lines [1992] OJ L165/27, Recital 4.

[136] Nenova 2007; Bauer 1999.

[137] 1995 Telephony ONP Directive, Article 12(2).

[138] It did use the term 'universal telephone service' once but in a hidden corner and in a very reluctant way. In Article 12(1), it provided that 'without prejudice to application of the principle of cost orientation, national regulatory authorities may impose on telecommunications organisations tariff constraints relating to the objectives of universal telephone—service accessibility, including town and county planning aspects': 1995 Telephony ONP Directive.

[139] Carey 1999.

First, the Telephony ONP Directive prescribes a minimum basic service package that Member States have the obligation to guarantee.[140] In this Directive, the scope of universal service obligation is confined within the area of telephony service.[141] This is in line with the approach taken in the liberalisation Directives. The basic requirement of universal service is to guarantee a connection to the fixed public telephone network.[142] It also includes certain other service elements that are closely related to telephony service provision, including the provision of directory services and public pay-telephones.[143]

Secondly, the social access elements of the universal service obligation is left to the free choice of Member States.[144] The Directive is against universal pricing. Indeed, the Directive is intended to break down the distorted price mechanism employed under traditional telecommunications operational models.[145] It prescribes that *cost orientation* is the basic tariff principle.[146]

As an exception to this general principle, the Directive did contain *certain elements concerning the affordability* of the voice telephony service. It allowed the national regulatory authorities (NRA) to impose tariff constraints on the provision of voice telephony service.[147] Another possibility available to Member States to guarantee social accessibility of voice telephony was to adopt special tariff schemes for low-usage users or specific social groups[148] and to draw specific conditions for disabled people and people with special needs.[149]

Different from the approach in the case of physical access, the fulfilment of the social element of universal service described immediately above is an *optional choice* for Member States, rather than a mandatory requirement. As a result, the real benefits for consumers still depend on the political will of the individual Member States.

The ONP Directives were adopted in the 1990s when the main task of the EU in the telecommunications market was still focused on the creation of a competitive

---

[140] 1995 Telephony ONP Directive, Article 3.

[141] De Streel 2003.

[142] Nenova 2007.

[143] 1995 Telephony ONP Directive, Articles 16 and 17; Kiessling and Blondeel 1998.

[144] Carey 1999; Naftel 1996.

[145] Under the traditional public service model in the telecommunications sector, the public monopolist charged a uniform price across the whole country regardless of the actual costs incurred in individual cases. This was against the basic commercial principle that price should reflect the actual cost.

[146] The Directive prescribes that tariff must be based on objective criteria and be transparent. It also rules that each item of the tariff should be listed separately for users: 1995 Telephony ONP Directive, Article 12.

[147] However, this must be done without prejudice to the application of the principle of cost orientation.

[148] This is categorised as 'socially useful services', which also include emergency services: 1995 Telephony ONP Directive, Article 14.

[149] Ibid., Article 18.

market. Meanwhile, the telephone was still the standard platform that was used by the majority of the population for communication. By 1999, 92% of the EU's households had a fixed telephone subscription. By contrast, only 43% of households had a mobile subscription. The penetration rate for the Internet was even lower, at only 12%.[150] Taking these into consideration, it is submitted that this narrow scope of USO suited the circumstance of the telecommunications sector prevailing at the time.

5.4.2 Insignificant Scope of USOs

The 2002 USO Directive contained the rules on the scope of USO and its funding mechanisms, which form the legal framework for the provision of USO in this new competitive telecommunications market. Universal service was defined as 'the provision of a defined minimum set of services to all end-users at an affordable price'.[151] A closer look shows that the scope of universal service obligation has remained the same as that contained in the 1995 Telephony ONP Directive.[152]

The USO Directive did *not enlarge or add new obligations* over its previous one. Rather, it only *repackaged* all the elements under a new title *without substantial changes*. The basic services that the Member States have a legal obligation to guarantee are confined to access to the network and telephony service, plus directory and public pay services.[153] On the other hand, the social element of the universal service, the issue of affordability, continued to be left as a voluntary option for Member States.[154] In fact, Directive 2002/21 did not intend to review and

---

[150] Commission of the European Communities, Annex to the Review of the Scope of Universal Service in Accordance with Article 15 of Directive 2002/22/EC, (Commission Staff Working Document), SEC (2005) 660, 24.05.2005.

[151] 2002 Universal Service Directive, Recital 4. This definition is not new but appeared in several harmonisation Directives, including:

(1) Directive 97/51/EC of the European Parliament and of the Council of 6 October 1997 amending Council Directives 90/387/EEC and 92/44/EEC for the purpose of adaptation to a competitive environment in telecommunications [1997] OJ L295/23;
(2) Directive 98/10/EC of the European Parliament and of the Council of 26 February 1998 on the application of Open Network Provision (ONP) to voice Telephony and on universal service for Telecommunications in a competitive environment [1998] OJ L101/24, Article 2;
(3) Directive 97/33/EC of the European Parliament and of the Council of 30 June 1997 on interconnection in Telecommunications with regard to ensuring universal service and interoperability through application of the principles of Open Network Provision (ONP) [1997] OJ L199/32, Article 2.

[152] Nenova 2007.

[153] Verhoest 2000; Nagy 2013.

[154] De Streel 2003.

redefine the USO regime, but rather to codify rules on USO into one legislation because the previous regulatory framework was fragmented.[155]

This minimum package of basic services as defined by EU Directives had been virtually achieved in Europe by the late 1990s.[156] This was particularly true regarding the physical access to the telephony network. As the telecommunications network in Europe has become mature,[157] access to the network and basic telephone service is not a significant issue any more.[158] As early as 1999, 92% of homes in the EU had been connected to the telephone network and had a telephone subscription.[159] Since then, however, with the advent of the mobile telephone, subscription to fixed telephone services has been in steady decline in recent years. Telephone penetration rates have dropped 10% in only five years, from 92% in 1999 to 82% in the EU by 2004.[160] This rate has dropped 11% more in the following seven years, to 71% in 2011.[161] By 2017, only 61% of the households in Europe had a fixed telephone.[162]

It is submitted that this narrow scope of USOs seems outdated in a new digital age.[163] Since market liberalisation, the telecommunications industry has undergone rapid development. The world has witnessed the advent of the digital age with the widespread usage of mobile phones and broadband Internet. Communications needs are increasingly being met by alternative technological platforms. Since 1999, more users began to switch to mobile usage.[164] By 2010, around 95% of the

[155] Rules on the scope of USO are found in Directive 95/62, which was later amended by 97/51 and repealed by 98/10. On the other hand, rules on the funding of USO are contained in 1996 Full Competition Directive and Directive 97/33/EC of the European Parliament and of the Council of 30 June 1997 on interconnection in Telecommunications with regard to ensuring universal service and interoperability through application of the principles of Open Network Provision (ONP) [1997] OJ L199/32.

[156] De Streel 2003.

[157] Milne 1998.

[158] Verhoest 2000.

[159] Commission of the European Communities, Universal Service in E-communications: Report on the Outcome of the Public Consultation and the Third Periodic Review of the Scope in Accordance with Article 15 of Directive 2002/22/EC, (Communication from the Commission to the European Parliament, the Council, the European Economic and Social Committee and the Committee of the Regions), COM (2011) 795 final, 23.11.2011, 8.

[160] Commission of the European Communities, Annex to the Review of the Scope of Universal Service in Accordance with Article 15 of Directive 2002/22/EC, (Commission Staff Working Document), SEC (2005) 660, 24.05.2005.

[161] Commission of the European Communities, Universal Service in E-communications: Report on the Outcome of the Public Consultation and the Third Periodic Review of the Scope in Accordance with Article 15 of Directive 2002/22/EC (Communication from the Commission to the European Parliament, the Council, the European Economic and Social Committee and the Committee of the Regions), COM (2011) 795 final, 23.11.2011, 8.

[162] Special Eurobarometer 462, E-Communications and Digital Single Market E-Communications and Digital Single Market, July 2018.

[163] Leith 2012; De Minico 2011; Nagy 2013.

[164] Ipsos 2004.

EU population had access to the Internet,[165] and 97% of the households had fixed broadband connection in 2018.[166] The same trend can be observed in the mobile phone sector, where the penetration rate has risen from 124.2% in 2010[167] to 145.6% in 2016.[168]

This has raised a very interesting question: whether the scope of universal service obligation should be expanded to include other services, such as mobile phone services and broadband Internet.[169] These issues involve complex economic and political assessments. It is a *political decision*, rather than one that should be left for *judicial assessment*. The Commission has been very cautious. The scope of USO has been reviewed four times, in 2005, 2008, 2011 and 2014, but remains unchanged.[170]

The Commission's approach is clearly in favour of market competition. First, it argues that, as a fundamental principle, 'regulation should be kept to a minimum'.[171] Regarding these advanced services, the Commission prefers to leave them to the market and confine State intervention only to the situation when the market

---

[165] Commission of the European Communities, Universal Service in E-communications: Report on the Outcome of the Public Consultation and the Third Periodic Review of the Scope in Accordance with Article 15 of Directive 2002/22/EC, (Communication from the Commission to the European Parliament, the Council, the European Economic and Social Committee and the Committee of the Regions), COM (2011) 795 final, 23.11.2011.

[166] European Commission (2019) Connectivity: Broadband market developments in the EU 2019, https://ec.europa.eu/newsroom/dae/document.cfm?doc_id=60010, p. 5.

[167] Commission of the European Communities, Universal Service in E-communications: Report on the Outcome of the Public Consultation and the Third Periodic Review of the Scope in Accordance with Article 15 of Directive 2002/22/EC (Communication from the Commission to the European Parliament, the Council, the European Economic and Social Committee and the Committee of the Regions), COM (2011) 795 final, 23.11.2011.

[168] European Commission (2016) Review of the scope of Universal Service—SMART 2014/0011. https://publications.europa.eu/en/publication-detail/-/publication/6eee3cb7-9adf-11e6-868c-01aa75ed71a1.

[169] Nenova 2007; Nagy 2013.

[170] Commission of the European Communities, On the Review of the Scope of Universal Service in accordance with Article 15 of Directive 2002/22/EC, COM (2005) 203 final, 24.5.2005; Commission of the European Communities, On the Second Periodic Review of the Scope of Universal Service in Electronic Communications Networks and Services in accordance with Article 15 of Directive 2002/22/EC, COM (2008) 572 final, 25.9.2008; Commission of the European Communities, Universal Service in E-communications: Report on the Outcome of the Public Consultation and the Third Periodic Review of the Scope in accordance with Article 15 of Directive 2002/22/EC, COM (2011) 795 final, 23.11.2011; European Commission (2016) Review of the scope of Universal Service—SMART 2014/0011. https://publications.europa.eu/en/publication-detail/-/publication/6eee3cb7-9adf-11e6-868c-01aa75ed71a1.

[171] Commission of the European Communities, Impact Assessment Report: Annex to the Report Regarding the Outcome of the Review of the Scope of Universal Service in accordance with Article 15(2) of Directive 2002/22/EC, (Commission Staff Working Document), SEC (2006) 445, 7.4.2006, 9.

fails to deliver.[172] This approach has been adopted in its practice in the assessment of state measures in support of broadband deployment, which has been discussed in Chap. 4. Second, limitation is also imposed on the Member States in relation to the funding of USO. Though Member States could expand the scope of USO, they are not allowed to require market undertakings to contribute to fund this part of USO.[173]

5.4.3 Scrutiny of USO Funding Through Infringement Procedure

The 1996 Full Competition Directive required Member States to withdraw all exclusive rights in the telecommunications sector, including voice telephony services, by 1 January 1998.[174] Together with this liberalisation process, the ONP Directives prescribed that telecommunication services tariffs must be based on the cost principle.[175] This essentially means that the traditional funding model of universal service provision cannot be sustained under EU law. An emerging issue is how to fund the provision of universal service after liberalisation. This was first pointed out by the Commission in its 1993 Universal Services Communication:

> As the traditional operators become increasingly *independent* and once the market is opened on the basis of *free competition* to new operators, it is *necessary* to determine the principles according to which the cost of universal service obligations can be shared amongst market participants. A clearer definition of universal service principle is *vital* to this process.[176] (emphasis added)

EU law has not established a uniform framework for USO funding.[177] It is left to NRA to decide such issues: (1) whether or not to provide funding for the provision

[172] The Commission states that one of the objectives of regulation is 'to ensure that objectives of general interest are met where they are not satisfied by market forces alone': Commission of the European Communities, Impact Assessment Report: Annex to the Report Regarding the Outcome of the Review of the Scope of Universal Service in accordance with Article 15(2) of Directive 2002/22/EC, (Commission Staff Working Document), SEC (2006) 445, 7.4.2006.

[173] 2002 Universal Service Directive, Article 32.

[174] 1996 Full Competition Directive; Bartosch 1999; Reiss 2011.

[175] 1995 Telephony ONP Directive; Commission of the European Communities, Universal Service for Telecommunications in the Perspective of Fully Liberalized Environment—An Essential Element of the Information Society, COM (96) 73 final, 13.03.1996; Carey 1999.

[176] Commission of the European Communities, Developing Universal Service for Telecommunications in a Competitive Environment, (Communication from the Commission to the Council, the European Parliament and the European Economic and Social Committee), COM (93) 543, 15.11.1993, 6.

[177] Nenova 2007.

of SGEI; (2) what procedures to be used to select the provider; (3) the calculation of the costs and what mechanisms are to be deployed to compensate such costs.[178]

In practice, the Member States have offered very diverse solutions.[179] In most Member States, the task of providing all USO services is still entrusted to the former incumbents without a public tendering procedure. Because of the limited scope of USO, in most cases, the costs of providing USO are born by the undertaking itself without additional State funding.[180] Meanwhile, only in a small number of Member States are the provider and the costs of providing f USO decided through a public tendering procedure.[181]

This does not mean the EU law has little influence over the funding of USO. Its concern has been focused on the *competition neutrality* of the funding measures implemented by Member States. What should be pointed out first is the procedural mechanism that is used by the Commission for such scrutiny. It has not demanded the use of the public tender procedure as it has in the provision of public service obligations (PSOs) in the air transport sector.[182] Nor has it used state aid control to examine USO funding. On the contrary, in its 1996 USO Funding Communication, the Commission expressly stated that compensation for USO provision did not constitute state aid. It stated that:

> Such funding should be transparent and should not exceed the net costs of the obligations calculated in line with guidelines provided in this Communication. In cases where it will be soundly established that there is no compensation of the cost of public service, there will normally be no state aid in the meaning of Article 92(1) EC Treaty [note: Article 107(1) TFEU].[183]

---

[178] Commission of the European Communities, Assessment Criteria for National Schemes for the Costing and Financing of Universal Service in Telecommunications and Guidelines for the Member States on Operation of such Schemes, COM (96) 608 final, 27.11.1996 (hereafter 1996 USO Funding Communication); Reiss 2011; Eliassen and From 2009.

[179] The Body of European Regulators for Electronic Communications has produced a detailed account on USO in 2010. See European Regulators for Electronic Communications, BEREC Report on Universal Service—Reflection for the Future (June 2010). http://berec.europa.eu/eng/document_register/subject_matter/berec/download/0/187-berec-report-on-universal-service-reflec_0.pdf.

[180] Seven Member States introduced USO funds, including France, Italy, Poland, Bulgaria, the Czech Republic and Romania. Among them only France, Italy and Romania actually paid out funding: Commission of the European Communities, The Commission's 2008 Report on the Scope of the Universal Service in Telecoms: Frequently Asked Questions, MEMO/08/583, 25.09.2008; Ladcomm Corporation (2013); Cassidy 1999.

[181] There are six Member States that have chosen to use open tender procedures to designate the USO provider: Cyprus, Czech Republic, Estonia, Hungary, Poland and Slovenia: Communications Alliance Ltd, 'Telecommunications Universal Service Obligation (USO) Review'. http://www.commsalliance.com.au/__data/assets/pdf_file/0016/1960/CommsAlliance-Subsmission_USO_Final.pdf.

[182] Nett 1998.

[183] 1996 USO Funding Communication, 5.

In the telecommunications sector, the Commission has used the infringement procedure under the Treaty to examine the validity of national USO funding measures.[184] The 2002 USO Directive requires Member States to notify all the transposition measures of EU telecommunications legislation.[185] This provides the opportunity for the Commission to assess national measures based on EU law. If the Commission has concerns about the validity of particular state measures, it can then send a 'Letter of Notice' and 'Reasoned Opinion' demanding that the Member State in question bring its national measures into compliance with the EU Directives.

The last resort of the procedure is that the Commission can refer the issue to the Court. Under Articles 258 and 260 of the TFEU, the Court can declare that a Member State is in breach of EU law, and in severe breaches it can even impose financial penalties.[186] Through this mechanism, the Commission has significant influence over the design and the administration of funding of USO provision in the Member States.[187]

5.4.4 *Competition Neutrality of USO Funding*

The focus of the EU has been on the competition neutrality of the funding measures of USO designed and implemented by the Member States.[188] In 1996, the Commission published a Communication on the funding issue of USO. It established detailed rules on the calculation of USO costs, the funding mechanism for USO and the operation of such funding. Great attention has been paid to the calculation of USO costs to rule out the possibility that the USO provider could gain advantage through the funding of the USO.[189] This has become the key

[184] Commission of the European Communities, The Commission's 2008 Report on the Scope of the Universal Service in Telecoms: Frequently Asked Questions, MEMO/08/583, 25.09.2008.

[185] 2002 USO Directive, Article 38.

[186] The Commission's 'Digital Agenda for Europe' website provides an overview of such procedures. https://ec.europa.eu/digital-agenda/en/infringements.

[187] There have been a significant number of infringement procedures initiated by the Commission against the Member States. The Commission often has to refer the Member States in question to the Court. The Commission has compiled two lists of such proceedings:

(1) Infringement Procedure Opened for Incorrect Implementation
https://ec.europa.eu/digital-agenda/sites/digital-agenda/files/Infringement%20procedures%20opened%20for%20incorrect%20implementation.pdf accessed 9 October 2014;
(2) Infringement Procedures Opened for Non-communication of Transposition Measures
https://ec.europa.eu/digital-agenda/sites/digital-agenda/files/Infringement%20procedures%20opened%20for%20non-communication%20of%20the%20revised%20framework.pdf accessed 9 October 2014.

[188] 2002 Universal Service Directive, Recital 4; Bauer 1999; Mueller 1993.

[189] Reiss 2011.

benchmark in the assessment of national USO funding measures.[190] In this way, the Commission can make sure that the proper functioning of the internal telecommunications market is not distorted by national USO funding models.

5.4.4.1 Market Failure Test

The Commission has adopted the principle of market failure as the precondition for State funding.[191] In other words, State funding is allowed only when the market has failed. As early as in 1993, the Commission argued that:

> Universal service obligations imposed by national legislation or authorisation regimes generally oblige market participants to provide a certain basic service to customers whom they may otherwise have *insufficient economic incentive* to service. [...] The so-called "economic cost" of universal service results from any additional expense incurred in serving such customers, where the needs of those customers would *not be met by market forces alone*.[192] (emphasis added)

This principle was clearly followed shortly afterwards in the 1997 Interconnection Directive, which lays down the formula for the calculation of the cost of USO.[193] These principles and rules were left virtually unchanged in the current 2002 Universal Service Directive.[194]

The market failure approach has significant implications for the scope of State funding. The scope of USO funding must only cover the provision of USO as defined by the 2002 Universal Service Directive. The Communication expressly prohibits certain services to be included in the calculation of the USO costs.[195]

On the other hand, USO funding covers only services that are provided at a loss or under cost conditions outside normal commercial standards. In practice, the

---

[190] Bauer 1999.

[191] Ibid.

[192] Commission of the European Communities, Developing Universal Service for Telecommunications in a Competitive Environment, (Communication from the Commission to the Council, the European Parliament and the European Economic and Social Committee), COM (93) 543, 15.11. 1993, 4.

[193] Directive 97/33/EC of the European Parliament and of the Council of 30 June 1997 on interconnection in telecommunications with regard to ensuring universal service and interoperability through application of the principles of Open Network Provision (ONP) [1997] OJ L199/32, Annex III.

[194] 2002 USO Directive.

[195] In the Communication, the Commission listed four categories as examples: measures for public security; communication service outside USO to schools, hospitals and libraries; refund payments; costs for network modernisation. 1996 USO Funding Communication, 14.

This list is not exhaustive. In December 2011, the Commission sent Denmark a 'reasoned opinion' and requested it to remove maritime emergency services from the scope of USO. Commission of the European Communities, Digital Agenda: Commission requests Denmark to change rules on financing of universal services (Press Release, IP/11/1106) http://europa.eu/rapid/press-release_IP-11-1106_en.htm.

operator has to identify specifically uneconomical customers that have generated a loss and also explicitly declare to the NRA that it would not serve those uneconomical customers without State funding.[196] These services (and therefore the costs involved) must be identifiable and specific under three categories: (1) uneconomical areas (geographical element of USO);[197] (2) uneconomical customers (social element of USO);[198] (3) uneconomical services (service element of USO).[199]

5.4.4.2 Competition Neutrality of the Calculation of USO Funds

Another aspect of the competition neutrality principle is related to the calculation of the net costs of the provision of USO. EU law has not required a competitive procedure for the appointment of the USO provider and the determination of the costs of its provision.[200] It has been left to national NRAs to calculate the net costs of the provision of USO and to choose the appropriate compensation mechanism.[201]

The fundamental rule is that the cost of USO only covers the *unavoidable net losses* incurred by an efficient operator in providing USO.[202] NRAs must take into account any benefits in connection with the provision of USOs, tangible or intangible.[203] The compliance with such detailed rules is to ensure that USO funding does not distort market competition. The Commission can impose adherence to such standards on Member States' funding of USO through the infringement procedure.

---

[196] 1996 USO Funding Communication, 13.

[197] 'The provision of a network and services throughout a specific geographical area, including, where required, averaged price, in that geographical area for the provision of that service': 2002 USO Directive, Annex IV.

[198] 'Provision of specific tariff options for consumers with low incomes or with special social needs': Ibid.

[199] 'This category may include service element such as access to emergency telephone services, provision of certain public pay telephones, provision of certain services or equipment for disabled people, etc.': Ibid.

[200] The Directive provides two options for Member States regarding the funding of the USO, including the establishment of sectoral fund or direct financial transfer from the State: Ibid.

[201] Some scholars argue that a competitive tender procedure for the allocation of USO costs could be a desirable alternative: Nett 1998; Milgrom 1996;

Some Member States have begun to use a competitive procedure to designate USO provider. International Telecommunication Union (2012), Sect. 3.1.2.

[202] The calculation and allocation of the USO costs is a very difficult task that requires detailed data and relevant expertise. The controversy over French USO fund offers a very good example. Its legality has been subject to the scrutiny of the Commission, the Court and also national courts. See Reiss 2011.

[203] This point has been confirmed by the Court in a Judgment concerning the French USO fund: Case C-146/00 *Commission of the European Communities v French Republic* [2001] ECR I-9767, 9818.

The French USO funding offers a very good example, which was subjected to the examination of the Commission and subsequently challenged before the Court.[204] Several aspects of the French USO funding measures were found incompatible with the EU Directives. First, the calculation of the USO costs failed to exclude profitable residential accounts from the calculation of the costs of the provision of USO.[205] Second, France adopted a flat-rate basis for certain components of USO and did not carry out specific calculation.[206] Third, it failed to take into account the benefits derived from the provision of USO.[207]

Furthermore, Member States are obliged to carry out individual and specific assessments regarding the costs of USO provision. This furthers limits Member States' freedom regarding the grant of USO funding. The case of Belgium USO funding offers a very appropriate illustration.[208] In 2005, Belgium adopted a new electronic communications law to transpose EU Directives. On the issue of USO funding, it provided that any loss making as a result of the provision of USO, taking into account any indirect benefits, constituted an unfair burden and would be compensated by the USO fund. The Commission was of the opinion that such a rule was in breach of the 2002 USO Directive.[209]

In the Judgment of the Court, the Belgium law was found to be incompatible with the 2002 USO Directive. Through the interpretation of the notion of 'unfair burden', the Court limited the discretion of the Member States on funding USO. In its ruling the Court held that:

> It [note: the Universal Service Directive] intended to exclude the possibility that any net costs of universal service provision automatically give rise to a right to compensation. In those circumstances, the unfair burden [...] is a burden which, for each undertaking concerned, is excessive in view of the undertaking's ability to bear it, account being taken of *all the undertaking's own characteristics*, in particular the quality of its equipment, its economic and financial situation and its market share.[210] (emphasis added)

By rejecting the idea of 'automatic right to compensation', the Court further limited the possibility of granting funding for the provision of USO. In other words, determination of compensation must be based on a case-by-case approach. In the Judgment, the Court ruled that 'individual assessment'[211]/'specific examination'[212]

---

[204] Ibid.

[205] Ibid., para 53.

[206] Ibid., paras 60–61.

[207] Ibid., paras 77–78.

[208] Case C-222/08 *European Commission v Kingdom of Belgium* [2010] ECR I-9017
The same issue is also the subject of a preliminary ruling procedure: Case *C-389/08 Base NV and Others v Ministerraad* [2010] ECR I-9073.

[209] It required the Belgium government to bring the law in compliance with the Directive by sending a 'letter of formal notice' and 'reasoned opinion'. Without receiving satisfactory results, it finally referred the case to the Court through the infringement procedure.

[210] Case C-222/08 *European Commission v Kingdom of Belgium* [2010] ECR I-9017, para 49.

[211] Ibid., para 50.

[212] Ibid., para 59.

for each USO operator is necessary for the determination of USO compensation. Such an exercise includes two aspects: (1) the net costs that the provision of USO represent for each undertaking responsible for it; and (2) whether such cost constitutes an excessive burden for the undertaking concerned, taking account of the characteristics of the undertaking concerned.

5.5 Conclusion

In the telecommunications sector, SGEI is defined via the notion of USO. This notion has long been established in the telecommunications sector. This research traces the roots of universal service and finds that it was not a clearly defined legal term but had strong political and economic implications.

The ideal of universal service had been at the heart of State intervention in the telecommunications sector. The modern version of universal service only began to come into being after World War II, under which basic telephony service was regarded as an essential service and associated with human rights. Under the notion, the State has the responsibility to ensure that everyone has access to its provision. Public undertakings were established under the control of the States. A uniform price was charged across the nation irrespective of the actual cost of service provision. In return, exclusive right was granted by the State to finance its provision, though in a non-transparent manner.

This traditional model contradicted the basic principle of EU law. In particular, the grant of exclusive rights eliminated competition and also divided the telecommunications sector along national borders. However, for three decades since the adoption of the Treaty of Rome, this situation was tolerated by the EU.

From 1985, the Commission began to promote market liberalisation and integration in the telecommunications sector. Liberalisation legislation was adopted on the basis of Article 106. The Commission used its power under Article 106(3) to require the Member State to withdraw the grant of exclusive rights. It found its legal basis in Article 106(1) as interpreted by the Court. As a result, EU law has transformed the telecommunications sector into an internal competitive market. It has essentially redefined and reshaped the relationship between the State and the market.

The development of the EU regime on SGEI in the telecommunications sector is closely associated with this process.[213] During the market liberalisation process, USO was defined very narrowly, limited only to physical access to the telephony network. It assumed exclusive right as a proper funding mechanism for USO. Meanwhile, it allowed the grant of exclusive right over telephony service, which accounted for 85–90% of the total revenue in the telecommunications sector. This approach towards the application of the necessity test essentially gave the Member

[213] Debusschere et al. 2010, p. 11.

States and the incumbent sufficient time to adjust to the coming competitive market environment.

After liberalisation, USO forms an essential component of the regulatory package for this new competitive market environment. The provision of USO has been redefined at the EU level. It recognises the provision of basic telephony service on a universal basis as a valid SGEI. The research finds that the current scope of USO in the telecommunications sector is very limited. It is confined to the universal provision of basic telephony service, which the Member States have an obligation to guarantee. This level of telecommunications service had been virtually achieved by the late 1990s. In the new digital age, communication needs are increasingly being met by other alternative technologies, including the Internet and the mobile phone. This finding is also supported by the fact that in most Member States USO is provided by incumbent operators without State funding.

In the telecommunications sector, full market liberalisation was achieved in 1999, which meant that exclusive right had to be withdrawn altogether. EU legislation has not adopted a uniform procedure for funding USOs in this new market environment. The calculation and design of funding measures have been left to the Member States. The necessity test has been translated such as to ensure the competitive neutrality of the USO funding. In the Commission's practice, its focus has been to ensure that USO funding is competition neutral.

References

Bartosch A (1999) EC Telecommunications Law: what aid does Article 90(2) of the EC Treaty offer to the former monopolists. Computer and Telecommunications Law Review 5(1):12–15

Bauer JM (1999) Universal service in the European Union. Government Information Quarterly 16 (4):329–343

Bauer JM (2010) Changing roles of the state in telecommunications. International Telecommunications Policy Review 17(1):1–36

Blackman CR (1995) Universal service: obligation or opportunity? Telecommunications Policy 19 (3):171–176

Buendia Sierra JL (2000) Exclusive rights and state monopolies under EC Law: Article 86 (former Article 90) of the EC Treaty. Oxford University Press, Oxford

Carey KD (1999) Competition law and the privatization of telecommunications markets in the European Union. Suffolk Transnational Law Review 22(2):747–774

Cassidy WP (1999) Universal service in a competitive telecommunications environment: the current state of universal service in the European Union and United States. North Carolina Journal of International Law and Commercial Regulation 25(1):107–166

De Minico G (2011) New European regulation on universal service and next generation networks or just a lifting of the old one? Computer and Telecommunications Law Review 17(5):135–147

De Streel A (2003) The protection of the European citizen in a competitive e-society: the new EU Universal Service Directive. Journal of Network Industries 4(2):189–223

Debusschere T, De Streel A, Moria L, Mourlon-Beernaert L, Villalobos J (2010) Final report for the study on the impact of EU policy options for revision of the universal service provision. http://ec.europa.eu/newsroom/dae/document.cfm?doc_id=1606

Economides N (2004) Telecommunications regulation: an introduction. Working Papers No 04–20, NET Institute. http://www.netinst.org/Telecommunications_Regulation.pdf

Eliassen KA, From J (2009) Deregulation, privatisation and public service delivery: universal service in telecommunications in Europe. Policy and Society 27(3):239–248

Gautier A, Wauthy X (2012) Competitively neutral universal service obligations. Information Economics and Policy 24(3–4):254–261

Hulsink W (1999) Privatisation and liberalisation in European telecommunications: comparing Britain, the Netherlands and France. Routledge, New York

International Telecommunication Union (2012) ICT regulation toolkit – module 4: universal access and services. http://www.ictregulationtoolkit.org/action/document/download?document_id=3606

Ipsos (2004) Telecoms Services Indicators 2004. Produced for the European Commission, DG Information Society. http://www.bandaancha.es/Informacion/Enlaces/Documents/report_telecom_2004_final_reduced.pdf

Jauk W (2000) The application of EC competition rules to telecommunications – selected aspects: the case of interconnection. International Journal of Communications Law and Policy 4:1–113

Jayakar KP, Sawhney H (2003) Universal service: beyond established practice to possibility space (Telecommunication Policy Research Conference). http://www.personal.psu.edu/kpj1/JayakarandSawhney1.pdf

Kiessling T, Blondeel Y (1998) The EU regulatory framework in telecommunications: a critical analysis. Telecommunication Policy 22(7):571–592

Ladcomm Corporation (2013) Universal service fund study. Conducted on behalf of the GSM Association, April 2013. https://www.gsma.com/publicpolicy/wp-content/uploads/2016/09/GSMA2013_Report_SurveyOfUniversalServiceFunds.pdf

Lando SD (1994) The European Community's road to telecommunications deregulation. Fordham Law Review 62(7):2159–2198

Larouche P (1999) Telecommunications. In: Geradin D (ed) The liberalization of state monopolies in European Union and beyond. Kluwer Law International, The Hague

Larouche P (2000) Competition law and regulation in European telecommunications. Hart Publishing, Oxford

Leith P (2012) Europe's information society project and digital inclusion: universal service obligations or social solidarity? International Journal of Law and Information Technology 20 (2):102–123

Locksley G (1994) From exclusive rights to access charges. Utilities Policy 4(3):223–228

Milgrom P (1996) Procuring universal service: putting auction theory to work. Lecture at the Royal Swedish Academy of Sciences, 9 December 1996. http://www.stanford.edu/~milgrom/publishedarticles/Procuring%20Universal%20Service%20Putting%20Auction%20Theory%20to%20Work,%201996.pdf

Millward R (2005) Private and public enterprise in Europe: energy, telecommunications and transport 1830–1990. Cambridge University Press, Cambridge, p 251

Millward R (2008) Business and the state. In: Jones G, Zeitlin J (eds) The Oxford handbook of business history. Oxford University Press, Oxford

Milne C (1998) Stages of universal service policy. Telecommunications Policy 22(9):775–780

Mueller M (1993) Universal service in telephone history: a reconstruction. Telecommunications Policy 17(5):352–369

Naftel JM (1992) The natural death of a natural monopoly: competition in EC telecommunications after the telecommunications terminals judgment. Emory International Law Review 6(2):449–494

Naftel JM (1996) European Commission: telecommunications – universal services. Computer and Telecommunications Law Review 2(3):89–92

Nagy CI (2013) The metamorphoses of universal service in the European telecommunications and energy sector: a trans-sectoral perspective. German Law Journal 14(9):1731–1756

Nenova MB (2007) The new concept of universal service in a digital networked communications environment. I/S: A Journal of Law and Policy for the Information Society 3(1):117–146

Nett L (1998) Auctions: an alternative approach to allocate universal service obligations. Telecommunications Policy 22(8):661–669

Prosser T (2000) Public service law: privatization's unexpected offspring. Law and Contemporary Problems 63(4):63–82

Rapp L (1996) Public service or universal service? Telecommunications Policy 20(6):391–397

Regan B (2008) Ushering universal service reform: politically feasible legislative principles. Common Law Conspectus 16(2):471–502

Reiss DR (2011) No innocents here: using litigation to fight against the costs of universal service in France. Creighton International and Comparative Law Journal 1(1):5–29

Sawhney H (1994) Universal service: prosaic motives and great ideals. Journal of Broadcasting & Electronic Media 38(4):375–396

Steinfield CW, Bauer JM, Caby L (1993) Telecommunications in transition: policies, services and technologies in the European Community. SAGE Publications, Thousand Oaks

Szyszczak E (2007) The regulation of the state in competitive markets in the EU. Hart Publishing, Oxford

Thatcher M (1999) The national politics of European Regulation: institutional reform in telecommunications. The 6th Biennial Conference of the European Union Studies Association, Pittsburgh, June 1999. http://aei.pitt.edu/2401/1/002904_1.PDF

Verhoest P (2000) The myth of universal service: hermeneutic considerations and political recommendations. Media Culture & Society 22(5):595–610

West LS (1996) Deregulating telecommunications: the conflict between competition and universal service. DePaul Business Law Journal 9(1):159–188

Wu T (2007) A brief history of American telecommunications regulation. http://ssrn.com/abstract=965860

Young M (2005) The future of universal service: does it have one? International Journal of Law and Information Technology 13(2):188–205

Chapter 6
Services of General Economic Interest in the Postal Sector

Contents

Abstract This chapter deals with services of general economic interest (SGEIs) in the postal sector. It first traces the history of universal postal service and finds that, although it was often taken for granted, the modern version of universal service obligation (USO) emerged only after World War II. This chapter then investigates how USO is treated during and after the market liberalisation process in the postal sector. This study suggests that universal postal services differ significantly from

L. Zhu, *Services of General Economic Interest in EU Competition Law*,
Legal Issues of Services of General Interest,
https://doi.org/10.1007/978-94-6265-387-0_6

their counterpart in the telecommunications sector. From the very beginning, universal service occupied a much more prominent position, and liberalisation was much delayed and prolonged. The EU managed to establish a minimum level of harmonisation regarding the definition of SGEI, and the Member States enjoy much freedom in regard to the scope of USO. While a significant amount of funding is still required for USO funding in the postal sector, the Commission has been using the state aid rules to ensure such funding does not lead to over-compensation.

Keywords liberalisation · postal reforms · universal postal service · postal monopoly · the *Altmark* criteria · the market failure test

6.1 Introduction

In the postal sector, SGEI has been defined through universal service obligation (USO), namely a guaranteed provision of basic postal services for everyone across the Member States. It is deeply rooted in national contexts. The ideal of universal postal service is relatively new. It came into existence only after World War II. The Universal Declaration of Human Rights in 1948 recognises the right to communicate as a basic human right. Since then, the postal services began to be associated with human rights as an essential channel for communication. Under this notion, the State has the obligation to ensure that everyone across the country has access to the postal services.

Right until the late 1980s, direct state control and provision of postal services was still the orthodox model of the postal systems across Member States. It was organised on a public service model rather than based on commercial and market principles. First, postal office was an integrated part of the public administration, whose staff enjoyed the status of civil servant. Second, postal operators did not have freedom to make Decisions over their operation. They were subject to various constraints from the State over investment, strategy and products. More importantly, pricing was determined by public authorities at an affordable level. Third, postal operation was used by the State to promote a wide range of public interest objectives, including employment, infrastructure and industrial policies. Universal availability was only one of their missions, and probably not the most important one.

The EU's involvement in the postal sector started only in the late 1980s, as part of its Internal Market integration programme. The concern was that the widespread monopoly in the postal sector essentially eliminated the prospect of private competition and divided the postal sector into national markets. This essentially meant free movement and market integration was impossible. It is through this process that the EU began to lay down rules on USO in the postal sector.

This chapter first provides an overview of the organisation of postal systems. The reason is that universal postal service is often taken for granted. However, this study finds that this notion is relatively new and had not been clearly defined. This study shows that postal services had long been organised as public services under the direct control of the State, rather than as a normal market activity. It finds that elements of universal postal service came into existence at different periods of the evolution of the postal systems.

The rest of this chapter focuses on how universal postal service was treated at the EU level. The third part of this chapter deals with the limited influence exercised by the EU over the definition of USO. On this issue, only a minimum level of harmonisation has been achieved at the EU level, and Member States still have wide freedom regarding the definition and scope of SGEIs in the postal sector. In practice, they have developed diverse solutions in this respect.

The fourth part examines the liberalisation process in the postal sector. The legislative process was much delayed; it took the EU more than two decades to gradually abolish postal monopolies. Full liberalisation was achieved only in 2013. Meanwhile, the Commission has been using its power under Article 106(3) to make liberalisation Decisions on a case-by-case basis.

The fifth part deals with the application of state aid rules in the postal sector. Although the postal Directive has devised three mechanisms for funding of SGEIs in the postal sector,[1] in practice it is mainly through direct compensation from public funds. The Commission has used the state aid rules to examine SGEI funding. Its Decisions provide a good example of how EU state aid rules on SGEI funding have evolved.

---

[1] There have been three postal Directives in the EU. The first postal Directive 97/67 allowed the grant of exclusive rights as the funding mechanism for the provision of USOs. In 2002, the EU adopted Directive 2002/39, which amended Directive 97/67 and reduced the scope of exclusive rights. In 2008, the EU adopted another amendment Directive 2008/6, which required the Member States to withdraw all exclusive rights by 2010. Meanwhile, Directive 2008/6 devised three possible funding mechanisms for the provision of USOs after full market liberalisation, including: (1) via public procurement procedure; (2) from public funds; and (3) sectoral compensation fund. These postal Directives are:

(1) Directive 97/67/EC of the European Parliament and of the Council of 15 December 1997 on common rules for the development of the Internal Market of Community postal services and the improvement of quality of service [1998] OJ L15/14;
(2) Directive 2002/39/EC of the European Parliament and of the Council of 10 June 2002 amending Directive 97/67/EC with regard to further opening of Community postal services to competition [2002] OJ L176/21;
(3) Directive 2008/6/EC of the European Parliament and of the Council of 20 February 2008 amending Directive 97/67/EC with regard to the full accomplishment of the Internal Market of Community postal services [2008] OJ L52/3.

A consolidated version of Directive 97/67 can be found on the EU's website: http://eur-lex.europa.eu/legal-content/EN/TXT/?uri=CELEX:01997L0067-20080227 accessed 9 October 2014 (hereafter Directive 97/67).

6.2 The Organisation of Postal Systems and Universal Postal Services

6.2.1 Early Postal Service Operation: By the State for the State

The postal service is as old as the State itself.[2] Its origin can be traced back to ancient Egypt, where official documents were carried by relay messengers on horseback. Before the advent of modern transport and communication technology, this form of communication was the only reliable means that the State had to dispatch official orders and information over long distances.[3] It had long been regarded as an essential part of state administration, and its services were provided by the State for the State.[4] It is not surprising that the Roman Empire had built the most advanced postal system in ancient Europe.

After the collapse of the Roman Empire, there was a brief period when postal services were provided outside state control. However, with the emergence of nation States in Europe, the State soon stepped in and took over the operation of the postal services and reserved the whole sector for the State itself as a monopoly.[5]

It is only later that state postal systems began to be open to the public for private usage. However, it had nothing to do with the modern idea of universal postal service. Postage was based on the distance a letter travelled and was paid by recipients. Price was set at a high level in order to increase state revenue.[6] Meanwhile, the content of posted letters was scrutinised by the State.[7] It had a good reason for doing so: the opening of the state postal service system to the public essentially turned it into an early broadcasting system through which ideas could be circulated.

6.2.2 The Origin of Universal Service

The modern version of the postal system that we are familiar with today did not come into existence until 1840, when England first reformed its postal system.[8] The proposal was made by Roland Hill. His concern was that the real revenue of postal

---

[2] For a brief review of the history of postal systems, see John 2001.

[3] Rawnsley and Lazar 1999.

[4] Campbell 1995.

[5] Crew and Kleindorfer 1991.

[6] In 1840 England, sending a letter could cost as much as a week's wages of a working class person: Rawnsley and Lazar 1999, p. 183.

[7] Campbell 1995.

[8] Crew and Kleindorfer 1991.

operations was in decline, taking into account the growth of the population and the development of the economy. He showed that the cost of transportation of mails was minor and insignificant. Therefore, he argued, postage should be reduced, and a uniform pricing policy should be adopted. He believed that this would increase the volume of letters carried and squeeze out illegal private postal carriers from the market. Roland Hill's reform idea on uniform pricing was adopted in England and later across the globe.

It seems that ideal of modern universal postal service was established in Roland Hill's postal reform. However, the reality is very different. In fact, Roland Hill made a crucial distinction between primary postal services and secondary postal services. The former was defined as the transportation of letters between postal towns and delivery within postal towns. His initial reform idea of universal pricing applied only to primary postal services, which covered only more populous towns that accounted for major postal traffic. For secondary postal services, he rejected the idea of universal pricing but argued the quality and pricing of service should be based on local circumstances and be financially self-sufficient.[9]

His concern was not to ensure that everyone in the country had guaranteed access to postal services, but rather that the revenue of the public postal operator was increased through price reduction,[10] which would lead to an increase in volume and therefore economics of scale.[11] Universal pricing across the whole country, which was later adopted by governments, was not Roland Hill's original intention.

6.2.3 Organising the Postal Sector as a Public Service and Universal Service

After Roland Hill's reform, for more than 100 years the organisation of the postal services sector did not change much.[12] Although the extent and actual performance might vary across countries, certain common themes could be found in almost all the postal systems across all Member States.

First, postal operators formed an integrated part of state administration, usually under the Ministry of Postal Services. Postal staff enjoyed the status of civil servants.[13] Second, postal services were regarded as public services rather than as normal commercial activities. Market competition did not exist because the postal sector was reserved for public operators under the protection of monopoly rights,

---

[9] Ibid.

[10] Rawnsley and Lazar 1999, p. 183.

[11] Crew and Kleindorfer 1991.

[12] Campbell 1995.

[13] Commission of the European Communities, 1st Commission Report to the European Parliament and the Council on the Application of the Postal Directive, COM (2002) 632 final, 25.11.2002; Comandini and Lettieri 2001.

even with criminal sanctions. Third, the operation of postal services did not follow commercial principles.[14] Postal operators did not have commercial freedom, and important decisions were made by governmental officials.[15]

In fact, the postal services sector was used by the State for a wide range of public interests that were not clearly defined and might evolve over time. First, the organisation of the postal sector had significant employment significance. As a labour- intensive industry, the public postal operators were often the largest single employer in Member States.[16] Second, the presence of the postal service also had political implications. In remote corners of the territory, the post office and postman could be the only representation of the State and the link with the outside world. A universal postal network is one way to promote national unity and national identity. In addition, before the advent of the modern communications era, postal services had been the only reliable network for long-distance communication. The postal network had been used by the State to spread information and political ideas on a nationwide scale.[17] Third, the operation of postal service also had significant fiscal significance for the State. A very good example can be found in the UK, where the government then significantly increased postage as an income source to fund its war efforts.[18] After the postal reform, although postage was reduced and became more affordable, the postal operation still generated a significant amount of revenue for the State. Fourth, the ideal of universal service advocates a guaranteed provision of postal services for everyone. Although it is often taken for granted and seems well-established in the postal sector, it emerged only after World War II. In 1948 the United Nations adopted the Universal Declaration of Human Rights, which recognises the right to communicate. Since then postal service began to be associated with basic human rights because of its function as an essential channel for communication. Therefore, the organisation of postal services acquired a new mandate.

Under this ideal, the State has an obligation to guarantee provision of basic postal service on a universal basis. This includes three dimensions. First, the maintenance of a nationwide physical postal network to ensure everyone can have

[14] Prosser 2001.

[15] Dobbenberg 1993.

[16] Campbell 1995; Ranganathan and Dey 1996.

[17] A good example can be found in the US during the founding period of the country: John 2008.

[18] During the Napoleonic wars, postage was greatly increased to raise state revenue. As a result, by the end of the Napoleonic wars, the net annual income of the post operation was six times its level in 1794. Postage increase also took place during the two World Wars. This is well-documented in Robinson's book. He pointed out that:

> The basic charge for letters was finally raised in June 1918 from 1d to 1.5 d; the Penny Post had finally become a war casualty and has since been unable to recover from the blow. In June 1920 the basic charge for letters became 2d; but in 1922 it returned to 1.2d, where it remained until 1940, when another war raised it to 2.5d.

Robinson 1953, pp 97, 239.

access to the network. Second, the State imposed constraints on the quality of service provided through the network. Postal operators were often required to provide clearance, transportation, sorting and delivery of postal services at least once a day to every address in the country. The third dimension is pricing, where a uniform price was charged irrespective of the individual profitability of each operation. Meanwhile, price was decided by the State to ensure it was affordable for everyone in society.

What is worthy of special attention is that the ideal of universal postal service as a human right did not fundamentally change the organisation of postal systems. It was pursued through political means rather than legal mechanisms. Universal service was not defined explicitly by law in quantitative terms.[19] It can hardly be regarded as an enforceable legal obligation. Its materialisation essentially depended on the *political will* of the government.

On the one hand, direct control by the State was regarded as necessary and sufficient to protect public interests, including universal postal service. Postal operators were owned and controlled by the State. The State had dominant and decisive influence over its operation, personnel and decision-making. On the other hand, although consumer interest organisations were set up to 'monitor' the performance of postal operations and to handle complaints, they could only make non-binding recommendations to the government.

Under the traditional model, it was hardly necessary to establish an explicit funding mechanism for universal services either. Monopoly rights were used to generate enough revenue to keep the postal system as a whole operational. As long as the accounts were in balance, or showed some profit, universal service could be maintained.[20]

In fact, as an integrated part of public administration, the financial responsibilities of postal operators were borne by the State. Revenues generated by the postal monopoly would ultimately go to the Treasury. Meanwhile, any losses of the postal service would be borne by the government. In fact, postal operators were allowed to expand their business into telegraph and savings, which generated significant profits to subsidise their postal operations.

Later, during liberalisation in the 1990s, monopoly rights were justified as a means of funding the provision of universal postal service because it protected the cross-subsidy flow from profitable areas to loss-making areas of the postal operation, often from urban to rural areas.[21] However, the argument was not tenable as there was scant evidence available to support it. Without comprehensive and

[19] Prosser 2001.

[20] Rawnsley and Lazar trace the history of postal monopoly and universal service and argue that 'historically we do not have postal monopolies in order to provide for universal service': Rawnsley and Lazar 1999, p. 184.

[21] Ranganathan and Dey 1996.

detailed accounting practice, it was not possible to work out what areas had generated how much losses/profits.[22] Contrary to the argument, it has been shown that the postal operation in rural areas was not necessarily loss making.

6.2.4 *Postal Reforms and the Issue of Universal Service Obligation*

From the late 1970s, the traditional organisational model of postal services began to face a crisis. The performance of postal operations had been poor and disappointing.[23] Operating as a public service under the protection of monopoly, State operators were often inefficient and not responsive to consumer needs, in particular to business users. In response to this market gap, private postal services first appeared in the US in the 1970s and later in Europe.[24] They competed with State postal operators by offering value-added services tailored to meet distinct consumer needs.[25] Public postal operators were ill-prepared for such commercial competition because of State control and intervention.

In addition, with the advent of modern telecommunications technology and advances in computing, communication needs began to be increasingly met by these alternative platforms.[26] This led to a steady decline in the post office's market share in the overall communications market in the EU, from 20% in 1995 to 15% by 2005.[27] As a result, postal operations generated a significant amount of deficit, which became a drain on public finances.[28] In 1988, only two out of twelve public postal operators in Europe generated minor profits—3.4% of total revenue in the UK, 2.6% in the Netherlands. The others were all in deficit, with Belgium having the highest, 48.3% of its total revenue.[29]

---

[22] This is the so-called 'internal cross-subsidisation': OECD Committee on Competition Law and Policy, 'Promoting Competition in Postal Services' (OECD Policy Roundtables 1999). www.oecd.org/daf/competition/sectors/1920548.pdf.

[23] Commission of the European Communities, 1st Commission Report to the European Parliament and the Council on the application of the Postal Directive, COM (2002) 632 final, 25.11.2002, 3.

[24] John 2001.

[25] Campbell 1993.

[26] Campbell 2001b; Campbell 2000;

OECD Committee on Competition Law and Policy, 'Promoting Competition in Postal Services' (OECD Policy Roundtables 1999). www.oecd.org/daf/competition/sectors/1920548.pdf.

[27] Commission of the European Communities, 1st Commission Report to the European Parliament and the Council on the Application of the Postal Directive, COM (2002) 632 final, 25.11.2002, p. 34.

[28] Ranganathan and Dey 1996.

[29] Commission of the European Communities, Green Paper on the Development of the Single Market for Postal Services, COM (91) 476 final, 11.06.1991.

In response to this situation, national governments in Europe began to reform their postal services sector in the late 1980s.[30] The extent and pace of reform varied significantly across countries.[31] However, certain common themes were widespread.[32] First, in regard to the institutional aspect, postal operators were separated from the state administration and transformed into autonomous market entities, often followed by the process of privatisation, whereby government sold its shareholdings to private hands. Second, in regard to the postal service market, governments began to abolish the monopoly structures and to allow gradual competition into the sector.

It is against this background that the EU began to actively promote competition and market integration in the postal sector in the late 1980s. It had strong reasons to do so. Postal services form an essential part of communications infrastructure, on which the development of an Internal Market depends. First, the EU was frustrated by the lack of harmonisation and poor performance of the postal sector, in particular in regard to intra-community postal services.[33] Second, the EU was concerned with how national postal monopolies wiped out competition and contradicted the basic cross-border market competition principle.[34] The postal sector was based on national markets and led to the fragmentation of the EU Internal Market: free movement in the postal sector was impossible. Accordingly, the EU intended to open up national postal markets to competition, which was an important aspect of its market integration programme launched in the late 1980s.[35]

It was an extremely challenging exercise for the EU.[36] Postal reform is a politically sensitive area, and the EU had not been granted explicit competence in this area.[37] The postal sector had been under the firm control of national governments. The EU's involvement in this process would erode the competence of Member States and constrain the freedom of national governments in organising the sector. This issue was of great significance, taking into account the scale of postal operations and its significance for employment.

On the other hand, it was politically desirable to ensure that a certain level of postal services was available throughout the EU. It was imperative that the EU resolve the issue in order to introduce competition and promote market integration

[30] Campbell 2000; Brandt 2007; Dieke et al. 2008.

[31] Campbell et al. 2008; Ranganathan and Dey 1996.

[32] For an overview of the issues on the postal reform, see Campbell 2001a; Universal Postal Union, 'Postal Regulation: Principles and Orientation' (Bern 2002); OECD Committee on Competition Law and Policy, 'Promoting Competition in Postal Services' (OECD Policy Roundtables 1999). www.oecd.org/daf/competition/sectors/1920548.pdf.

[33] Zepos 1992, p. 222; Commission of the European Communities, 1st Commission Report to the European Parliament and the Council on the application of the Postal Directive, COM (2002) 632 final, 25.11.2002.

[34] Crew et al. 2008.

[35] Van Der Horst 2005.

[36] Reay 1997; Von Danwitz 2002.

[37] Smith 2005.

into the sector.[38] It was feared that private operators would only *cherry-pick* profitable areas of the market and leave the non-profitable sections to the public operator. This would worsen the financial status of the public operators and put universal service in jeopardy.

This concern found its legal basis in the landmark *Corbeau* case,[39] where the Court held that the grant of exclusive rights is justified if it is necessary for the provision of SGEI under economically acceptable conditions. However, more crucial questions remained unanswered. What postal service would be so basic and essential as to require that it be made available to everyone? What are the costs of maintaining universal service? What areas of the postal sector fall within the scope of monopoly to fund the provision of USO?

6.3 EU Harmonisation of Universal Postal Service Provision

6.3.1 The Legal Basis for EU Postal Legislation: Article 100, not Article 106(3)

The blueprint for EU postal policy was laid down in the Green Paper published in 1992.[40] The Commission indicated that it might use its power under Article 106(3) to adopt Commission Directives to introduce competition in the sector.[41] This position was explicitly confirmed by the Competition Commissioner in its speech.[42]

The implications were significant. The Commission had adopted this approach in the telecommunications sector, which abolished all monopoly rights in just ten years, as under Article 106(3), the Commission was entitled to adopt Directives of general application without the involvement of the Council or the Parliament. This enabled the Commission to avoid the lengthy legislative process and also potentially political resistance from Member States.

Although the legitimacy of the legislative power of Article 106(3) had been upheld by the Court in the telecommunications sector, its usage turned out to be politically impossible in the postal services sector.[43] Both the Parliament and the Council explicitly rejected the use of the Article 106(3) Directive approach. In response to the

[38] Rawnsley and Lazar 1999, p. 85.

[39] Case C-320/91 *Paul Corbeau* [1993] ECR I-2533.

[40] Commission of the European Communities, Green Paper on the Development of the Single Market for Postal Services, COM (91) 476 final, 11.06.1991; Chung 1994.

[41] Commission of the European Communities, Green Paper on the Development of the Single Market for Postal Services, COM (91) 476 final, 11.06.1991, p. 55.

[42] Britain 1992.

[43] Smith 2005, p. 133.

Commission's 1991 Green Paper,[44] the Parliament passed a resolution that was 'opposed to any transposition of measures on the basis of Article 106(3) of the Treaty' and 'insisted that the legal basis should be Article 100 of the Treaty'.[45] The same position was taken by the Council, which 'reaffirmed that a political agreement with the full participation of both the European Parliament and the Council is the best way of encouraging the implementation of the future Community policy in the postal sector'.[46]

This had profound implications for the EU's postal reform process. Under the co-decision procedure of Article 100 of the Treaty, the Member States, through the Council, could have significant influence over the process and results of the postal liberalisation legislative process. It is in this context that the political will of Member States became influential. Although globally, postal reform started in the late 1980s, Member States had not reached a political consensus on how to undertake this reform.[47] This explains why EU postal liberalisation was much delayed.

It was out of this process that universal postal service began to emerge and consolidate at the EU level. Actually, it has become a pivotal point of the EU postal reform agenda, because universal postal service provided the very justification for the existence of postal monopolies.[48] From the very beginning, the EU had accepted that the grant of exclusive rights was a legitimate funding mechanism. The Commission pointed out that:

> The Green Paper considers that the universal service objective can justify the establishment of a set of reserved services, which would help to ensure the financial viability of the universal service network. In this way, the public service mission, which is and will remain a feature of universal postal services, would be guaranteed.[49]

Full liberalisation was much delayed and achieved only in 2013. Exclusive rights were allowed to provide funding for the provision of universal postal service. However, this does not stand up to any serious legal reasoning. Instead, it was a political decision. It essentially gave public postal operators enough time to adjust to the new market environment.[50]

---

[44] Commission of the European Communities, Green Paper on the Development of the Single Market for Postal Services, COM (91) 476 final, 11.06.1991.

[45] The European Parliament, Resolution on the Green Paper on the Development of the Single Market for Postal Services' (Resolution A3-039/92) [1993] OJ C42/240.

[46] The Council of the European Union, Council Resolution of 7 February 1994 on the Development of Community Postal Services (94/C 48/02) [1994] OJ C48/3.

[47] Campbell 2001b.

[48] Chung 1994; Smith 2005, p. 127.

[49] Commission of the European Communities, Green Paper on the Development of the Single Market for Postal Services, COM (91) 476 final, 11.06.1991, 8.

[50] Major changes include: (1) transformation from part of State administration to independent market entity; (2) merger and acquisitions on the market; (3) diversion of revenue sources; (4) more focus on cost efficiency, profitability and customers' needs; and (5) increase in productivity. As a result, most public postal operators had become profitable by 2000: Commission of the European Communities, 1st Commission Report to the European Parliament and the Council on the application of the Postal Directive, COM (2002) 632 final, 25.11.2002, 26–28.

The political nature of this process had profound implications for the definition of USO and also the pace of liberalisation. A crucial point for the EU, in particular for the Commission, was to reach a solution that was acceptable to all stakeholders. The EU regime on universal postal services was a direct result of this political compromise. It prescribed only a minimum level of USO that the Member States have an obligation to guarantee.[51] Meanwhile, it left much freedom for the Member States to decide what is beyond this level of harmonisation.

6.3.2 Minimum Level of Harmonisation

From the very beginning, the maintenance of the universal postal service has been a priority of the EU's postal reform agenda.[52] In fact, the EU had assumed universal postal service as a valid and legitimate objective. This issue did not receive much attention from the EU. The non-economic objectives pursued by universal postal service were defined only in very broad and general terms:

> Since they constitute an essential instrument for communication and information exchange, postal services fulfil a vital role which contributes to the objectives of social, economic and territorial cohesion in the Union. Postal networks have important territorial and social dimensions which make universal access to essential local services possible.[53]

The EU's regime on USO has two aspects. The first is a universal postal network. This is related to the territorial presence of the postal infrastructure itself. It requires the permanent and standby presence of postal access facilities across the whole territory of Member States. In this respect, Directive 97/67 did not prescribe a uniform standard for all Member States, but laid down only a very general obligation and left it to the discretion of each individual Member State to implement. The wording of the Directive reads as follows:

> To this end, Member States shall take steps to ensure that the density of the points of contact and of the access points takes account of the needs of users.[54]

In practice, what this meant is that Member States often translated this as an obligation placed on the USO provider to maintain a certain level of presence across the whole country, irrespective of its profitability.[55] The actual level of universality

---

[51] Commission of the European Communities, 1st Commission Report to the European Parliament and the Council on the application of the Postal Directive, COM (2002) 632 final, 25.11.2002, 3.

[52] Universal Postal Union, 'Postal Regulation: Principles and Orientation' (Bern 2002).

[53] Directive 2008/6/EC of the European Parliament and of the Council of 20 February 2008 amending Directive 97/67/EC with regard to the full accomplishment of the Internal Market of Community postal services [2008] OJ L52/3, Recital 5.

[54] Directive 97/67.

[55] This implies that extra funding is often necessary to maintain the sustainability of such network. State funding for the universal postal network has become one of the major issues in the application of state aid control to SGEIs in the postal sector.

varies significantly across Member States.[56] It is not within the scope of this study to conduct a complete survey on this aspect.[57] But some examples will be given to illustrate this variation across Member States. In this respect, the Commission's state aid Decisions offer a very good window on how USO is defined by Member States in practice. Its Decisions concerning Poland, Belgium and the UK are very good examples, in which different levels of requirements have been imposed by national authorities and which have been recognised as valid SGEIs by the Commission (Table 6.1).

Another aspect of USOs is related to the actual provision of certain postal products itself. The Directive obliges Member States to guarantee a permanent provision of certain postal services of a specific quality at an affordable price for all users, irrespective of the profitability of each individual service. It established a minimum level of provision of basic postal service across Member States. It essentially imposed constraints on three dimensions, which are essential to the universality of the postal service.[58]

The first dimension is the scope of the postal products covered by the obligation. It includes postal items up to 2 kg, postal packages up to 20 kg and registered items and insured items.[59] Secondly, the Directive also established the minimum quality level of the universal service. It requires one clearance and one delivery to the home or premises of every natural or legal person on every working day and not less than five days a week.[60]

What is worthy of special attention is the EU rule on the third dimension of universal service constraint, namely price. The Directive requires Member States to ensure that the price of universal postal service is affordable, rather than uniform.[61] This is a clear divorce from uniform pricing policy under the traditional notion of universal service. It also implies that the price of universal postal service should be cost oriented.

The Directive does not set quantitative standards on the affordability of universal postal service. Such an exercise is not desirable at the EU level, taking into consideration the huge diversity of the postal service sector across Member States. This issue is essentially left to Member States to decide at the national level.

In practice, there are considerable differences across Member States in regard to universal postal service.[62] Most Member States still require the provision of

[56] Borsenberger et al. 2011.

[57] NERA, 'Costing and Financing of Universal Services in the Postal Sector in the European Union' (Study Commissioned by the European Commission 1998).

[58] Gautier and Paolini 2011.

[59] Directive 97/67, Article 3(4).

[60] Ibid., Article 3(3).

[61] Ibid., Article 3(1).

[62] Universal Postal Union, 'Postal Regulation: Principles and Orientation' (Bern 2002).

Table 6.1 Universal postal network requirements in Poland, Belgium and the UK

Country	Density requirements
Poland[a]	(1) A post office for each cluster of 7000 inhabitants in urban areas; (2) a post office for each 65 km^2 in rural areas; and (3) a post office for each county of over 2500 inhabitants
Belgium[b]	(1) 95% of the population within 5 km of the nearest post service points; (2) 98% of the population within 10 km of the nearest post service points; at least one post office in each of the 589 municipalities of the country; and total number requirement: 1300 postal service points and 650 postal offices
The UK[c]	(1) 90% of the population to be within 1 mile of their nearest post office; (2) 99% of the UK population to be within 3 miles of the nearest post office; (3) 99% of the total population in deprived urban areas to be within 1 mile of the nearest post office; (3) 95% of the total rural population to be within 3 miles of the nearest post office; (4) 95% of the total urban population (and 99% of the total population in deprived urban areas) to be within 1 mile of their nearest post office

Source The author

[a]2010/815/EU: Commission Decision of 15 December 2009 on state aid C 21/05 (ex PL 45/04), which Poland plans to implement for Poczta Polska as compensation of universal postal service obligations [2010] OJ L347/29

[b]State Aid SA.31006 (2013/N)—Belgium State compensations to Bpost for the delivery of public services over 2013–2015, C (2013) 1909 final, 02.05.2013

[c]Its funding measures have been the subject of several Commission state aid Decisions

(1) State Aid No 252/2002—United Kingdom reinvention of the urban Post Office network, C (2002) 3341 fin, 18.09.2002

(2) State Aid N 784/2002—United Kingdom Government rural network support funding, debt payment funding and rolling working capital loan to Post Office Limited, C (2003) 1652 fin, 27.05.2003

(3) State Aid N 166/2005—United Kingdom Government rural network support funding to Post Office Limited (POL) for 2006–2008, C (2006) 434 final, 22.02.2006

(4) State Aid SA.33054—United Kingdom Post Office Limited (POL) compensation for net costs incurred to keep a non-commercially viable network for the period 2012–15 and the continuation of a working capital facility, C (2012) 1905 final, 28.03.2012

universal postal services at a uniform price. Meanwhile, different mechanisms have been devised by Member States for price control.[63] Such variations also exist regarding the scope and the quality dimensions of the universal postal service.[64] The Directive establishes only a minimum level of universal postal service, whereas in practice, Member States often go further than that. National variations have a direct impact on the costs of universal postal service provision: the more constraints it requires, the more costly it becomes. This is illustrated by the following diagram: the bigger the box is, the higher the cost USO involves (Fig. 6.1).

[63]Campbell et al. 2008; Ambrosini et al. 2006.

[64]Von Danwitz 2002; Ambrosini et al. 2006.

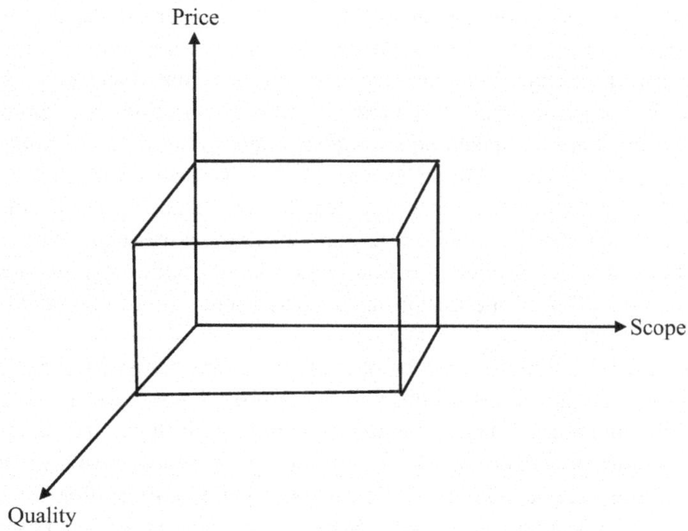

Fig. 6.1 Dimensions of universal postal services. *Source* Ambrosini et al. (2006)

6.3.3 Funding of USO Through the Grant of Exclusive Rights

In the 1992 Green Paper, the Commission concluded that a preferred approach is a balance between gradual liberalisation and harmonisation of USO. This is in line with the approach formulated by the Court in the *Corbeau* case, in which the Court ruled that monopoly was justified if it was necessary for the provision of universal postal services under economically acceptable conditions.[65] Unlike the more stringent least restrictive means test, the EAC test does not challenge the appropriateness of exclusive right as a funding measure for SGEI. In the 1992 Green Paper, the Commission was of the opinion that USOs 'can only be achieved through the granting of some special and exclusive rights'.[66] This approach is further elaborated as follows:

> The Green Paper considers that the universal service objective can justify the establishment of a set of reserved services, which would help to ensure the financial viability of the universal service network. In this way, the public service mission, which is and will remain a feature of universal postal service, would be guaranteed.[67]

[65] Case C-320/91 *Paul Corbeau* [1993] ECR I-2533.

[66] Ibid., 11.

[67] Commission of the European Communities, Green Paper on the Development of the Single Market for Postal Services, COM (91) 476 final, 11.06.1991, 8.

The next issue the Commission had to address concerned the scope of such exclusive rights. In its 1992 Green Paper, the Commission pointed out that 'the scope of reserved area should be directly proportional to the objective'.[68] However, this is not an economic issue, but rather a political question that requires compromises among various stakeholders whose interests may be in conflict. Such political consensus is very difficult to reach.[69] This is clearly reflected in the prolonged legislation process of the postal legislation. After the publication of the Green Paper, it took the EU another five years to adopt its first legislation, Directive 97/67.[70] This had a very limited effect on market liberalisation and integration. It is estimated that only 3% of the postal market was opened up to competition by the Directive.[71]

It did not establish a uniform scope of exclusive rights across Member States but only established certain limits within which Member States have the discretion to decide. On the one hand, it laid down the maximum limit that could be reserved in the domestic correspondence market[72]—350 g and 5 times the basic tariff. The domestic letter market outside this scope must be open to competition. This seemed a significant liberalisation effort: many Member States reserved letters up to 2 kg for public postal operators in 1990[73], but in practice this had little impact on the position of the postal monopolists in the market. By 2000, they still occupied 84% of the market, and private operators took up a very insignificant share.

On the other hand, it also prescribed whether a sub-section of the postal sector can be reserved by Member States. It expressly prohibited Member States from doing so in the market of document exchange, self-provision and any new services. In the Directive, it allowed the Member States to reserve cross-border mail and direct mail services under the protection of exclusive rights.[74]

While the actual liberalisation impact of the Directive was limited, Directive 97/67 essentially paved the way towards further liberalisation. It defined a set of postal services as covered by USOs. With an explicit USO scope in place, it would be possible to review the scope of monopoly. In addition, it established a timetable to review the sector and to promote further liberalisation. This also gave time for the public incumbent to adjust to the liberalisation process.

---

[68] Ibid., 8.

[69] Griffiths 2000.

[70] Directive 97/67/EC of the European Parliament and of the Council of 15 December 1997 on common rules for the development of the Internal Market of Community postal services and the improvement of quality of service [1998] OJ L15/14.

[71] Ibid.

[72] Commission of the European Communities, 1st Commission Report to the European Parliament and the Council on the application of the Postal Directive, COM (2002) 632 final, 25.11.2002, p. 3.

[73] Commission of the European Communities, Green Paper on the Development of the Single Market for Postal Services, COM (91) 476 final, 11.06.1991, p. 41.

[74] Directive 97/67, Article 7(2). This was criticised as unjustified and unsatisfactory: Campbell 2001b.

6.4 EU Efforts Towards Full Market Liberalisation

While it was politically very difficult to push liberalisation through EU legislation,[75] the Commission had been pursuing this policy long before Directive 97/67: since the late 1980s, it had been using its power under Article 106(3) to adopt Decisions against individual Member States. In its Decisions, it applied the SGEI derogation under Article 106(1) very strictly.[76] A similar approach could also be found in the Court's case law interpreting Directive 97/6. It essentially adopted a pro-competition attitude and further limited the scope of exclusive rights.[77] These efforts all contributed to the final abolishment of all exclusive rights in EU postal legislation. These will now be considered.

6.4.1 Liberalisation Through Commission Decisions Under Article 106

While liberalisation through EU legislation was difficult to progress, the Commission has been using its power under Article 106(3) to adopt Decisions against Member States on a case-by-case basis. The focus of the Commission had been on the newly emerging areas of the market, such as express courier services and hybrid mail services. There had been significant market development in these areas, where private operators offered value-added services and competed with public postal operators. The concern of the Commission was that Member States adopted legislation reclaiming the scope of postal monopoly as covering these areas and consequently drove out competition.[78]

---

[75] Chung 1994.

[76]
(1) 90/16/EEC: Commission Decision of 20 December 1989 concerning the provision in the Netherlands of express delivery services [1990] OJ L10/47;
(2) 90/456/EEC: Commission Decision of 1 August 1990 concerning the provision in Spain of international express courier services [1990] OJ L 233/19;
(3) 2001/176/EC: Commission Decision of 21 December 2000 concerning proceedings pursuant to Article 86 of the EC Treaty in relation to the provision of certain new postal services with a guaranteed day-or time-certain delivery in Italy [2001] OJ L63/59;
(4) COMP/F-1/39.562: Commission Decision of 7 October 2008 on the Slovakian law on hybrid mail services [2008] OJ C322/10.

[77] Case C-162/06 *International Mail Spain SL v Administración del Estado and Correos* [2007] ECR I-9911.

[78] While the adoption of state measures reserving certain areas of the postal market under postal monopoly is a *direct and obvious* obstacle to market liberalisation and the creation of an internal postal market, what is equally damaging but *less obvious and hidden* is that certain State measures or conduct of the incumbent *potentially have the effect of* squeezing commercial competitors out of the market and therefore jeopardising the development of competition. This practice was also subject to the scrutiny of competition law. Examples include:

(1) Article 102: abusive conduct that eliminates competition

Public postal operators might engage in abusive conduct to drive out private competitors from the market, which was in breach of Article 102. The Commission's Decision concerning the public postal operator in Germany, Deutsche Post AG, is a good example. Deutsche Post enjoyed an exclusive right over the postal market weighing less than 200 g. Meanwhile, it was active in the parcel delivery services market, which was open to market competition. The Commission found that it had engaged in abusive conduct in the parcel delivery services market through fidelity rebates and predatory pricing, which had the effect of eliminating competition in the market.
2001/354/EC: Commission Decision of 20 March 2001 relating to a proceeding under Article 82 of the EC Treaty (Case COMP/35.141—Deutsche Post AG) [2001] OJ L125/44.

(1) state aid rules: financial grants from the Member States

The Commission used state aid control mechanisms to scrutinise financial grants by the Member States to public postal operators. The concern of the Commission is that public postal operators might gain an advantage over their commercial competitors. This issue often arises in two circumstances. First, the Member States granted funding for the provision of SGEIs. This will be discussed in Sect. 6.5 of this chapter.
Second, the Member States granted pension relief for civil servants working in public postal operators. The prolonged investigation on financial transfers from Germany to its public postal operator, Deutsche Poste AG, offers a good example. In its latest Decision SA.17653, the Commission found that the social security contribution borne by Deutsche Poste was lower than private competitors and concluded that it constituted incompatible state aid and must be recovered. The Decision was later challenged by Germany and Deutsche Poste before the Court of First Instance. Meanwhile, the Commission also brought a case against Germany before the Court for its failure to comply with the Decision. These cases are still pending.
2012/636/EU: Commission Decision of 25 January 2012 Measures C 36/07 (ex NN 25/07) implemented by Germany for Deutsche Post AG [2012] OJ L289/1; Case T-143/12 *Germany v Commission*; Case T-152/12 *Deutsche Post v Commission*; Case C-674/13 Commission v Germany (not yet reported). http://curia.europa.eu/juris/liste.jsf?language=en&td=ALL&num=C-674/13#

(2) Article 106(1) in conjunction with Article 102: State measures leading to competitive advantages

State measures that put public postal operators in an advantageous position have been the subject of the case law. The principle established by the Court in the *TNT Traco* case is very important. In this case, the Italian legislation required all express mail service providers to pay a postal due to the public postal operator, Poste Italiane, to fund the provision of universal postal services. In the Judgment, the Court ruled that the total proceeds from the postal dues must not exceed the amount necessary to offset the costs of USO provision and that Poste Italiane must pay the same postal due when it provided express mail services.
Case C-340/99 *TNT Traco SpA v Poste Italiane SpA and Others* [2001] ECR I-4109.

This issue was also the concern of the Commission in its Decisions. Its Decision concerning mail preparation services in France is a good example. The French public postal operator, La Poste, enjoyed an exclusive right over the basic postal service. It was also active on the mail preparation service market, which is an upstream market to its reserved area. The Commission found that La Poste had the power to decide price conditions and technical standards for private mail preparation operators. The Commission concluded that La Poste was in a conflict of interest position because it also competed with other private undertakings on the mail

Even before the publication of its Green Paper, the Commission had intervened in the market of express courier services, where public postal monopolists claimed that their postal monopoly rights also covered this area and tried to prevent competition from private operators that began to emerge and develop quickly in this area.[79] The Commission made Decisions against several Member States, including Germany, Belgium, France, Ireland, Italy, the Netherlands, Denmark and Spain.[80] As a result, by 1992 express postal service had been opened to competition in all Member States.[81]

Only in the case of Spain[82] and the Netherlands[83] did the Commission make and publish its formal Decisions. The Decision concerning the Netherlands is very illustrative.[84] It shows the difficulties and dilemmas in applying Article 106(1) to challenge the grant of exclusive rights by Member States. The Decision was made in 1989, two years before the Court ruled on how Article 106(1) is interpreted and applied.

In Decision 90/16/EEC, the Dutch Postal Office, PTT Post BV (hereafter PTT), had held a comprehensive postal monopoly over the whole postal sector based on a 1954 law. However, in practice, despite this statutory monopoly right, an express courier service market for domestic and international postal services developed and grew to a considerable size (employing 4000 persons). This essentially eroded the monopoly right held by PTT. It was tolerated by the Dutch authorities until 1988,

---

preparation market and that France was therefore in breach of Article 106(1) in conjunction with Article 102.

2002/344/EC: Commission Decision of 23 October 2001 on the lack of exhaustive and independent scrutiny of the scales of charges and technical conditions applied by La Poste to mail preparation firms for access to its reserved services [2002] OJ L120/19.

[79] Zepos 1992, p. 260.

[80] The Commission did not make formal decisions against these Member States. Only brief summaries were reported in its annual Competition Policy Report: Commission of the European Communities, Fifteenth Report on Competition Policy 1985, 202–3; Commission of the European Communities, Nineteenth Report on Competition Policy 1990, 201; Commission of the European Communities, Twentieth Report on Competition Policy 1991, 207–209; Commission of the European Communities, Twenty-First Report on Competition Policy 1992, 188–189.

[81] Commission of the European Communities, Green Paper on the Development of the Single Market for Postal Services, COM (91) 476 final, 11.06.1991, 42, 56–57.

[82] 90/456/EEC: Commission Decision of 1 August 1990 concerning the provision in Spain of international express courier services [1990] OJ L 233/19.

[83] 90/16/EEC: Commission Decision of 20 December 1989 concerning the provision in the Netherlands of express delivery services [1990] OJ L10/47.

[84] The legal reasoning in these two decisions is essentially the same. Its Decision against the Netherlands was later challenged before the Court. The Court declared the Commission's decision void because of its procedural flaws. However, it upheld the Commission's power to make decisions under Article 106(3). It did not discuss how Article 106(1) and (2) shall be applied. Interestingly, the Commission's application of Article 106(1) in conjunction with Article 102 was heavily criticised by the Advocate General in his Opinion: Joined Cases C-48/90 & C-66/90 *Kingdom of the Netherlands, Koninklijke PTT Nederland NV and PTT Post BV v Commission of the European Communities* [1992] ECR 1-565.

when new legislation was adopted, which redefined the postal monopoly more clearly in terms of weight (postal items up to 500 g) and price (lower than a minimum price). The effect of this new legislation was to drive out express courier services from this reserved area of the postal sector.

The Commission found its legal basis through a combined application of Article 106(1) and Article 102. The difficulty lies in the fact that Article 106(1), as a reference rule, does not contain any substantive obligations for Member States. Meanwhile Article 102 is devised to deal with abusive behaviour of undertakings in a dominant position. It does not prohibit the existence of dominant position and is not applicable to Member States. Therefore, in order to hold Member State responsible, a causal link needed to be established between the grant of exclusive right by Member States and an undertaking's abusive behaviour under Article 102.

The Commission did not provide any factual findings regarding whether PTT (the monopolist) actually committed abusive conduct under Article 102. Instead, it focused on *the effects of exclusive rights* on competition. First, it found the new legislation constituted an *extension of PTT's monopoly rights*. The approach of the Commission was to break down the monopoly structure into two separate markets, the market for basic postal services and the market for express delivery services. In its Decision, it argued as follows:

> The *effect of the new law* is to reserve for PTT the section of the express delivery market [...] in which, prior to the entry into force of the law, it competed against private express delivery undertakings.[85] (emphasis added)

Secondly, it found that the grant of exclusive rights over express courier services led to the *restriction of supply*. Surprisingly, the Commission did not mention its legal basis. However, what is clear is that the concern of the Commission was the grant of the exclusive right itself, rather than any abuse carried out by PTT under Article 102. In its Decision, it pointed out that:

> The new measure will adversely affect the number of providers and the quality of the service. Since private couriers can no longer provide their services, their customers no longer have a service of the same quality, as the Netherlands post office and its EMS service are not as yet offering an express delivery service of comparable reliability or speed.[86]

Following this approach, postal monopoly beyond basic postal service will be very likely to be found in breach of the Treaty because they will extend the monopoly over basic postal service to ancillary services, which is inherently restrictive. This approach was very controversial and was criticised by the Advocate General in the appeal procedure.[87]

---

[85] 90/16/EEC: Commission Decision of 20 December 1989 concerning the provision in the Netherlands of express delivery services [1990] OJ L10/47, para 11.

[86] Ibid., para 13.

[87] Opinion of the Advocate General, Joined Cases C-48/90 & C-66/90 K*ingdom of the Netherlands, Koninklijke PTT Nederland NV and PTT Post BV v Commission of the European Communitie*s [1992] ECR 1-565.

The Commission's approach regarding the incompatibility of the monopoly's extension was supported by the Court in its case law in 1991. Two cases are particularly relevant in the postal sector. In the *GB Inno* case,[88] the Court ruled that the grant of exclusive rights leading to an extension of dominant position was incompatible with the Treaty.[89] In the *Höfner* case,[90] the Court ruled that a Member State was in breach of the Treaty if the grant of exclusive right limits the supply of service to consumers.[91] These two cases put the Commission in a legally sound position to challenge postal monopolies in the Member States. Since 1991, the Commission adopted two more liberalisation Decisions, against Italy in 2001[92] and against Slovak in 2008.[93] In both Decisions, it referred explicitly to these two Court Judgments as a legal basis for concluding that State legislation was in breach of Article 106(1) in conjunction with Article 102.

With the grant of exclusive right becoming increasingly easy to be found incompatible with the Treaty, the application of SGEI derogation under Article 106 (2) had become more important. The Commission applied the economically acceptable conditions test developed by the Court in the *Corbeau* case to evaluate whether the reservation of some segments of the postal sector is justified. In its decision practice, it has adopted an economic analysis approach. The inquiry is twofold: it examines the impact of market liberalisation on the financial equilibrium of the SGEI operation and also the competitive status of the SGEI operator on the market.

The Commission has made four liberalisation Decisions in the postal sector, and its approach to the application of the EAC test has been consistent. [94] For example,

---

[88]Case C-18/88 *Régie des Télégraphes et des Téléphones v GB-Inno-BM SA* [1991] ECR I-5941.

[89]The case is dealt with in more detail in Sect. 3.2.4 of Chap. 3.

[90]Case C-41/90 *Klaus Höfner and Fritz Elser v Macrotron GmbH* [1991] ECR I-1979.

[91]The case is dealt with in more detail in Sect. 3.2.2 of Chap. 3.

[92]2001/176/EC: Commission Decision of 21 December 2000 concerning proceedings pursuant to Article 86 of the EC Treaty in relation to the provision of certain new postal services with a guaranteed day- or time-certain delivery in Italy [2001] OJ L63/59.

[93]COMP/F-1/39.562: Commission Decision of 7 October 2008 on the Slovakian law on hybrid mail services [2008] OJ C322/10.

[94]

(1) 90/16/EEC: Commission Decision of 20 December 1989 concerning the provision in the Netherlands of express delivery services [1990] OJ L10/47;
The Decision was overturned by the General Court of the EU because of procedural defects. Joined cases C-48/90 and C-66/90, *Kingdom of the Netherlands, Koninklijke PTT Nederland NV and PTT Post BV v Commission of the European Communities,* [1992] ECR I-565
(2) 90/456/EEC: Commission Decision of 1 August 1990 concerning the provision in Spain of international express courier services [1990] OJ L233/19;
(3) 2001/176/EC: Commission Decision of 21 December 2000 concerning proceedings pursuant to Article 86 of the EC Treaty in relation to the provision of certain new postal services with a guaranteed day- or time-certain delivery in Italy [2001] OJ L63/59;
(4) COMP/F-1/39.562: Commission Decision of 7 October 2008 on the Slovakian law on hybrid mail services [2008] OJ C322/10.

Table 6.2 The application of the EAC test in the Commission's Postal liberalisation decisions

Decision name	Legal reasoning
90/456/EEC International express courier service in Spain[a]	(1) Financial equilibrium of SGEI provision—international express mail service represented *only 0.00039%* of its total postal volume (2) Financial position on the market—the SGEI provider's revenue grew *35%* annually
90/16/EEC Express delivery service in the Netherlands[b]	(1) Financial position of the SGEI provider—substantial amount of profits on the market of basic postal service market and express delivery service (2) Competitive position on the market—the SGEI provider withstood market competition very well
2001/176/EC Guaranteed day- or time-certain delivery in Italy[c]	Financial position of SGEI provider (1) The SGEI provider did not suffer any loss of revenue because it did not offer such service; (2) The guaranteed day- or time-certain delivery was distinct from traditional postal service and would not reduce its revenue in the basic postal service market; (3) No cherry-picking because the guaranteed day- or time-certain delivery covered a whole province
COMP/F-1/39.562 Hybrid mail services in Slovakia[d]	(1) Financial equilibrium of SGEI provision—the SGEI operator remained profitable in the preceding three years and was in a solid financial position (2) Competitive position on the market—the SGEI operator would still occupy a dominant position after market liberalisation

Source The author

[a]90/456/EEC: Commission Decision of 1 August 1990 concerning the provision in Spain of international express courier services [1990] OJ L233/19

[b]90/16/EEC: Commission Decision of 20 December 1989 concerning the provision in the Netherlands of express delivery services [1990] OJ L10/47

[c]2001/176/EC: Commission Decision of 21 December 2000 concerning proceedings pursuant to Article 86 of the EC Treaty in relation to the provision of certain new postal services with a guaranteed day- or time-certain delivery in Italy [2001] OJ L63/59

[d]COMP/F-1/39.562: Commission Decision of 7 October 2008 on the Slovakian law on hybrid mail services [2008] OJ C322/10

in its Decision 90/456, it found that the opening international express mail courier service in the Netherlands would not jeopardise the financial viability of the SGEI operation because of its insignificant share in the total volume of the postal operation (0.00039%). Meanwhile, with a steady growth of market share in the international mail market (35%), the SGEI operator was in a solid position to face competition. Therefore, the Commission concluded that the derogation was not applicable and the international express courier service in the Netherlands must be opened to competition. Other factors may also suggest the lack of economic necessity to maintain the exclusive right for the provision of SGEI. This is summarised in Table 6.2.

The Decision was upheld by the General Court of the EU and also by the EUCJ in the appeal procedure. T-556/08 - Slovenská pošta v Commission. http://curia.europa.eu/juris/liste.jsf?num=T-556/08&language=en#; Case C-293/15 P, Slovenská pošta a.s. v European Commission. http://curia.europa.eu/juris/liste.jsf?num=C-293/15&language=en.

Meanwhile, it was the Member States that had the burden of proving the EAC test was satisfied. Under the doctrine of limitation of supply and the extension of dominant position, it was very likely that a postal monopoly would be found incompatible with the Treaty. As a consequence, Member States increasingly have to discharge such obligation in order to maintain such exclusive rights in the postal sector. If a Member State fails to prove it is necessary to maintain the exclusive right for SGEI, the Commission will conclude that the SGEI derogation is not applicable and that therefore Article 106(1) is breached by the Member State.[95] This is the very case in the Decision COMP/F-1/39.562, where Slovak failed to provide economic evidence regarding the cost of universal postal service and the impact of the liberalisation of hybrid mail services.

The implications are significant: Article 106 has effectively become a stick in the hand of the Commission to push Member States to withdraw exclusive rights in the postal services sector. In particular, in newly emerged service markets such as express mail services and hybrid mail services, it would be very difficult for Member States to extend postal monopoly beyond traditional postal services. Using Article 106, the Commission has effectively confined postal monopoly structure within traditional basic postal services. This power is significant, especially when it was still difficult to reach a consensus on liberalisation during the legislative process.

6.4.2 Pro-liberalisation Interpretation of Directive 97/67 by the Court

As discussed earlier, the text of the Directive 97/67 itself has very limited liberalisation effect. It still allows Member States to grant exclusive rights in certain areas of the postal service sector. However, this freedom was greatly constrained by the Court when it was asked to interpret Directive 97/67 by national courts.

This is well-illustrated in the *International Mail Spain* case.[96] The case was concerned with cross-border mail services. Directive 97/67 explicitly allows the Member States to grant exclusive rights to SGEI providers over this area of the market. Spain utilised this option and reserved cross-border postal service for letters and postcards to its public postal operator. In this main proceeding, International

[95] The Commission's Decision against Slovak offers a very good example. In its decision the Commission first found that Slovak was in breach of Article 106(1) because it extended the exclusive right from traditional letter service to hybrid mail service. Though Slovak proposed some data to justify it under SGEI derogation, the Commission regarded such data as not reliable or sufficient. It concluded that the Slovakian law was incompatible with the Treaty and must be amended: COMP/F-1/39.562: Commission Decision of 7 October 2008 on the Slovakian law on hybrid mail services [2008] OJ C322/10.

[96] Case C-162/06 *International Mail Spain SL v Administración del Estado and Correos* [2007] ECR I-9911.

Mail Spain, as a private commercial operator, provided cross-border postal services for postcards in main Spanish tourist locations. It was fined and prohibited from carrying out such business because of its breach of Spanish postal legislation. The Court was asked whether the reservation of cross-border mail service by Spanish postal legislation was compatible with Directive 97/67.

In its Judgment, the Court took the objective of the Directive into consideration, i.e. 'gradual and controlled opening of postal service to competition'.[97] The key lies in the application of the necessity test under Article 106(2) SGEI derogation. It essentially adopted a pro-market approach, by significantly reducing the discretion of the Member State in two ways.

First, it explicitly ruled that the Member States have the burden of proof to prove the necessity test.[98] Secondly, the criteria under the necessity test are very strict and difficult to meet. The wording of the Judgment reads as follows:

> Article 7(2) of Directive 97/67 is to be interpreted as allowing Member States to reserve cross-border mail to the universal postal service provider only in so far as they establish
>
> – (1) that, *in the absence of such a reservation, achievement of that universal service would be precluded*, or
>
> – (2) that reservation is necessary to enable that service to be carried out under economically acceptable condition.[99] (emphasis added)

The Court did not articulate how these conditions were to be applied in practice.[100] These conditions were left to the Spanish Court to apply. What is certain is that, following the Commission's practice,[101] it was very likely that Spain would fail to fulfil the test. The reason was that the Spanish public postal operator's competitive position on the market was very strong. Meanwhile, cross-border postal services accounted for only a small portion of its operations in terms of both traffic and revenue. Therefore, opening up this part of the sector would not threaten its provision of SGEIs.

---

[97] Directive 97/67, Recital 8.

[98] In the *Corbeau* case in 1993, the Court ruled that Article 106(2) permits the grant of exclusive right by the Member States insofar as restrictions on competition, or even the exclusion of all competition, are necessary to ensure the performance of an SGEI task: Case C-320/91 *Paul Corbeau* [1993] ECR I-2533.

[99] Case C-162/06 *International Mail Spain SL v Administración del Estado and Correos* [2007] ECR I-9911, para 50.

[100] According to this case, Member States can satisfy the necessity test by proving that either one of the two scenarios is met. What is worthy of attention is the fact that the standard under scenario (1) is much higher than that under scenario (2). Under scenario (1), Member States need to compare different means for the provision of SGEI and choose the least restrictive one. This would suggest that the exclusive right is not justified because it is the most restrictive mechanism for SGEI provision and there are less restrictive means without the grant exclusive rights to secure SGEI provision, such as direct public funding without granting an exclusive right. By contrast, under scenario (2) it is assumed that the grant of the exclusive rights is a proper mechanism for SGEI funding.

[101] 90/456/EEC: Commission Decision of 1 August 1990 concerning the provision in Spain of international express courier services [1990] OJ L233/19.

6.4.3 *The Shrinking and Final Abolition of Exclusive Rights*

The EU adopted the so-called controlled and gradual liberalisation approach. In its Directives, it stated that the reserved area is 'necessary to ensure the maintenance of universal service'.[102] It has never been clear how this necessity test was applied by the EU in its postal legislation. In fact, the EU had been very generous towards the grant of exclusive rights. Its first liberalisation Directive 97/67 in 1997 had a very limited liberalisation effect. By allowing a reserved area over postal service for letters weighing less than 350 g and priced less than 5 times the public tariff, it is estimated that only 3% of the market was opened up to competition by the Directive.

By delaying the liberalisation process, the EU essentially gave the public postal operators enough time to adjust to a new market environment. By 2000, most of them were making a significant amount of profit. On the other hand, they were still the dominant players on the traditional letter market, with a market share of 84%, while expanding into the new courier and express mail service with a market share of 40%.[103]

It is submitted that the pace of liberalisation was a political one.[104] The key issue was not how this necessity test was applied, but what was an acceptable solution for all stakeholders.[105] It took another two Directives to abolish all exclusive rights: first, Directive 2002/39 reduced the scope of exclusive rights further (to 100 g and less than 3 times the public tariff from 1 January 2003, and 50 g and less than 2.5 times from 1 January 2006);[106] and second, Directive 2008/6/EC required the

[102] Directive 97/67/EC of the European Parliament and of the Council of 15 December 1997 on common rules for the development of the Internal Market of Community postal services and the improvement of quality of service [1998] OJ L15/14.

The wording remains the same in the following amending Directives:

(1) Directive 2002/39/EC of the European Parliament and of the Council of 10 June 2002 amending Directive 97/67/EC with regard to the further opening of Community postal services to competition[2002] OJ L176/21;
(2) Directive 2008/6/EC of the European Parliament and of the Council of 20 February 2008 amending Directive 97/67/EC with regard to the full accomplishment of the Internal Market of Community postal services [2008] OJ L52/3.

[103] Commission of the European Communities, 41st Commission Report to the European Parliament and the Council on the application of the Postal Directive, COM (2002) 632 final, 25.11.2002.

[104] Von Danwitz 2002.

[105] Griffiths 2000.

[106] Directive 2002/39/EC of the European Parliament and of the Council of 10 June 2002 amending Directive 97/67/EC with regard to the further opening to competition of Community postal services [2002] OJ L176/21.

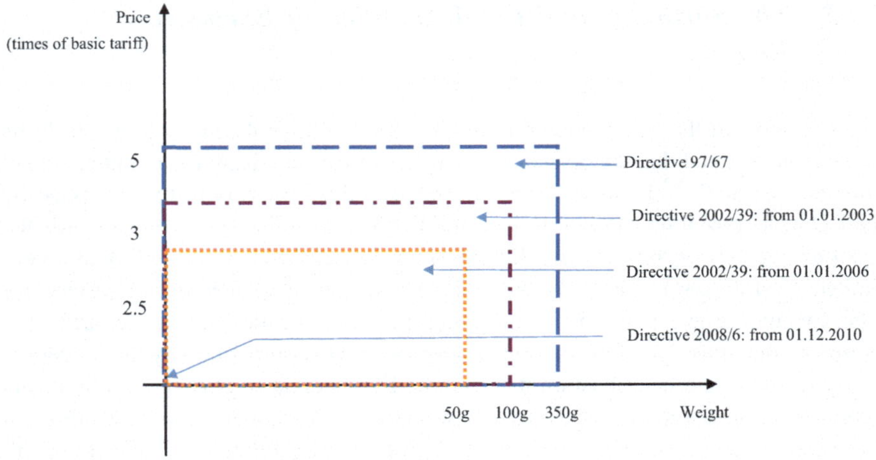

Fig. 6.2 The shrinking scope of exclusive rights in the postal sector. *Source* The author

Member States to withdraw all exclusive rights in the postal sector from 31 December 2010.[107] The shrinking scope of postal monopoly is illustrated in Fig. 6.2.

6.5 Funding SGEIs in Competitive Postal Markets and State Aid Law

6.5.1 SGEI Funding Mechanisms After Market Liberalisation

The final liberalisation of the postal sector means that the Member States are not allowed to grant exclusive rights to fund universal postal services.[108] The postal Directive[109] draws lessons from the EU's experience in the telecommunications

[107] The withdrawal of exclusive rights does not necessarily mean market competition will develop in reality: Jonsson and Selander 2006; Burns et al. 2002.

It also grants a derogation for certain Member States and allows them to maintain postal monopoly until 31 December 2012: Directive 2008/6/EC of the European Parliament and of the Council of 20 February 2008 amending Directive 97/67/EC with regard to the full accomplishment of the Internal Market of Community postal services [2008] OJ L52/3, Article 3.

[108] Bergum 2008; Eccles 2011.

[109] Directive 97/67.

sector[110] and offers three alternative options for the funding of USO in the postal sector:[111]

(1) the provider and the amount of USO to be decided through public procurement procedures;
(2) sector compensation fund through which the net cost of USO is shared by all postal service providers/users; or
(3) direct compensation from public funds.

What is interesting to observe is the fact that the first two options do not have much practical significance in the postal sector. *Public procurement* is almost irrelevant for the provision of USO in the postal sector.[112] This is because USO provision requires a nationwide postal network and permanent standby presence across the country. Across Member States, it is only the former postal incumbent that can fulfil this requirement. This essentially means no alternative provider exists, which deprives public procurement of any value.[113] Consequently, public procurement has not been used in Member States for the provision of USO in the postal sector.[114] In practice, it is still the former incumbent that is designated as the universal postal service provider without public procurement.

Meanwhile, *sectoral compensation fund* also has very limited application in the postal sector.[115] Many Member States have rules on the possibility of establishing a sectoral compensation fund as a funding mechanism in its postal legislation.[116] Until now, only Italy has activated its postal compensation fund;[117] but its contribution to USO funding is insignificant.[118] The majority of USO funding in Italy still comes from public funds.

[110] Comandini and Lettieri 2001.

[111] During market liberalisation, exclusive rights were allowed to provide funding for USO provision. Alternative funding mechanisms (instead of exclusive rights) became an issue only after full market liberalisation: Directive 2008/6/EC of the European Parliament and of the Council of 20 February 2008 amending Directive 97/67/EC with regard to the full accomplishment of the Internal Market of Community postal services [2008] OJ L52/3.

[112] Van Der Horst 2005.

[113] Calzada et al. 2010.

[114] The only example is found in New Zealand, where contractors were selected through public tender for the provision of rural delivery service: Oxera Consulting Ltd. 2007.

[115] Universal Postal Union, 'Postal Regulation: Principles and Orientation' (Bern 2002).

[116] Including Germany, the Netherlands, Spain, France, Finland, Belgium, Cyprus, Denmark, the UK, Italy, Latvia, Portugal and Slovenia: WIK-Consult 2011; Oxera Consulting Ltd. 2007.

[117] Oxera Consulting Ltd. 2007.

[118] Gautier & Paolini 2011; Consumer Postal Council, 'Universal Postal Service in Major Economies'. https://www.postalconsumers.org/wp-content/uploads/2018/01/June-2015-CPC-Universal-Postal-Service-Report.pdf.

In the postal sector, SGEI funding comes mainly from *public funds*. It involves the direct transfer of state funds to the SGEI provider. It is against this background that the issue of state aid has arisen. The Commission has been using the state aid rules to examine state funding of SGEIs in the postal sector.

6.5.2 The Application of State Aid Law in the Postal Sector

The Commission has not adopted specific rules for the postal sector. Without such rules, it is the *Altmark* criteria and the Commission's subsequent Monti and Almunia Packages that are applicable. Its Decisions in the postal sector provide a good example of how these rules are applied and what the implications are.

On the issue of *notification obligation*, besides the *Altmark* criteria, the Almunia Package contains two other documents that exempt the Member States from such obligation.[119] However, they are not applicable in the postal sector. On the one hand, the *de minimis* Regulation 360/2012[120] granted a derogation from the notification obligation for SGEI funding not exceeding EUR 500,000 for three years. The postal sector is very unlikely to be covered by the Regulation because of the sheer amount of funding involved. On the other hand, Commission Decision 2012/21 also grants exemption from the notification obligation for certain compatible SGEI funding.[121] The postal sector is not included in the list.

Consequently, it is still the *Altmark* criteria that are applied to examine the issue of definition in the postal sector. In the Commission's practice, the application of the *Altmark* criteria has turned out to be fairly easy and straightforward in the postal sector. [122] In 12 out of its 13 Decisions, the Commission found that *Altmark* (4) has not been fulfilled simply because: (1) the Member State has not used a public tender procedure or (2) the Member State has not discharged its burden of proof on a typical well-run market undertaking.[123]

---

[119] On the issue of notification, the Monti Package included a Decision that exempted certain SGEI funding from the notification obligation because they are *compatible* state aid. The Almunia Package updated the Decision and added a new Regulation that exempts certain SGEI funding from notification because they do not affect intra-community trade owing to the insignificant amount of funding. Because the Monti Package was repealed, here the author only looks at rules in the Almunia Package.

[120] Commission Regulation (EU) No 360/2012 of 25 April 2012 on the application of Articles 107 and 108 of the Treaty on the Functioning of the European Union to *de minimis* aid granted to undertakings providing services of general economic interest [2012] OJ L114/8.

[121] Commission Decision of 20 December 2011 on the application of Article 106(2) of the Treaty on the Functioning of the European Union to state aid in the form of public service compensation granted to certain undertakings entrusted with the operation of services of general economic interest [2012] OJ L7/3.

[122] Van Der Horst 2005.

[123] The Commission's Decisions applying the *Altmark* criteria will be summarised in the form 'the Commission's Decisions Applying State Aid Rules to SGEI Funding in the Postal Sector after the *Altmark* Case' at the end of this section.

The reason is that in the postal sector public tender procedures are not practical. Across Member States, it is still the former incumbents that are the only operators that have maintained a country-wide universal postal network and that therefore have the capacity to provide SGEI tasks on a universal basis. In practice, Member States entrust SGEI tasks to former incumbents without a public tender procedure, through designation, licence or contract.[124]

Meanwhile, the second scenario, i.e. comparison with a typical well-run market undertaking, is also extremely difficult to satisfy in the postal sector.[125] The reason lies in the lack of benchmark market undertaking in the postal sector.[126] The Commission argues that former incumbents cannot be regarded as typical well-run undertakings because they had been under the protection of exclusive rights. This essentially means that such 'efficient undertaking' is nowhere to be found.[127] This explains why, in most Decisions, the Member States have failed to prove this criterion is satisfied.

Altmark does not deal with the issue of compatibility. Failure to satisfy the *Altmark* criteria only means that the funding measure constitutes state aid and that therefore it falls within the scope of the EU state aid control regime. It does not mean that SGEI funding is incompatible with the Treaty. Instead, its compatibility is subject to review by the Commission, based on the necessity test under SGEI contained in Article 106(2). The Court has long established that for the SGEI derogation to apply, three conditions must be met: (1) there must be a clearly defined SGEI task; (2) the SGEI task must have been entrusted by public authorities; and (3) a necessity test must be satisfied.[128] The Commission's approach to the application of Article 106(2) is found in its two frameworks contained in the Monti and Almunia Packages.[129] While the 2005 Framework was largely a codification of existing rules and practices, its 2012 Framework followed all these rules and also introduced some new interesting developments.

---

[124] Calzada et al. 2010.

[125] In the Commission's practice in the postal sector, there is only one decision in which it concluded that this scenario was met and concluded the SGEI funding measure did not constitute state aid: State Aid C49/2006 on a state aid scheme implemented by Italy to remunerate Poste Italiane for distributing postal savings certificates, C (2008) 5585 final, 21 October 2008.

[126] Eccles 2011.

[127] Comandini et al. 2010; Fratini and Filpo 2006.

[128] Case C-320/91 *Paul Corbeau* [1993] ECR I-2533. In the context of state aid law, the issue was first discussed by the Court in the *FFSA* case. Case T-106/95 *Federation Française des Societes d'Assurances (Ffsa) and Others v E.C. Commission* [1997] ECR II-229.

[129] Community framework for state aid in the form of public service compensation [2005] OJ C297/4;

Communication from the Commission, European Union framework for state aid in the form of public service compensation [2012] OJ C8/15.

Table 6.3 The Commission's decisions applying state aid rule to SGEI funding in the postal sector after the *Altmark* Case

Decisions	Valid SGEI tasks	The issue of definition	The issue of compatibility
C21/2005[a] (15.12.2009) Poland	(1) Universal postal services; (2) universal postal network: a post office should be operated for every 7000 inhabitants in urban areas and for every 65 km^2 in rural areas; and (3) handling of postal money orders	*Altmark* (4) is not satisfied	No over-compensation —compatible
N642/05[b] (22.11.2006) Sweden	Basic cashier services, including bank deposits and withdrawals, payment in and out, daily business receipt management and money orders	*Altmark* (4) is not satisfied	Compatible
NN24/08[c] (30.04.2008) Italy	Universal postal services	*Altmark* (4) is not satisfied	SGEI funding does not exceed its costs—compatible
C49/2006[d] (21.10.2008) Italy	Placement of postal saving certificate[e]	*Altmark* criteria are fulfilled—not state aid	
SA 33989[f] (20.11.2012) Italy	Obligations to offer reduced tariffs to publishers, not-for-profit organisation and electoral materials	*Altmark* (4) is not satisfied	SGEI funding does not exceed its costs—compatible
C36/2007[g] (25.01.2012) Germany	(1) Universal postal service; and (2) universal postal network: at least 12,000 post offices throughout Germany	*Altmark* (4) is not satisfied.	SGEI funding is below its costs—compatible
SA 14588[h] (25.01.2012) Belgium	(1) Universal postal network; (2) postal services, which include universal postal service; distribution of newspapers, periodicals, electoral material; special tariffs for NGOs; free postal services for royal and other special correspondence; international postal services; (3) universal Financial services; (4) sales of stamps; and (5) other public services, including social role of the postman, appropriate information to the public, printing and delivery of electronic mail, message certification services, service carried out for state accountants, sale of revenue and penalty stamps, cooperation in the distribution of voting packages and ballot papers	Constitutes state aid	SGEI funding led to over-compensation and therefore incompatible
SA 31006[i] (02.05.2013) Belgium		*Altmark* (4) is not satisfied	No over-compensation —compatible
SA 14588[j] (25.01.2012) Belgium	(1) Universal postal network; (2) postal services, which include universal postal service; distribution of newspapers, periodicals, electoral material; special tariffs for NGOs; free postal services for royal and other special correspondence; international postal services; (3) universal financial services; (4) sales of stamps; and (5) other public services, including social role of the postman, appropriate information to the public, printing and delivery of electronic mail, message certification services, service carried out for state accountants, sale of revenue and penalty stamps, cooperation in the distribution of voting packages and ballot papers	Constitutes state aid	SGEI funding led to over-compensation and therefore incompatible
SA 31006[k] (02.05.2013) Belgium		*Altmark* (4) is not satisfied	No over-compensation —compatible

(continued)

Table 6.3 (continued)

Decisions	Valid SGEI tasks	The issue of definition	The issue of compatibility
N166/2005[l] (22.2.2006) N822/2006[m] (07.03.2007) N388/2007[n] (28.11.2007) N508/2010[o] (23.03.2011) SA 33054[p] (28.03.2012) the UK	(1) Rural postal network requirements, including 84% of the people in rural areas to live within a mile of a post office and over two-thirds of villages with between 500 and 1000 inhabitants to have a post office; and (2) SGEIs through the postal network, including postal services, universal access to basic cash and banking facilities and government savings instruments, universal cash payments for public utilities, processing of social benefits, tax payments, national identity and licensing schemes	*Altmark* (4) is not satisfied	No over-compensation —compatible

Source The author

[a]2010/815/EU: Commission Decision of 15 December 2009 on state aid C 21/05 (ex PL 45/04), which Poland plans to implement for Poczta Polska as compensation of universal postal service obligations [2010] OJ L347/29'

[b]State Aid N 642/05—Sweden Compensation to Posten AB for providing basic payment and cash facilities services, C (2006) 5481 fin, 22.11.2006

[c]State Aid NN 24/08—Italy Poste Italiane SpA State compensation for universal postal service obligations 2006–2008, C (2008) 1606 fin, 30.04.2008

[d]State Aid C 49/2006 on a state aid scheme implemented by Italy to remunerate Poste Italiane for distributing postal savings certificates, C (2008) 5585 final, 21.10.2008

[e]It is a financial instrument for fund raising with a guaranteed payment by the State. It allows the saver to request repayment at a predetermined price at any time during the life of the certificate

[f]State Aid SA.33989 (2012/NN)—Italy State compensation for the delivery of the universal service over 2009–2011; State compensation for reduced tariffs offered to publishers, not-for-profit organisations and electoral candidates over 2009–2011, C (2012) 8230 final, 20.11.2012

[g]State Aid C 36/2007 Measures implemented by Germany for Deutsche Post AG, 25.01.2012

[h]2012/321/EU: Commission Decision of 25 January 2012 on the measure SA.14588 (C 20/09) implemented by Belgium in favour of De Post-La Poste (now Bpost) [2012] OJ L170/1

[i]State Aid SA.31006 (2013/N)—Belgium State compensations to Bpost for the delivery of public services over 2013–2015, C (2013) 1909 final, 02.05.2013

[j]2012/321/EU: Commission Decision of 25 January 2012 on the measure SA.14588 (C 20/09) implemented by Belgium in favour of De Post-La Poste (now Bpost) [2012] OJ L170/1

[k]State Aid SA.31006 (2013/N)—Belgium State compensations to Bpost for the delivery of public services over 2013–2015, C (2013) 1909 final, 02.05.2013

[l]State Aid N 166/2005—United Kingdom Government rural network support funding to Post Office Limited (POL) for 2006–2008, C (2006) 434 final, 22.02.2006

[m]State Aid N 822/2006—United Kingdom Debt payment funding to Post Office Limited (POL) for 2007–2008, C (2007) 653 final, 07.03.2007

[n]State Aid N 388/2007—United Kingdom Post Office Limited (POL) transformation programme, C (2007) 5623 final, 28.11.2007

[o]State Aid N 508/2010—United Kingdom Post Office Limited (POL): continuation of network subsidy payment and working capital facility, C (2011) 1770 final, 23.03.2011

[p]State Aid SA.33054—United Kingdom Post Office Limited (POL): compensation for net costs incurred to keep a non-commercially viable network for the period 2012–15 and the continuation of a working capital facility, C (2012) 1905 final, 28.03.2012

The Commission's Decisions evaluating the compatibility of SGEI funding will be examined in the next three sections. These Decisions will be first summarised in Table 6.3 above. They offer a very good example of the intricate relationship between the *Altmark* criteria and SGEI derogation under Article 106(2). In 11 out of its 13 Decisions, the Commission found that SGEI funding measures were compatible with the Treaty (even though they did not satisfy the *Altmark* criteria).[130] The essential criterion is that the amount of funding must not exceed the costs of SGEI provision.

6.5.3 Wide Range of SGEI Tasks in the Postal Sector

On the issue of what constitutes valid SGEIs, the Commission largely respects the wide freedom of Member States on this issue. It does not apply a *market failure test*.[131] The Commission often assumes the validity of the SGEI tasks as defined by the Member States without any discussion on the non-economic values behind. A rare example is found in a Decision concerning Italy.[132] In the Decision, the Italian government required its national postal operator to offer reduced postal tariff for publishers, not-for-profit organisations and electoral materials. The Commission recognised this task as a valid SGEI and expressly mentioned the underlying non-economic values including 'the pluralism of press, promoting democracy and supporting officially recognised not-for-profit organisations'.[133]

In practice, the actual SGEI tasks entrusted to public postal operators vary significantly across Member States.[134] Besides their traditional role as the provider of universal postal services and the operator of the universal postal network, public postal operators are often entrusted with the provision of basic financial services through the network. This is the case, for example, in Poland, Sweden, Belgium, the UK and Italy.

In addition, certain functions of public authorities are also entrusted to the postal operator. For example, in the UK, government entrusts the Royal Mail to process

---

[130] The conclusions of the Commission in the remaining two Decisions are as follows:

(1) In Decision C 49/2006, the Commission found that the *Altmark* criteria were satisfied and that therefore the measure did not constitute state aid.
State Aid C 49/2006 on a state aid scheme implemented by Italy to remunerate Poste Italiane for distributing postal savings certificates, C (2008) 5585 final, 21.10.2008.

(2) In decision SA.14588, the Commission found that the funding measure led to overcompensation and was therefore incompatible with the Treaty.
2012/321/EU: Commission Decision of 25 January 2012 on the measure SA.14588 (C 20/09) implemented by Belgium in favour of De Post-La Poste (now Bpost) [2012] OJ L170/1.

[131] This approach is very similar to that in the public service broadcasting sector. But it is in sharp contrast to that in the broadband sector, where a very stringent market failure test has been adopted by the Commission. The Commission's Decisions in the public service broadcasting and broadband sectors are discussed in Sect. 4.4 of Chap. 4.

[132] State Aid SA.33989 (2012/NN)—Italy State compensation for the delivery of the universal service over 2009–2011; State compensation for reduced tariffs offered to publishers, not-for-profit organisations and electoral candidates over 2009–2011, C (2012) 8230 final, 20.11.2012,

[133] Ibid., para 78.

[134] For the wide range of SGEI tasks recognised by the Commission as valid, see the form 'the Commission's Decisions Applying State Aid Rule to SGEI Funding in the Postal Sector after the *Altmark* Case' on the preceding page.

social benefits, tax payments, national identity and licensing schemes. A similar example can also be found in Belgium, where the public postal operator is entrusted with disseminating information to the public; to carry out services for state accountants; to sell revenue and penalty stamps; and to distribute voting packages and ballot papers. These tasks have all been regarded as valid SGEI tasks by the Commission without question.

On this issue, *a market failure test* has been introduced by the Commission in the 2012 Framework.[135] The Commission argues that:

> Member States *cannot* attach specific public service obligations to services that are already provided or can be provided satisfactorily and under conditions, such as price, objective quality characteristics, continuity and access to the service, consistent with the public interest, as defined by the State, by undertakings operating *under normal market conditions.*[136] (emphasis added)

Meanwhile, it indicates that the Commission would not apply such a strict market failure test as in the broadband sector. Its assessment is only limited to a manifest error test:

> As for the question whether a service can be provided by the market, the Commission's assessment is limited to checking whether the Member States' definition is vitiated by a *manifest error*, unless provisions of Union law provide a stricter standard.[137] (emphasis added)

It is not clear how this new market failure test will be applied by the Commission. What is certain is that the Commission enjoys wide discretion on this issue. Its practice in the postal service sector shows that the effect of this market failure test is very limited. The Commission's Decisions concerning SGEIs in Belgium and the UK offer very good examples.[138] The same SGEI tasks have been

---

[135] Communication from the Commission: European Union framework for state aid in the form of public service compensation [2012] OJ C8/15.

[136] Ibid., para 13.

[137] Ibid.

[138] Regarding Belgium, Decision SA.14588 was made before the introduction of this market failure test, and Decision SA.31006 was made afterwards: 2012/321/EU: Commission Decision of 25 January 2012 on the measure SA.14588 (C 20/09) implemented by Belgium in favour of De Post-La Poste (now Bpost) [2012] OJ L170/1; State Aid SA.31006 (2013/N)—Belgium State compensations to Bpost for the delivery of public services over 2013–2015, C (2013) 1909 final, 02.05.2013.

Regarding the UK, four Decisions were made before the introduction of this market failure test, including:

(1) State Aid N 166/2005—United Kingdom Government rural network support funding to Post Office Limited (POL) for 2006–2008, C (2006) 434 final, 22.02.2006;
(2) State Aid N 822/2006—United Kingdom Debt payment funding to Post Office Limited (POL) for 2007–2008, C (2007) 653 final, 07.03.2007;
(3) State Aid N 388/2007—United Kingdom Post Office Limited (POL) transformation programme, C (2007) 5623 final, 28.11.2007;
(4) State Aid N 508/2010—United Kingdom Post Office Limited (POL): continuation of network subsidy payment and working capital facility, C (2011) 1770 final, 23.03.2011.

dealt with by the Commission under both the 2005 Framework and the 2012 Framework. The adoption of the above market failure test did not make any difference to the results of the Decisions. In fact, the Commission did not even mention this market failure test at all.

6.5.4 The Crucial Role of Entrustment Act

On the second condition of the SGEI derogation under Article 106(2), namely entrustment of SGEIs from public authorities, the Commission's approach under the 2012 Framework remains essentially the same as that under its 2005 Framework. In this respect, the EU does not prescribe what format the relevant national entrustment act should take—that shall be decided by the Member States. Typical examples include legislation, administrative regulation, licence and contract.

This does not mean that the entrustment act is of little importance. On the contrary, it has become crucial in the application of Article 106(2). The reason lies in the fact that Member States have very diverse arrangements on the content and scope of SGEIs entrusted to the postal operator. In the Commission' practice, the entrustment act has become the very basis for ascertaining the scope of SGEIs, and, consequently, for calculating the costs of SGEI provision.

The importance of the entrustment act in the compatibility test is well-illustrated in the Commission Decision concerning Belgium.[139] In Belgium, a wide range of SGEI tasks have been assigned to the public postal operator, Bpost, through management contract, which specifies what constitute SGEI tasks and what SGEI tasks would be funded by the State. Four contracts were signed between 1992 and 2010.

In its Decision, the Commission examined these contracts separately. It found that in the first management contract (1992–1996), all SGEI tasks, without distinction, were covered by State funding, which included universal postal service and universal financial services. By contrast, in the other three management contracts, universal postal services were not included in the list of SGEI tasks eligible for state funding. Therefore, when calculating the cost of SGEIs, the Commission included the cost of universal postal service provision under the first management

---

One Decision concerning the UK was made after the introduction of this market failure test, that is:

State Aid SA.33054—United Kingdom Post Office Limited (POL): compensation for net costs incurred to keep a non-commercially viable network for the period 2012–15 and the continuation of a working capital facility, C (2012) 1905 final, 28.03.2012.

[139] 2012/321/EU: Commission Decision of 25 January 2012 on the measure SA.14588 (C 20/09) implemented by Belgium in favour of De Post-La Poste (now Bpost) [2012] OJ L170/1.

contract but excluded it under the other three contracts. This significantly reduced the amount of necessary funding. This was the very reason why the Commission found that Bpost was over-compensated by 415 million Euros, which must therefore be recovered by Belgium.

6.5.5 New Efficiency Test in the 2012 Framework

The issue of over-compensation has been the very focus of the Commission in the evaluation of the compatibility of SGEI funding under the EU state aid regime. This has been elaborated in its 2005 Framework. This basic principle has remained unchanged in the latest 2012 Framework, which only explains it in more detail. In practice, this involves a very complicated economic exercise, demanding substantial economic expertise.[140] On the one hand, one needs to calculate the net avoided cost of SGEI provision.[141] On the other hand, it also involves the calculation of any benefits (including intangible benefits) and revenues from SGEI provision. What make it more difficult is that SGEI provider is also allowed to gain a reasonable profit. Such an exercise can be very controversial in practice.[142] The result often depends on the benchmark and methodology used in the calculation.

What is worthy of special attention is the fact the 2012 Framework has added two new conditions into the compatibility evaluation, which essentially echoes the efficiency requirement under *Altmark* (4). The first one is an efficiency incentive: it requires Member States to introduce incentives for the efficient provision of SGEI.[143] From the Commission's practice in the postal sector so far, this

---

[140] Eccles 2011; Gautier and Paolini 2011.

[141] The 2012 Framework defines 'net avoided cost' as follows:

> Under the net avoided cost methodology, the net cost necessary, or expected to be necessary, to discharge the public service obligations is calculated as the difference between the net cost for the provider of operating with the public service obligation and the net cost or profit for the same provider of operating without that obligation.

Communication from the Commission, European Union framework for state aid in the form of public service compensation [2012] OJ C8/15.

Other methods have been proposed by economists for the calculation of the costs of USO provision, including entry pricing and profitability cost: Bergum 2008; Gautier and Paolini 2011.

[142] Universal Postal Union, 'Postal Regulation: Principles and Orientation' (Bern 2002) http://www.prc.gov/PRC-Docs/aboutprc/IPR/UPU%20Postal%20Regulation%20publication.pdf; Fratini and Filpo 2006.

[143] In the 2012 Framework, the Commission provides two examples on how this requirement can be satisfied:

> Member States can define upfront a fixed compensation level which anticipates and incorporates the efficiency gains that the undertaking can be expected to make over the lifetime of the entrustment act. Alternatively, Member States can define productive efficiency targets in the entrustment act whereby the level of compensation is made dependent upon the extent to which the targets have been met.

requirement seems easy to satisfy and does not create much of a burden for Member States. A good example is found in its Decision concerning funding for rural postal networks in the UK. The Commission concluded that the efficiency incentive test was met simply because the amount of funding was a fixed upfront one, which is less than the expected net costs of the SGEI.[144] Another example is found in its Decision regarding Belgium, which allowed the SGEI provider to keep 67% of the realised efficiency gain under an efficiency sharing mechanism. The Commission accepted this mechanism as fulfilling the efficiency incentive test.[145]

The second new condition to the compatibility test introduced by the 2012 Framework is more problematic, namely compliance with EU public procurement rules. The wording suggests that such requirement is compulsory. Failure to comply with this condition would mean that SGEI funding is incompatible with the Treaty and would be prohibited. It points out that:

> Aid will be considered compatible with the Internal Market on the basis of Article 106(2) of the Treaty *only* where the responsible authorities, when entrusting the provision of the service to the undertaking in question, has complied or commits to comply with the applicable Union rules in the area of public procurement. [....] Aid that does not comply with such rules and requirements is considered to affect the development of trade to an extent that would *be contrary to the interests of the Union* within the meaning of Article 106(2) of the Treaty.[146] (emphasis added)

These implications are significant. It would further limit the freedom of Member States and force them to put SGEI provision into tender. The reason lies in the fact that if Member States entrust SGEIs to undertakings through public service contracts or concessions, they are subject to EU public procurement Directives. Even in areas where no specific procurement Directives are applicable, they must comply with general principles of EU law, including transparency, equal treatment and non-discrimination.

Its effects have been felt in the postal sector. The Commission's Decisions regarding postal SGEIs in the UK[147] and Belgium[148] are very good examples. In

---

Communication from the Commission: European Union framework for state aid in the form of public service compensation [2012] OJ C8/15, paras 40–41.

[144] State Aid SA.33054—United Kingdom Post Office Limited (POL): compensation for net costs incurred to keep a non-commercially viable network for the period 2012–15 and the continuation of a working capital facility, C (2012) 1905 final, 28.03.2012.

[145] State Aid SA.31006 (2013/N)—Belgium State compensations to Bpost for the delivery of public services over 2013–2015, C (2013) 1909 final, 02.05.2013.

[146] Communication from the Commission: European Union framework for state aid in the form of public service compensation [2012] OJ C8/15, para 19.

[147] State Aid SA.33054—United Kingdom Post Office Limited (POL): compensation for net costs incurred to keep a non-commercially viable network for the period 2012–15 and the continuation of a working capital facility, C (2012) 1905 final, 28.03.2012.

[148] State Aid SA.31006 (2013/N)—Belgium State compensations to Bpost for the delivery of public services over 2013-2015, C (2013) 1909 final, 02.05.2013.

the UK, Royal Mail was entrusted with the SGEI tasks via an entrustment letter and a funding agreement. The Commission argued that it constituted a public service contract and that therefore public procurement Directive 2004/18 is applicable.[149] However, in the postal sector, the Directive would not apply to its full extent. Because of its unique network nature, it would be covered by the sole provider exemption in the Directive. In its Decision, the Commission points out that:

> At present, POL [note: Postal Office Ltd, which owns and operates the postal network, is a subsidiary of the Royal Mail Group.] is the only operator whose network and contractual relationships actually satisfy the requirements for the provision of the network SGEI, as described in the entrustment. In these circumstances, the Commission considers that the negotiated procedure without prior publication, which is followed to entrust POL with the network SGEI, is justified under Article 1(1)(b) of Directive 2004/18 and therefore can be considered compliant with EU public procurement rules.[150]

This does not necessarily mean that the effect is modest, but potentially far-reaching. The underlying logic of the Commission is that the incumbent is the only candidate because the SGEI in question can be provided only through its unique network. This implies, on the one hand, that a competitive tender procedure would be desirable if other operators have developed such networks and are capable of SGEI provision, and, on the other hand, that if a particular SGEI product can be disassociated from the network, it is not covered by the sole provider exemption. In such circumstances, Member States are obliged to organise its provision in full compliance with EU procurement Directives.

This is well-illustrated in the Commission's Decision concerning Belgium postal SGEI.[151] In this Decision, Bpost was entrusted with various SGEI tasks under a management contract. In its Decision, the Commission distinguished press distribution SGEI from traditional postal USOs. The reason lies in the fact that the Belgium State required newspapers to be delivered before 7.30 am from Monday to Friday. This meant that press distribution as required by the Belgium State was *time sensitive* and had a *value-added commercial service feature*, which could be potentially provided by private undertakings on the market. The Commission argued that:

---

[149] Directive 2004/18/EC of the European Parliament and of the Council of 31 March 2004 on the coordination of procedures for the award of public works contracts, public supply contracts and public service contracts [2004] OJ L134/114.

Directive 2004/18 was repealed by Directive 2014/24. Directive 2014/24/EU of the European Parliament and of the Council of 26 February 2014 on public procurement and repealing Directive 2004/18/EC [2014] OJ L94/65.

[150] State Aid SA.33054—United Kingdom Post Office Limited (POL): Compensation for net costs incurred to keep a non-commercially viable network for the period 2012–15 and the continuation of a working capital facility, C (2012) 1905 final, 28.03.2012, para 67.

[151] State Aid SA.31006 (2013/N)—Belgium State compensations to Bpost for the delivery of public services over 2013–2015, C (2013) 1909 final, 02.05.2013.

> As regards the press distribution SGEI, which is *not delivered through this unique logistic and retail network*, the Belgian authorities committed to organise a competitive, transparent and non-discriminatory tendering procedure with a view to award a service concession at national level by end of 2014.[152] (emphasis added)

The Commission's influence in pushing Member States to organise SGEI through public procurement is observable. Following the state aid investigation, Belgium would have to organise a public procurement procedure for press distribution SGEI by the end of 2014. The UK has an even more ambitious plan. It is committed to reviewing all its SGEI contracts by the end of 2017 to ensure full compliance with EU public procurement rules.[153] It would be interesting to see if such an exercise will be a satisfactory solution and how the Commission will apply this new condition in the future.

The Commission's approach is problematic and creates further uncertainties. The real benefits of a public tender procedure in the postal sector are still doubtful. Even though the postal market has been open to competition, it is still the former incumbents that are dominant on the market.[154] More importantly, they are often the only operators that maintain an extensive nationwide network in the Member States and are therefore the only candidates for the provision of network-based SGEIs.

Furthermore, organising public procurement for SGEIs in the postal sector is a challenging task.[155] The costs of SGEI provision depend largely on national and even local circumstances. The former incumbent, as the long-term historical provider of SGEI, has a great advantage in this respect. Without a large amount of reliable data, it would be very difficult for new entrants to estimate the costs of SGEI provision and to make sensible bids. This poses great challenges for the Member States in the actual design and organisation of public procurement procedure in the postal sector, given the fact that they have very limited experience in this respect.[156]

6.6 Conclusion

This chapter first reviews the history of the organisation of postal systems. It shows that it had not been organised on the basis of a competitive market. Instead, the State had a dominant influence over its provision. The modern version of postal

[152] Ibid., para 141.

[153] State Aid SA.33054 – United Kingdom Post Office Limited (POL): compensation for net costs incurred to keep a non-commercially viable network for the period 2012–15 and the continuation of a working capital facility, C (2012) 1905 final, 28.03.2012, para 23.

[154] WIK-Consult 2011; Gautier and Paolini 2011.

[155] Comandini and Lettieri 2001; Calzada et al. 2010.

[156] Calzada et al. 2010; Oxera Consulting Ltd 2007.

organisation began to take shape only after Roland Hill's postal reforms in the mid-1800 s. Postal services were provided by entities owned and controlled by the State under the protection of monopoly rights. Postal operations were used by the State to pursue a wide range of public policies, among which universal postal service eventually emerged.

The idea of a universal postal service, i.e. a guaranteed provision of postal services for everyone in society, is often taken for granted. This chapter reveals that it is relatively new: it came into existence only after World War II. Since then, basic postal services began to be associated with human rights, which the State has a responsibility to guarantee.

The provision of universal postal services is often used to justify the national postal incumbents' funding mechanism for USO—the grant of exclusive rights. This study argues that such justification existed only in theory without sound economic analysis. The reason lies in the fact that under the traditional model, it was not possible to work out how much loss was incurred in the provision of the universal postal service.

Similar to that of the telecommunications sector, the EU began to promote market liberalisation and integration policies in the postal sector in the late 1980 s. However, this process was undertaken not via Article 106(3), but via the harmonisation legislation procedure under Article 100. This has profound implications because under the Article 100 procedure the Member States, via the Council, can have a significant influence over the pace and extent of market liberalisation.

In the postal sector, SGEI is also defined through the notion of USO. This study finds that a very different regime on USO has been developed in the postal sector. From the very beginning, the priority of the reform agenda was universal postal service, rather than market liberalisation. On the content and scope of USO, EU law managed to achieve only a minimum level of harmonisation on the scope and quality level of postal services covered by USO. Meanwhile, many issues were left to the Member States to decide, including the density level of the postal network, the scope of the services to be provided over the postal network and the price dimension of the USO.

During the market liberalisation process, the EU assumed the grant of exclusive rights as an appropriate funding mechanism for USO provision. The necessity test under SGEI was applied very generously: the first liberalisation directive, Directive 97/67, opened up only 3% of the postal market to competition.

While it was very difficult to reach a political consensus in the harmonisation legislative process, the EU had been pushing its liberalisation agenda through two other channels. On the one hand, the Commission used its power under Article 106 (3) to make Decisions against individual Member States. It challenged the grant of exclusive rights in the valued-added postal services market. On the other hand, the Court adopted a pro-market approach to the interpretation of Directive 97/67. Both contributed to the adoption of two other pieces of liberalisation legislation: full market liberalisation was finally achieved in 2010.

After liberalisation, the EU drew lessons from its experience in the telecommunications sector and devised three new possible funding mechanisms for USO in the postal sector: through public procurement procedure, sectoral compensation fund, and direct public funding. However, owing to the unique feature of the postal sector, only the third mechanism is the main funding source deployed by the Member States.

The Commission has been using state aid as a control procedure to scrutinise SGEI funding. On the application of the *Altmark* criteria, the Commission adopts a formalist approach, by focusing on its fourth condition. In the postal sector, public tender procedures are not practical because the former incumbent is often the only entity that has the capability to fulfil USOs. Meanwhile, a typical well-run undertaking is nowhere to be found in the postal sector, and the Commission argues that former monopolists cannot be used as benchmark undertakings.

Regarding the application of the SGEI derogation under Article 106(2), this study finds that the Commission applies the necessity test very differently in the postal sector from the way it does in the telecommunications sector. In the postal sector, a wide range of non-economic values have been recognised as legitimate SGEIs. Therefore the Member States enjoy wide freedom in deciding what constitutes SGEIs. The 2012 Framework has introduced a market failure test. However, it seems that its practical effects are very limited.

The focus of the Commission has been to ensure the SGEI funding does not lead to over-compensation. Its 2012 Framework introduced an efficiency test. It began to require the Member States to follow public procurement rules. This would further limit the Member States' freedom in the organisation of SGEI, by pushing them to conduct public tenders. It remains to be seen how it will be applied in the postal sector.

References

Ambrosini X, Boldron F, Roy B (2006) Universal service obligations in the postal sector: economic learnings from cross-country comparisons. In: Crew MA, Kleindorfer PR (eds) Progress toward liberalization of the postal and delivery sector. Springer, Boston

Bergum K (2008) Calculating the net cost of the USO: a practical example from Norway. In: Crew MA, Kleindorfer PR, Campbell JI (eds) Handbook of worldwide postal reform. Edward Elgar Publishing, Cheltenham & Northampton

Borsenberger C, Joram D, Roy B (2011) How many outlets if the USP does not face any USO? A cross-country comparison. In: Crew MA, Kleindorfer PR (eds) Reinventing the postal sector in an electronic age. Edward Elgar Publishing, Cheltenham & Northampton

Brandt T (2007) Liberalisation, privatisation and regulation of postal services in Europe – first international experiences in the run-up to new European regulations. WSI Discussion paper. https://www.boeckler.de/pdf/wsi_pj_piq_post_europe.pdf

Britain L (1992) Competition policy and post and telecommunications. Speech/92/50, Speech of Sir Leon Britain at the Centre for European Policy Studies, Brussels, 19.05.1992. http://europa.eu/rapid/press-release_SPEECH-92-50_en.htm

Burns P, Carslake I, Houpis G (2002) Brand loyalty and limited entry in postal markets. In: Crew MA, Kleindorfer PR (eds), Postal and delivery services: delivering on competition. Springer, Boston

Calzada J, Jaag C, Trinkner U (2010) Universal service auctions in liberalized postal markets. In: Crew MA, Kleindorfer PR, Campbell JI (eds) Heightening competition in the postal and delivery sector. Edward Elgar Publishing, Cheltenham & Northampton

Campbell JI (1993) Couriers and the European postal monopolies: policy challenges of a newly emerging industries. In: Van Schendelen R (ed) National public and private EC lobbying. Dartmouth Publishing, Aldershot & Brookfield

Campbell JI (1995) A review of efforts to develop a new policy framework for postal services in the European Union. In: Crew MA, Kleindorfer PR (eds) Commercialization of postal and delivery services: national and international perspectives. Springer, Boston

Campbell JI (2000) Global postal reform movement. In: Hudgins EL (ed) Mail at the millennium: will the postal service go private? Cato Institute, Washington

Campbell JI (2001a) Remailing – catalyst for liberalising the European postal markets? In: Kulenkampff G, Smit H (eds) Liberalisation of postal markets: papers presented at the 6th Königswinter Seminar Königswinter, 19-21 February (WIK)

Campbell RM (2001b) Regulatory and governance changes in liberalized commercialized postal environments. In: Crew MA, Kleindorfer PR (eds) Future directions in postal reform. Kluwer Academic Publishers, Boston

Campbell JI, Dieke AK, Niederprüm A (2008) National postal policies in Europe on the eve of the third directive. In: Crew MA, Kleindorfer PR, Campbell JI (eds) Handbook of worldwide postal reform. Edward Elgar Publishing, Cheltenham & Northampton

Chung CM (1994) Recent developments in EC postal liberalisation. European Competition Law Review 4(15):217–224

Comandini VV, Lettieri C (2001) Comparing postal and telecommunication networks: similarities and differences. Journal of Network Industries 2(2):163–206

Comandini VV, Consiglio A, Gori S, Piccinin E, Pierleoni MR (2010) The Altmark ruling and approaches to measuring efficiency of postal operators. In: Crew MA, Kleindorfer PR, Campbell JI (eds) Heightening competition in the postal and delivery sector. Edward Elgar Publishing, Cheltenham & Northampton

Crew MA, D'Alcantara G, Kleindorfer PR, Claeys P, Kuypers B (2008) Economic factors underlying postal reform in the European Union. In: Crew MA, Kleindorfer PR, Campbell JI (eds) Handbook of worldwide postal reform. Edward Elgar Publishing, Cheltenham & Northampton

Crew MA, Kleindorfer PR (1991) Rowland hill's contribution as an economist. In: Crew MA, Kleindorfer PR (eds) Competition and innovation in postal services. Springer, Boston

Dieke AK, Niederprüm A, Campbell JI (2008) Universal service and postal monopoly in other countries. Study on Universal Postal Service and the Postal Monopoly. George Mason University, November. http://digilib.gmu.edu/dspace/handle/1920/3477

Dobbenberg P (1993) The international mail market in the 1990s. In: Crew MA, Kleindorfer PR (eds) Regulation and the nature of postal and delivery services. Springer, Boston

Eccles R (2011) State funding and cost sharing of the USO under the 2008 EU postal services directive. In: Crew MA, Kleindorfer PR (eds) Reinventing the postal sector in an electronic age. Edward Elgar Publishing, Cheltenham & Northampton

Fratini A, Filpo F (2006) The new EC framework for state aid to public service and the postal sector: where do we stand now? In: Crew MA and Kleindorfer PR (eds) Progress toward liberalization of the postal and delivery sector. Springer, Boston, MA

Gautier A, Paolini D (2011) Universal service financing in competitive postal markets: one size does not fit all. Review of Network Economics 10(3):Article 6

Griffiths M (2000) Failing to install effective competition in postal services – the limited impact of EC law. European Competition Law Review 21(9):399–407

John RR (2001) Postal systems. In: Smelser NJ, Baltes PB (eds) International encyclopedia of social & behavioral sciences. Elsevier, Amsterdam & New York

John RR (2008) History of universal service and the postal monopoly. Study on universal postal service and the postal monopoly, George Mason University, November. https://academiccommons.columbia.edu/doi/10.7916/D8V99RQT/download

Jonsson P, Selander S (2006) The "real" graveyard spiral: experiences from the liberalized Swedish postal market. In: Crew MA, Kleindorfer PR (eds) Progress toward liberalization of the postal and delivery sector. Springer, Boston
Oxera Consulting Ltd (2007) Funding universal service obligations in the postal sector. A study prepared for La Poste, De Post-La Poste, Hellenic Post, Poste Italiane, P&T Luxembourg, Correos, Magyar Posta, Cyprus Post, Poczta Polska. http://www.oxera.com/Oxera/media/Oxera/Funding-the-USO-in-the-postal-sector.pdf?ext=.pdf
Prosser T (2001) Regulating public enterprises. Public Law (Aut):505–526
Ranganathan K, Dey R (1996) Redirecting mail: postal sector reform. Private Sector Development Department of the World Bank, in Collaboration with Universal Postal Union, August. http://documents.worldbank.org/curated/en/1998/06/693346/redirecting-mail-postal-sector-reform
Rawnsley D, Lazar N (1999) Managing the universal service obligation. In: Crew MA, Kleindorfer PR (eds) Emerging competition in postal and delivery services. Kluwer Academic Publishers, Boston
Reay I (1997) The structure of postal markets. In: Crew MA, Kleindorfer PR (eds) Emerging competition in postal and delivery services. Kluwer Academic Publishers, Boston
Robinson H (1953) Britain's Post Office: A history of development from the beginnings to the present day. Oxford University Press, Oxford
Smith MP (2005) States of Liberalization: redefining the public sector in integrated Europe. State University of New York Press, Albany
Van Der Horst M (2005) Postal liberalization in the EU: a small step in weights, a giant leap for the market. In: Crew MA, Kleindorfer PR (eds) Regulatory and economic challenges in the postal and delivery sector. Kluwer Academic Publishers, New York
Von Danwitz T (2002) The new directive on the further liberalization of postal markets in Europe. In: Crew MA, Kleindorfer PR (eds) Postal and delivery services: delivering on competition. Springer, Boston
WIK-Consult (2011) Universal postal service and competition: experience from Europe. Study for TNT Post UK. http://www.wik-consult.com/uploads/media/Universal_Postal_Service.pdf
Zepos CJ (1992) Liberalizing the "sacred cows": telecommunications and postal services in the EC. Duke Journal of Comparative & International Law 3(1):203–234

Chapter 7
Service of General Economic Interest in Transport

Contents

Abstract Service of general economic interest (SGEI) in the transport sector has been developed under the notion of public service obligation (PSO) within the framework of Common Transport Policy. This chapter explores the treatment of SGEIs in the transport sector. It begins with PSO in air transport, where the pursuit of regional economic development has been recognised as a valid SGEI objective and the public tendering procedure must be used. The second part of this chapter discusses PSO in

L. Zhu, *Services of General Economic Interest in EU Competition Law*,
Legal Issues of Services of General Interest,
https://doi.org/10.1007/978-94-6265-387-0_7

inland transport, where Member States still enjoy much freedom and have been granted derogation from the public tendering procedure. It further studies PSO in the maritime transport sector, where transport links to islands have been regarded as valid SGEIs by the EU. The analysis shows that the concern of the EU is to ensure state intervention is competition neutral.

Keywords public tendering · public transport services · public service obligation · liberalisation in transport · market viability test · exclusive right · market failure test

7.1 Introduction

In the transport sector, the concept of service of general economic interest in transport (SGEI) appears through the notion of 'public service obligation (PSO)'. Under the Common Transport Policy, the Treaty grants a derogation for the Member States from state aid rules. Article 93 TFEU provides that 'aids shall be compatible with this Treaty if they represent reimbursement for the discharges of certain *obligations inherent in the concept of a public service*'. It is this notion of 'PSO' that is the equivalent of SGEI in the transport sector.

The EU does not have an explicit and independent competence over the definition and organisation of SGEI in transport. Its involvement in the provision of SGEI is closely linked with the development of the Common Transport Policy. From the Treaty of Rome in 1957, the transport sector gained a special position in the Treaty. The Treaty provided that transport is subject to the Common Transport Policy owing to its distinctive features.[1] For the first three decades following the Treaty of Rome, EU law had little influence in the organisation of the transport sector. The transport sector was largely outside the reach of EU rules on free movement and competition.[2] This essentially meant that the organisation of the transport sector was still in the hands of the Member States.

The organisation of the transport industry in the Member States did not sit very well with EU rules on free movement and competition. On inland transport, for both goods and passengers, market access was based on a quota system, whereby a limited number of authorisations were granted by national authorities every year. In the air transport sector, international air transport was based on bilateral agreements and dominated by large national flag carriers based on exclusive rights over the routes.[3] Regarding

[1] Greaves 2000, pp. 1–2.

[2] The Treaty itself made explicit derogation for the transport sector from the application of free movement and state aid rules. The Council also declared that Articles 101 and 102 did not apply to the transport sector: Title VI on Transport, TFEU; Regulation No 141 of the Council exempting transport from the application of Council Regulation No 17 [1962] OJ L124/2751.

[3] Kawagoe 2008.

maritime transport, the concern of the EU was that certain Member States had adopted a closed system that allowed only their own nationals to access their maritime market.[4]

During this period, the Council had adopted a harmonisation approach aimed at eliminating the disparities between the operating conditions in different Member States.[5] However, the results were far from a comprehensive Common Transport Policy, and the Court declared, in 1985 that the Council had failed to fulfil its obligations under the Treaty.[6]

This case marked a turning point in the development of a Common Transport Policy. Since then, the EU began to promote competition and market integration in the transport sector. The EU adopted a piecemeal approach. Market integration was developed on the basis of different modes of transport, starting with air transport[7]

---

[4] This was exactly the case in Member States such as Greece, Italy, France, Spain and Portugal: Brooks (2009).

[5] 65/271/EEC: Council Decision of 13 May 1965 on the harmonisation of certain provisions affecting competition in transport by rail, road and inland waterway [1965] OJ 88/1500.

[6] Case 13/83 *European Parliament v Council of the European Communities* [1985] ECR-1513.

[7] Three packages of EU legislation were adopted between 1987 and 1992 to introduce competition and market integration in the air transport sector gradually.

(1) The first package was adopted in 1987, including:

   (a) Council Regulation (EEC) No 3975/87 of 14 December 1987 laying down the procedure for the application of the rules on competition to undertakings in the air transport sector [1987] OJ L374/1;
   (b) Council Regulation (EEC) No 3976/87 of 14 December 1987 on the application of Article 85 (3) of the Treaty to certain categories of agreements and concerted practices in the air transport sector [1987] OJ L374/9;
   (c) Council Directive 87/601/EEC of 14 December 1987 on fares for scheduled air services between Member States; and
   (d) 87/602/EEC: Council Decision of 14 December 1987 on the sharing of passenger capacity between air carriers on scheduled air services between Member States and on access for air carriers to scheduled air-service routes between Member States [1987] OJ L374/19.

(2) The second package was adopted in 1990, including:

   (a) Council Regulation (EEC) No 2342/90 of 24 July 1990 on fares for scheduled air services [1990] OJ L217/1;
   (b) Council Regulation (EEC) No 2343/90 of 24 July 1990 on access for air carriers to scheduled intra-Community air service routes and on the sharing of passenger capacity between air carriers on scheduled air services between Member States [1990] OJ L217/8;
   (c) Council Regulation (EEC) No 2344/90 of 24 July 1990 amending Regulation (EEC) No 3976/87 on the application of Article 85 (3) of the Treaty to certain categories of agreements and concerted practices in the air transport sector [1990] OJ L217/15.

(3) The third package was adopted in 1992, including:

   (a) Council Regulation (EEC) No 2407/92 of 23 July 1992 on licensing of air carriers [1992] OJ L240/1;
   (b) Council Regulation (EEC) No 2408/92 of 23 July 1992 on access for Community air carriers to intra-Community air routes [1992] OJ L240/8;

and maritime liberalisation[8] and then moving to inland transport.[9] Within each transport mode, liberalisation was undertaken step by step. Ultimately, a supranational regulatory framework was established at the EU level and is still evolving.

The essence of this process is the withdrawal of unjustified state intervention in the market and the restoration of the functioning of free competition and the independence of transport undertakings. On the one hand, it is an exercise in

---

(c) Council Regulation (EEC) No 2409/92 of 23 July 1992 on fares and rates for air services [1992] OJ L240/15.

Rules in the third package were consolidated into Regulation 1008/2008. Regulation (EC) No 1008/2008 of the European Parliament and of the Council of 24 September 2008 on common rules for the operation of air services in the Community (Recast) [2008] OJ L293/3.

[8]The main legislation for liberalisation and market integration in the maritime sector is Regulation 3577/92. It granted exemptions for certain Member States and therefore introduced liberalisation gradually: Council Regulation (EEC) No 3577/92 of 7 December 1992 applying the principle of freedom to provide services to maritime transport within Member States (maritime cabotage) [1992] OJ L364/7.

[9]EU legislation is adopted on the basis of different modes and areas of inland transport.

(1) For carriage of goods by road, market liberalisation and integration was introduced by Regulation 881/92 in 1992, which was replaced by Regulation 1072/2009.
Council Regulation (EEC) No 881/92 of 26 March 1992 on access to the market in the carriage of goods by road within the Community to or from the territory of a Member State or passing across the territory of one or more Member States [1992] OJ L95/1;
Regulation (EC) No 1072/2009 of the European Parliament and of the Council of 21 October 2009 on common rules for access to the international road haulage market [2009] OJ L300/72.
(2) For carriage of passengers by road, market liberalisation and integration was introduced by Regulation 684/92 and Regulation 12/98, which were replaced by Regulation 1073/2009.
Council Regulation (EEC) No 684/92 of 16 March 1992 on common rules for the international carriage of passengers by coach and bus [1992] OJ L74/1;
Council Regulation (EC) No 12/98 of 11 December 1997 laying down the conditions under which non-resident carriers may operate national road passenger transport services within a Member State [1992] OJ L74/10;
Regulation (EC) No 1073/2009 of the European Parliament and of the Council of 21 October 2009 on common rules for access to the international market for coach and bus services, and amending Regulation (EC) No 561/2006 [2009] OJ L300/88.
(3) For inland water transport, market liberalisation and integration was introduced by Regulation 1356/96.
Council Regulation (EC) No 1356/96 of 8 July 1996 on common rules applicable to the transport of goods or passengers by inland waterway between Member States with a view to establishing freedom to provide such transport services [1996] OJ L175/7.
For railway transport sector, market liberalisation and integration was much delayed. The first Directive 91/440 on market access was adopted in 1991. Market access has been one of the subjects in the following three packages of EU rules for internal railway market, adopted in 2001, 2004 and 2007. The latest (fourth) package has been proposed by the Commission and is still in the legislative process. For a list of railway legislation, see the Commission's website: http://ec.europa.eu/transport/modes/rail/packages/index_en.htm accessed 9 October 2014.
Council Directive 91/440/EEC of 29 July 1991 on the development of the Community's railways [1991] OJ L237/25.

deregulation; EU legislation requires the withdrawal of state intervention/regulation to restore commercial freedom. On the other hand, it is a process of liberalisation, in that it breaks down national constraints on market access to facilitate free movement of transport services between the Member States. It inevitably leads to the erosion of national sovereign power and competence transfer to the EU.

It is during this process that PSOs began to be defined and regulated at the EU level. The PSO concept forms an essential component of the new regulatory framework because it is concerned with the destiny of state intervention in the market. In this respect, the Member States have long been involved with the provision of public transport services under the broad notion of universal service. Although the actual extent and organisation of state intervention varies across Member States, the principle behind it is the same: the State assumes the responsibility to guarantee affordable public transport services for everyone.

This chapter examines the treatment of SGEI in the transport sector. It starts from the PSO regime in the area of air transport, where the EU has been very successful in promoting competition and liberalisation. It recognises the pursuit of regional economic development through PSO air links as a valid SGEI objective. Meanwhile, it limits state intervention to what is strictly necessary by using the market viability test. The Member States are also obliged to use a public tender procedure for any form of state funding, which is assumed to be able to avoid overcompensation.

The second part of this chapter examines the organisation of public transport systems, in which Member States have long been involved under the notion of universal service. This activity had been immune from the market integration process owing to its local nature. This approach was reflected in Regulation 1191/69,[10] which essentially exempted public transport services from its application. The latest EU Regulation, 1370/2007, intends to promote competition in this sector,[11] although it recognises the organisation of public transport systems as a whole to be an SGEI and grants several derogations from public tender procedures to this sector.

The last part of the chapter will investigate the application and the development of PSOs in the maritime sector, where transport links to islands have been defined as valid SGEIs. However, EU law has failed to provide a framework for its organisation. In practice, the Commission has been using the state aid control mechanism to ensure the competition neutrality of such measures by focusing on the issue of overcompensation and cross-subsidisation.

[10] Regulation (EEC) No 1191/69 of the Council of 26 June 1969 on action by Member States concerning the obligations inherent in the concept of a public service in transport by rail, road and inland waterway [1969] OJ L156/1.

[11] Regulation (EC) No 1370/2007 of the European Parliament and of the Council of 23 October 2007 on public passenger transport services by rail and by road and repealing Council Regulations (EEC) Nos 1191/69 and 1107/70 [2007] OJ L315/1.

7.2 Public Service Obligations in Air Transport

The air transport sector is covered by the common transport policy. However, it has been subject to a distinct set of rules from inland transport. The Treaty of Rome originally provided that the Council may, acting unanimously,[12] decide whether and to what extent and by what procedure, appropriate provisions may be laid down for air transport. Since the adoption of the Treaty of Rome, air transport had essentially remained outside the reach of the Treaty's rules on competition and free movement.[13] EU law had little influence over the air transport sector until the late 1980s, when it began to challenge the traditional structure of the air transport sector in Member States.

It was through this liberalisation process that the concept of SGEI came within the scope of EU air transport law. With liberalisation, the EU has established a new regulatory framework, which also defines under what circumstances, and in which way, state intervention in the market is legitimate.

In this section of the chapter, first the change of regulatory framework in the air transport sector and the role of the SGEI concept in this process will be considered; then the non-economic values underpinning the provision of public service air links will be examined; and finally, the arrangements for the accommodation of these non-economic values (the market viability test before State funding, exclusive right as a way of funding, the compulsory nature of the public tendering procedure) will be discussed.

7.2.1 Market Integration and Liberalisation in Air Transport

The traditional organisational model of the air transport sector did contradict the rules on free movement and the principles of free competition. Air space was regarded as being under national sovereignty, and the State had absolute freedom to decide how to organise its aviation sector.[14] Main European airline operators were owned or controlled by the Member States.[15] Normally, they were the only

---

[12] Article 84, EEC Treaty. Since the adoption of the EC Treaty, it has been subjected to the normal legislative procedure, which requires only a qualified majority: Article 80 EC Treaty and Article 100 TFEU.

[13] Regulation No 141 of the Council exempting transport from the application of Council Regulation No 17 [1962] OJ L124/2751.

[14] Commission of the European Communities, Civil Aviation Memorandum No. 2: Progress towards the Development of a Community Air Transport Policy, COM (84) 72 final, 15.03.1984, Annex II, para 2.

[15] Ibid.

operators holding licences in national markets and thus had a de facto monopoly position in domestic air transport markets.[16]

Meanwhile, international air transport was based on an international cartel system. Bilateral agreements were signed on the operation of air transport links between States. It was usually the public air operators, the so-called national flag carriers, that were licensed under these bilateral agreements to operate these routes and thus enjoy exclusive rights over them. In addition, capacity, ticket fares and revenue allocations were decided by these bilateral agreements. Globally, it was the International Air Transport Association (IATA) that facilitated this international cartel practice. It was a 'protected, fragmented and highly regulated structure'.[17] Therefore, a genuine EU internal air transport market did not exist, but only a collection of national air transport markets.[18]

This anti-competition structure had created considerable tension with the Internal Market, which is based on free market and competition. The Court had a chance to deal with this issue only in 1986 in the *Asjes* case.[19] In its Judgment, the Court favoured the pro-market approach[20] and confirmed that the air transport sector, and indeed the transport sector as a whole, is subject to EU competition rules.[21]

---

[16] Kawagoe 2008.

[17] Ibid., p. 161.

[18] Commission of European Communities, European Experience of Air Transport Liberalisation. http://www.icao.int/sustainability/CaseStudies/StatesReplies/EuropeLiberalization_En.pdf accessed 9 October 2014, para 3.1.

[19] The case was concerned with the organisation of the air transport sector in France. The French air transport sector had been subjected to tight state control: both access to the market and ticket tariffs were subject to compulsory ministerial approval. In the main proceedings, the defendant was accused of selling tickets at a price different from the approved one, which was punishable by criminal penalties under French law. The case was referred to the Court for a preliminary ruling, asking whether the air transport sector was subject to competition law and, if so, whether such French regime was compatible with these rules: Joined Cases 209 to 213/84 *Criminal proceedings against Lucas Asjes and others, Andrew Gray and others, Andrew Gray and others, Jacques Maillot and others and Léo Ludwig and others* [1986] ECR-1425.

[20] It is quite interesting to note the disagreements between the Member States. On the one hand, Britain together with the Commission took a more pro-competition approach. They argued that Title IV of the Treaty on the Common Transport Policy did not render air transport beyond the reach of competition law. On the other hand, France and Italy took the opposite stance. Therefore, the interpretation of the Treaty by the Court was crucial in this debate.

[21] The reason for that lies in the lack of express exclusion from competition law by the Treaty for the transport sector. The Court ruled that:

> It should also be noted that where the Treaty intended to remove certain activities from the ambit of the competition rules, it made an express derogation to that effect. […] As regards transport there is no provision in the Treaty which excludes the application of the competition rules or makes it subject to a decision by the Council.

Joined Cases 209 to 213/84 *Criminal proceedings against Lucas Asjes and others, Andrew Gray and others, Andrew Gray and others, Jacques Maillot and others and Léo Ludwig and others* [1986] ECR-1425, para 40.

The Court ruled that Member States might be in breach of competition law if they encouraged or facilitated anti-competitive behaviour prohibited by Articles 101 and 102. This suggested that the very organisational structure of national air transport sector might be in breach of Treaty rules and have to be abolished. Therefore, this case essentially made the traditional national approaches to air transport sector organisation vulnerable to attack under the Treaty.

Although some took the view that the Judgment was of limited significance,[22] the Judgment should be read in the broader context at the end of the 1980s, when the EU began to be more active in the market integration programme. The Judgment was delivered in 1986 and signalled the beginning of the change of the Court's approach towards the compatibility of exclusive rights under EU law. Five years later, in a series of cases, the Court ruled (admittedly not in transport-specific cases) that the very existence of state monopoly was in breach of EU competition law.[23]

The *Asjes* case rendered support to the commencement of the application of the market integration process in the air transport sector. It was not a coincidence that the market integration programme in air transport took off after this Judgment. The EU adopted a piecemeal approach, through which three packages of Council legislation were passed to break down constraints from Member States and to create a competitive market structure in the EU air transport sector.[24] Following this

---

[22] The significance of the Judgment itself is limited; it has not been cited by the Court in later cases. The reason lies in the fact that the questions were not properly formulated by the French court: Rodger 2008, p. 179.

[23] Case C-41/90 *Klaus Höfner and Fritz Elser v Macrotron GmbH* [1991] ECR I-1979; Case C-260/89 *Elliniki Radiophonia Tileorassi AE (Ert) (Panellinia Omospondia Syllogon Prossopikou Ert intervening) v Dimotiki Étairia Pliroforissis (Dep) and Sotirios Kouvelas (Nicolaos Avdellas and Others intervening)* [1991] ECR I-02925; Case C-260/89 *Elliniki Radiophonia Tileorassi AE (Ert) (Panellinia Omospondia Syllogon Prossopikou Ert intervening) v Dimotiki Étairia Pliroforissis (Dep) and Sotirios Kouvelas (Nicolaos Avdellas and Others intervening)* [1991] ECR I-02925; Case C-179/90 *Merci Convenzionali Porto di Genova SpA v Siderurgica Gabrielli SpA* [1991] ECR I-05889. This issue has been discussed in Sect. 3.2 of Chap. 3.

[24] Three packages of EU legislation were adopted between 1987 and 1992 to introduce competition and market integration in the air transport sector gradually.

(1) The first package was adopted in 1987, including:

    (a) Council Regulation (EEC) No 3975/87 of 14 December 1987 laying down the procedure for the application of the rules on competition to undertakings in the air transport sector [1987] OJ L374/1;
    (b) Council Regulation (EEC) No 3976/87 of 14 December 1987 on the application of Article 85 (3) of the Treaty to certain categories of agreements and concerted practices in the air transport sector [1987] OJ L374/9;
    (c) Council Directive 87/601/EEC of 14 December 1987 on fares for scheduled air services between Member States; and
    (d) 87/602/EEC: Council Decision of 14 December 1987 on the sharing of passenger capacity between air carriers on scheduled air services between Member States and on access for air carriers to scheduled air-service routes between Member States [1987] OJ L374/19.

market liberalisation and market creation process was an EU re-regulation exercise. A comprehensive framework for the functioning of internal air transport market would be established and updated at the EU level.[25]

7.2.2 *PSO as a Necessary Component of a New Regulatory Framework*

It was during this transition process that PSO began to feature at the EU level. The first liberalisation package was adopted by the Council in 1987 and only laid down rules on capacity sharing,[26] fares for scheduled services[27] and the application of

---

(2) The second package was adopted in 1990, including:

(a) Council Regulation (EEC) No 2342/90 of 24 July 1990 on fares for scheduled air services [1990] OJ L217/1;
(b) Council Regulation (EEC) No 2343/90 of 24 July 1990 on access for air carriers to scheduled intra-Community air service routes and on the sharing of passenger capacity between air carriers on scheduled air services between Member States [1990] OJ L217/8;
(c) Council Regulation (EEC) No 2344/90 of 24 July 1990 amending Regulation (EEC) No 3976/87 on the application of Article 85 (3) of the treaty to certain categories of agreements and concerted practices in the air transport sector [1990] OJ L217/15.

(3) The third package was adopted in 1992, including:

(a) Council Regulation (EEC) No 2407/92 of 23 July 1992 on licensing of air carriers [1992] OJ L240/1;
(b) Council Regulation (EEC) No 2408/92 of 23 July 1992 on access for Community air carriers to intra-Community air routes [1992] OJ L240/8;
(c) Council Regulation (EEC) No 2409/92 of 23 July 1992 on fares and rates for air services [1992] OJ L240/15.

Rules in the third package were consolidated into one Regulation 1008/2008 in 2008. Regulation (EC) No 1008/2008 of the European Parliament and of the Council of 24 September 2008 on common rules for the operation of air services in the Community (Recast) [2008] OJ L293/3. Dempsey 1992.

[25] Commission of the European Communities, European Civil Aviation Handbook: Part I. Regulations and Directives:

http://ec.europa.eu/transport/modes/air/internal_market/handbook/part1_en.htm accessed 9 October 2014.

[26] 87/602/EEC: Council Decision of 14 December 1987 on the sharing of passenger capacity between air carriers on scheduled air services between Member States and on access for air carriers to scheduled air-service routes between Member States [1987] OJ L374/19.

[27] Council Directive 87/601/EEC of 14 December 1987 on fares for scheduled air services between Member States [1987] OJ L374/12.

Articles 101 and 102 to air transport operators.[28] It did not deal with market access and also did not mention PSO at all.

It was only with the adoption of the second package, in 1990, on market access that rules on PSOs began to emerge at the EU level.[29] Substantive rules were prescribed in Regulation 2408/92 in the third package on full liberalisation of the air transport in 1992.[30] It laid down detailed rules on the definition and conditions for PSOs. It also established a procedural framework through which PSOs could be organised by the Member States. The latest Regulation, 1008/2008, did not change these rules substantially but only upgraded them in more detail.[31]

The rules on PSOs formed a necessary component of this new EU regulatory framework since it dealt with the relationship between the Member States and the market.[32] On the one hand, PSOs essentially involved state intervention in the market, justifiable in 'limited circumstances',[33] i.e. where the market otherwise fails to provide certain air transport links deemed desirable for the sake of the public interest. On the other hand, PSO air links often need funding from the State. Left unregulated in the hands of Member States, it might distort the proper functioning of the newly established Internal Market on air transport, which would naturally concern the EU.

7.2.3 Freedom to Establish PSOs for Regional Economic Development

The non-economic values pursued in the air transport sector are quite different from those in the maritime transport and the public passenger transport sectors, where it is used to guarantee a basic transport service to everyone in society. In the air

---

28 Council Regulation (EEC) No 3975/87 of 14 December 1987 laying down the procedure for the application of the rules on competition to undertakings in the air transport sector [1987] OJ L374/1.

29 Council Regulation (EEC) No 2343/90 of 24 July 1990 on access for air carriers to scheduled intra-Community air service routes and on the sharing of passenger capacity between air carriers on scheduled air services between Member States [1990] OJ L217/8.

30 Council Regulation (EEC) No 2408/92 of 23 July 1992 on access for Community air carriers to intra-Community air routes [1992] OJ L240/8.

31 Regulation (EC) No 1008/2008 of the European Parliament and of the Council of 24 September 2008 on common rules for the operation of air services in the Community [2008] OJ L293/3.

32 It is very interesting to note that Article 5 on PSOs is titled as 'relations between a Member State and carriers of other Member States'. Council Regulation (EEC) No 2343/90 of 24 July 1990 on access for air carriers to scheduled intra-Community air service routes and on the sharing of passenger capacity between air carriers on scheduled air services between Member States [1990] OJ L217/8.

33 Council Regulation (EEC) No 2343/90 of 24 July 1990 on access for air carriers to scheduled intra-Community air service routes and on the sharing of passenger capacity between air carriers on scheduled air services between Member States [1990] OJ L217/8, Recital 7.

transport sector, the concept of PSO is used to pursue regional economic development, rather than the ideal of universal service. The concern of the Commission is that the market alone would fail to provide air links to certain peripheral regions, based on a purely commercial basis because of low traffic demand.[34]

On the other hand, it is the State (through its public authorities) that decides to maintain a particular route, even though it is not commercially viable.[35] The existence of a PSO route is regarded as necessary for economic development considerations, i.e. regional economic development. The importance of regular air links to these peripheral regions is deemed to be self-explanatory by the Commission.[36] It points out that regular air links to these uneconomical regions is a prerequisite for developing good economic and other relations between the community and the rest of the world.[37] This approach was expressed clearly in the Commission's explanatory memorandum for the third package for air transport liberalisation:

> It may serve to establish closer and quicker links not only between central regions but also *between peripheral and central parts of the Community*. The latter point is of particular importance because air links *may* help to overcome disadvantages for peripheral regions and facilitate, thereby, *regional economic development*, in particular, in the field of services including *tourism*.[38] (emphasis added)

This is the initial argument put forward by the Commission in 1991 for the establishment of the PSO regime in the air transport sector. The term 'regional economic development' itself has been defined in a broad way, with reference to social integration and promotion of tourism.[39] Air transport links may contribute to or facilitate these goals. However, there has not been direct scientific evidence to support the *causal link* between the existence of these uneconomical routes and the advancement of regional economic development.[40] In essence, it is a *political decision* made by the legislation, in this case Regulation 2408/92.

The EU legislation has decided that regional economic development is a legitimate public interest goal that could be pursued in the air transport sector. However, there is no EU legislation or institution to decide which routes should be designated as public service routes. This approach is very different from how SGEIs are viewed in the telecommunications and postal sectors, where Member States have an obligation to guarantee a minimum level of service for everyone, prescribed by EU legislation.

---

[34] Under the previous monopoly structure, national air transport network covering these regions was maintained through cross-subsidy from profitable routes to unprofitable ones.

[35] Williams and Pagliari 2004.

[36] Commission of the European Communities, Completion of the Civil Aviation Policy in the European Communities towards Single Market Conditions, COM (1991) 275 final, 18.09.1991, p. 3.

[37] Ibid.

[38] Ibid., p. 2.

[39] Williams 2005.

[40] Graham 1998.

This illustrates unique public interest considerations in the application of PSOs in the air transport sector: regional economic development through the maintenance of air transport link. Transport by air has not been regarded as a basic service to be protected as a human right.[41] It is more concerned with national economic policy in the Member States, linked to a Community objective. Therefore, in the air transport sector, there is little discussion on universal access and affordability at the EU level.

The actual design and organisation of PSO links is largely left to the Member States: the EU legislation does not oblige the Member States to impose PSOs to guarantee economic development for certain regions. It leaves the establishment of PSOs for the Member States to decide. The Member States have the *option and freedom* to decide whether or not, and on what route, to impose PSOs.[42]

EU regulation does not lay down uniform and detailed criteria for the establishment of PSOs. Rather, it only prescribes certain very broad and subjective elements that should be taken into consideration by the Member States.[43] A Member State may impose a PSO as follows:

> (1) in respect of scheduled air services between an airport in the Community and an airport serving a *peripheral or development region* in its territory
> (2) on *a thin route* on its territory any such route being considered *vital for the economic and social development of the region* which the airport serves.[44] (emphasis added)

It depends on the political will of public authorities in the Member States on whether to maintain certain air routes although they are not commercially viable. Essentially, it is a decentralised administration system. The real contribution to regional economic development by PSO air links still depends on national governments, rather than on EU law.[45]

---

[41] This is also true in the energy sector, where PSOs cover a wide range of public interests such as security of supply and environmental protection: Directive 2009/72/EC of the European Parliament and of the Council of 13 July 2009 concerning common rules for the internal market in electricity and repealing Directive 2003/54/EC [2009] OJ L211/55, Article 3(2); Directive 2009/73/EC of the European Parliament and of the Council of 13 July 2009 concerning common rules for the internal market in natural gas and repealing Directive 2003/55/EC [2009] OJ L211/94, Article 3(2).

[42] Williams 2005.

[43] This approach could also be observed in the Regulation 2408/92, where the term public interest is used to allow Member States to assess its needs to impose PSOs: Council Regulation (EEC) No 2408/92 of 23 July 1992 on access for Community air carriers to intra-Community air routes [1992] OJ L240/8, Article 4(1).

[44] Regulation (EC) No 1008/2008 of the European Parliament and of the Council of 24 September 2008 on common rules for the operation of air services in the Community [2008] OJ L293/3, Article 16.

[45] Williams and Pagliari 2004; Reynolds-Feighan suggests that the EU should adopt a centralised administrative system where PSO air links would be decided and funded at the EU level: Reynolds-Feighan 1995.

7.2.4 *The Market Viability Test as a Precondition for State Funding*

Without much control over the content of PSOs, the key concern of EU law has focused on the way PSOs are delivered by Member States. The EU has established a uniform procedural framework that enables Member States to pursue regional economic development policy through PSO air links.

The precondition for any state funding is that the market has actually failed to deliver the service under normal conditions. Regulation 1008/2008 requires Member States to first impose PSOs without any state funding.[46] Relevant information is published in the Official Journal of the EU.[47] In practice, it acts as an invitation to a route that is initiated or encouraged by public authorities.

The market viability test limits state intervention to the minimum level necessary to guarantee that an air link will function and reach a certain level of continuity, regularity, pricing or minimum capacity. Without the imposition of PSOs, the market, left to itself, might not reach the desired level of service requirements. In this sense, state intervention is necessary.

However, this does not necessarily justify further state intervention in the form of state funding, which might distort market competition. If operators can reach that level of service requirements without state funding, it shows that the service is viable under normal market conditions. In fact, 87 among the published 226 PSO routes are commercially viable without any state funding.[48] Consequently, Member States are not allowed to fund these through the grant of exclusive rights or direct compensation. Imposition of PSOs without funding is a weaker form of state intervention in the market. On the one hand, no exclusivity is involved. Any Community air carrier[49] is permitted to commence the air link at any time if it meets all the public service requirements.[50] On the other hand, no operator is chosen to be

---

[46] Regulation (EC) No 1008/2008 of the European Parliament and of the Council of 24 September 2008 on common rules for the operation of air services in the Community [2008] OJ L293/3.

[47] With no extra conditions or constraints; this procedure is compulsory.

[48] Cranfield University 2007.

[49] A Community air carrier is an air operator that holds a valid operating licence that is granted by any Member State. See Regulation (EC) No 1008/2008 of the European Parliament and of the Council of 24 September 2008 on common rules for the operation of air services in the Community [2008] OJ L293/3, Article 2.

[50] Regulation (EC) No 1008/2008 of the European Parliament and of the Council of 24 September 2008 on common rules for the operation of air services in the Community [2008] OJ L293/3, Article 16(8).

In the Commission Decision 2007/332, the Italian authority imposed a deadline for the acceptance of the PSOs, within 30 days. The Commission concluded that this practice was unduly restrictive and disproportionate: 2007/332/EC: Commission Decision of 23 April 2007 on public service obligations on certain routes to and from Sardinia under Article 4 of Council Regulation (EEC) No 2408/92 on access for Community air carriers to intra-Community air routes [2007] OJ L125/16.

responsible for the delivery of the PSO link.[51] In fact, they are free to withdraw from the route.[52] As a result, there is no guarantee that the air link would be maintained by the market itself.

7.2.5 *Exclusive Right as a Mechanism of Funding PSO*

Only if no carrier is willing to provide the air link does Regulation 1008/2008 allow the Member States to step into provide funding. The Regulation uses public tendering procedures as the framework that enables the Member States to choose a PSO provider and to determine the amount of funding needed. Two forms of funding mechanism are possible under the Regulation: exclusive right over that particular route or financial compensation.[53]

The treatment of exclusive rights in the air transport sector is worthy of special attention. Instead of promoting full competition in the air transport sector, the Council has chosen a limited competition or controlled competition approach. This dates back to the second liberalisation package in 1990. As an exception to the opening of national air transport markets to all the Community carriers, Regulation 2343/90 allowed the Member States 'under limited circumstances'[54] to reserve a PSO route to one carrier. This essentially allowed Member States to grant exclusive rights on certain routes and thus to prevent competition.

This was the result of the political compromise between Member States and the EU over the control of the air transport sector. On the one hand, the Council, consisting of national Governments, preferred to give national Governments more control over the national air transport market.[55] On the other hand, the Commission was more in favour of a fully competitive market. In the Commission's two proposals for Regulation 2343/90, there was no provision that permitted the grant of

[51] These requirements are obligatory in the sense that any carrier operating on that route must reach that level of service as decided by the public authorities.

[52] Case C-205/99 *Asociación Profesional de Empresas Navieras de Líneas Regulares (Analir) and Others v Administración General del Estado* [2001] ECR I-1271, para 64.

[53] Regulation (EC) No 1008/2008 of the European Parliament and of the Council of 24 September 2008 on common rules for the operation of air services in the Community [2008] OJ L293/3, Article 16(1).

[54] Council Regulation (EEC) No 2343/90 of 24 July 1990 on access for air carriers to scheduled intra-Community air service routes and on the sharing of passenger capacity between air carriers on scheduled air services between Member States [1990] OJ L217/8, Recital 7.

[55] This could also be observed from the very broad term 'public interest' used as a criterion for the decision of PSOs by Member States.

exclusive rights over a route.[56] The exception on PSO routes was added to the text by the Council as one option that allowed a Member State to delay or avoid market liberalisation.[57]

In the transport sector, the Commission cannot overrule the Council to establish a more liberal market: it is the Council that has exclusive legislative competence in the air transport sector.[58] The Commission had no other choice but to compromise. This was evident in the treatment of PSO in the third package of liberalisation. Instead of the abolition of exclusive rights altogether, the Commission tolerated its existence. In its proposal for the third liberalisation legislation Regulation 2408/92, the Commission recognised that:

> This opening of market access [...] *may* make life more difficult for new entrants and it does not ensure the establishment of air services from some regions where they should exist for *regional policy* reasons. In order to address these problems a possibility already exists to protect an airline on a new route for up to 2 years and to introduce a public service obligation for a limited period. These provisions should be *retaine*d and, where necessary, *developed further*.[59] (emphasis added)

Neither the Council nor the Commission provided any analysis over the necessity of the exclusive rights. Indeed there are other alternative ways—direct financial support without the grant of exclusive rights. A good example comes from the essential air service programme in the US, which operates without exclusive right over the route. A comparison between these two regimes by commentators illustrates that the US approach is more favourable from a competition perspective.[60]

It is submitted that the compatibility of the exclusive right under EU law in the air transport sector has been determined *politically* rather than as a matter of law. The question has been decided in the EU legislative process, which involves compromises between the Member States and EU institutions, rather than via the

---

[56] Commission of the European Communities, Proposal for a Council Regulation (EEC) on access for air carriers to scheduled intra-Community air service routes and on the sharing of passenger capacity between air carriers on scheduled air services between Member States, COM (89) 373 final, 11.10.1989; Commission of the European Communities, Amendment to the proposal for a Regulation on access for air carriers to scheduled intra-Community air service routes and on the sharing of passenger capacity between air carriers on scheduled air services between Member States, COM (90) 234 final, 05.07.1990.

[57] Both Regulations provide several exceptions that Member States could use to avoid the introduction of competition. This also creates problems in their interpretation. The latest example is found in case 181/00: Case C-181/00 *Flightline Ltd v Secretário de Estado dos Transportes e Comunicações and Transportes Aéreos Portugueses SA (TAP)* [2002] ECR I-6139.

[58] This is very different from the approach as in the telecommunications sector, where the Commission was dominant in the legislative process under Article 106(3). See Sect. 5.3 of Chap. 5.

[59] Commission of the European Communities, Completion of the Civil Aviation Policy in the European Communities towards Single Market Conditions, COM (1991) 275 final, 18.09.1991, p. 13.

[60] Reynolds-Feighan 1995.

judicial process of the Court applying the necessity test. In this process, the public interest of regional economic development has triumphed over the promotion of full competition. Member States are allowed to grant exclusive rights as a funding mechanism for the fulfilment of PSO. This approach has remained the same in the latest Regulation, 1008/2008.[61]

7.2.6 The Compulsory Nature of the Public Tendering Procedure

The tight control lies on the procedural side: in order to award any form of state funding, an EU-wide public tendering procedure must be observed.[62] Regulation 1008/2008 set up a framework enabling the Member States to choose the provider for a particular PSO route and also to determine the amount of compensation. Public funding granted following this Regulation is assumed to be free from advantage and is exempt from the notification procedure under state aid control.[63]

The public tendering procedure is compulsory in nature; failure to comply with it means that state funding granted will be examined under state aid rules. More importantly, it is very likely that state funding granted outside the framework of Regulation 1008/2008 will be regarded as incompatible with EU law. This approach is clearly shown in the Commission Decision 2005/351/EC, in 2004, regarding a Spanish air scheme for PSOs.[64]

In that Decision, the Spanish local authority intended to maintain a scheduled air link between Madrid and the city of Gerona. It contacted several air carriers individually to inform them about this opportunity, without publishing it in the Official Journal of the EU. The local authority concluded that only one carrier, Intermed, would and could provide that route. It then signed a contract with Intermed to provide a scheduled service between the two cities. In the contract, the level of services and the method of calculating the costs were also specified.

In the Commission's Decision, it did not challenge the PSO nature of the air transport link. Instead, it focused on *the way compensation was granted* by the

---

[61] Regulation (EC) No 1008/2008 of the European Parliament and of the Council of 24 September 2008 on common rules for the operation of air services in the Community [2008] OJ L293/3.

[62] Commission of the European Communities, Guidelines on the application of Articles 92 and 93 of the EC Treaty and Article 61 of the EEA Agreement to state aids in the aviation sector [1994] OJ C350/5, para 18.

[63] Commission of the European Communities, Commission Decision of 20 December 2011 on the application of Article 106(2) of the Treaty on the Functioning of the European Union to state aid in the form of public service compensation granted to certain undertakings entrusted with the operation of services of general economic interest [2012] OJ L7/3, Article 2(4).

[64] 2005/351/EC: Commission Decision of 20 October 2004 concerning the aid scheme implemented by the Kingdom of Spain for the airline Intermediación Aérea SL [2005] OJ L110/56 (hereafter the *Intermed* Decision).

Spanish authority. Its reasoning dealt with the very complicated issues of the treatment of state funding of PSOs under the *Altmark* criteria under state aid law and the SGEI derogation contained in Article 106(2).[65]

The first issue the Commission had to address was the existence of advantage. The presumption of the non-existence of advantage does not apply because the Spanish authority failed to comply with the procedural rules as prescribed in Article 17 of Regulation 1008/2008.[66] In such a case, the measure will be examined according to general state rules. This is when the *Altmark* criteria comes into play, in which the Court rules that compensation for performance of a PSO does not constitute state aid if four conditions are met.

In assessing whether *Altmark* criteria are satisfied, the Commission took into account the public tender procedure prescribed by Regulation 1008/2008 for PSOs in the air transport sector. The second condition of the *Altmark* criteria requires that parameters for compensation be established in advance in an objective and transparent manner. In the air transport sector, EU secondary legislation Regulation 1008/2008 has established this method, which Spain failed to follow. This led the Commission to conclude that the second condition of *Altmark* was not satisfied.[67]

Meanwhile, the Regulation also played a significant role in the assessment of the third condition of the *Altmark* criteria, which prescribes that compensation cannot exceed what is necessary for the provision of SGEI. Again, the Commission argued that EU legislation has established a mechanism in Regulation 1008/2008 to fulfil that purpose, i.e. to avoid overcompensation. The Commission argued that, without strict compliance with such compulsory rules, it would be difficult to rule out the possibility of overcompensation and potential existence of advantage. Therefore, it pointed out that the third condition was not fulfilled.[68]

The message from the Commission is clear: a tendering procedure in compliance with Regulation 1008/2008 is *indispensable* to satisfy the *Altmark* criteria in the air transport sector. This approach is in line with the general trend in its practice that the public tendering procedure is the preferred mechanism for the organisation of SGEI. This is particularly true in the air transport sector, where the EU has adopted secondary legislation to establish a public tendering procedure for the award of PSOs. Such a regime serve the same objective as that of the *Altmark* criteria, i.e. to

[65] In the *Corbeau* case, the Court established that for the SGEI derogation to apply, three conditions must be met: (1) there must be a clearly defined SGEI task; (2) the SGEI task must have been entrusted by public authorities; (3) a necessity test must be satisfied. In the context of state aid law, the essential requirement under the necessity test is that the amount of SGEI funding does not exceed the costs of SGEI provision: Case C-320/91 *Paul Corbeau* [1993] ECR I-2533.

[66] And compliance with that Regulation presumes the non-existence of financial advantages. The procedure used by Spanish government was found to be flawed in several aspects. It did not inform the Commission of the imposition of the PSOs, nor did it consult other Member States. In addition, neither the content of the PSOs nor the invitation to tender was published in the Official Journal of the EU.

[67] The *Intermed* Decision, paras 64–65.

[68] The *Intermed* Decision, paras 66–69.

rule out the possibility of advantage. Strict compliance with the Regulation will provide legal certainty that PSO funding does not involve advantage. The compulsory nature of the Regulation would be compromised if a funding measure failing to comply with such rules could still be regarded as free from advantage under the *Altmark* criteria.

Then the Commission examined whether there was a possible justification under Article 106(2).[69] The Decision did not articulate what criteria it applied. Its Decision shows that the Commission adopts a very strict approach. In the Decision, the Commission agreed that the amount of aid was *less than the deficit* that was actually incurred by *Intermed* in fulfilling the contract.[70] Nevertheless, the requirement went further than that. The Commission argued that:

> In the absence of objective means of establishing the level of compensation pursuant to the mandatory rules laid down by the Council, *it cannot be ruled out that* other companies would have been able to offer the service in question with a *lower level of subsidy*.[71] (emphasis added)

This approach has profound implications for the application of the SGEI derogation in the air transport sector. It essentially means that state funding for the PSO in the air transport sector would be impossible to justify under the SGEI derogation if it were not granted through the procedural framework in Regulation 1008/2008. This approach is explicitly stated by the Commission in its Decision:

> The conditions of these other provisions [note: Article 4 of Regulation 2408/92] would be *added to the compatibility requirement* arising from Article 106. In addition, it is clear that a state aid procedure *must never* lead to a result which is contrary to the *specific provisions* of the Treaty, or to Community regulations adopted on the basis of such provisions. [....] It is *not possible* to declare aid compatible if the arrangements for granting it have not complied with Article 4 of Regulation (EEC) No 2408/92.[72] (emphasis added)

Consequently, Article 16 of Regulation 1008/2008 has become the specific provision in relation to the *Altmark* criteria and the SGEI derogation in the air transport sector. Member States must be in strict compliance with it when they

---

[69] It is only after a state measure is regarded as state aid that the issue of compatibility will arise: whether it could be justified under Article 106(2). The *Altmark* criteria decide whether a state measure is a state aid; by contrast, SGEI derogation under Article 106(2) determines whether a state aid measure can be justified. For the interplay between EU state aid law and SGEI, see Chap. 4.

[70] The Commission has applied less strict criteria in applying the necessity test in the postal service sector. In its State Aid Decision NN 135/92 concerning a French tax concession to La Poste, the Commission decided the State Aid could be justified under Article 106(2) because it was less than the additional cost of PSOs: Commission of the European Communities, State Aid NN 135/92 France [1995] OJ C 262/11, 14.

[71] The *Intermed* Decision, para 97.

[72] Ibid., paras 98–99.

establish any public service air link.[73] It is quite unlikely that compensation granted outside Regulation 1008/2008 could be justified by the *Altmark* criteria in state aid law or under the SGEI derogation contained in Article 106(2). Therefore, they are largely irrelevant in the examination of PSOs in the air transport sector. The procedural framework contained in Regulation 1008/2008 has become *the only way* to legitimately establish PSO routes by the Member States in the air transport sector.[74]

7.3 The Organisation of Public Transport Systems

In the three decades following the adoption of the Treaty of Rome, the public transport sector was immune from the EU's development of Common Transport Policy owing to its local nature. Right until the late 1980s, public transport services were still operated by local undertakings for the local public.[75] This lack of intra-community element did not justify EU action in this area. Public transport services had been excluded from the scope of market integration legislation in inland transport.[76]

During this period, the only document that touched upon PSOs was Regulation 1191/69.[77] From the late 1980s onwards, the Member States had been introducing competition in the sector, and European operators began to emerge. Public transport services began to have an EU dimension, which justified EU regulation. In 2007, the EU adopted Regulation 1370/2007 to promote competition and market integration in the public transport services sector.[78]

This study first traced the roots of the organisation of public transport systems as SGEI in the Member States and the non-economic considerations behind state

---

[73] 2007/332/EC: Commission Decision of 23 April 2007 on public service obligations on certain routes to and from Sardinia under Article 4 of Council Regulation (EEC) No 2408/92 on access for Community air carriers to intra-Community air routes [2007] OJ L125/16.

[74] The *Intermed* Decision, para 55.

[75] Gwilliam and Van De Velde 1990; Commission of the European Communities, Revised Proposal for a Regulation of the European Parliament and of the Council on Public Passenger Transport Services by Rail and by Road, COM (2005) 319 final, 20.07.2005, p. 3.

[76] The latest Regulation on cabotage passenger transport provides that 'cabotage operations shall be authorised for with the exception of regular service meeting the needs of an urban centre or conurbation, or transport needs between it and the surrounding areas': Regulation (EC) No 1073/2009 of the European Parliament and of the Council of 21 October 2009 on common rules for access to the international market for coach and bus services, and amending Regulation (EC) No 561/2006 [2009] OJ L300/88, Article 15(c).

[77] Regulation (EEC) No 1191/69 of the Council of 26 June 1969 on action by Member States concerning the obligations inherent in the concept of a public service in transport by rail, road and inland waterway [1969] OJ L156/1.

[78] Regulation (EC) No 1370/2007 of the European Parliament and of the Council of 23 October 2007 on public passenger transport services by rail and by road and repealing Council Regulations (EEC) Nos 1191/69 and 1107/70 [2007] OJ L315/1.

intervention. It then shows that EU law had little influence in this area until 2007: Regulation 1191/69, as the relevant EU legislation during this period, took extra care of public transport service and granted exemption for public transport services from the ongoing market liberalisation and integration process.[79] The final part of this section will look at the current EU regime in this area: Regulation 1370/2007.[80] This study finds that the immediate impacts of this Regulation on the organisation of public transport systems are still very limited.

7.3.1 State Involvement in the Organisation of Public Transport Systems

The involvement of public authorities in the provision of passenger transport services started in the late 1890s and early 1900s with the advent of tram services.[81] The justification behind the public involvement was not well-defined and differed across the Member States. It was driven partly by the uneasy relationship between public authorities and transport undertakings at the early stage of transport development and partly by the attractiveness of the potential profitability arising from the operation of the public tram system.[82]

This was still an age when the majority of the population in Europe did not have access to motor cars and relied on public transport services for their mobility needs. For example, in Britain in 1952, 85% of households still did not have regular use of a car, and buses were used to cover 42% of total travel distances.[83] High ridership of the public transport system in combination with the protection of monopoly rights essentially guaranteed economical scale and its sustainability without the need to call on extra State funding.

State involvement in the public transport systems grew even stronger after World War II under the influence of the welfare State and the ideal of universal service. The public transport service was regarded as an essential service and a basic service that should be made available for everyone.[84] Therefore, public authorities assumed

[79] Regulation (EEC) No 1191/69 of the Council of 26 June 1969 on action by Member States concerning the obligations inherent in the concept of a public service in transport by rail, road and inland waterway [1969] OJ L156/1.

[80] Regulation (EC) No 1370/2007 of the European Parliament and of the Council of 23 October 2007 on public passenger transport services by rail and by road and repealing Council Regulations (EEC) Nos 1191/69 and 1107/70 [2007] OJ L315/1.

[81] Costa and Fernandes 2012.

[82] Amaral 2008.

[83] Office for National Statistics, 'Social Trends' (No. 40, 2010 edition): http://www.ons.gov.uk/ons/rel/social-trends-rd/social-trends/social-trends-40/social-trends-40-full-report.pdf.

[84] Hidson and Müller 2003.

responsibility for its organisation and delivery. Networks were expanded to achieve full territorial coverage, and price was kept artificially low to make it affordable to users.[85]

This massive development in human progress involved the design of a nationwide transport network and the deployment of different transportation means to meet the collective demand of the general public.[86] The actual forms of its organisation differed hugely across Member States and evolved over time, depending on national settings and local circumstances. Therefore, it is more appropriate to use the term 'public transport systems' rather than 'public transport services'.

This diversity can be found in various ways. First, in terms of technology, different means of transport have been used, including bus, tram, rail and underground.[87] Second, the institutional arrangements varied across Member States.[88] Public transport systems were organised by public authorities at the municipal, local, regional or national level. They might establish public undertakings to deliver the services or even through public administrations themselves. Public transport services were also delivered by private undertakings. Public authorities exerted their influence through the authorisation system. Undertakings intending to provide public transport services were required by law to obtain a licence to operate. As a condition for a licence, PSOs were frequently imposed on the undertaking, including obligations on matters concerning routes, timetable and fares.

The organisation of public transport systems, as described earlier, began to run into trouble in the 1960s, when the majority of the population began to own private cars.[89] This posed new challenges. First, more cars on the road led to more pollution and more traffic congestion.[90] The expansion of the national road networks simply could not keep pace with the growth of car usage. Meanwhile, this move to cars essentially made public transport services commercially unviable in many instances, since more and more individuals opted out because their individual mobility needs began to be met increasingly by the use of private cars. As early as the 1970s, car transport accounted for 73.8% of the total travel distance, which steadily rose to 78.2% in 2001. In contrast, the use of public transport services has declined from 24.7% to 16%.[91] As a result, the operating costs of public transport could not be covered by the ticket revenue generated.

---

[85] Isotope 1997.

[86] Commission of the European Communities, The Citizens' Network—Fulfilling the Potential of Public Passenger Transport in Europe (European Commission Green Paper), COM (95) 601 final, 29.11.1995 (hereafter 1995 Citizens' Network Green Paper).

[87] Costa and Fernandes 2012.

[88] For a detailed discussion, see Van De Velde 1999.

[89] Karlaftis and McCarthy 1998.

[90] 1995 Citizens' Network Green Paper.

[91] Ibid., para 1.

In these new market conditions, public authorities still decided to maintain, and even to expand, public transport systems for two main non-economic reasons. The first reason is the ideal of universal service, which is still regarded as an essential and valid objective in the organisation of a public transport system. Its emphasis began to shift towards building a safety net for the vulnerable, which might include the poor, the elderly and the disabled, who had no other choice but to use the public transport services.[92] Secondly, public authorities also intend to improve the quality of the public transport system to attract more people from private car usage, thereby, relieving traffic congestion and air pollution caused by the increasing usage of private cars.[93]

In this new market reality, public transport systems, as defined by universal coverage and affordable price, was simply not sustainable on commercial terms. Even though the grant of monopoly meant that all revenues could be pooled together, it could not cover the full operating costs because of the decreasing use of public transport systems. This is a widespread problem in virtually all public transport systems in Member States. For example, in Rome, in 1993 revenues covered only 10% of the operating costs.[94] As a result, extra funds are granted by public authorities to maintain the operation of public transport system.

What can be observed is that the involvement of public authorities in the organisation and delivery of public transport system is a *political choice*. It is the public authorities that decide that the public transport system should be maintained, and even expanded, for non-economic reasons in spite of deteriorating market conditions. These non-economic aims are wide ranging and loosely defined and are associated with national circumstances, including providing universal service, protecting the environment and relieving traffic congestion.

7.3.2 Limited Influence of Regulation 1191/69 During Market Liberalisation

Since the late 1980s, the EU began to adopt legislation to break down national restraints on access to inland transport markets.[95] During this process, the only EU legislation that was relevant to the organisation of public transport systems was Regulation 11191/69.[96] The potential impacts of this Regulation on the organisation of public transport services seemed significant. Article 1 required Member

---

92 Viegas 1999.

93 Isotope 1997.

94 1995 Citizens' Network Green Paper, 56.

95 For a description of the EU market liberalisation process, see Greaves 2000.

96 Regulation (EEC) No 1191/69 of the Council of 26 June 1969 on action by Member States concerning the obligations inherent in the concept of a public service in transport by rail, road and inland waterway [1969] OJ L156/1.

States to terminate all obligations inherent in the concept of a public service. Potentially, this could force the Member States to hand over public transport service and let free market competition take over the provision of public transport services. However, a close scrutiny shows that the significance of this Regulation on the provision of public transport service was very limited. It virtually left the public transport sector untouched by the market integration process in inland transport.

In the Regulation, the term 'PSO' itself was used in a very unique setting and meant something very different. It essentially covered all state interventions in the transport sector, rather than just SGEI. This could be observed from the very rationale behind the Regulation. The initial approach of the Council towards the Common Transport Policy was harmonisation rather than market integration. As early as 1965, the Council had adopted a Decision that set as the objectives of the common transport policy the elimination of disparities and harmonisation of national laws in regard to taxation, state intervention and social legislation.[97] The concern of the EU then was that state control and intervention in the transport undertaking obstructed the *commercial freedom* of the undertaking,[98] without which free competition was not possible. This was particularly true in the railway sector.

It is in this harmonisation framework that the first legislation on PSO was adopted. Regulation 1191/69 covered all compulsory requirements from the State, including the obligations to operate and to carry and tariff obligations. As a general principle, it required Member States to terminate all these obligations inherent in the concept of a public service and to restore commercial freedom in these undertakings.[99] However, this Regulation was designed to apply to the rail transport sector. It allowed the Member States to exclude public transport services from its scope. In Recital (20) of the original text, it acknowledges that:

> This regulation is at present to apply to rail transport operations of the six national railway undertakings of the Member States and, as regards other transport undertakings, to undertakings *not* mainly providing *transport service of a local or regional character.*[100] (emphasis added)

Indeed, as the implementation report of the Commission shows, most of the Member States applied this Regulation only to their railway undertakings.[101] This exclusion was made clearer by its subsequent amendment in 1991, which in Article

[97] 65/271/EEC: Council Decision of 13 May 1965 on the harmonisation of certain provisions affecting competition in transport by rail, road and inland waterway [1965] OJ 88/1500.

[98] Opinion of Advocate General, Case 36/73 *NV Nederlandse Spoorwegen v Minister van Verkeer en Waterstaat* [1973] ECR-1299.

[99] Regulation (EEC) No 1191/69 of the Council of 26 June 1969 on action by Member States concerning the obligations inherent in the concept of a public service in transport by rail, road and inland waterway [1969] OJ L156/1, Article 1.

[100] Ibid., Recital 20.

[101] Commission of the European Communities, Second report on the implementation of Council Regulation (EEC) No 1191/69 of 26 June 1969, relating to the action by Member States concerning the obligations inherent in the concept of a public service in transport by rail, road and

1(2) granted an escape mechanism that the Member States could make use of,[102] by allowing the Member States *to exclude* public transport undertakings from the scope of this Regulation.

Even if the Member States do not utilise the exclusion mechanism, Regulation 1191/69 then also granted an exception/derogation regarding the provision of public transport services, namely the concept of *adequacy of transport services*, which is equivalent to the concept of SGEIs in the inland transport sector. As an exception to the overall prohibition, state intervention can be maintained in order to ensure adequate transport services. However, EU law does not clearly define the term. Rather, 'it merely provides certain factors for assessing it':[103]

> The adequacy of transport services shall be assessed having regard to: (a) the *public interest*; (b) the possibility of having recourse to other forms of transport and the ability of such forms to meet *the transport needs* under consideration; (c) *the transport rates and conditions* which can be quoted to users.[104]

These factors are extremely broad and vague, and no detailed guideline has been issued by any EU institution either as to their interpretation or meaning. Meanwhile, the Regulation does not provide rules on how state funding in public transport systems should be awarded. This actually grants Member States extremely wide discretion regarding the organisation of public transport services. Through this very broad term, public transport systems were virtually under the complete control of the Member States, outside the influence of EU law. The *Kainuun* case concerning the bus service in Finland is a good illustration of this approach.[105]

In Finland, the operation of scheduled bus services was subject to licensing from public authorities. The Ministry of Transport granted a licence to a transport undertaking, Kainuun, for the operation of a regional scheduled service between Kajanni and Rukatunturi, a distance of about 275 km. It also set the specific timetables for the service. In the main proceeding, Kainuun was unwilling to provide service on certain parts of the route because of their loss-making nature and applied to terminate those parts.

The case was referred to the Court for a preliminary ruling, and the main issue was whether the Regulation entitles a transport undertaking to obtain termination of

---

inland waterway, and of Council Regulation (EEC) No 1192/69 of 26 June 1969, relating to the normalisation of the accounts of railway undertakings, SEC (74) 2219 final, 18.06.1974.

[102] Council Regulation (EEC) No 1893/91 of 20 June 1991 amending Regulation (EEC) No 1191/69 on action by Member States concerning the obligations inherent in the concept of a public service in transport by rail, road and inland waterway [1991] OJ L169/1.

[103] Case C-412/96 *Kainuun Liikenne Oy and Oy Pohjolan Liikenne Ab* [1998] ECR I-5141, para 32.

[104] Regulation (EEC) No 1191/69 of the Council of 26 June 1969 on action by Member States concerning the obligations inherent in the concept of a public service in transport by rail, road and inland waterway [1969] OJ L156/1.

[105] Case C-412/96 *Kainuun Liikenne Oy and Oy Pohjolan Liikenne Ab* [1998] ECR I-5141.

its obligation. In other words, whether it forced/obliged the Member States to withdraw its intervention in the sector. In the Judgment, the Court explicitly stated that:

> It should be noted that under Article 4(1) of the Regulation a transport undertaking may apply for the termination of all or any part of a public service obligations, but that *no provision of that regulation obliges* the Member States to grant that application, even if the undertaking shows that maintaining it involves economic disadvantages within the meaning of Article 5 of the Regulation. On the contrary, [...] the competent authorities of the Member States are *entitled to maintain* in whole or in part a public service obligation which they consider necessary to ensure *the provision of adequate transport services*.[106] (emphasis added)

The Court did not define what could be regarded as 'adequate transport service' but left its interpretation to the Member States. The attitude of the Court is clear: public authorities are permitted to impose compulsory requirements for the provision of adequate transport service. Therefore, the Member States still have almost absolute freedom in organising their public transport services.

7.3.3 Introduction of Competition by the Member States

The landscape changed dramatically from 1986 onwards, when Britain first opened up its public transport service market to market competition.[107] Without EU initiatives, 11 out of 15 Member States had introduced competition in the public transport system.[108] The actual extent differs across the Member States.[109] Countries such as the UK deregulated the public transport service market and allowed full access to the market, where provision of public transport services fully depends on market mechanisms. Market undertakings bear full financial responsibilities; they decide what routes they will provide and also set ticket fares. This essentially means a withdrawal of the State from the public transport service sector.[110] Other countries (for example, Sweden, Denmark and Germany) were more cautious and adopted the so-called controlled competition approach.[111] This allows Member States to have control over the planning and design over the routes and fares of public transport services. Meanwhile, providers and the amount of public subsidy are decided through public tendering procedures.

---

[106] Ibid., paras 26–27.

[107] Van De Velde 2001.

[108] Commission of the European Communities, Proposal for a Regulation of the European Parliament and of the Council on action by Member States concerning public service requirements and the award of public service contracts in passenger transport by rail, road and inland waterway, COM (2000) 7 final, 26.07.2001, p. 4.

[109] Hidson and Müller 2003.

[110] Van De Velde 2001.

[111] Ibid.

With the opening up of these national markets, public transport services are not merely based on national markets any more. Operators from other European countries could increasingly participate in the provision of local public transport services, which essentially meant that the organisation of public transport services began to have a European dimension.[112]

In the Treaty, there was no specific provision relating to this hugely complicated issue. Nor were there any rules concerning the competence of the EU in this area. The only provision of relevance was found in Article 93 TFEU, which declares that state aid for PSO is compatible with the Treaty. This exception allows state funding for public transport services to be brought outside the reach of the state aid control regime. On the other hand, there were no rules on how compensation for PSO in public transport shall be awarded. Without much oversight from EU law or institution, state funding for public transport systems could potentially lead to over-compensation and distortion of the market. The other issue that comes to the attention of competition law is the widespread usage of exclusive rights. It does not sit easily either with the market integration programme in the transport sector or with the principle of free competition. Its compatibility has been challenged by the Court under Article 106(1).[113]

In this environment, the initial intention of the Commission was to implement free movement rules and to introduce competition in the sector. At the same time, the Commission had to grapple with the non-economic dimensions prevailing in the provision of public transport services. This has turned out to be very controversial. It took ten years for the EU to adopt its Regulation on public transport services, Regulation 1370/2007.[114]

The balancing exercise resulted in the triumph of non-economic values over the application of competition law and market integration principles. The EU has recognised the wide non-economic values pursued by public authorities in the organisation of national public transport systems. It did not introduce full

[112]Transport service operator Arriva is a good example of this. It is headquartered in the UK but owned by Deutsche Bahn, a German railway company. It operates public transport services in 14 European countries. See the company's official website: Arriva Official Website, 'Transport Services: Overview.' http://www.arriva.co.uk/business_activities/transport_services/overview_1.aspx.

[113]Case C-41/90 *Klaus Höfner and Fritz Elser v Macrotron GmbH* [1991] ECR I-1979; Case C-260/89 *Elliniki Radiophonia Tileorassi AE (Ert) (Panellinia Omospondia Syllogon Prossopikou Ert intervening) v Dimotiki Étairia Pliroforissis (Dep) and Sotirios Kouvelas (Nicolaos Avdellas and Others intervening)* [1991] ECR I-02925; Case C-260/89 *Elliniki Radiophonia Tileorassi AE (Ert) (Panellinia Omospondia Syllogon Prossopikou Ert intervening) v Dimotiki Étairia Pliroforissis (Dep) and Sotirios Kouvelas (Nicolaos Avdellas and Others intervening)* [1991] ECR I-02925. This issue has been discussed in Chap. 3.

[114]The efforts started from 1995, when it published a Green Paper on this issue: 1995 Citizens' Network Green Paper.

competition in this sector. Instead, in order to provide funding for the provision of public transport services, it allowed the existence of exclusive rights. Furthermore, it also granted derogations for Member States from the public tendering procedure.[115]

7.3.4 *Market Failure and Wide Range of Non-economic Values*

The blueprint for the application of EU rules in the public transport system was laid down by the Commission's 1995 Citizens' Network Green Paper.[116] It acknowledged the market failure problem in the public transport systems. As pointed out by the Commission, the usage of the private car as a means of passenger transport had increased significantly and accounted for 75% of the distances travelled by citizens in 1993. By contrast, bus transport took up only 8%.[117] In 10 out of 15 European cities tickets revenues covered less than half of the operational costs by. The recovery rate ranges from only 10%, in Rome, to 45%, in Frankfurt.[118] As a result, revenues generated by tickets alone cannot cover its full operational costs, and the very existence of public transport service depends on state funding.

On the other hand, the Commission also recognised the wide range of non-economic considerations that justify state intervention to maintain the public transport systems.[119] However, it did not define it in detail. In the 1995 Citizens' Network Green Paper, the Commission pointed out that:

> It is generally recognised that in the transport field market forces alone do not ensure in all situations the level, coverage and quality of transport service provision required for *fulfilment of essential economic, social and regional policy goals*. This is particularly valid in the field of urban, and regional public transport services.[120] (emphasis added)

What stands out from these wide non-economic values is the ideal of universal service, i.e. the provision of public transport service to everyone in society. In the Green Paper, the Commission expressly recognised that:

> In particular, there should be further consideration of the notion of public service obligations. Ideally, public transport should be *accessible, affordable and available to all citizens*.[121] (emphasis added)

---

[115] Regulation (EC) No 1370/2007 of the European Parliament and of the Council of 23 October 2007 on public passenger transport services by rail and by road and repealing Council Regulations (EEC) Nos 1191/69 and 1107/70 [2007] OJ L315/1.

[116] 1995 Citizens' Network Green Paper.

[117] Ibid.

[118] Ibid.

[119] Delle Site and Salucci 2009.

[120] 1995 Citizens' Network Green Paper, para 99.

[121] Ibid., para 89.

It provided a quality checklist that was essentially based on the ideal of universal service. The first on the list is universal access,[122] which takes consideration of 'the needs of people of reduced mobility' and 'linking rural and peripheral regions'.[123] The second element is affordability, which focuses on fare levels. In practice, this essentially means low fare prices, which could not even cover the operational costs of the public transport services. This principle of universality and affordability corresponds to the very ideal of universal service found in the telecommunications sector.

Surprisingly, even this broad definition of non-economic values was not contained in the Regulation 1370/2007, which followed. Regulation 1370/2007 does not specify what non-economic considerations justify state intervention in the market. In fact, the Regulation takes the non-economic considerations for granted and does not intend to challenge or confine Member States' freedom in this respect.

The EU does not establish a minimum service requirement package that the Member States have the legal obligation to guarantee. It essentially left many issues regarding non-economic values in organising the transport systems to the discretion and freedom of the Member States. These include: (1) what non-economic values they will pursue in organising their public transport systems; (2) to what extent these non-economic consideration will be materialised; and (3) to what values priority will be given if there is a conflict between these non-economic values. Unregulated by EU law, these issues still remain in the hands of the Member States. Therefore, the actual achievement of these non-economic values still depends on the political will of each individual Member State. EU law has little influence in this respect.

7.3.5 Limited Competition Approach: The Compatibility of Exclusive Rights

The aim of the Regulation is to establish a framework for the grant of compensation and/or exclusive rights. On the issue of exclusive rights, similarly to those in the air transport sector, EU law does not introduce full competition in the public transport sector, but rather adopts the limited competition approach. In fact, as early as in 1995 in its Green Paper, the Commission indicated that the *controlled competition*

---

[122] It did not use the term 'universal access' or 'universal service'; instead it adopted the term 'system accessibility': 1995 Citizens' Network Green Paper.

[123] Ibid.

approach is the future choice for the organisation of public transport services in the EU.[124] This approach is adopted in Regulation 1370/2007, in which it recognises exclusive right as a funding pathway for the provision of public transport services.[125]

The Commission's reasoning on the compatibility of exclusive rights under the Treaty is very interesting. It points out the anti-competitive nature of exclusive right: it is in conflict with competition law and also contradicts the basic freedom of the Treaty. Meanwhile, it also recognises that it might be justified under Article 106 (2) on SGEI under the necessity test:

> Granting exclusive rights which affect trade between Member States limits market access and thus infringes – albeit indirectly – the principle of freedom of establishment. Interventions by Member States restricting market access must, in accordance with Article 10(2), be *proportionate* and therefore should limit or harm competition *only to the degree necessary* to obtain the public benefits aimed at.[126] (emphasis added)

In its 1995 Citizens' Network Green Paper, the Commission did not articulate what standard would be applied in the test. It indicated that a wide range of factors would be examined under the necessity test, including the length of time, the geographical area covered, the competing services excluded and the public service requirements decided by public authorities. A thorough investigation would potentially challenge the organisation of public transport service in the Member States, as is shown by the Commission's practice in PSO in the air transport sector.

Surprisingly, the Commission does not apply this necessity test to examine the compatibility of exclusive rights at all, let alone comprehensive economic evaluation. Instead, it adopts a very generous approach to the grant of exclusive rights. It does not challenge the very existence of exclusive rights but simply *assumes* the compatibility of exclusive rights as an appropriate funding mechanism. In its proposal for the Regulation 1370/2007, it states that:

> Exclusive rights are also widespread in the public transport sector. […] Where *properly applied* by competent authorities, they can enable *the finance of loss-making* and of commercially viable services to be pooled in ways that *benefit the general interest*. It follows that access to the public transport market depends, in reality, on access to public financing and to exclusive rights.[127] (emphasis added)

In nature it is a *political decision* rather than serious legal reasoning. This political nature could be observed well from the lengthy legislative process that

---

[124] Ibid.

[125] Regulation (EC) No 1370/2007 of the European Parliament and of the Council of 23 October 2007 on public passenger transport services by rail and by road and repealing Council Regulations (EEC) Nos 1191/69 and 1107/70 [2007] OJ L315/1, Recital 5.

[126] Commission of the European Communities, Proposal for a Regulation of the European Parliament and of the Council on action by Member States concerning public service requirements and the award of public service contracts in passenger transport by rail, road and inland waterway, COM (2000) 7 final, 26.07.2001.

[127] Ibid., p. 6.

preceded the adoption of Regulation 1370/2007.[128] The Commission first proposed its draft in 2000,[129] and the EU institutions took seven years to pass the Regulation in 2007 after another two drafts.[130]

7.3.6 Derogations from Competitive Tendering Procedures

Without challenging the compatibility of exclusive rights itself, the concern of the EU law has focused on how they are granted. From the EU's perspective, an EU-wide public procurement procedure can open up national public transport markets to EU operators based in other Member States and thus enable freedom of establishment and competition. Meanwhile, a transparent and properly conducted public procurement process is assumed to guarantee that state funding does not lead to overcompensation and distortions of market competition. Therefore, as a general principle, any state funding for public transport services, i.e. the grant of exclusive rights and/or compensation, is subject to competitive tendering procedure and EU procurement Directives.[131]

Meanwhile, the accommodation of non-economic values in the public transport systems has taken precedence, which is then translated as derogations from the public tendering procedure. First, the Regulation grants a ten-year transition period for the implementation of public tendering procedures for the sector. Although the Regulation came into effect in 2009, it requires Member States to comply with this rule only from 2019.[132] Second, it allows the so-called 'in house' provision, where direct award without tendering is permitted by the Regulation.[133] The Member States may opt to provide public transport services through an entity that it actually controls without public tendering procedures.[134]

---

[128] Van De Velde 2008.

[129] Commission of the European Communities, Proposal for a Regulation of the European Parliament and of the Council on action by Member States concerning public service requirements and the award of public service contracts in passenger transport by rail, road and inland waterway, COM (2000)7 final, 26.07.2001.

[130] Commission of the European Communities, Amended proposal for a Regulation of the European Parliament and of the Council on action by Member States concerning public service requirements and the award of public service contracts in passenger transport by rail, road and inland waterway, COM (2002) 107 final, 21.02.2002; Commission of the European Communities, Revised Proposal for a Regulation of the European Parliament and of the Council on Public Passenger Transport Services by Rail and by Road, COM (2005) 319 final, 20.07.2005.

[131] Maczkovics et al. 2010.

[132] Regulation (EC) No 1370/2007 of the European Parliament and of the Council of 23 October 2007 on public passenger transport services by rail and by road and repealing Council Regulations (EEC) Nos 1191/69 and 1107/70 [2007] OJ L315/1, Article 8(2).

[133] Ibid., Article 5(2).

[134] It is not clear to what extent this public control should be to qualify for this exception. Thus, it has created interpretation difficulties and uncertainty in practice. The Court has not addressed this

Although 'in house' provision of public transport service is immune from the application of public procurement rules, EU law can still have significant implications over its organisation and funding, through the state aid control regime. The reason is that without following EU public procurement law, state funding for public transport services is very likely to fall within the scope of state aid rules: on the issue of whether it constitutes state aid or not, the essential benchmark is the *Altmark* criteria, which turn out to be extremely difficult to satisfy.[135] So far, the Commission has made eight Decisions concerning the provision of public transport services, and none of them were found to have fulfilled the *Altmark* criteria.[136] Consequently, the Commission concluded that the funding measures constituted state aid.

After finding that the funding measure constitutes state aid, the Commission would proceed to examine whether it is compatible with the Treaty. On this issue, Regulation 1370/2007 lays down rules that all PSO funding in the public transport sector has to comply with.[137] These rules constituted the *lex specialis* in the area of public transport in relation to Article 106(2) and are therefore the benchmark for

---

issue in the context of Regulation 1370/2007. However, this question has been discussed by the Court in the context of public procurement rules and tends to be problematic: See Maczkovics et al. 2010; Kekelekis and Rusu 2010.

[135] For a discussion of the application of the *Altmark* criteria, see Sect. 4.2 of Chap. 4.

[136]

(1) 2009/845/EC: Commission Decision of 26 November 2008 on state aid granted by Austria to the company Postbus in the Lienz district C 16/07 (ex NN 55/06) [2009] OJ L306/26;
(2) 2009/325/EC: Commission Decision of 26 November 2008 on State Aid C 3/08 (ex NN 102/05)– Czech Republic concerning public service compensations for Southern Moravia Bus Companies [2009] OJ L97/14;
(3) 2009/973/EC: Commission Decision of 13 July 2009 on the restructuring aid for Combus A/S [2009] OJ L345/28;
(4) 2011/3/EU: Commission Decision of 24 February 2010 concerning public transport service contracts between the Danish Ministry of Transport and Danske Statsbaner [2011] OJ L7/1;
(5) 2011/501/EU: Commission Decision of 23 February 2011 on State Aid C 58/06 (ex NN 98/05) implemented by Germany for Bahnen der Stadt Monheim (BSM) and Rheinische Bahngesellschaft (RBG) in the Verkehrsverbund Rhein-Ruhr [2011] OJ L210/1;
(6) 2014/201/EU: Commission Decision of 2 October 2013 on compensation to be paid to Simet SpA for public transport services provided between 1987 and 2003 [2014] OJ L114/48;
(7) SA.34155 Regional law on the compensation of school bus transport in the Land Rhineland-Palatinate, C (2014) 133, 22.01.2014;
(8) Commission Decision of 15 October 2014 on State Aid SA.20580 (C 31/2007) (ex NN 17/2007) implemented by Ireland for Córas Iompair Éireann Bus Companies (Dublin Bus and Irish Bus), C (2014) 7275 final, 15.10.2014.

[137] Article 6 of the Regulation provides that:

All compensation connected with a general rule or a public service contract shall comply with the provisions laid down in Article 4, irrespective of how the contract was awarded. All compensation, of whatever nature, connected with a public service contract awarded directly in accordance with Article 5(2), (4), (5) or (6) or connected with a general rule shall also comply with the provisions laid down in the Annex.

assessing the compatibility of such measures with state aid law.[138] On the one hand, Article 4 of the Regulation lays down mandatory content for all public service contacts. It requires that public service contract shall:

> (1) clearly define the public service obligations with which the public service operator is to comply, and the geographical areas concerned; (2) establish in advance, in an objective and transparent manner, (i) the parameters on the basis of which the compensation payment, if any, is to be calculated, and (ii) the nature and extent of any exclusive rights granted, in a way that prevents overcompensation; and (3) determine the arrangements for the allocation of costs connected with the provision of services.[139]

Its Decisions show that these rules would have profound significance over the organisation of public transport services by the Member States (even though they are not subject to the EU procurement Directive). Its Decision concerning a planned funding measure by Italy to an interregional bus service operator, Simet, is a good example.[140] In the Decision, the Commission found that the compensation parameters were not established in advance and that compensation was therefore calculated ex post. Consequently, the Commission concluded that the proposed funding measure did not comply with Regulation 1370/2007 and was therefore incompatible with the Treaty.

On the other hand, the Annex of the Regulation also establishes principles and detailed rules on how compensation shall be determined.[141] The Commission has been using these rules to scrutinise Member States' funding of public transport services. The substantive requirement is to ensure that funding does not lead to overcompensation, and therefore grant an advantage to the recipient undertaking. In other words, any overcompensation by the Member State would be regarded as incompatible and must be recovered.

Its impact is well-illustrated in the Commission's Decision concerning Danish funding for public transport services provided by its public rail operator *Danske Statsbaner* (hereafter DSB).[142] In this case, Denmark concluded contracts with DSB to provide public transport services from 2005 to 2014. The amount of payment was fixed in advance on the basis of a ten-year budget. In the Commission's Decision, it found that DSB had reduced the costs of PSO provision significantly owing to the improvement in its financial situation and efficiency, which had not been taken into account when the compensation amount was determined. Consequently, the Commission argued that DSB gained excessive

---

[138] See, for example, 2011/501/EU: Commission Decision of 23 February 2011 on State Aid C 58/06 (ex NN 98/05) implemented by Germany for Bahnen der Stadt Monheim (BSM) and Rheinische Bahngesellschaft (RBG) in the Verkehrsverbund Rhein-Ruhr [2011] OJ L210/1, para 218.

[139] Regulation 1370/2007, Article 4.

[140] 2014/201/EU: Commission Decision of 2 October 2013 on compensation to be paid to Simet SpA for public transport services provided between 1987 and 2003 [2014] OJ L114/48.

[141] Regulation 1370/2007, Annex.

[142] 2011/3/EU: Commission Decision of 24 February 2010 concerning public transport service contracts between the Danish Ministry of Transport and Danske Statsbaner [2011] OJ L7/1.

profit that led to overcompensation (hence, incompatible with the Treaty).[143] Furthermore, in its Decision, the Commission required Denmark to introduce a clawback refund mechanism to adjust the amount of compensation every year, to ensure that the PSO provider did not gain excessive profit.[144]

7.4 Public Service Obligations in Maritime Transport

Maritime activity has been subject to the Common Transport Policy in the Treaty. The application of free movement rules and competition law in this sector depends on the implementing legislation adopted by the Council. For three decades since the Treaty of Rome, the maritime sector had been exempted from these rules.[145] It was only in December 1986, when the Council adopted Regulation 4055/86, that the maritime transport sector began to be subject to the Treaty's rules on free movement and competition.[146]

This Regulation did not change the organisational structure of the maritime sector adopted by the Member States. While some Member States adopted an open regime on maritime transport (where the sector was open to foreign operators), the closed regime in certain Member States had created serious tension with the ongoing market integration programme. Under such national regimes, the maritime transport market was reserved only for national operators but was not open to undertakings from other Member States. This was the very case in Member States such as Greece, Italy, France, Spain and Portugal.[147]

This closed regime had been the major concern of the EU, as it was in contradiction to the principle of non-discrimination and free movement of services. From the market integration perspective, the consequences are essentially the same

---

[143] In the Decision, the Commission did not require Denmark to recover the incompatible state aid because DSB was a 100% state-owned company, and overcompensation was neutralised by the collection of dividends by Denmark: Ibid., para 347.

[144] The refund mechanism was proposed by Denmark and approved by the Commission, which will be incorporated into all PSO contracts between Denmark and DSB. The refund mechanism did not eliminate the possibility of profit-gain by DSB but to control it within a reasonable level. The actual design of the refund mechanism also introduced an incentive element for DSB to improve efficiency: Ibid., paras 350–364.

[145] Greaves 2009.

[146] Council Regulation (EEC) No 4055/86 of 22 December 1986 applying the principle of freedom to provide services to maritime transport between Member States and between Member States and third countries [1988] OJ L117/33.

[147] Brooks 2009.

as in the case of exclusive rights in the telecommunications and postal service sectors. It led to market fragmentation and isolation; a genuine Internal Market on maritime transport did not yet exist.[148]

The focus of market integration in the maritime sector has been the breakdown of these national barriers by the rules on free movement of services. This has created significant controversy and reluctance among these Member States owing to the significance of the sector for national economies and employment.[149] It took three years for the EU institutions to adopt Regulation 3577/92 to apply the free movement rules in this sector.[150] Meanwhile, the Regulation made many derogations and exemptions for Member States; full maritime cabotage has been possible only since 2002.

As part of this new regulatory framework, rules on SGEI began to be established by EU institutions for the first time. The interest of the EU in this matter arise because the imposition of certain SGEI obligations might restrict the free movement of services. Therefore, it was largely seen as an exception.

This section will focus on the treatment of the SGEI concept in the maritime sector, as in Regulation 3577/92. It discusses how SGEIs are defined at the EU level and shows how the Regulation fails to provide a comprehensive framework for the organisation of SGEIs in the maritime sector.

7.4.1 Transport Link for Islands as an SGEI

The Recital of Regulation 3577/92 stipulates that state intervention in the market is justified in order to guarantee *adequacy* of regular transport service for islands.[151] This does not suggest the genuine underlying non-economic considerations but rather the *conditions* for state intervention, i.e. the market itself fails to provide adequate transport services. In its Interpretation Communication, the Commission itself points out that:

---

[148] In the maritime sector, there was a competitive market, but it existed only at the national level. This is different from that in the telecommunications and postal sectors, where the grant of exclusive rights eliminated competition at the national and EU levels.

[149] Greaves 2009.

[150] In 1989 the Commission made a proposal to the Council on the application of rules on freedom of movement to the maritime sector: Commission of the European Communities, Proposal for a Council Regulation applying the principle of freedom to provide services to maritime transport within Member States [1989] OJ L263/17.

[151] This includes transport services from, to and between islands: Council Regulation (EEC) No 3577/92 of 7 December 1992 applying the principle of freedom to provide services to maritime transport within Member States [1992] OJ L364/7.

> The maritime transport of passenger and goods is *vital for the inhabitants of Europe's islands*. That is why a special set of rules was drawn up to protect some of these maritime links n*ot adequately served by the market*.[152] (emphasis added)

From the Commission's perspective, transport link for islands per se needs special attention and deserves exception from market integration. The importance of the transport link for islands seems obvious. The problem associated with island transport is very unique: maritime transportation is normally the only practical and reliable regular means of transport. A reliable and regular ferry service for islands is often regarded as their lifeblood.[153]

The recognition of non-economic values at the EU level has its roots at the national level in the Member States, which have long been involved in the provision of transport links for islands in Europe, linked to a wide range of non-economic values.[154] At the EU level, there is no uniform rule on what non-economic values should be achieved by the Member States. In the Commission's practice, it has expressly recognised the following as legitimate: regional economic development, social cohesion and territorial continuity.[155] In nature, it is a political issue that will be decided at the national level. The actual design and management of these ferry links vary across Member States.[156] A common theme that can be found is the establishment of public undertakings and the grant of substantial public funding.[157]

Similarly to other areas of the transport sector, the EU legislation does not oblige Member States to guarantee the provision of PSO for islands. The decision to

---

[152] Commission of the European Communities, Communication on the interpretation of Council Regulation (EEC) No 3577/92 applying the principle of freedom to provide services to maritime transport within Member States (maritime cabotage), COM (2003) 595 final, 22.12.2003.

[153] Chlomoudis et al. 2007.

[154] For example, in Scotland ferry services for islands dated back to 1851: Morton 2011, p. 8; Bennett 2006.

[155] 2013/435/EU: Commission Decision of 2 May 2013 on State Aid SA.22843 (2012/C) (ex 2012/NN) implemented by France in favour of Société Nationale Maritime Corse-Méditerranée [2013] OJ L220/20 (hereafter the *SNCM* Decision), paras 145–146.

[156] For a survey of the organisation of PSO links for islands in Member States, see Commission of the European Communities, Report from the Commission—Third report of the implementation of Council Regulation 3577/92 applying the principle of freedom to provide services to maritime cabotage (1997–1998), COM (2000) 99 final, 24.02.2000.

[157] Commission Decisions provide a window to the organisation of ferry service for islands in the Member States. The application of EU competition law and state aid law has produced a lot of controversy. See for example:

(1) 2001/156/EC: Commission Decision of 19 July 2000 on the state aid implemented by Spain in favour of the maritime transport sector (new maritime public service contract) [2001] L57/32 (hereafter the *Transmed* Decision);
(2) 2011/98/EC: Commission Decision of 28 October 2009 on the state aid C 16/08 (ex NN 105/05 and NN 35/07) implemented by the United Kingdom of Great Britain and Northern Ireland —Subsidies to CalMac and NorthLink for maritime transport services in Scotland [2011] OJ L45/33 (hereafter the *CalMac* Decision).

establish and fund a particular PSO link is made at the national level.[158] It is the Member States that have the freedom to decide the scope of PSOs (whether it might include passenger/car/freight) and the actual organisation and delivery.[159] The Commission seldom challenges State measures regarding the compatibility of the non-economic objectives pursued by the Member States. Its evaluation has been confined to whether a transport link for island regions fulfils the market failure test.[160]

7.4.2 *Lack of Procedural Framework for the Organisation of SGEIs at EU Level*

The treatment of PSOs in the maritime sector has not received much attention in the market integration legislation. In fact, it was largely neglected. The funding issue was not even envisaged by the original proposal of the Regulation 3577/92. In the proposal, there was only one mechanism available for the Member States, the imposition of PSOs.[161] Even in the amended version of the proposal, it did not mention public service contracts or the funding issues. Without much debate, public service contracts and funding were only added to the final version of the Regulation by the Council.

For the first decade since the adoption of the Regulation 3577/92, the focus of the EU had been predominantly on market integration issues. In the first three reports on the implementation of the Regulation, the issue of PSOs was not mentioned at all.[162] It was only in 2002, when market integration had been essentially achieved, that the Commission began to examine the issue of PSOs in more detail. In its fourth report, for the first time it surveyed the actual organisation of PSO by

158 Chlomoudis et al. 2007.

159 Baird and Wilmsmeier 2011.

160 See Sect. 7.4.3 of this chapter.

161 Commission of European Communities, Proposal for a Council Regulation applying the principle of freedom to provide services to maritime transport within Member States [1989] OJ L263/17.

162 Commission of the European Communities, Commission Report on the implementation of Regulation (EEC) 3577/92 applying the principle of freedom to provide services to maritime transport within Member States—1993–1994, COM (95) 383, 06.09.1995; Commission of the European Communities, Commission Report for 1995–96 on the implementation of Regulation 3577/92 applying the principle of freedom to provide services to maritime transport within Member States (maritime cabotage), and on the economic and social impact of the liberalisation of island cabotage, COM (97) 296 final, 17.06.1997; Commission of the European Communities, Report from the Commission—Third report of the implementation of Council Regulation 3577/92 applying the principle of freedom to provide services to maritime cabotage (1997–1998), COM (2000) 99 final, 24.02.2000.

the Member States in the maritime transport sector.[163] Until this time, maritime transport links for islands were still organised by Member States at the national level, without much influence from EU law.

More importantly, rules on PSO in Regulation 3577/92 have not been carefully designed to be a comprehensive framework for the organisation of PSOs. The framework contained in the Regulation is seriously inadequate: there is only one provision dealing with this very complex issue. It allows Member States to intervene when the market fails to provide adequate transport service for islands by imposition of PSOs or by conclusion of public service contract.[164] Article 4 of the Regulation provides that:

> A Member State may conclude public service contracts with or impose public service obligations as a condition for the provision of cabotage services, on shipping companies participating in regular services to, from and between islands.
>
> Whenever a Member State concludes public service contracts or impose public service obligations, it shall do so on a non-discriminatory basis in respect of all community shipowners.
>
> In imposing public service obligations, Member States shall be limited to requirements concerning ports to be served, regularity, continuity, frequency, capacity to provide the service, rates to be charged and manning of the vessel.
>
> Where applicable, any compensation for public service obligations must be available to all Community ship owners.

Unlike in the air transport sector, the Regulation has not adopted the public tendering procedure to rule out the possibility of advantages.[165] The Regulation has failed to provide a procedural framework for the establishment of PSOs for the maritime sector. This has significant implications for the treatment of maritime PSO funding under the EU's state aid regime. Without public tendering in place, the presumption of non-existence of advantage element does not apply. Consequently, the Commission has been using the state aid control regime to examine state funding measures for PSOs in the maritime sector.[166]

The Commission's approach was reflected in its soft law documents. In its 1997 Maritime state aid Guidelines, it lays down detailed rules on the conditions for PSO funding to be exempted from the notification procedure[167] and how state funding will be examined by the Commission. Strangely, its current State Aid Guidelines

---

[163] Commission of the European Communities, Report from the Commission—Fourth Report on the implementation of Council Regulation 3577/92 applying the principle of freedom to provide services to maritime cabotage (1999–2000), COM (2002) 203 final, 24.04.2002.

[164] Baird 2012.

[165] In practice, several Member States have been using the public tendering procedure to procure ferry services for islands. The practice in Denmark, Sweden, Greece and Norway has attracted much attention: Baird and Wilmsmeier 2011; Baird et al. 2010.

[166] Baird and Wilmsmeier 2011, p. 93.

[167] These Guidelines were adopted much before the *Altmark* ruling. However, the Commission's approach in these Guidelines was very similar to the *Altmark* criteria: Community guidelines on state aid to maritime transport [1997] OJ C205/5.

adopted in 2004 are far less detailed and practical.[168] Apart from that, PSO forms a very significant part of its 2003 Interpretation Communication on Regulation 3577/92.[169] These are the rules that have real effect regarding the compatibility of state measures for organising PSOs under EU law in the maritime sector.

The Commission examines state measures under its state aid regime on a case-by-case basis. The key concern of the Commission is the legitimacy of the state funding under state aid rules. The benchmark is Article 106(2) where it granted a derogation from the application of state aid rules.[170] Through the application of Article 106(2), the Commission can have profound influence over the organisation of PSOs in Member States.[171]

7.4.3 Transport Links for Islands in the Maritime Sector: Market Failure Test

Regarding the definition of PSO in the maritime sector, the Regulation has adopted a market failure test as a benchmark for legitimate state intervention in the market. In other words, state intervention in the market is allowed only when the market fails to provide a transport link to the island region. This is also reflected in the 1997 Maritime State Aid Guidelines, in which it expressly mentioned that:

> A PSO is defined as any obligation imposed upon a carrier to ensure the provision of a service satisfying fixed standards of continuity, regularity, capacity and pricing, which standards the carrier would not assume if it were solely considering its economic interest.
>
> PSOs may be imposed for scheduled services to ports serving peripheral regions of the Community of thinly served routes considered vital for the economic development of that region, in cases where the operation of market forces would not ensure a sufficient service level.[172]

In the practice of the Commission, it adopts a case-by-case approach by examining the market competition situation of a particular PSO route. This can potentially challenge the establishment organisation of PSO island links in the

[168] Community guidelines on state aid to maritime transport [2004] OJ C13/3.

[169] Commission of the European Communities, Communication on the interpretation of Council Regulation (EEC) No 3577/92 applying the principle of freedom to provide services to maritime transport within Member States, COM (2003) 595 final, 22.12.2003.

[170] The *Altmark* ruling does not substantially change its approach regarding the application of state aid to SGEI funding. The interplay between the provision of SGEIs and EU state aid law has been dealt with in Chap. 4.

[171] The reason lies in the fact that national programmes organising the delivery of PSO have not taken full account of the development of EU competition law and state aid law. This is the very case in the design of Scottish ferry policy. For a brief introduction to the evolution of Scottish ferry policy, see Kay 2009.

[172] Community guidelines on state aid to maritime transport [1997] OJ C205/5, p. 13.

Member States. Its Decisions concerning PSOs' link to Spanish islands[173] and French island Corsica[174] are good illustrations of its market failure approach. In both Decisions, public authorities in both Member States faced the same problems regarding transport link to islands. The traffic to the islands was highly seasonal: the majority of the demand and revenue was generated during summer holidays. Different solutions were offered by local authorities in these two countries.

In the *Transmed* Decision, the Spanish authority intended to maintain an all-year-round transport link to the islands. It concluded a public service contract with operator Transmed, where service requirements were specified. In its Decision, the Commission recognised it as an SGEI task because the transport link required by the public authority could not be provided under normal conditions. It pointed out that:

> It follows that there is no significant competitor covering passenger/car traffic on the lines in question who could offer a service satisfying the criteria of frequency, capacity and continuity all year round and the ability to provide a replacement vessel in around 24 hours as required by the public service contract.[175]

By contrast, in its Decision in May 2013 concerning French funding measures for Corsica island ferries,[176] the Commission found that a manifest error was committed in defining SGEI because of the absence of the market failure element.[177] In the 2007–2013 public service contract, a distinction was made between two different transport services. On the one hand, basic services guaranteed passenger and freight services to the island throughout the year. This service package is essentially the same as that found in the *Transmed* Decision. On the other hand, additional passenger services for the summer peak periods (from May to September) were also included in the public service contract and funded by the French government.[178]

In its Decision, the Commission recognised that state intervention for the provision of basic services was justified to pursue territorial continuity because market

---

[173] The *Transmed* Decision.

[174] The *SNCM* Decision.

[175] The *Transmed* Decision, para 87.

[176] In France, Maritime transport link for Corsica (departing from Marseille) has been guaranteed by the French State since as early as 1976 through the establishment of the public undertaking (SNCM) and the grant of State funding.

[177] Two months after the Decision was made, it was challenged by France before the Court. The case is still pending. For a summary of the case, see Case T-366/13 *France v Commission* [2013] OJ C252/42.

[178] Transport service for peak period was also covered in the basic service package but subject to very specific obligations on timetable, frequency. This is very similar to that in the *Transmed* Decision.

On the other hand, for additional services package, the French authority did not impose such obligations but only specify a minimum capacity requirement, which is deemed 'weak' by the Commission. Therefore, the Commission argued that basic and additional services were distinct services and must be treated separately. See the *SNCM* Decision, paras 14 and 152.

forces alone were unable to provide the services. By contrast, the Commission rejected the provision of the additional services as a legitimate SGEI task. It found that the demand could have been actually met under normal market conditions without state funding.[179] Therefore, the Commission concluded that the inclusion of the additional services did not meet the market failure test[180] and that state funding for that route was not compatible with the Treaty. This market failure test is clearly spelled out in its Decision:

> In this regard, the Commission considers in particular that Member States may not impose specific public services that are already provided or can be provided satisfactorily in conditions that are compatible with the public interest, as defined by the State, by companies operating under normal market conditions.[181]

This narrow approach can limit state intervention to what is strictly necessary and meanwhile utilise market competition to its full extent. This issue has become more important as incumbent PSO providers[182] face competition from the market after liberalisation. An excessively wide scope of PSOs would potentially suffocate the development of market competition. Through the application of the market failure test, the Commission can prohibit unjustified state intervention in the market and facilitate market competition.

7.4.4 Competition Neutrality Test and the Push for a Public Tendering Procedure

In the Commission's practice, another substantive requirement under Article 106(2) is to ensure the competition neutrality of the state funding.[183] In other words, state funding must not distort market competition. In this regard, the Commission focuses on two aspects of the design of a particular funding measure in Member

[179] In its Decision, it compared the maritime transport services departing from a nearby town, Toulon, without state funding with the additional services (from Marseille to Corsica ports) in question. It found that Toulon-Corsica was a substitute service to the Marseille to Corsica link. It took into account several factors: (1) the short distance between Marseille and Toulon, which is 50 km and needs only 35 min; (2) journey time—maritime link from Marseille to Corsica takes up to 10 h, while departing from Toulon needs only 5 h 45 min; and (3) actual traffic flow—actual flow on additional service has declined by 208,213 passengers, while a comparable increase was found on the Toulon route by 324,466 passengers.

[180] The inclusion of additional services could not be justified as providing funding towards basic service because of its loss-making nature: the *SNCM* Decision, para 47.

[181] The *SNCM* Decision, para 166.

[182] They are often public undertakings owned and controlled by public authorities in Member States. This is exactly the case in the *SNCM* Decision, the *Transmed* Decision and the *CalMac* Decision.

[183] This is particularly the case if the recipient has engaged in anti-competitive conduct prohibited by Articles 101 and 102.

States.[184] The first is the issue of overcompensation. In its Decisions, the Commission investigates whether the amount of funding is strictly necessary for the provision of the PSO links. State funding is compatible with the Treaty only if funding is equivalent to or less than the costs of PSO provision. The second issue is that which arises if the operator also undertakes commercial activity outside its PSO mission: in this situation the Commission also looks at the issue of cross-subsidisation. The concern is that PSO funding might be used to cross-subsidise its commercial activity, which gives PSO undertakings an advantage over their competitors in commercial operations. In this respect, account separation is an essential precondition. State funding will be regarded as incompatible with the Treaty if it is used to cross-subsidise commercial activities.

Competition neutrality is the common theme found in the Commission's Decisions on the application of EU state aid rules to the provision of SGEIs, which has been discussed in Chap. 4. What is unique in the maritime sector is the Commission's push for public tendering as a preferred mechanism for the organisation of PSOs.[185] From the Commission's perspective, the adoption of a proper public tender procedure itself is enough to ensure the competition neutrality of the funding measure.[186] In its 1997 guidelines, the Commission pointed out that state funding following a public tender procedure would not constitute state aid.[187]

In practice, the Commission has been using state aid control to push/force the Member States to adopt public tendering procedures for the delivery of PSO links for islands.[188] In its state aid Decisions, the adoption of public tendering is often included as an additional requirement for the PSOs. This can be observed in several Decisions concerning both compatible[189] and incompatible[190] state funding measures.

The use of public tendering procedures can open up local PSO ferry services to competition. On the other hand, a properly designed tender procedure can rule out the possibility of advantage. However, the Commission's approach is not without

[184]Community guidelines on state aid to maritime transport [1997] OJ C205/5.

[185]The Commission 'considers that launching an open Community-wide invitation to tender is in principle the best way to ensure non-discrimination': Commission of the European Communities, Communication on the interpretation of Council Regulation (EEC) No 3577/92 applying the principle of freedom to provide services to maritime transport within Member States (maritime cabotage), COM (2003) 595 final, 22.12.2003, p. 15.

[186]Bennett 2006.

[187]In the 2004 Guidelines, the Commission does not mention this point. The Commission has adopted a formalist approach regarding the application of the *Altmark* criteria. It essentially means that in most cases, state funding for PSOs still constitutes state aid, and Member States have the obligation to notify. This issue has been discussed in Sect. 4.3.3 of Chap. 4.

[188]Without mandatory requirements from the EU law, some Member States have been using the public tendering procedure for the delivery of PSO ferry links for islands, as, for example, in Denmark, Greece, Sweden and Norway. For a discussion on the practice in these countries, see Baird and Wilmsmeier 2011.

[189]See, for example, the *CalMac* Decision.

[190]See, for example, the *Transmed* Decision.

problems and has produced much controversy.[191] This is due to the special feature of the maritime sector: meaningful competition on the provision of PSOs' ferry services is often weak and even absent. This issue has emerged in the procurement practice in Norway, Sweden, Denmark and Scotland.[192] Very often it is still the former incumbent that wins the tender.[193] This seems to explain why there is no uniform requirement for the adoption of the public tendering procedure for the provision of PSO links in the maritime sector.

7.5 Conclusion

In the transport sector, the EU's regime on SGEI has been developed in the framework of Common Transport Policy, under the notion of 'PSO'. It has been closely associated with the evolution of the Common Transport Policy as a whole. For three decades since the adoption of the Treaty of Rome, EU law had very limited influence in the transport sector. It was not until the late 1980s that the Common Transport Policy began to take shape.

The concern of the EU was that different forms of state interventions in the sector essentially made free movement and competition impossible. The priority of the EU was to promote market competition and integration in the sector. It has adopted a mode-specific approach: EU rules are adopted on the basis of different modes of transport, including air, inland, maritime and railway. There are no overarching rules covering all areas of the transport sector.

It is a political process. On the one hand, compromise needed to be reached between different stakeholders, in particular the EU and the Member States. On the other hand, lawmakers had to take into account a wide range of economic, political and social factors. As a result, different regimes have been established in different areas of the transport sector.

It is as part of this process that rules on SGEI in the transport sector are established at the EU level. This has profound implications for SGEIs in the transport sector. The EU has developed different regimes for SGEI provision on the basis of modes of transport, and the EU's influence varied in different sectors. In addition, compared with that in the telecommunications and postal services sectors, the balancing exercise under SGEI in the transport sector is more in favour of the Member States and the pursuit of non-economic values.

On the one hand, EU rules do not impose obligations for the Member States to guarantee the provision of certain SGEIs (as in the telecommunications and the postal sectors). EU rules prescribe only what constitute legitimate SGEIs. The pursuit of such SGEIs is only optional for the Member States, rather than

[191] Morton 2011.
[192] Baird and Wilmsmeier 2011; Cowie 2012; Hervi and Sunde 2001.
[193] Hauge 1999.

obligatory. In other words, it is the Member States that have the freedom to decide whether or not they will organise a particular SGEI in the transport sector. On the other hand, the EU has been unable to promote full market liberalisation in the transport sector: the grant of exclusive right is still allowed to provide funding for the provision of SGEIs.

In the air transport sector, regional economic development through PSO links to peripheral regions is recognised as valid general interest. While the Member States enjoy wide freedom to decide which routes constitute PSO links, the EU imposes tight control over the funding aspect of PSO air links. First, as a precondition for any form of funding, the Member States must first publish intended PSO links in the Official Journal of the EU. Only if such routes are unviable on the market is state funding allowed.

Second, EU regulation also establishes a framework that enables the Member States to choose the PSO provider and to determine the amount of funding needed: through public tendering. Such a procedure is mandatory. In the Commission's Decisions, state funding that does not follow this procedure would not satisfy the *Altmark* criteria or the SGEI derogation under Article 106(2); therefore, it is prohibited under state aid law.

In the inland transport sector, the organisation of public transport systems as a whole is recognised as SGEI. However, the EU's influence in this area is very limited. For a long time, the local nature of public transport services did not justify the EU's involvement. It was only after the Member States began to open up this sector to competition that the organisation of the public transport systems gained an EU dimension.

EU legislation in this area was much delayed: Regulation 1370/2007 was adopted only in 2007. Although it introduced public tendering as the procedure to award funding, its effects are insignificant: it granted a ten-year transition period for the Member States and also exempted an 'in house' provision from its application.

In the maritime transport sector, transport links for islands are regarded as valid SGEI by EU law. However, the EU has failed to establish a procedural framework for its organisation. In practice, the Commission uses the state aid control mechanism to examine state funding for PSOs in the maritime transport sector.

The focus of the Commission's Decision has been to ensure that state intervention is proportionate. On the one hand, it imposes a market failure test on the issue of what constitute legitimate PSO links. In other words, if market forces alone can provide the island transport link, state intervention is not allowed. On the other hand, state funding must not lead to overcompensation or cross-subsidisation. What is also worthy of attention is the fact that, in the maritime sector, the Commission has been pushing the Member States to award PSO funding through the public tendering procedure.

References

Amaral M (2008) Public vs private management of public utilities – the case of urban public transport in Europe. Research in Transportation Economics 22(1):85–90

Baird A, Wilmsmeier G, Boglev Y (2010) Scottish ferries review –final report part A: methods of ferry service delivery and operation, competition and procurement and environmental issues. www.scotland.gov.uk/Resource/Doc/935/0105632.doc

Baird AJ (2012) Comparing the efficiency of public and private ferry services on the Pentland Firth between mainland Scotland and the Orkney Islands. Research in Transportation Business and Management 4(1):78–89

Baird AJ, Wilmsmeier G (2011) Public tendering of ferry services in Europe. European Transport 49:90–111

Bennett P (2006) Competing for the island lifeline: European law, state aid and regional public services. Regional Studies 40(8):953–966

Brooks MR (2009) Liberalisation in maritime transport. International Transport Forum 2009: transport for a global economy – challenges and opportunities in the downturn. www.internationaltransportforum.org/2009/.../ws1-Brooks.pdf

Chlomoudis CI, Pallis PL, Papadimitriou S, Tzannatos ES (2007) The liberalisation of maritime transport and the island regions in EU – evidence from Greece. European Transport 37:1–15

Costa Á, Fernandes R (2012) Urban public transport in Europe: technology diffusion and market organization. Transportation Research Part A: Policy and Practice 46(2): 269–284

Cowie J (2012) The cost of remote transport services in the single European market – the case of the Scottish western Isles ferries. Research in Transportation Business & Management 4:90–96

Cranfield University (2007) Air transport: quarterly report No. 15, 2nd quarter, April to June 2007. http://ec.europa.eu/transport/modes/air/observatory_market/doc/atv_q22007_15.pdf

Delle Site P, Salucci MV (2009) Thematic research summary: urban transport. European Research Knowledge Centre, European Commission DG Energy and Transport. http://transport-research.info/sites/default/files/thematic-analysis/20100215_145249_66950_TRS%20Urban%20Transport.pdf

Dempsey PS (1992) European aviation regulation: flying through the liberalisation labyrinth. Boston College International and Comparative Law Review 15(2):311–374

Graham B (1998) Liberalization, regional economic development and the geography of demand for air transport in the European Union. Journal of Transport Geography 6(2):87–104

Greaves R (2000) EC transport law. Longman, Harlow, England & New York

Greaves R (2009) Application of the EC common rules on competition to cabotage, including island cabotage. In: Antapassis A, Athanassiou LI, Rosaeg E (eds) Competition and regulation in shipping and shipping related industries. Martinus Nijhoff Publishers, Leiden & Boston

Gwilliam KM, Van De Velde DM (1990) The potential for regulatory change in European bus markets. Journal of Transport Economics and Policy 24(3):333–350

Hauge O (1999) Experimental tendering. An analysis of experiences from the road/ferry sector in Norway. https://thredbo-conference-series.org/downloads/thredbo6_papers/Thredbo6-theme1-Hauge.pdf

Hervi A, Sunde Ø (2001) An evaluation of competitive tendering in the ferry sector in Norway. http://www.thredbo-conference-series.org/downloads/thredbo7_papers/thredbo7-workshopA-Hervik-Sunde.pdf

Hidson M, Müller M (2003) Better public transport for Europe through competitive tendering a good practice guide – a good practice guide. The International Council for Local Environmental Initiatives. https://www.bkb.admin.ch/dam/bkb/de/dokumente/Oeffentliches_Beschaffungswesen/Nachhaltige_Beschaffung/leitfaden_beschaffung.pdf.download.pdf/Leitfaden%20Beschaffung%20%C3%B6ffentlicher%20Transportleistungen%20A%20Good%20Practice%20Guide.pdf

Isotope (1997) Improved structure and organisation for urban transport operations of passengers in Europe. Transport Research Fourth Framework Programme Urban Transport VII-51, 1997. http://bookshop.europa.eu/en/fourth-framework-programme-pbC30897581/downloads/C3–08-97-581-EN-C/C30897581ENC_001.pdf?FileName=C30897581ENC_001.pdf&SKU=C30897581ENC_PDF&CatalogueNumber=C3-08-97-581-EN-C

Karlaftis MG, McCarthy P (1998) Operating subsidies and performance in public transit: an empirical study. Transportation Research Part A: Policy and Practice 32(5):359–375

Kawagoe M (2008) Air transport deregulation in the EU: study from the European perspective. Paper for presentation at the IPSA RC-3 Symposium on European Integration between the Past and the Present, Hokkaido University, Sapporo, Japan, 6 September 2008. http://eprints.lib.hokudai.ac.jp/dspace/bitstream/2115/43684/1/2_161-180.pdf

Kay N (2009) Scottish ferry policy. http://www.strath.ac.uk/media/departments/economics/fairse/backissues/Fraser_of_Allander_Economic_Commentary_Vol_32,_No_3[1].pdf

Kekelekis M, Rusu IE (2010) The award of public contracts and the notion of "internal operator" under regulation 1370/2007 on public passenger transport services by rail and by road. Public Procurement Law Review 19(6):198–216

Maczkovics C, Van Calster G, Martens B (2010) Study on the implementation of regulation (EC) N° 1370/2007 on public passenger transport services by rail and by road. https://ec.europa.eu/transport/sites/transport/files/themes/pso/studies/doc/2010-pso.pdf

Morton A (2011) The impact of European Union competition policy on public transport policy and provision in the UK. http://www.european-services-strategy.org.uk/news/2011/essu-launches-a-new-series-of-european-public/eu-public-transport-policy.pdf

Reynolds-Feighan A (1995) European air transport public service obligations: a periodic review. Fiscal Studies 16(1):58–74

Rodger B (2008) Article 234 and competition law – an analysis. Wolters Kluwer, Alphen aan den Rijn, The Netherlands

Van De Velde DM (2008) A new regulation for the European public transport. Research in Transportation Economics 22(1):78–84

Van De Velde DM (1999) Organisational forms and entrepreneurship in public transport: classifying organisational forms. Transport Policy 6(3):147–157

Van De Velde DM (2001) The evolution of organisational forms in European public transport. 7th Conference on Competition and Ownership in Land Passenger Transport, Molde, Norway, 25–28 June 2001. http://thredbo.econ.usyd.edu.au/downloads/thredbo7_papers/thredbo7-workshopE-Velde.pdf

Viegas JM (1999) Public transport in the sustainable urban transport policy package: taking an integral policy approach. Prepared for the ECMT/OECD Workshop on Implementing Strategies to Improve Public Transport for Sustainable Urban Travel, Athens, Greece, 3–4 June 1999. http://www.kas.de/upload/dokumente/megacities/sustainable_urban_transport.pdf

Williams G (2005) European experience with direct subsidization of air services. Public Money and Management 25(3):155–161

Williams G, Pagliari R (2004) A comparative analysis of the application and use of public service obligations in air transport within the EU. Transport Policy 11(1):55–66

Chapter 8
Conclusions

Contents

Abstract This chapter summarises the major findings of the research. It draws conclusions on this research and proposes answers to the research question formulated in Chap. 1 of the book. It also compares and contrasts diverse solutions for service of general economic interest (SGEI) provision developed across different sectors and highlights the features of the European Union regime on SGEI. It ends with some insights and reflections on the implications of this research.

Keywords service of general economic interest · public service obligation · universal service obligation · exclusive rights · liberalisation · market failure · competition-neutral

8.1 Summary of the Research

The European Union (EU) notion of service of general economic interest (SGEI) is rooted in the tradition of public services common to the Member States, which has strong egalitarian and citizenship implications. Access to telephone services, postal

L. Zhu, *Services of General Economic Interest in EU Competition Law*,
Legal Issues of Services of General Interest,
https://doi.org/10.1007/978-94-6265-387-0_8

services, public transport service, water supply and electricity supply were regarded as basic and essential that must be guaranteed for everyone in the society. This is reflected in the notion of universal service, which was used to justify widespread state intervention in these sectors through the establishment of public undertakings and the grant of monopoly rights.

From the late 1980s, the EU began to promote market liberalisation and integration into these sectors, which transformed these sectors into competitive markets. These measures caused serious concerns and generated debate over the fate of public services and citizenship. The debate led to the ever-increasing significance of the SGEI in the EU. SGEI has been recognised as a shared value of the EU, with 'a high level of quality, safety and affordability, equal treatment and the promotion of universal access and of user rights'.[1] Furthermore, access to SGEI has been endorsed as a fundamental right.[2] This provides the mandate and obligation for the Member States and the EU to put into place measures to ensure its organisation and delivery.[3]

On the other hand, SGEI is provided through the market mechanism, thus economic in nature. The provision of SGEI may have adverse impacts on market competition. In the landmark *Corbeau* case, the Court ruled that restriction and even the exclusion of competition is justified if it is necessary for the provision of SGEI under economically acceptable conditions.[4] The key issue is to strike a balance between the non-economic values embedded in the notion of citizenship and public services and on the other hand, the economic values underpinning functioning of undistorted competitive markets. It is the aim of this research to investigate whether the right balance has been struck by the current EU regime on SGEI.

The EU framework on SGEI is developed alongside two lines. The first is in general EU competition law (relevant to all SGEIs), in particular Article 106(1) on exclusive rights and state aid rules. These rules regulate how SGEIs are organised and funded. The Court played a critical role on the interpretation of these rules. Regarding the compatibility of exclusive rights, it developed legal doctrines which held that the grant of exclusive rights was incompatible with the Treaty (discussed in Chap. 3). Thus the Member States' freedom to grant exclusive rights in the organisation of SGEIs is much limited. On state aid rules, the Court established the *Altmark* criteria, which formulated strict criteria on when SGEI funding does not constitute state aid. Rules adopted afterwards regulate the way SGEI is funded by the Member States (discussed in Chap. 4).

---

[1] Article 1, Protocol on Service of General Interest, TEU.

[2] Article 36, Charter of Fundamental Rights of the European Union [2012] OJ C326/391.

[3] Article 16 TFEU provides that "the Community and the Member States, each within their respective powers and within the scope of application of this Treaty, shall take care that such services operate on the basis of principles and conditions which enable them to fulfil their missions."

[4] Case C-320/91 *Paul Corbeau* [1993] ECR I-2533.

The second is through sector-specific rules developed in the market liberalisation and integration process. In sectors such as telecommunication, postal services and transport, the EU has set up frameworks for the provision of SGEIs (discussed in Chaps. 5–7). It prescribes what constitutes legitimate SGEIs, what mechanisms are allowed for its delivery and the respective competence of the EU and the Member States in the organisation of SGEI.

8.2 Research Findings

8.2.1 State Functions and Economic and Non-economic Distinction of SGI

The concept of SGEI has been in the Treaty since 1957. A relatively new concept is 'service of general interest' (SGI), adopted by the Lisbon Treaty. As an overarching term, SGI covers both SGEI (which is economic in nature) and NSGI (which is non-economic in nature). EU law makes a crucial distinction between economic and non-economic SGI, which dictates two very important issues: *competence allocation* and *the application of competition law*. First, the Treaty of Lisbon grants a new legislative competence regarding SGEI, while it confirms that the Member States still retain exclusive competence in the area of NSGI. Second, SGEI is of economic nature, and consequently, it is subject to EU competition law. By contrast, NSGI is non-economic in nature and so falls outside the scope of EU competition law.

This research traced the historical root of SGI to the great expansion of State functions after World War II into two areas: welfare provision and direct intervention in the economy. These activities were not regarded as normal market activity subject to competition forces and commercial principles. Instead, they were organised based on a completely different model and logic from that of the market. The power to decide what functions the State performs and how it is organised is inherent in national sovereignty. This is at the heart of the reason why the application of EU competition law in these areas has caused much controversy and debate.

In the Treaty, there has been *a strong assumption that State intervention in the economy shall be subject to EU competition law*. This is also reflected in the case law: the Court often assumed the economic nature of SGEI without any discussion. In this way, it brings SGEI within the scope of competition law. This has significant implications: the application of EU competition law, in particular Article 106, would have far-reaching ramifications.

By contrast, regarding *the welfare functions* of the State, the Court has been more cautious. The research found that the Court has not adopted the so-called *potentiality test*. Instead, it used *the principle of solidarity* to exclude the organisation of public healthcare systems from EU competition law. It has translated this principle into workable rules: (1) the lack of linkage between contribution and benefits; and (2) State control over the amount of contribution and benefits. This is essentially a *functional approach*. In this way, the EU respects national political choices regarding the organisation of national public healthcare systems and excludes them from the application of competition law.

8.2.2 The Grant of Exclusive Rights Under Article 106

The provision of SGEI was often organised under a monopolistic structure through the grant of exclusive right by the Member States. Such measure is inherently anticompetitive because it eliminates market competition, which would naturally cause concern from the EU. A fundamental change regarding the compatibility of exclusive rights could be observed in the evolution of EU law. The Treaty of Rome took State intervention in the economy for granted and did not challenge the grant of exclusive rights by the Member States. This approach was also reflected in the early case law on the interpretation of Article 106 by the Court before the 1990s. The Court adopted the absolute sovereignty approach in the *Sacchi* case in 1974 by ruling that it was compatible with the Treaty for the Member States to grant or to extend an exclusive right.

The Court fundamentally changed its approach on the interpretation of Article 106 in the early 1990s. On the compatibility of exclusive rights, it delivered four Judgments in 1991 and ruled that *the very structure of exclusive rights could be incompatible with competition law*. Consequently, it was very likely that the Member States would be in breach of the Treaty if they granted undertaking exclusive rights in circumstances where this would place the undertaking in a position where breach of EU competition law would be likely.

This revolutionary approach would *potentially challenge the model of mixed economy* that was widespread in the Member States. It also undermined the provision of SGEIs, because exclusive rights were used to provide funding for its provision. This created serious tensions over competence allocation between the EU and the Member States, and over the application of competition law and the protection of certain public interests. It is against this background that the Court in the *Corbeau* case in 1993 ruled that the restriction of competition by the Member States can be justified, if it is necessary for the provision of SGEI under economically acceptable conditions.

The necessity test also provides the legal framework to restrict market competition in order to accommodate non-economic values. During market liberalisation, it justified the Member States' measures to retain certain exclusive rights. Therefore, it controlled the pace of market liberalisation, and the market was opened to competition gradually. Following market liberalisation, the necessity test allows the Member States to intervene in the market in order to secure the provision of SGEIs.

8.2.3 The Application of State Aid Rules to SGEI Funding

The provision of SGEI is often not commercially viable under normal market conditions and thus requires funding from the State. The concern of the EU is that the Member States might grant excessive compensation beyond the mere cost of SGEI provision, which will give the recipient an advantage and consequently distort market competition. The first issue is whether SGEI funding constitutes state aid. This issue has been settled in the famous *Altmark* case. It grants an exemption for SGEI funding from the scope of state aid under very strict conditions. In the Commission's Decisions, it focuses on the fourth condition which uses public procurement or comparison to a typical well run undertaking as a benchmark. In most Decisions, the Commission found that this condition was not met, and therefore the SGEI funding measures constituted state aid.

Failure to satisfy the *Altmark* criteria does not necessarily mean SGEI funding would be prohibited by EU state aid law. The compatibility of SGEI funding is examined in the framework of SGEI derogation under three conditions: (1) there must be genuine SGEI tasks; (2) entrustment from public authorities; (3) necessity test. The Commission's approach in applying these conditions is reflected in its soft law documents—it has published Guidelines or Communications in the maritime transport, broadband and broadcasting sectors. In areas without sector-specific rules, it applies its Framework on SGEI Funding. The focus of the scrutiny has been to ensure the competition neutrality of SGEI funding—the absence of overcompensation and cross-subsidisation of commercial activity.

8.2.4 USO in the Telecommunications Sector

In the telecommunications sector, market liberalisation was undertaken under Article 106(3) where the Commission has dominant influence. Liberalisation was swift: the Commission adopted a series of six Directives in less than a decade to introduce full competition into the sector (1988–1996). During this period, SGEI was defined very narrowly, being confined to a universal physical telephony network. While all exclusive rights had to be withdrawn, EU law did allow the Member States to maintain exclusive rights over telephony services as a funding mechanism for the provision of SGEI.

Exclusive rights over telephony services were abolished in 1996 and therefore full market competition was introduced in the telecommunications sector. In this new competitive market, SGEI was defined as 'universal service obligations' (USOs), i.e. a guaranteed provision of basic telecommunications services. It consisted of two aspects. The first aspect is universal access to the physical telephony network and basic telephony services (plus directory and public pay services), which the Member States have a legal obligation to guarantee. This research found that the scope of this set of basic telephony services is limited and insignificant, because it had already been achieved from the late 1990s, as the European telephony network (fixed line) became mature.

The second aspect is the *social element* of USO, i.e. affordability of the basic telephony service. The EU did not establish a uniform standard at the EU level, but left its implementation to the hands of the Member States. The extent and real benefits achieved largely depend on the political will of individual Member State in this area.

Regarding the issue of USO funding, EU legislation has left it to the Member States to decide. The Commission has been using the infringement procedure to scrutinise funding measures in the Member States. It has adopted *a market failure test* to limit the scope of funding. Meanwhile, its focus has been to ensure USO funding is competition-neutral, i.e. USO funding should not lead to overcompensation or cross-subsidisation.

8.2.5 SGEI in the Postal Services Sector

Though USO has also been the choice for SGEI in the postal services sector, EU law has developed a very different regime for SGEI in the postal sector. First, EU postal legislation was not adopted on the basis of Article 106(3), but rather through Article 100. This had profound implications. Under Article 100 the priority of EU legislation was *harmonisation rather than liberalisation* and the Member States retained a significant say in the decision-making process via Article 100.

On the issue of SGEI, the EU only managed to prescribe certain aspects of USO at the EU level, namely, the minimum level of the scope of postal products covered and frequency of delivery: the Member States being obliged to assure these were guaranteed. Other aspects of USOs, including the density of the postal network, the affordability of USO, are left to the Member States to decide and to implement.

Second, liberalisation was much delayed in the postal sector. The Commission first published its Green Paper in 1992, which set up the blueprint for EU postal reform. However, full liberalisation was only achieved almost two decades later, from December 2010. During this period, the maintenance of exclusive rights over a large part of the postal market was allowed to provide funding for USOs.

Third, following full liberalisation, EU postal legislation learned from its experience in the telecommunications sector and devised similar funding mechanisms. However, in practice, direct State funding continued to be the main funding source in the postal sector. The Commission has been using state aid control procedures to examine State funding measures in the postal sector.

8.2.6 Public Service Obligations in the Transport Sector

In the transport sector, SGEI has been developed under a distinctive pattern and approach. From the Treaty of Rome in 1957, the transport sector has been subject to a special set of rules, the Common Transport Policy. Under the Common Transport Policy, the Treaty grants derogation for compensation of public service obligations (PSO) from state aid rules. It is this notion of PSO that is the equivalent of SGEI in the transport sector.

EU rules on SGEI have been closely associated with the development of the Common Transport Policy itself. The priority of the Common Transport Policy has been to promote market integration in the sector. The exercise has been undertaken based on different modes of transportation, including air, inland and maritime. It is during this process that the EU decides what constitutes legitimate SGEIs and the mechanisms for its provision. There are no overarching rules in the transport sector to covering SGEIs in all sections of the transport sector. In fact, EU rules on SGEI vary significantly across different areas of transport, i.e. air, inland and maritime.

Compared with the telecommunications and postal services sectors, the influence of EU law in the transport sector is *less significant*. On the one hand, unlike in the telecommunications and postal services sectors (where all exclusive rights have been withdrawn and full liberalisation has been achieved), in the transport sector, exclusive rights are still allowed as a funding generator for the provision of SGEI. Unlike in the telecommunications and postal service sectors (where EU law obliges the Member States to guarantee certain SGEIs), in the transport sector there is no such mandatory requirement at EU level: in the transport sector, the pursuit of SGEI is an *optional choice* for public authorities in the Member States. EU law only *defines* what constitutes legitimate SGEIs, and establishes a framework for their organisation. It is left to the Member States *to decide* whether or not to utilise this option.

In the *air transport sector*, regional economic development through PSO air transport links has been recognised as SGEI. The EU has established a procedural framework for its organisation in Regulation 1008/2008. It applies a *strict market failure test* by requiring the Member States to publish planned PSO routes in the EU Official Journal to see if the market forces alone can provide the particular air services without extra State funding. Only if such PSO routes are not commercially viable does EU law allow the Member States to provide extra funding. Such funding must follow an EU-wide public tendering procedure. Failure to comply with such procedure would mean that such funding cannot satisfy the *Altmark* criteria or SGEI derogation under Article 106(2). Therefore, it would be prohibited under EU state aid law.

In the *inland transport sector*, the organisation of public transport systems as a whole is regarded as SGEIs, which has been used by the Member States to pursue a wide range of non-economic values including universal services, environmental protection and relief of traffic congestion. Public transport services had long been outside the reach of EU Internal Market law. It was not until Regulation 1370/2007 that the EU began to lay down rules for the organisation of public transport systems. It promotes market competition in the sector by introducing competitive tendering procedures into the sector. However, the influence of Regulation 1370/2007 is limited, because it permits a ten-year transition period for the Member States and also exempts in-house provision from its application.

In the *maritime transport sector*, transport link for islands is regarded as a valid SGEI under EU law. However, the EU has failed to establish a procedural framework for its organisation. In practice, the Commission uses state aid as a control mechanism to examine State funding for PSOs in the maritime transport sector. The focus of the Commission's Decisions has been to ensure State intervention is proportionate. On the one hand, it imposes a market failure test on the issue of what constitutes legitimate PSO links (in other words, if the market alone can provide the island transport link, State intervention is not allowed). On the other hand, State funding must not lead to *overcompensation or cross-subsidisation*. What is also worthy of attention is the fact that, in the maritime sector, the Commission has been pushing the Member States to award PSO funding through public tendering procedures.

8.3 Implications of the Research

The development of the EU's regime on SGEI could not have been anticipated by the founding fathers of the EEC Treaty back in 1957. In the first three decades following the Treaty of Rome, the EU largely respected, or at least tolerated, the realities of State intervention in major sectors of the economy, such as the telecommunications, postal services, transport and energy. In these sectors, the Member State often established public undertakings and State monopolies to pursue a wide range of public interests. The underlying principle is universal service and citizenship: these basic and essential services must be guaranteed for everyone in the society. During this period, the EU had little influence over the organisation of SGEIs.

From the late 1980s, the provision of SGEI has increasingly come under the scrutiny and regulation from the EU law. The major concern of the EU law is to ensure that SGEI provision does not distort market competition. This is evident in setting the boundaries and limits on the grant of exclusive rights and the award of funding for the provision of SGEI by the Member States. Also, the process of market liberalisation and integration pushed the logic of market competition further into new frontiers. It transformed the organisation of these sectors into competitive markets and redefined the relationship between the state and the market.

What also emerged from this research is the existence of wide disparities in the provision of SGEI across the Member States. The EU does not have meaningful control over the content of SGEI. The extent of SGEI provision and its real benefits for citizens largely depend on the Member States. In areas without sector-specific legislation, the EU does not prescribe what SGEIs must be provided. It is the

Member States that define, organise and fund the provision of SGEI at the national level. Even in areas with sector legislation, the extent of harmonisation over SGEI has been limited. For example, universal telephony service as defined by EU law has become obsolete and outdated because communication needs are increasingly being met by alternative means and the use of telephone is in steady decline. It is upon the Member States to decide whether or not to include more advanced electronic communication services, such as broadband, to be guaranteed as part of USO.

This lack of real influence over the level of SGEI service provision is also prominent in the transport sector. The EU does not lay down a uniform standard at the EU level, but only recognises certain non-economic values as valid SGEI and leaves its implementation to the Member States. It is upon the Member States to decide whether they would provide such SGEI services in the first place and if so, what level of services they would like to undertake and how much funding will be allocated.

It seems that the current EU regime has failed to strike the right balance by focusing its priority on the market competition aspect of SGEI without putting sufficient safeguards over the non-economic values at the EU level. As a result, the notion of SGEI as EU citizenship is still thin and shallow. There is no uniform level of SGEI guaranteed at the EU level; the materialisation of SGEI largely remains in the domain of the Member States. This could be a particular concern from the perspective of public services as Member States are subject to increasing constraints on public finance. This might lead to cuts on public spending on SGEI and thus the shrinking scope of its provision, which would have negative implications for the citizenship values underlying it.

Developing SGEIs into full-fledged EU citizenship would require deeper integration, in particular in the social and political arenas. This seems to be the direction of future evolution of SGEI as the EU has acquired a new constitutional mandate in the Lisbon Treaty, which recognises SGEI as a shared value and a fundamental right of EU citizenship. On this respect, the legislation competence of the EU under Article 14 TFEU (Treaty on the Functioning of the European Union) lays the very foundation and holds great potential for the future development of SGEI. Such development is desirable but likely to be difficult and controversial as SGEI is closely connected with the concept of political identity. This would call for an EU-wide debate and dialogue to rethink and reflect on the nature, purpose and destiny of the EU as an ever closer union.

Table of Treaties, Legislation, Decisions, Cases and Soft Law Documents

Treaties

- Consolidated Version of the Treaty on European Union [2012] OJ C326/13
- Consolidated Version of the Treaty on the Functioning of the European Union [2012] OJ C326/47
- Protocol (No 26) on Services of General Interest, TFEU
- Protocol (No 27) on the Internal Market and Competition, TFEU
- Protocol (No 29) on the System of Public Broadcasting in the Member States, TFEU
- Charter of Fundamental Human Rights of the European Union [2012] OJ C326/391
- Single European Act [1987] OJ L169/1.

Legislation

Regulations of the European Parliament and of the Council

- Regulation (EC) No 1370/2007 of the European Parliament and of the Council of 23 October 2007 on public passenger transport services by rail and by road and repealing Council Regulations (EEC) Nos 1191/69 and 1107/70 [2007] OJ L315/1
- Regulation (EC) No 1008/2008 of the European Parliament and of the Council of 24 September 2008 on common rules for the operation of air services in the Community [2008] OJ L293/3
- Regulation (EC) No 1072/2009 of the European Parliament and of the Council of 21 October 2009 on common rules for access to the international road haulage market [2009] OJ L300/72

L. Zhu, *Services of General Economic Interest in EU Competition Law*,
Legal Issues of Services of General Interest,
https://doi.org/10.1007/978-94-6265-387-0

- Regulation (EC) No 1073/2009 of the European Parliament and of the Council of 21 October 2009 on common rules for access to the international market for coach and bus services, and amending Regulation (EC) No 561/2006 [2009] OJ L300/88.

Council Regulations

- Regulation No 141 of the Council exempting transport from the application of Council Regulation No 17 [1962] OJ L124/2751
- Regulation (EEC) No 1191/69 of the Council of 26 June 1969 on action by Member States concerning the obligations inherent in the concept of a public service in transport by rail, road and inland waterway [1969] OJ L156/1
- Council Regulation (EEC) No 4055/86 of 22 December 1986 applying the principle of freedom to provide services to maritime transport between Member States and third countries [1988] OJ L117/33
- Council Regulation (EEC) No 3975/87 of 14 December 1987 laying down the procedure for the application of the rules on competition to undertakings in the air transport sector [1987] OJ L374/1
- Council Regulation (EEC) No 3976/87 of 14 December 1987 on the application of Article 85 (3) of the Treaty to certain categories of agreements and concerted practices in the air transport sector [1987] OJ L374/9
- Council Regulation (EEC) No 2342/90 of 24 July 1990 on fares for scheduled air services [1990] OJ L217/1
- Council Regulation (EEC) No 2343/90 of 24 July 1990 on access for air carriers to scheduled intra-Community air-service routes and on the sharing of passenger capacity between air carriers on scheduled air services between Member States [1990] OJ L217/8
- Council Regulation (EEC) No 2344/90 of 24 July 1990 amending Regulation (EEC) No 3976/87 on the application of Article 85 (3) of the Treaty to certain categories of agreements and concerted practices in the air transport sector [1990] OJ L217/15
- Council Regulation (EEC) No 1893/91 of 20 June 1991 amending Regulation (EEC) No 1191/69 on action by Member States concerning the obligations inherent in the concept of a public service in transport by rail, road and inland waterway [1991] OJ L169 /1
- Council Regulation (EEC) No 684/92 of 16 March 1992 on common rules for the international carriage of passengers by coach and bus [1992] OJ L74/1
- Council Regulation (EEC) No 881/92 of 26 March 1992 on access to the market in the carriage of goods by road within the Community to or from the territory of a Member State or passing across the territory of one or more Member States [1992] OJ L95/1
- Council Regulation (EEC) No 2407/92 of 23 July 1992 on licensing of air carriers [1992] OJ L240/1

- Council Regulation (EEC) No 2408/92 of 23 July 1992 on access for Community air carriers to intra-Community air routes [1992] OJ L240/8
- Council Regulation (EEC) No 2409/92 of 23 July 1992 on fares and rates for air services [1992] OJ L240/15
- Council Regulation (EEC) No 3577/92 of 7 December 1992 applying the principle of freedom to provide services to maritime transport within Member States (maritime cabotage) [1992] OJ L364/7
- Council Regulation (EC) No 1356/96 of 8 July 1996 on common rules applicable to the transport of goods or passengers by inland waterway between Member States with a view to establish freedom to provide such transport services [1996] OJ L175/7
- Council Regulation (EC) No 12/98 of 11 December 1997 laying down the conditions under which non-resident carriers may operate national road passenger transport services within a Member State [1992] OJ L74/10.

Commission Regulations

- Commission Regulation (EU) No 360/2012 of 25 April 2012 on the application of Articles 107 and 108 of the Treaty on the Functioning of the European Union to *de minimis* aid granted to undertakings providing services of general economic interest [2012] OJ L114/8.

Directives of the European Parliament and of the Council

- Directive 95/62/EC of the European Parliament and of the Council of 13 December 1995 on the application of Open Network Provision (ONP) to voice telephony [1995] OJ L321/6
- Directive 97/33/EC of the European Parliament and of the Council of 30 June 1997 on interconnection in telecommunications with regard to ensuring universal service and interoperability through application of the principles of Open Network Provision (ONP) [1997] OJ L199/32
- Directive 97/51/EC of the European Parliament and of the Council of 6 October 1997 amending Council Directives 90/387/EEC and 92/44/EEC for the purpose of adaptation to a competitive environment in telecommunications [1997] OJ L295/23
- Directive 97/67/EC of the European Parliament and of the Council of 15 December 1997 on common rules for the development of the Internal Market of Community postal services and the improvement of quality of service [1998] OJ L15/14
- Directive 98/10/EC of the European Parliament and of the Council of 26 February 1998 on the application of Open Network Provision (ONP) to voice

Telephony and on universal service for Telecommunications in a competitive environment [1998] OJ L101/24

- Directive 2002/22/EC of the European Parliament and of the Council of 7 March 2002 on universal service and users' rights relating to electronic communications networks and services [2002] OJ L108/51
- Directive 2002/39/EC of the European Parliament and of the Council of 10 June 2002 amending Directive 97/67/EC with regard to the further opening to competition of Community postal services [2002] OJ L176/21
- Directive 2006/111/EC of 16 November 2006 on the transparency of financial relations between Member States and public undertakings as well as on financial transparency within certain undertakings [2006] OJ L318/17
- Directive 2008/6/EC of the European Parliament and of the Council of 20 February 2008 amending Directive 97/67/EC with regard to the full accomplishment of the Internal Market of Community postal services [2008] OJ L52/3
- Directive 2009/72/EC of the European Parliament and of the Council of 13 July 2009 concerning common rules for the internal market in electricity and repealing Directive 2003/54/EC [2009] OJ L211/55
- Directive 2009/73/EC of the European Parliament and of the Council of 13 July 2009 concerning common rules for the internal market in natural gas and repealing Directive 2003/55/EC [2009] OJ L211/94
- Directive 2009/136/EC of the European Parliament and of the Council of 25 November 2009 amending Directive 2002/22/EC on universal service and users' rights relating to electronic communications networks and services, Directive 2002/58/EC concerning the processing of personal data and the protection of privacy in the electronic communications sector and Regulation (EC) No 2006/2004 on cooperation between national authorities responsible for the enforcement of consumer protection laws [2009] OJ L337/11.

Council Directives

- Council Directive 75/439/EEC of 16 June 1975 on the disposal of waste oils [1975] OJ L194/23
- Council Directive 87/601/EEC of 14 December 1987 on fares for scheduled air services between Member States [1987] OJ L374/12
- Council Directive 89/552/EEC of 3 October 1989 on the coordination of certain provisions laid down by law, regulation or administrative action in Member States concerning the pursuit of television broadcasting activities [1989] OJ L298/23
- Council Directive 90/387/EEC of 28 June 1990 on the establishment of the Internal Market for telecommunications services through the implementation of Open Network Provision [1990] OJ L192/1
- Council Directive 91/440/EEC of 29 July 1991 on the development of the Community's railways [1991] OJ L237/25

- Council Directive 92/25/EEC of 31 March 1992 on the wholesale distribution of medicinal products for human use [1992] OJ L113/1
- Council Directive 92/44/EEC of 5 June 1992 on the application of Open Network Provision to leased lines [1992] OJ L165/27.

Commission Directives

- Commission Directive 80/723/EEC of 25 June 1980 on the transparency of financial relations between Member States and public undertakings [1980] OJ L195/35
- Commission Directive 85/413/EEC of 24 July 1985 amending Directive 80/723/EEC on the transparency of financial relations between Member States and public undertakings [1985] OJ L229/20
- Commission Directive 88/301/EEC of 16 May 1988 on competition in the markets in telecommunications terminal equipment [1988] OJ L131/73
- Commission Directive 90/388/EEC of 28 June 1990 on competition in the markets for telecommunications services [1990] OJ L192/10
- Commission Directive 93/84/EEC of 30 September 1993 amending Directive 80/723/EEC on the transparency of financial relations between Member States and public undertakings [1993] OJ L254/16
- Commission Directive 94/46/EC of 13 October 1994 amending Directive 88/301/EEC and Directive 90/388/EEC in particular with regard to satellite communications [1994] OJ L268/15
- Commission Directive 95/51/EC of 18 October 1995 amending Directive 90/388/EEC with regard to the abolition of the restrictions on the use of cable television networks for the provision of already liberalised telecommunications services [1995] OJ L256/49
- Commission Directive 96/19/EC of 13 March 1996 amending Directive 90/388/EEC with regard to the Implementation of full competition in Telecommunications Markets [1995] OJ L256/49
- Commission Directive 96/2/EC of 16 January 1996 amending Directive 90/388/EEC with regard to mobile and personal communications [1996] OJ L20/59
- Commission Directive 2000/52/EC of 26 July 2000 amending Directive 80/723/EEC on the transparency of financial relations between Member States and public undertakings [2000] OJ L193/75
- Commission Directive 2005/81/EC of 28 November 2005 amending Directive 80/723/EEC on the transparency of financial relations between Member States and public undertakings as well as on financial transparency within certain undertakings [2005] OJ L312/47
- Commission Directive 2006/111/EC of 16 November 2006 on the transparency of financial relations between Member States and public undertakings as well as on financial transparency within certain undertakings [2006] OJ L318/17.

Council Decisions

- 65/271/EEC: Council Decision of 13 May 1965 on the harmonisation of certain provisions affecting competition in transport by rail, road and inland waterway [1965] OJ 88/1500
- 87/602/EEC: Council Decision of 14 December 1987 on the sharing of passenger capacity between air carriers on scheduled air services between Member States and on access for air carriers to scheduled air-service routes between Member States [1987] OJ L374/19.

Judgments

Court of Justice of the European Union

- Joined Cases 6 & 7–73 *Istituto Chemioterapico Italiano S.p.A. and Commercial Solvents Corporation v Commission of the European Communities* [1974] ECR-223
- Case 120/73 *Gebrüder Lorenz GmbH v Federal Republic of Germany et Land de Rhénanie-Palatinat* [1973] ECR-1471
- Case 155/73 *Giuseppe Sacchi* [1974] ECR-409
- Case 94/74 *Industria Gomma Articoli Vari IGAV v Ente nazionale per la cellulosa e per la carta ENCC* [1975] ECR-699
- Case 78/76 *Steinike & Weinlig v Federal Republic of Germany* [1977] ECR-595
- Case 258/78 *L.C. Nungesser KG and Kurt Eisele v Commission of the European Communities* [1982] ECR-2015
- Case 149/79 *Commission of the European Communities v Kingdom of Belgium* [1982] ECR-1845
- Joined cases 188 to 190/80 *French Republic, Italian Republic and United Kingdom of Great Britain and Northern Ireland v Commission of the European Communities* [1982] ECR-2545
- Case 13/83 *European Parliament v Council of the European Communities* [1985] ECR-1513
- Case 41/83 *Italian Republic v Commission of the European Communities* [1985] ECR-873
- Case 240/83 *Procureur de la République v Association de défense des brûleurs d'huiles usagées d (ADBHU)* [1985] ECR-531
- Case 107/84 *Commission of the European Communities v Federal Republic of Germany* [1985] ECR-2655
- Joined Cases 209 to 213/84 *Criminal proceedings against Lucas Asjes and Others, Andrew Gray and Others, Andrew Gray and Others, Jacques Maillot and Others and Léo Ludwig and Others* [1986] ECR 1425

- Case 311/84 *Centre belge d'études de marché – Télémarketing (CBEM) v SA Compagnie luxembourgeoise de télédiffusion (CLT) and Information publicité Benelux (IPB)* [1985] ECR-3261
- Case 118/85 *Re the Amministrazione Autonoma dei Monopoli di Stato: E.C. Commission v Italy* [1988] ECR-2599
- Case 66/86 *Ahmed Saeed Flugreisen and Silver Line Reisebüro GmbH v Zentrale zur Bekämpfung unlauteren Wettbewerbs e.V.* [1989] ECR-803
- Case 263/86 *Belgian State v René Humbel and Marie-Thérèse Edel* [1988] ECR-5365
- Case-301/87 *French Republic v Commission of the European Communities* [1990] ECR-307
- Case C-18/88 *Régie des Télégraphes et des Téléphones v GB-Inno-BM SA* [1991] ECR I-5941
- Case C-202/88 *French Republic v Commission of the European Communities* [1991] ECR I-1223
- Case C-260/89 *Elliniki Radiophonia Tileorassi AE (Ert) (Panellinia Omospondia Syllogon Prossopikou Ert intervening) v Dimotiki Étairia Pliroforissis (Dep) and Sotirios Kouvelas (Nicolaos Avdellas and Others intervening)* [1991] ECR I-02925
- Case C-41/90 *Klaus Höfner and Fritz Elser v Macrotron GmbH* [1991] ECR I-1979
- Joined Cases C-48/90 & C-66/90 *Kingdom of the Netherlands, Koninklijke PTT Nederland NV and PTT Post BV v Commission of the European Communitie*s [1992] ECR 1-565
- Case C-179/90 *Merci Convenzionali Porto di Genova SpA v Siderurgica Gabrielli SpA* [1991] ECR I-05889
- Joined cases C-271/90, C-281/90 & C-289/90 *Kingdom of Spain, Kingdom of Belgium and Italian Republic v Commission of the European Communities* [1992] ECR I-5833
- Case C-354/90 *Fédération Nationale du Commerce Extérieur des Produits Alimentaires and Syndicat National des Négociants et Transformateurs de Saumon v French Republic* [1991] ECR I-5505
- Case C-69/91 *Criminal proceedings against Francine Gillon, née Decoster* [1993] ECR I-5335
- Joined cases C-159/91 & C-160/91 *Christian Poucet v Assurances Générales de France and Caisse Mutuelle Régionale du Languedoc-Roussillon* [1993] ECR I-637
- Joined cases C-241/91 P & C-242/91 P *Radio Telefis Eireann (RTE) and Independent Television Publications Ltd (ITP) v Commission of the European Communities* [1995] ECR I-743
- Case C-320/91 *Paul Corbeau* [1993] ECR I-2533
- Case C-364/92 *SAT Fluggesellschaft mbH v Eurocontrol* [1994] ECR I-43
- Case C-393/92 *Municipality of Almelo and Others v NV Energiebedrijf Ijsselmij* [1994] ECR I-1477

- Case C-157/94 *Commission of the European Communities v Kingdom of the Netherlands* [1997] ECR I-5699
- Case C-244/94 *Fédération Française des Sociétés d'Assurance, Société Paternelle-Vie, Union des Assurances de Paris-Vie and Caisse d'Assurance et de Prévoyance Mutuelle des Agriculteurs v Ministère de l'Agriculture et de la Pêche* [1995] ECR I-4013
- Case C-242/95 *GT-Link A/S v De Danske Statsbaner (DSB)* [1997] ECR I-4449
- Case 343/95 *Diego CalÃ & Figli Srl v Servizi Ecologici Porto di Genova SpA (SEPG)* [1997] ECR I-1547
- Case C-67/96 *Albany International BV v Stichting Bedrijfspensioenfonds Textielindustrie* [1999] ECR I-575
- C-158/96 *Kohll v Union des Caisses de Maladie* [1998] ECR I-1931
- Case C-412/96 *Kainuun Liikenne Oy and Oy Pohjolan Liikenne Ab* [1998] ECR I-5141
- Joined Cases C-147/97 & C-148/97 *Deutsche Post AG v Gesellschaft für Zahlungssysteme mbH (GZS) (C-147/97) and Citicorp Kartenservice GmbH (C-148/97)* [2000] ECR I-825
- Case C-174/97 P *Fédération française des sociétés d'assurances and Others v Commission of the European Communities* [1998] I-130
- Joined Cases C-180/98 to C-184/98 *Pavlov and Others v Stichting Pensioenfonds Medische Specialisten* [2001] ECR I-6497
- Case C-205/99 *Asociación Profesional de Empresas Navieras de Líneas Regulares (Analir) and Others v Administración General del Estado* [2001] ECR I-1271
- Case C-340/99 *TNT Traco SpA v Poste Italiane SpA and Others* [2001] ECR I-4109
- Case C-475/99 *Firma Ambulanz Glöckner v Landkreis Südwestpfalz* [2001] ECR I-8089
- Case C-53/00 *Ferring SA v Agence centrale des organismes de sécurité sociale (ACOSS)* [2001] ECR I-09067
- Case C-146/00 *Commission of the European Communities v French Republic* [2001] ECR I-9767
- Case C-181/00 *Flightline Ltd v Secretário de Estado dos Transportes e Comunicações and Transportes Aéreos Portugueses SA* (TAP) [2002] ECR I-6139
- Case C-218/00 *Cisal di Battistello Venanzio & Co. Sas v Istituto Nazionale Per L'Assicurazione Contro Gli Infortuni Sul Lavoro (INAIL)* [2002] ECR I-691
- Case C-280/00 *Altmark Trans GmbH and Regierungspräsidium Magdeburg v Nahverkehrsgesellschaft Altmark GmbH, and Oberbundesanwalt beim Bundesverwaltungsgericht* [2003] ECR I-7747
- Case C-82/01 P *Aéroports de Paris v Commission of the European Communities* [2002] I-9297
- Case C-126/01 *Ministère de l'Économie, des Finances et de l'Industrie v GEMO SA* [2003] ECR I-13769

- Joined cases C-264/01, C-306/01, C-354/01 & C-355/01 *AOK Bundesverband, Bundesverband der Betriebskrankenkassen (BKK), Bundesverband der Innungskrankenkassen, Bundesverband der landwirtschaftlichen Krankenkassen, Verband der Angestelltenkrankenkassen eV, Verband der Arbeiter-Ersatzkassen, Bundesknappschaft and See-Krankenkasse v Ichthyol-Gesellschaft Cordes, Hermani & Co* [2004] ECR I-2493
- Case C-205/03 *Federación Española de Empresas de Tecnología Sanitaria (FENIN) v Commission of the European Communities* [2006] ECR I-6295
- C-372/04 *R. (on the application of Watts) v Bedford Primary Care Trust* [2006] ECR I-4325
- Case C-76/05 *Herbert Schwarz and Marga Gootjes-Schwarz v Finanzamt Bergisch Gladbach* [2007] ECR I-6879
- Case C-162/06 *International Mail Spain SL v Administración del Estado and Correos* [2007] ECR I-9911
- Case C-350/07 *Kattner Stahlbau GmbH v Maschinenbau- und Metall-Berufsgenossenschaft* [2009] ECR I-1513
- Case C-222/08 *European Commission v Kingdom of Belgium* [2010] ECR I-9017
- Case C-389/08 *Base NV and Others v Ministerraad* [2010] ECR I-9073
- Case C-437/09 *AG2R Prévoyance v Beaudout Père et Fils SARL* [2011] ECR I-973
- C-108/10 *Ivana Scattolon v Ministero dell'Istruzione, dell'Università e della Ricerca* [2011] ECR I-7491
- Case C 138/11 *Compass-Datenbank GmbH v Republik Österreich* (not yet reported). https://eur-lex.europa.eu/legal-content/EN/ALL/?uri=CELEX%3A62011CJ0138
- C-288/11 P *Mitteldeutsche Flughafen and Flughafen Leipzig-Halle v Commission* (not yet reported). http://curia.europa.eu/juris/liste.jsf?num=C-288/11&language=EN
- Case C-674/13 *Commission v Germany* (not yet reported). http://curia.europa.eu/juris/liste.jsf?language=en&td=ALL&num=C-674/13#
- Case C-74/16 *Congregación de Escuelas Pías Provincia Betania v Ayuntamiento de Getafe* (not yet reported). http://curia.europa.eu/juris/liste.jsf?language=en&num=C-74/16.

Advocate General Opinions

- Opinion of Advocate General, Case 36/73 *NV Nederlandse Spoorwegen v Minister van Verkeer en Waterstaat* [1973] ECR-1299
- Opinion of Advocate General, Case 155/73 *Giuseppe Sacchi* [1974] ECR-409
- Opinion of Advocate General, Joined cases 188 to 190/80 *French Republic, Italian Republic and United Kingdom of Great Britain and Northern Ireland v Commission of the European Communities* [1982] ECR-2545

- Opinion of Advocate General, Case 311/84 *Centre belge d'études de marché – Télémarketing (CBEM) v SA Compagnie luxembourgeoise de télédiffusion (CLT) and Information publicité Benelux (IPB)* [1985] ECR-3261
- Opinion of Advocate General, Case 66/86 *Ahmed Saeed Flugreisen and Silver Line Reisebüro GmbH v Zentrale zur Bekämpfung unlauteren Wettbewerbs e.V.* [1989] ECR-803
- Opinion of Advocate General, Case C-202/88 *French Republic v Commission of the European Communities* [1991] ECR I-1223
- Opinion of Advocate General, Case C-260/89 *Elliniki Radiophonia Tileorassi AE (Ert) (Panellinia Omospondia Syllogon Prossopikou Ert intervening) v Dimotiki Étairia Pliroforissis (Dep) and Sotirios Kouvelas (Nicolaos Avdellas and Others intervening)* [1991] ECR I-02925
- Opinion of Advocate General, Case C-41/90 *Klaus Höfner and Fritz Elser v Macrotron GmbH* [1991] ECR I-1979
- Opinion of the Advocate General, Joined Cases C-48/90 & C-66/90 *Kingdom of the Netherlands, Koninklijke PTT Nederland NV and PTT Post BV v Commission of the European Communities* [1992] ECR 1-565
- Opinion of Advocate General, Case C-218/00, *Cisal di Battistello Venanzio & Co. Sas v Istituto Nazionale Per L'Assicurazione Contro Gli Infortuni Sul Lavoro (INAIL)* [2002] ECR I-691
- Opinion of Advocate General, Case C-126/01 *Ministère de l'Économie, des Finances et de l'Industrie v GEMO SA* [2003] ECR I-13769
- Opinion of the Advocate General, C-372/04 *R. (on the application of Watts) v Bedford Primary Care Trust* [2006] ECR I-4325.

General Court (Court of First Instance)

- Case T-69/89 *Radio Telefis Eireann v Commission of the European Communities* [1991] ECR II-485
- Case T-76/89 *Independent Television Publications Ltd v Commission of the European Communities* [1991] ECR II-575
- Case T-106/95 *Federation Française des Societes d'Assurances (Ffsa) and Others v E.C. Commission* [1997] ECR II-229
- Case T-46/97 *SIC – Sociedade Independente de Comunicação SA v Commission of the European Communities* [2000] ECR II-2125
- Case T-289/03 *British United Provident Association Ltd (BUPA), BUPA Insurance Ltd and BUPA Ireland Ltd v Commission of the European Communities* [2008] ECR II-8
- Case T-155/04 *Selex Sistemi Integrati SpA v Commission of the European Communities* [2006] ECR II-4803
- Case T-143/12 *Germany v Commission* (pending)
- Case T-152/12 *Deutsche Post v Commission* (pending)

- Case T-138/15 *Aanbestedingskalender BV and Others v European Commission* (not yet reported). http://curia.europa.eu/juris/liste.jsf?language=en&num=T-138/15
- Case T-216/15 *Dôvera zdravotná poist'ovňa, a.s. v European Commission* (not yet reported). http://curia.europa.eu/juris/liste.jsf?language=en&num=T-216/15.

Commission Decisions

- 78/823/EEC: Commission Decision of 21 September 1978 relating to a proceeding under Article 85 of the EEC Treaty (IV/28.824—Breeders' rights—maize seed) [1978] OJ L286/23
- 82/861/EEC: Commission Decision of 10 December 1982 relating to a proceeding under Article 86 of the EEC Treaty (IV/29.877—British Telecommunications) [1982] OJ L360/36
- 85/276/EEC: Commission Decision of 24 April 1985 concerning the insurance in Greece of public property and loans granted by Greek State-owned banks [1985] OJ L152/25
- 87/359/EEC: Commission Decision of 22 June 1987 concerning reductions in air and sea transport fares available only to Spanish nationals resident in the Canary Islands and the Balearic Islands [1987] OJ L194/28
- 88/518/EEC: Commission Decision of 18 July 1988 relating to a proceeding under Article 86 of the EEC Treaty (Case No IV/30.178 Napier Brown—British Sugar) [1988] OJ L284/41
- 89/205/EEC: Commission Decision of 21 December 1988 relating to a proceeding under Article 86 of the EEC Treaty (IV/31.851—Magill TV Guide/ITP, BBC and RTE) [1989] OJ L78/43
- 89/536/EEC: Commission Decision of 15 September 1989 relating to a proceeding under Article 85 of the EEC Treaty (IV/31.734—Film purchases by German television stations) [1989] OJ L284/36
- 90/16/EEC: Commission Decision of 20 December 1989 concerning the provision in the Netherlands of express delivery services [1990] OJ L10/47
- 90/456/EEC: Commission Decision of 1 August 1990 concerning the provision in Spain of international express courier services [1990] OJ L 233/19
- State Aid Decision NN 135/92—France tax arrangements applicable to the French postal administration [1995] OJ C262/11
- 94/666/EC: Commission Decision of 6 July 1994 concerning compensation in respect of the deficit incurred by TAP on the routes to the Autonomous Regions of the Azores and Madeira [1994] OJ L260/27
- State Aid Decision NN 141/95—Portugal financing of the Portuguese public television service [1997] OJ C67/10
- 95/364/EC: Commission Decision of 28 June 1995 relating to a proceeding pursuant to Article 90 (3) of the Treaty [1995] OJ L216/8

- 97/745/EC: Commission Decision of 21 October 1997 relating to a proceeding pursuant to Article 90 (3) of the EC Treaty regarding the tariffs for piloting in the Port of Genoa [1997] OJ L301/27
- State Aid No NN 88/98—United Kingdom financing of a 24-hour advertising-free news channel out of the licence fee by the BBC, SG (99) D/10201, 14.12.1999
- 2001/156/EC: Commission Decision of 19 July 2000 on the State Aid implemented by Spain in favour of the maritime transport sector (new maritime public service contract) [2001] L57/32
- 2001/176/EC: Commission Decision of 21 December 2000 concerning proceedings pursuant to Article 86 of the EC Treaty in relation to the provision of certain new postal services with a guaranteed day- or time-certain delivery in Italy [2001] OJ L63/59
- 2001/354/EC: Commission Decision of 20 March 2001 relating to a proceeding under Article 82 of the EC Treaty (Case COMP/35.141—Deutsche Post AG) [2001] OJ L125/44
- State Aid Decision N 514/2001: United Kingdom "modernisation of the UK benefit payment system and provision of access to universal banking services through post offices" shortened as Universal Banking Services or UBS, C (2002) 311 final, 13.02.2002
- State Aid No N 631/2001—United Kingdom BBC licence fee, C (2002) 1886 fin, 22.05.2002
- State Aid Decision N 650/01—Ireland: equity injection to An Post for the purpose of restructuring the counter network, C (2002) 941 final, 12.03.2002
- Statligt Stöd Nr N 749/01—Sverige Posten AB (publ); girobetalningstjänster, nedan grundläggande kassaservice, C (2002) 2402 final, 2.07.2002
- State Aid No 252/2002—United Kingdom Reinvention of the urban Post Office network, C (2002) 3341 fin, 18.09.2002
- 2002/344/EC: Commission Decision of 23 October 2001 on the lack of exhaustive and independent scrutiny of the scales of charges and technical conditions applied by La Poste to mail preparation firms for access to its reserved services [2002] OJ L120/19
- 2002/782/EC: Commission Decision of 12 March 2002 on the aid granted by Italy to Poste Italiane SpA (formerly Ente Poste Italiane) [2002] OJ L 282/29
- State Aid N 784/2002—United Kingdom government rural network support funding, debt payment funding and rolling working capital loan to Post Office Limited, C (2003) 1652 fin, 27.05.2003
- State Aid No N 244/2003—United Kingdom credit union provision of access to basic financial services in Scotland, C (2005) 977 final, 06.04.2005
- State Aid No N 37/2003—United Kingdom BBC digital curriculum, C (2003) 3371 fin, 01.10.2003
- State Aid Decision N 46/2003—Ireland risk equalisation scheme in the Irish health insurance market, C (2003) 1322 final, 13.05.2003
- 2004/339/EC: Commission Decision of 15 October 2003 on the measures implemented by Italy for RAI SpA [2004] OJ L119/1

- Aide d'Etat N 381/2004—France: projet de réseau de telécommunication haut débit des Pyrénées-Atlantiques, C (2004) 4343 final, 16.11.2004
- Aide d'Etat N° N 382/2004—France: mise en place d'une infrastructure haut débit sur le territoire de la région Limousin (DORSAL), C (2005) 1170 final, 03.05.2004
- 2004/838/EC: Commission Decision of 10 December 2003 on State Aid implemented by France for France 2 and France 3 [2004] OJ L361/21
- Commission Decision of 28 November 2005 on the application of Article 86(2) of the EC Treaty to State Aid in the form of public service compensation granted to certain undertakings entrusted with the operation of services of general economic interest, [2005] OJ L312/67
- State Aid N 166/2005—United Kingdom Government rural network support funding to Post Office Limited (POL) for 2006–2008, C (2006) 434 final, 22.02.2006
- 2005/217/EC: Commission Decision of 19 May 2004 on measures implemented by Denmark for TV2/Danmark [2006] OJ L85/1
- State Aid N 284/2005—Ireland regional broadband programme: Metropolitan Area Networks ("MANs"), phases II and III, C (2006) 436 final, 08.03.2006
- 2005/351/EC: Commission Decision of 20 October 2004 concerning the aid scheme implemented by the Kingdom of Spain for the airline Intermediación Aérea SL [2005] OJ L110/56
- Commission Decision on the measure N° C 35/2005 (ex N 59/2005) which the Netherlands are planning to implement concerning broadband infrastructure in Appingedam, C (2006) 3226 final, 19.07.2006
- State Aid N642/05—Sweden Compensation to Posten AB for providing basic payment and cash facilities services, C (2006) 5481 final, 22.11.2006
- State Aid C49/2006 on a State Aid scheme implemented by Italy to remunerate Poste Italiane for distributing postal savings certificates, C (2008) 5585 final, 21.10.2008
- Commission Decision of 23 February 2011 on State Aid No C 58/2006 (ex NN 98/2005) implemented by Germany for Bahnen der Stadt Monheim (BSM) and Rheinische Bahngesellschaft (RBG) in the Verkehrsverbund Rhein-Ruhr, C (2011) 632 final, 23.2.2011
- State Aid N 822/2006—United Kingdom debt payment funding to Post Office Limited (POL) for 2007–2008, C (2007) 653 final, 07.03.2007
- State Aid NN 8/2007 (ex N 840/2006)—Spain financing of workforce reduction measures of RTVE, C (2007) 641 final, 07.03.2007
- Commission Decision of 15 October 2014 on State Aid SA.20580 (C 31/2007) (ex NN 17/2007) implemented by Ireland for Córas Iompair Éireann Bus Companies (Dublin Bus and Irish Bus), C (2014) 7275 final, 15.10.2014
- State Aid C 36/2007 Measures implemented by Germany for Deutsche Post AG, 25.01.2012
- 2007/217/EC: Commission Decision of 22 November 2006 on State Aid implemented by France for the Laboratoire national de métrologie et d'essais [2007] OJ L95/25

- 2007/332/EC: Commission Decision of 23 April 2007 on public service obligations on certain routes to and from Sardinia under Article 4 of Council Regulation (EEC) No 2408/92 on access for Community air carriers to intra-Community air routes [2007] OJ L125/16
- State Aid N 388/2007—United Kingdom Post Office Limited (POL) transformation programme, C (2007) 5623 final, 28.11.2007
- COMP/F-1/39.562: Commission Decision of 7 October 2008 on the Slovakian law on hybrid mail services [2008] OJ C322/10
- State Aid NN 24/08—Italy Poste Italiane SpA State compensation for universal postal service obligations 2006–2008, C (2008) 1606 fin, 30.04.2008
- Aide d'Etat N 331/2008—France: compensation de charges pour une Délégation de Service Public (DSP) pour l'établissement et l'exploitation d'un réseau de communications électroniques à très haut débit dans le Département des Hauts-de-Seine, C (2009) 7426 final, 30.09.2009
- State Aid No N 582/2008—Ireland health insurance intergenerational solidarity relief, C (2009) 3572 final, 17.06.2009
- 2009/325/EC: Commission Decision of 26 November 2008 on State Aid C 3/08 (ex NN 102/05)—Czech Republic concerning public service compensations for Southern Moravia Bus Companies [2009] OJ L97/14
- 2009/554/EC: Commission Decision of 21 October 2008 on a State Aid scheme implemented by Italy to remunerate Poste Italiane for distributing postal savings certificates (C 49/06 (ex NN 65/06)) [2009] OJ L189/3
- State Aid No E 2/2005 and N 642/2009—The Netherlands existing and special project aid to housing corporations, C (2009) 9963 final, 15.12.2009
- 2009/845/EC: Commission Decision of 26 November 2008 on State Aid granted by Austria to the company Postbus in the Lienz district C 16/07 (ex NN 55/06) [2009] OJ L306/26
- 2009/973/EC: Commission Decision of 13 July 2009 on the restructuring aid for Combus A/S [2009] OJ L345/28
- State Aid No N 109/2010—Belgium Vlaamse Mediamaatschappij—Subsidie live ondertiteling "Het Nieuws"—Project iWATCH, C (2010) 7679 final, 17.11.2010
- State Aid No N 178/2010—Spain public service compensation linked to a preferential dispatch mechanism for indigenous coal power plants, C (2010) 4499, 29.09.2010
- State Aid N 196/2010—Estonia establishment of a sustainable infrastructure permitting Estonia-wide broadband Internet connection (EstWin project), C (2010) 4943 final, 20.7.2010
- State Aid N 508/2010—United Kingdom Post Office Limited (POL): continuation of network subsidy payment and working capital facility, C (2011) 1770 final, 23.03.2011
- 2010/815/EU: Commission Decision of 15 December 2009 on State Aid C 21/05 (ex PL 45/04) which Poland plans to implement for Poczta Polska as compensation of universal postal service obligations [2010] OJ L347/29

- 2011/1/EU: Commission Decision of 20 July 2010 on the State Aid scheme C 38/09 (ex NN 58/09) which Spain is planning to implement for Corporación de Radio y Televisión Españla (RTVE) [2011] OJ L1/9
- 2011/3/EU: Commission Decision of 24 February 2010 concerning public transport service contracts between the Danish Ministry of Transport and Danske Statsbaner [2011] OJ L7/1
- State Aid No SA.32019—Denmark Danish radio channel FM4, C (2011) 1376 final, 23.03.2011
- 2011/98/EC: Commission Decision of 28 October 2009 on the State Aid C 16/08 (ex NN 105/05 and NN 35/07) implemented by the United Kingdom of Great Britain and Northern Ireland—Subsidies to CalMac and NorthLink for maritime transport services in Scotland [2011] OJ L45/33
- 2011/140/EU: Commission Decision of 20 July 2010 on State Aid C 27/09 (ex N 34/B/09) budgetary grant for France Télévisions which the French Republic plans to implement in favour of France Télévisions [2011] OJ L59/44
- 2011/501/EU: Commission Decision of 23 February 2011 on State Aid C 58/06 (ex NN 98/05) implemented by Germany for Bahnen der Stadt Monheim (BSM) and Rheinische Bahngesellschaft (RBG) in the Verkehrsverbund Rhein-Ruhr [2011] OJ L210/1
- Commission Decision of 20 December 2011 on the application of Article 106 (2) of the Treaty on the Functioning of the European Union to State Aid in the form of public service compensation granted to certain undertakings entrusted with the operation of services of general economic interest [2012] OJ L7/3
- State Aid SA.33054—United Kingdom Post Office Limited (POL) compensation for net costs incurred to keep a non-commercially viable network for the period 2012–15 and the continuation of a working capital facility, C (2012) 1905 final, 28.03.2012
- State Aid SA.33989 (2012/NN)—Italy State compensations for the delivery of the universal service over 2009–2011; State compensations for reduced tariffs offered to publishers, not-for-profit organisations and electoral candidates over 2009–2011, C (2012) 8230 final, 20.11.2012
- 2012/321/EU: Commission Decision of 25 January 2012 on the measure SA.14588 (C 20/09) implemented by Belgium in favour of De Post-La Poste (now Bpost) [2012] OJ L170/1
- 2012/636/EU: Commission Decision of 25 January 2012 Measures C 36/07 (ex NN 25/07) implemented by Germany for Deutsche Post AG [2012] OJ L289/1
- State Aid SA.31006 (2013/N)—Belgium State compensations to Bpost for the delivery of public services over 2013–2015, C (2013) 1909 final, 02.05.2013
- State Aid SA.34515 (2013/NN)—Ireland risk equalisation scheme for 2013, C (2013) 793 final, 20.02.2013
- 2013/435/EU: Commission Decision of 2 May 2013 on State Aid SA.22843 (2012/C) (ex 2012/NN) implemented by France in favour of Société Nationale Maritime Corse-Méditerranée [2013] OJ L220/20

- 2014/201/EU: Commission Decision of 2 October 2013 on compensation to be paid to Simet SpA for public transport services provided between 1987 and 2003 [2014] OJ L114/48
- SA.34155—Regional law on the compensation of school bus transport in the Land Rhineland-Palatinate, C (2014) 133, 22.01.2014
- Commission Decision (EU) 2015/248 of 15 October 2014 on the measure SA.23008 (2013/C) (ex 2013/NN) implemented by Slovak Republic for Spoločná zdravotná poisťovňa, a. s. (SZP) and Všeobecná zdravotná poisťovňa, a. s. (VZP) [2015] OJ L41/25.

Soft Law Instruments

Commission Communications

- 1992 Review of the Situation in the Telecommunications Services Sector, SEC (92) 1048 final, 21.10.1992
- Developing Universal Service for Telecommunications in a Competitive Environment, (Communication from the Commission to the Council, the European Parliament and the European Economic and Social Committee), COM (93) 543, 15.11.1993
- Service of General Interest in Europe, COM (96) 43 final, 11.09.1996
- Service of General Interest in Europe, [2001] OJ C17/04
- Communication from the Commission on the application of State Aid rules to public service broadcasting [2001] OJ C320/5
- Communication on the interpretation of Council Regulation (EEC) No 3577/92 applying the principle of freedom to provide services to maritime transport within Member States COM(2003) 595 final, 22.12.2003
- Community framework for State Aid in the form of public service compensation [2005] OJ C297/4
- Services of General Interest, including Social Services of General Interest: A New European Commitment' (Communication from the Commission to the European Parliament, the Council, the European Economic and Social Committee and the Committee of the Regions), COM (2007) 725 final, 20.11.2007
- Communication from the Commission on the application of State Aid rules to public service broadcasting [2009] OJ C257/1
- Communication from the Commission on the application of the European Union State Aid rules to compensation granted for the provision of services of general economic interest [2012] OJ C8/4
- Communication from the Commission, European Union framework for State Aid in the form of public service compensation [2012] OJ C8/15

Commission Reports

- Second report on the implementation of Council Regulation (EEC) No 1191/69 of 26 June 1969, relating to the action by Member States concerning the obligations inherent in the concept of a public service in transports by rail, road and inland waterway and of Council Regulation (EEC) No 1192/69 of 26 June 1969, relating to the normalization of the accounts of railway undertakings, SEC (74) 2219 final, 18.06.1974
- Fifteenth Report on Competition Policy 1985
- Nineteenth Report on Competition Policy 1990
- Twentieth Report on Competition Policy 1991
- Twenty-First Report on Competition Policy 1992
- Commission Report on the implementation of Regulation (EEC) 3577/92 applying the principle of freedom to provide services to maritime transport within Member States—1993 to 1994, COM (95) 383, 06.09.1995
- Commission Report for 1995–1996 on the implementation of Regulation 3577/92 applying the principle of freedom to provide services to maritime transport within Member States (maritime cabotage) and on the economic and social impact of the liberalisation of island cabotage, COM (97) 296 final, 17.06.1997
- Report from the Commission—Third report of the implementation of Council Regulation 3577/92 applying the principle of freedom to provide services to maritime cabotage (1997–1998), COM (2000) 99 final, 24.02.2000
- Service of General Interest (Report to the Laeken European Council), COM (2001) 598 final, 17.10.2001
- Report from the Commission—Fourth report on the implementation of Council Regulation 3577/92 applying the principle of freedom to provide services to maritime cabotage (1999–2000), COM (2002) 203 final, 24.04.2002
- First Commission Report to the European Parliament and the Council on the application of the Postal Directive, COM (2002) 632 final, 25.11.2002
- On the Review of the Scope of Universal Service in accordance with Article 15 of Directive 2002/22/EC, COM (2005) 203 final, 24.5.2005
- Annex to the Review of the Scope of Universal Service in Accordance with Article 15 of Directive 2002/22/EC (Commission Staff Working Document) SEC (2005) 660, 24.05.2005
- Impact Assessment Report: Annex to the Report Regarding the Outcome of the Review of the Scope of Universal Service in accordance with Article 15(2) of Directive 2002/22/EC (Commission Staff Working Document), SEC (2006) 445, 7.4.2006
- The Commission's 2008 Report on the Scope of the Universal Service in Telecoms: Frequently Asked Questions, MEMO/08/583, 25.09.2008
- On the Second Periodic Review of the Scope of Universal Service in Electronic Communications Networks and Services in accordance with Article 15 of Directive 2002/22/EC, COM (2008) 572 final, 25.9.2008

- Universal Service in E-communications: Report on the Outcome of the Public Consultation and the Third Periodic Review of the Scope in accordance with Article 15 of Directive 2002/22/EC, COM (2011) 795 final, 23.11.2011.

Commission Green Papers

- Television without Frontiers: Green Paper on the Establishment of the Common Market for Broadcasting, especially by Satellite and Cable, COM (84) 300 final, 14.06.1984
- Towards a Dynamic European Economy: Green Paper on the Development of the Common Market for Telecommunication Services and Equipment COM (87) 290 final, 30.06.1987
- Green Paper on the Development of the Single Market for Postal Services, COM (91) 476 final, 11.06.1991
- The Citizens' Network—Fulfilling the Potential of Public Passenger Transport in Europe, COM (95) 601 final, 29.11.1995.

Commission White Papers

- White Paper from the Commission to the European Council: Completing the Internal Market, COM (85) 310 final, 14.06.1985
- White Paper on Services of General Interest, COM (2004) 374 final, 12.5.2004.

Commission Guidelines

- Guidelines on the Application of EEC Competition Rules in the Telecommunications Sector [1991] OJ C233/2
- Guidelines on the application of Articles 92 and 93 of the EC Treaty and Article 61 of the EEA Agreement to State Aids in the aviation sector [1994] OJ C350/5
- Assessment Criteria for National Schemes for the Costing and Financing of Universal Service in Telecommunications and Guidelines for the Member States on Operation of such Schemes, COM (96) 608 final, 27.11.1996
- Community guidelines on State Aid to maritime transport [1997] OJ C205/5
- Community guidelines on State Aid to maritime transport [2004] OJ C13/3
- Community Guidelines for the application of State Aid rules in relation to rapid deployment of broadband networks [2009] OJ C235/7
- EU Guidelines for the application of State Aid rules in relation to the rapid deployment of broadband networks [2013] OJ C25/1

Commission Proposals

- Proposal for a Council Regulation applying the principle of freedom to provide services to maritime transport within Member States [1989] OJ L263/17
- Proposal for a Council Regulation (EEC) on access for air carriers to scheduled intra-Community air-service routes and on the sharing of passenger capacity between air carriers on scheduled air services between Member States, COM (89) 373 final, 11.10.1989
- Amendment to the proposal for a Regulation on access for air carriers to scheduled intra-Community air-service routes and on the sharing of passenger capacity between air carriers on scheduled air services between Member States, COM (90) 234 final, 05.07.1990
- Proposal for a Regulation of the European Parliament and of the Council on action by Member States concerning public service requirements and the award of public service contracts in passenger transport by rail, road and inland waterway, COM (2000) 7 final, 26.07.2001
- Amended proposal for a Regulation of the European Parliament and of the Council on action by Member States concerning public service requirements and the award of public service contracts in passenger transport by rail, road and inland waterway, COM (2002) 107 final, 21.02.2002
- Revised Proposal for a Regulation of the European Parliament and of the Council on Public Passenger Transport Services by rail and road, COM (2005) 319 final, 20.07.2005
- Proposal for a Regulation of the European Parliament and of the Council repealing Regulation (EEC) No 1192/69 of the Council on common rules for the normalisation of the accounts of railway undertakings, COM (2013) 26 final, 30.1.2013
- Proposal for a Regulation of the European Parliament and of the Council amending Regulation (EC) No 1370/2007 concerning the opening of the market for domestic passenger transport services by rail, COM (2013) 28 final, 30.1.2013
- Proposal for a Directive of the European Parliament and of the Council on railway safety, COM (2013) 31 final, 30.1.2013.

Bibliography

Allum P (1995) State and society in Western Europe. Polity Press, Cambridge

Amaral M (2008) Public vs private management of public utilities – the case of urban public transport in Europe. Research in Transportation Economics 22(1):85–90

Ambrosini X, Boldron F, Roy B (2006) Universal service obligations in the postal sector: economic learnings from cross-country comparisons. In: Crew MA, Kleindorfer PR (eds) Progress toward liberalization of the postal and delivery sector. Springer, Boston

Auricchio V (2001) Services of general economic interest and the application of EC competition law. World Competition 24(1):65–91

Bacon K (1997) State regulation of the market and EC competition rules: Articles 85 and 86 compared. European Competition Law Review 18(5):283–291

Baird A, Wilmsmeier G, Boglev Y (2010) Scottish ferries review –final report part A: Methods of ferry service delivery and operation, competition and procurement and environmental issues. www.scotland.gov.uk/Resource/Doc/935/0105632.doc

Baird AJ (2012) Comparing the efficiency of public and private ferry services on the Pentland Firth between mainland Scotland and the Orkney Islands. Research in Transportation Business and Management 4(1):78–89

Baird AJ, Wilmsmeier G (2011) Public tendering of ferry services in Europe. European Transport 49:90–111

Bartosch A (1999) EC Telecommunications Law: what aid does Article 90(2) of the EC Treaty offer to the former monopolists. Computer and Telecommunications Law Review 5(1):12–15

Bartosch A (2003) Clarification or confusion? How to reconcile the ECJ's rulings in Altmark and Chronopost? European State Aid Law Quarterly 2(3):375–386

Bauer JM (1999) Universal service in the European Union. Government Information Quarterly 16 (4):329–343

Bauer JM (2010) Changing roles of the state in telecommunications. International Telecommunications Policy Review 17(1):1–36

Bavasso AF (2002) Public service broadcasting and state aid rules: between a rock and a hard place. European Law Review 27(3):340–350

Behrens P (2001) Public services and the internal market – an analysis of the commission's communication on services of general interest in Europe. European Business Organisation Law Review 2(4):469–492

Bekkedal T (2011) Article 106 TFEU is dead. Long live Article 106 TFEU! In: Szyszczak E, Davies J, Andenæs M, Bekkedal T (eds) Developments in services of general interest. T.M.C. Asser Press, The Hague, pp 61–102

L. Zhu, *Services of General Economic Interest in EU Competition Law*,
Legal Issues of Services of General Interest,
https://doi.org/10.1007/978-94-6265-387-0

Bell J (1999) France: the concept of public service under threat from Europe? An illustration from energy law. European Public Law 5(2):189–198

Bennett P (2006) Competing for the island lifeline: European law, state aid and regional public services. Regional Studies 40(8):953–966

Bergum K (2008) Calculating the net cost of the USO: a practical example from Norway. In: Crew MA, Kleindorfer PR, Campbell JI (eds) Handbook of worldwide postal reform. Edward Elgar Publishing, Cheltenham & Northampton

Blackman CR (1995) Universal service: obligation or opportunity? Telecommunications Policy 19 (3):171–176

Blum F (2000) The recent case law of the European Court of Justice on state monopolies and its implication for network industries. Journal of Network Industries 1(1):55–87

Blum F, Logue A (1998) State monopolies under EC law. Wiley, New Jersey

Boeger N (2007) Solidarity and EC competition law. European Law Review 32(3):319–340

Boeger N (2010) Public service, autonomy and community law. In: Nickel R (ed) Conflict of laws and laws of conflict in Europe and beyond: patterns of supranational and transnational juridification. Intersentia Publishing, Antwerp

Borre O, Goldsmith M (1995) The scope of government. In: Borre O, Scarbrough E (eds) The scope of government. Oxford University Press, Oxford

Borre O, Viegas J M (1995) Government intervention in the economy. In: Borre O, Scarbrough E (eds) The scope of government. Oxford University Press, Oxford

Borsenberger C, Joram D, Roy B (2011) How many outlets if the USP does not face any USO? A cross-country comparison. In: Crew MA, Kleindorfer PR (eds) Reinventing the postal sector in an electronic age. Edward Elgar Publishing, Cheltenham & Northampton

Bovis C (2003) Public procurement, state aid and public services: between symbiotic correlation and asymmetric geometry. European State Aid Law Quarterly 2(4):553–569

Bovis CH (2005) Public service obligations in the transport sector: the demarcation between state aids and services of general interest under EU Law. European Business Law Review 16 (6):1329–1347

Bovis CH (2005) The application of state aid rules to the European Union transport sector. Columbia Journal of European Law 11(3):557–604

Brandt T (2007) Liberalisation, privatisation and regulation of postal services in Europe – first international experiences in the run-up to new European regulations. WSI Discussion paper. https://www.boeckler.de/pdf/wsi_pj_piq_post_europe.pdf

Bright C (1993) Article 90, Economic policy and the duties of member states. European Competition Law Review 14(6):263–272

Britain L (1992) Competition policy and post and telecommunications. Speech/92/50, Speech of Sir Leon Britain at the Centre for European Policy Studies, Brussels, 19.05.1992. http://europa.eu/rapid/press-release_SPEECH-92-50_en.htm

Broberg MP, Fenger N (1995) National organisation of regulatory powers and community competition law. European Competition Law Review 16(6):364–375

Brooks MR (2009) Liberalisation in maritime transport. International Transport Forum 2009: Transport for a Global Economy – Challenges and Opportunities in the Downturn. https://www.itf-oecd.org/sites/default/files/docs/09fp02_0.pdf

Bruijn HD, Dicke W (2006) Strategies for safeguarding public values in liberalized utility sectors. Public Administration 84(3):717–735

Buelens C, Garnier G, Meiklejohn R, Johnson M (2007) The economic analysis of state aid: some open questions. Economic Papers No. 286, Directorate-General for Economic and Financial Affairs, European Commission. http://ec.europa.eu/economy_finance/publications/publication9549_en.pdf

Buendia Sierra JL (2000) Exclusive rights and state monopolies under EC Law: Article 86 (formerly Article 90) of the EC Treaty, Oxford University Press, Oxford

Burns P, Carslake I, Houpis G (2002) Brand loyalty and limited entry in postal markets. In: Crew MA, Kleindorfer PR (eds) Postal and delivery services: delivering on competition. Springer, Boston

Cahill D (2010) The ebb and flow, the doldrums and the raging tide: single market law's ebb and flow over services of general economic interest, the legal doldrums over services of general interest, and the raging tide of Article 106(2) (ex Art 86(2)) over state aid & public procurement. European Business Law Review 21(5):629–662

Calzada J, Jaag C, Trinkner U (2010) Universal service auctions in liberalized postal markets. In: Crew MA, Kleindorfer PR, Campbell JI (eds) Heightening competition in the postal and delivery sector. Edward Elgar Publishing, Cheltenham & Northampton

Camenen FX (1996) Public undertakings and public service activities in the European Union. European Parliament, Directorate General for Research, Working document, Economic Affairs Series, W - 21. http://www.europarl.europa.eu/workingpapers/econ/pdf/w21_en.pdf

Campbell JI (1993) Couriers and the European postal monopolies: policy challenges of a newly emerging industries. In: Van Schendelen R (ed) National public and private EC lobbying. Dartmouth Publishing. Aldershot & Brookfield

Campbell JI (1995) A review of efforts to develop a new policy framework for postal services in the European Union. In: Crew MA, Kleindorfer PR (eds) Commercialization of postal and delivery services: national and international perspectives. Springer, Boston

Campbell JI (1997) The roots of deregulation: why aviation and telecommunications but not the Postal Office? In: Crew MA, Kleindorfer PR (eds) Managing change in the postal and delivery industries. Springer, Boston

Campbell JI (2000) Global postal reform movement' In: Hudgins EL (ed) Mail at the millennium: will the postal service go private? Cato Institute, Washington

Campbell JI (2001) Remailing – catalyst for liberalising the European postal markets? In: Kulenkampff G, Smit H (eds) Liberalisation of postal markets: papers presented at the 6th Königswinter Seminar Königswinter, 19–21 February (WIK). https://www.jcampbell.com/Articles/2002_Remail_as_Catalyst.pdf

Campbell JI, Dieke AK, Niederprüm A (2008) National postal policies in Europe on the eve of the third directive. In: Crew MA, Kleindorfer PR, Campbell JI (eds) Handbook of worldwide postal reform. Edward Elgar Publishing, Cheltenham & Northampton

Campbell RM (2001) Regulatory and governance changes in liberalized commercialized postal environments. In: Crew MA, Kleindorfer PR (eds) Future directions in postal reform. Kluwer Academic Publishers, Boston

Campbell RM (2002) The politics of postal transformation: modernizing postal systems in the electronic and global world. McGill Queens University Press, Montreal

Carey KD (1999) Competition law and the privatization of telecommunications markets in the European Union. Suffolk Transnational Law Review 22(2):747–774

Cassidy WP (1999) Universal service in a competitive telecommunications environment: the current state of universal service in the European Union and United States. North Carolina Journal of International Law and Commercial Regulation 25(1):107–166

Charles MB, Dicke W, Koppenjan J, Ryan N (2007) Public values and safeguarding mechanisms in infrastructure policies: a conceptual and theoretical exploration. http://eprints.qut.edu.au/9283/1/PT_Infrastructure_Charles%2520Dicke%2520Koppenjan%2520Ryan.pdf

Chlomoudis CI, Pallis PL, Papadimitriou S, Tzannatos ES (2007) The liberalisation of maritime transport and the island regions in EU – evidence from Greece. European Transport 37:1–15

Chung CM (1994) Recent developments in EC postal liberalisation. European Competition Law Review 4(15):217–224

Coleman JA, Rollet B (1997) Television in Europe. Intellect Ltd, Bristol

Comandini VV, Lettieri C (2001) Comparing postal and telecommunication networks: similarities and differences. Journal of Network Industries 2(2):163–206

Comandini VV, Mazzarella F (2011) Competition and regulation in the Italian postal market. In: Crew MA, Kleindorfer PR (eds) Reinventing the postal sector in an electronic age. Edward Elgar Publishing, Cheltenham & Northampton

Comandini VV, Consiglio A, Gori S, Piccinin E, Pierleoni MR (2010) The Altmark ruling and approaches to measuring efficiency of postal operators. In: Crew MA, Kleindorfer PR, Campbell JI (eds) Heightening competition in the postal and delivery sector. Edward Elgar Publishing, Cheltenham & Northampton

Conway G (2010) Conflicts of competence norms in EU law and the legal reasoning of the ECJ. German Law Journal 11(9):966–1005

Costa Á, Fernandes R (2012) Urban public transport in Europe: technology diffusion and market organization. Transportation Research Part A: Policy and Practice 46(2):269–284

Cowie J (2012) The cost of remote transport services in the single European market – the case of the Scottish Western Isles ferries. Research in Transportation Business & Management 4:90–96

Craig P (2010) The Lisbon Treaty: law, politics, and treaty reform. Oxford University Press, Oxford

Cranfield University (2007) Air transport: Quarterly report No. 15, 2nd quarter, April to June 2007. http://ec.europa.eu/transport/modes/air/observatory_market/doc/atv_q22007_15.pdf

Crew MA, D'Alcantara G, Kleindorfer PR, Claeys P, Kuypers B (2008) Economic factors underlying postal reform in the European Union. In: Crew MA, Kleindorfer PR, Campbell JI (eds) Handbook of worldwide postal reform. Edward Elgar Publishing, Cheltenham & Northampton

Crew MA, Kleindorfer PR (1991) Rowland hill's contribution as an economist. In: Crew MA, Kleindorfer PR (eds) Competition and innovation in postal services. Springer, Boston

Cruz JB (2005) Beyond competition: services of general interest and European community law. In: De Búrca G (ed) EU Law and the welfare state: in search of solidarity. Oxford University Press, Oxford, pp 169–212

Cseres KJ (2008) What has competition done for consumers in liberalised markets? The Competition Law Review 4(2):77–121

Cygan A (2008) Public healthcare in the European Union: still a service of general interest? International and Comparative Law Quarterly 57(3):529–560

Damjanovic D, De Witte B (2009) Welfare integration through EU Law: the overall picture in the light of the Lisbon Treaty. In: Neergaard UB, Nielsen R, Roseberry LM (eds) Integrating welfare functions into EU Law: From Rome to Lisbon. DJØF Publishing, Copenhagen

Danner CR (1999) Postal service and the telecommunications analogy. In: Crew MA, Kleindorfer PR (eds) Emerging competition in postal and delivery services. Kluwer Academic Publishers, Boston

Davies G (2009) What does article 86 actually do? In: Krajewski M, Neergaard U, Van de Gronden J (eds) The changing legal framework for services of general interest in Europe: between competition and solidarity. T.M.C. Asser Press, The Hague

De Minico G (2011) New European regulation on universal service and next generation networks or just a lifting of the old one? Computer and Telecommunications Law Review 17(5):135–147

De Streel A (2003) The protection of the European citizen in a competitive e-society: the new EU Universal Service Directive. Journal of Network Industries 4(2):189–223

De Vries SA (2008) Harmonization of services of general economic interest: where there's a will there's a way! In: Van de Gronden J (ed) The EU and WTO law on services: limits to the realization of general interest policies within the services markets? Kluwer Law International, Alphen aan den Rijn

Debusschere T, De Streel A, Moria L, Mourlon-Beernaert L, Villalobos J (2010) Final report for the study on the impact of EU policy options for revision of the universal service provision. http://ec.europa.eu/newsroom/dae/document.cfm?doc_id=1606

Defeuilley C (1999) Competition and public service obligations: regulatory rules and industries games. Annals of Public and Cooperative Economics 70(1):25–48

Delle Site P, Salucci MV (2009) Thematic research summary: urban transport. European Research Knowledge Centre, European Commission DG Energy and Transport. http://transport-research.info/sites/default/files/thematic-analysis/20100215_145249_66950_TRS%20Urban%20Transport.pdf

Dempsey PS (1992) European aviation regulation: flying through the liberalisation labyrinth. Boston College International and Comparative Law Review 15(2):311–374

Depypere S, Broche J, Tigchelaar N (2004) State aid and broadcasting: state of play. Competition Policy Newsletter (1):71–73

Depypere S, Tigchelaar N (2004) The commission's state aid policy on activities of public service broadcasters in neighbouring Markets. Competition Policy Newsletter (2):19–22

Deringer A (1965) The interpretation of Article 90 (2) of the E.E.C. Treaty. Common Market Law Review 2(2):129–138

Dieke AK, Niederprüm A, Campbell JI (2008) Universal service and postal monopoly in other countries. Study on Universal Postal Service and the Postal Monopoly, George Mason University. http://mars.gmu.edu/handle/1920/3477

Dobbenberg P (1993) The international mail market in the 1990s. In: Crew MA, Kleindorfer PR (eds) Regulation and the nature of postal and delivery services. Springer, Boston

Donders K (2009) State aid and public service broadcasting: how future-proof is the remit of public broadcasting organisations? http://www.ies.be/files/IES%20Working%20paper%201_2009%20Karen%20Donders.pdf

Dreyfus M (2009) France. In: Krajewski M, Neergaard U (eds) The changing legal framework for services of general interest in Europe: between competition and solidarity. T.M.C. Asser Press, The Hague

Eccles R (2008) United Kingdom postal services regulation. In: Crew MA, Kleindorfer PR, Campbell JI (eds) Handbook of worldwide postal reform. Edward Elgar Publishing, Cheltenham & Northampton

Eccles R (2011) State funding and cost sharing of the USO under the 2008 EU postal services directive. In: Crew MA, Kleindorfer PR (eds) Reinventing the postal sector in an electronic age. Edward Elgar Publishing, Cheltenham & Northampton

Economides N (2004) Telecommunications regulation: an introduction. Working Papers No 04–20, NET Institute, 2004. http://www.netinst.org/Telecommunications_Regulation.pdf

Edward D, Hoskins M (1995) Article 90: Deregulation and EC Law. Reflections arising from the XVI FIDE conference. Common Market Law Review 32(1):157–186

Ehlermann CD (1993) Managing monopolies: the role of the state in controlling market dominance in the European Community. European Competition Law Review 14(2):61–69

Eliassen KA, From J (2009) Deregulation, privatisation and public service delivery: universal service in telecommunications in Europe. Policy and Society 27(3):239–248

Ellis E (ed) (1999) The principle of proportionality in the laws of Europe. Hart Publishing, Oxford

Ewing KD (2001) Constitutional reform and human rights: unfinished business? Edinburgh Law Review 5(3):297–324

Ferrera M (2005) Towards an 'open' social citizenship? the new boundaries of welfare in the European Union. In: De Búrca G (ed) EU Law and the welfare state: in search of solidarity. Oxford University Press, Oxford, pp 11–38

Fiedziuk N (2011) Services of general economic interest and the Treaty of Lisbon: opening doors to a whole new approach or maintaining the 'status quo'. European Law Review 36(2):226–242

Fratini A, Filpo F (2006) The new EC framework for state aid to public service and the postal sector: where do we stand now? In: Crew MA, Kleindorfer PR (eds) Progress toward liberalization of the postal and delivery sector. Springer, New York

Freedland M, Sciarra S (eds) (1998) Public services and citizenship in European law: public and labour law perspectives. Oxford University Press, Oxford

Freeman R (1998) Competition in context: the politics of health care reform in Europe. International Journal for Quality in Health Care 10(5):395–401

Friederiszick HW, Röller LH, Verouden V (2008) European state aid control: an economic framework. In Buccirossi P (ed) Handbook of antitrust economics. MIT Press, Cambridge

Gallet-Rybak C, Moreno C, Nadal D, Toledano J (2008) The French postal market in the wake of the postal law of 2005. In: Crew MA, Kleindorfer PR, Campbell JI (eds) Handbook of worldwide postal reform. Edward Elgar Publishing, Cheltenham & Northampton

Gardner A (1995) The velvet revolution: Article 90 and the triumph of the free market in Europe's regulated sectors. European Competition Law Review 16(2):78–86

Gautier A, Paolini D (2011) Universal service financing in competitive postal markets: one size does not fit all. Review of Network Economics 10(3): Article 6

Gautier A, Wauthy X (2012) Competitively neutral universal service obligations. Information Economics and Policy 24(3–4):254–261

Geradin D (2006) Twenty years of liberalization of network industries in the European Union: where do we go now? http://papers.ssrn.com/sol3/papers.cfm?abstract_id=946796

Gerber DJ (1994) The transformation of European Community Law? Harvard International Law Journal 35(1):97–138

Giaimo S (2014) Cost containment vs. solidarity in the welfare state: the case of German and American health care reform. American Institute for Contemporary German Studies: Policy Papers No. 6, 1998. http://webdoc.sub.gwdg.de/ebook/lf/2003/aicgs/publications/PDF/giaimo.pdf

Gómez-Barroso JL, Marbán-Flores R (2013) Basic financial services: a new service of general economic interest? Journal of European Social Policy 23(3):332–339

Graham B (1998) Liberalization, regional economic development and the geography of demand for air transport in the European Union. Journal of Transport Geography 6(2):87–104

Graham C (2010) Social-economic rights and essential services: a new challenge for the regulatory state. In: Oliver D, Prosser T, Rawlings R (eds) The regulatory state: constitutional implications. Oxford University Press, Oxford

Greaves R (2000) EC transport law. Longman, Harlow & New York

Greaves R (2009) Application of the EC common rules on competition to cabotage, including island cabotage. In: Antapassis A, Athanassiou LI, Rosaeg E (eds) Competition and regulation in shipping and shipping related industries. Martinus Nijhoff Publishers, Leiden & Boston

Greer I, Breidahl NK, Knuth M, Larsen F (2017) The Marketization of employment services: the dilemmas of Europe's work-first welfare state. Oxford University Press, Oxford

Griffiths M (2000) Failing to install effective competition in postal services – the limited impact of EC law. European Competition Law Review 21(9):399–407

Gwilliam KM, Van De Velde DM (1990) The potential for regulatory change in European bus markets. Journal of Transport Economics and Policy 24(3):333–350

Gyselen L (1993) Anti-competitive state measures under the EC Treaty: towards a substantive legality standard. European Law Review Supp. (Competition Law Checklist):55–89

Gyselen L (2010) Services of general economic interest and competition under European Law – a delicate balance. Journal of European Competition Law & Practice 1(6):491–499

Haffner A (2005) United States Postal Service v Flamingo Industries (USA) Ltd: does the USA have the answer to the 'undertaking problem' in Europe? European Competition Law Review 26(7):397–402

Hall D (2001) EU competition policies and public services. http://www.psiru.org/sites/default/files/DHepsuConfFinal.doc

Hammerschmid G, Van de Walle S, Andrews R, Mostafa A (2019) New Public Management reforms in Europe and their effects: findings from a 20-country top executive survey. International Review of Administrative Sciences 85(3):399–418

Hancher L (1999) Community, state and market. In: Craig P, De Búrca G (eds) The evolution of EU Law. Oxford University Press, Oxford

Hancher L, Larouche P (2010) The coming age of EU regulation of network industries and services of general economic interest. Tilburg Law and Economics Center Law and Economics Discussion Paper No. 2010–024. http://papers.ssrn.com/sol3/papers.cfm?abstract_id=1628573

Hanretty C (2012) Public service broadcasting's continued rude health. http://www.britac.ac.uk/templates/asset-relay.cfm?frmAssetFileID=11221

Harrison J, Woods LM (2001) Defining European public service broadcasting. European Journal of Communication 16(4):477–504

Hatzopoulos V (2005) Health law and policy: the impact of the EU. In: De Búrca G (ed) EU Law and the welfare state: in search of solidarity. Oxford University Press, Oxford, pp 111–168

Hatzopoulos V (2009) Service of general interest in healthcare: an exercise in deconstruction. In: Neergaard UB, Nielsen R, Roseberry LM (eds) Integrating welfare functions into EU law: from Rome to Lisbon. DJØF Publishing, Copenhagen

Haucap J, Schwalbe U (2014) Economic principles of state aid control. In: Sacker FJ, Montag F (eds) European state aid law: a commentary. Hart Publishing, Oxford

Hauge O (1999) Experimental tendering. an analysis of experiences from the road/ferry sector in Norway. https://thredbo-conference-series.org/downloads/thredbo6_papers/Thredbo6-theme1-Hauge.pdf

Henry C (1993) Public service and competition in the European community approach to communications networks. Oxford Review of Economic Policy 9(1):45–66

Héritier A (2001) Market integration and social cohesion: the politics of public services in European regulation. Journal of European Public Policy 8(5):825–852

Hermans HEGM (2008) Cross-border health care in the European Union: recent legal implications of 'Decker and Kohl'. Journal of Evaluation in Clinical Practice 6(4):431–439

Hervey TK (2007) EU law and national health policies: problem or opportunity? Health Economics, Policy and Law 2(1):1–6

Hervey TK (2011a) If only it were so simple: public health services and EU law. In: Cremona M (ed) Market integration and public services in the European Union. Oxford University Press, Oxford, pp 179–310

Hervey TK (2011b) The impacts of European Union law on the health care sector: institutional overview. Eurohealth 16(4):5–7

Hervey TK, McHale JV (2004) Health law and the European Union. Cambridge University Press, Cambridge

Hervi A, Sunde Ø (2001) An evaluation of competitive tendering in the ferry sector in Norway. http://www.thredbo-conference-series.org/downloads/thredbo7_papers/thredbo7-workshopA-Hervik-Sunde.pdf

Hidson M, Müller M (2003) Better public transport for Europe through competitive tendering a good practice guide – a good practice guide. The International Council for Local Environmental Initiatives. https://www.bkb.admin.ch/dam/bkb/de/dokumente/Oeffentliches_Beschaffungswesen/Nachhaltige_Beschaffung/leitfaden_beschaffung.pdf.download.pdf/Leitfaden%20Beschaffung%20%C3%B6ffentlicher%20Transportleistungen%20A%20Good%20Practice%20Guide.pdf

Holmes J (2004) Fixing the limits of EC competition law: state action and the accommodation of the public services. Competition Law and Policy 57(1):149–174

Hordijk EP (1995) EC Law versus legal monopolies: a tense relationship. International Business Law Journal 11 (5):595–614

Houben I (2008) Public service obligations: moral counterbalance of technical liberalization legislation? European Review of Private Law 16(1):7–27

Huffschmid J (ed) (2005) Economic policy for a social Europe a critique of neo-liberalism and proposals for alternatives. Palgrave, Macmillan

Hulsink W (1999) Privatisation and liberalisation in European telecommunications: comparing Britain, the Netherlands and France. Routledge, New York

Humphreys P (1996) Mass media and media policy in Western Europe. Manchester University Press, Manchester

Humphreys P (2005) The EU and audiovisual regulation: an agency for de-regulation or re-regulation – a research agenda. http://regulation.upf.edu/ecpr-05-papers/phumphreys.pdf

International Telecommunication Union (2012) ICT regulation toolkit – module 4: universal access and services. http://www.ictregulationtoolkit.org/action/document/download?document_id=3606

Iosifidis P (2009) Plurality of public service provision in the UK and beyond. Interactions: Studies in Communication & Culture 1(2):253–267

Ipsos (2004) Telecoms Services Indicators 2004. Produced for the European Commission, DG information society. http://europa.eu.int/information_society/topics/ecomm/doc/useful_information/librar%20y/studies_ext_consult/inra_%20year2004/report_telecom_2004_fi%20nal_reduced.pdf

Isotope (1997) Improved structure and organisation for urban transport operations of passengers in Europe. Transport Research Fourth Framework Programme Urban Transport VII-51. http://bookshop.europa.eu/en/fourth-framework-programme-pbC30897581/downloads/C3-08-97-581-EN-C/C30897581ENC_001.pdf?FileName=C30897581ENC_001.pdf&SKU=C30897581ENC_PDF&CatalogueNumber=C3-08-97-581-EN-C

Jacobi O, Kowalsky W (2002) Regulated and controlled liberalisation: a means to reconcile market efficiency and social cohesion? Transfer: European Review of Labour and Research 8(2):185–197

Jauk W (2000) The application of EC competition rules to telecommunications – selected aspects: the case of interconnection. International Journal of Communications Law and Policy 4:1–113

Jayakar KP, Sawhney H (2003) Universal service: beyond established practice to possibility space. Telecommunication Policy Research Conference. http://www.personal.psu.edu/kpj1/JayakarandSawhney1.pdf

John RR (2001) Postal systems. In: Smelser NJ, Baltes PB (eds) International encyclopedia of social & behavioral sciences. Elsevier, Amsterdam & New York

John RR (2008) History of universal service and the postal monopoly. Study on universal postal service and the postal monopoly, George Mason University, November. http://digilib.gmu.edu/dspace/handle/1920/3477. Accessed 9 October 2014

Jonsson P, Selander S (2006) The "real" graveyard spiral: experiences from the liberalized Swedish postal market. In: Crew MA, Kleindorfer PR (eds) Progress toward liberalization of the postal and delivery sector. Springer, Boston

Karayigit MT (2009) The notion of service of general economic interest revisited. European Public Law 15(4):575–595

Karayigit MT (2009) Under the triangle rules of competition, state aid and public procurement: public undertakings entrusted with the operation of services of general economic interest. European Competition Law Review 30(11):542–564

Karlaftis MG, McCarthy P (1998) Operating subsidies and performance in public transit: an empirical study. Transportation Research Part A: Policy and Practice 32(5):359–375

Kaufmann FX, Veit-Wilson J (trans.) (2012) European foundations of the welfare state. Berghahn Books, New York & Oxford

Kawagoe M (2008) Air transport deregulation in the EU: study from the European perspective. Paper for presentation at the IPSA RC-3 Symposium on European Integration between the Past and the Present, Hokkaido University, Sapporo, Japan, 6 September 2008. http://eprints.lib.hokudai.ac.jp/dspace/bitstream/2115/43684/1/2_161-180.pdf

Kay N (2009) Scottish ferry policy. http://www.strath.ac.uk/media/departments/economics/fairse/backissues/Fraser_of_Allander_Economic_Commentary_Vol_32,_No_3[1].pdf

Kekelekis M, Rusu IE (2010) The award of public contracts and the notion of "internal operator" under regulation 1370/2007 on public passenger transport services by rail and by road. Public Procurement Law Review 19(6):198–216

Kenny M (2009) Freezing the state out of the market: the three degrees of state incapacity in Europe. http://www.jura.uni-bremen.de/lib/download.php?file=0abf581818.pdf&filename=wp7_2009.pdf

Kerf M (1993) The policy of the commission of the E.E.C. toward national monopolies – an analysis of the measures adopted on the basis of Article 90 § 3 of the E.E.C. Treaty. World Competition 17(1):73–111

Keune M, Leschke J, Watt A (2008) Privatisation and liberalisation of public services in Europe: an analysis of economic and labour market impacts. European Trade Union Institute, Brussels

Kiessling T, Blondeel Y (1998) The EU regulatory framework in telecommunications – a critical analysis. Telecommunication Policy 22(7):571–592

Klasse M (2013) The impact of Altmark: the European commission case law responses. In: Szyszczak E, Van de Gronden JW (eds) Financing services of general economic interest: reform and modernization. T.M.C. Asser Press, The Hague

Kociubiński J (2011) Services of general economic interest – towards a European concept of public services. Wroclaw Review of Law, Administration and Economics 1(2):49–64

Koenig C, Fechter S (2009) The European Commission's hidden asymmetric regulatory approach in the field of broadband infrastructure funding. European State Aid Law Quarterly 8(4):463–472

Krajewski M (2006) Background paper on a legal framework for services of general (economic) interest. https://www.epsu.org/sites/default/files/article/files/Paper%20legal%20framework%20SGI_M_Krajewski_2006.pdf

Krajewski M (2008) Providing legal clarity and securing policy space for public services through a legal framework for services of general economic interest: squaring the circle? European Public Law 14(3):377–398

Kronenberger V (2001) A model of the transformation process of statutory monopolies in European community law: from practice to theory. European Business Organization Law Review 2(2):301–338

Ladcomm Corporation (2013) Universal service fund study. Conducted on behalf of the GSM Association

Lando SD (1994) The European Community's road to telecommunications deregulation. Fordham Law Review 62(7):2159–2198

Lang JT (1989) European community competition law and member state action. Northwestern Journal of International Law & Business 10(1):114–132

Lang JT (2005) Privatisation of social welfare: European Union competition law rules. In: Spaventa E, Dougan M (eds) Social welfare and EU Law. Hart Publishing, Oxford

Larouche P (1999) Telecommunications. In: Geradin D (ed) The liberalization of state monopolies in European Union and beyond. Kluwer Law International, The Hague

Larouche P (2000) Competition law and regulation in European telecommunications. Hart Publishing, Oxford

Lasok KPE (2004) When is an undertaking not an undertaking? European Competition Law Review 25(7):383–385

Leith P (2012) Europe's information society project and digital inclusion: universal service obligations or social solidarity? International Journal of Law and Information Technology 20 (2):102–123

Lenaerts K (2012) Defining the concept of 'services of general interest' in light of the 'checks and balances' set out in the EU treaties. Jurisprudence 19(4):1247–1267

Llorens-Maluquer C (2002) The European Union policy, pluralism and public service. Paper presented at the RIPE@2002 Conference

Locksley G (1994) From exclusive rights to access charges. Utilities Policy 4(3):223–228

Louri V (2002) "Undertaking" as a jurisdictional element for the application of EC competition rules. Legal Issues of Economic Integration 29(2):143–176

Lundahl BW, Kunz C, Brownell C, Harris N, Vleet RV (2009) Prison privatization: a meta-analysis of cost and quality of confinement indicators. http://rsw.sagepub.com/content/19/4/383

Lynskey O (2007) The application of article 86(2) EC to measures which do not fulfil the Altmark criteria; institutionalising incoherence in the legal framework governing state compensation of public service obligations. World Competition 30(1):153–168

Maas W (2007) Creating European citizens. Rowman & Littlefield, Washington

Maczkovics C, Van Calster G, Martens B (2010) Study on the implementation of regulation (EC) N° 1370/2007 on public passenger transport services by rail and by road. https://ec.europa.eu/transport/sites/transport/files/themes/pso/studies/doc/2010-pso.pdf

Majone G (1997) From the positive to the regulatory state: causes and consequences of changes in the mode of governance. Journal of Public Policy 17(2):139–167

Marenco G (1983) Public sector and community law. Common Market Law Review 20(3):495–527

Marshall TH (1950) Citizenship and social class, and other essays. Cambridge University Press, Cambridge

Martin R, Roma M, and Vansteenkiste I (2005) Regulatory reforms in selected EU network industries. Occasional Paper Series No. 28. https://www.ecb.europa.eu/pub/pdf/scpops/ecbocp28.pdf.

Martinsen DS (2005) Social security regulation in the EU: the de-territorialization of welfare. In: De Búrca G (ed) EU Law and the welfare state: In search of solidarity. Oxford University Press, Oxford

Mendel T (2013) Public service broadcasting: a comparative legal survey. UNESCO, Paris

Menéndez AJ (2003) The rights' foundations of solidarity: social and economic rights in the Charter of Fundamental Rights of the European Union. Working Papers 03/1, Advanced Research on the Europeanisation of the Nation-State, University of Oslo

Milgrom P (1996) Procuring universal service: putting auction theory to work. Lecture at the Royal Swedish Academy of Sciences, 9 December 1996. http://www.stanford.edu/~milgrom/publishedarticles/Procuring%20Universal%20Service%20Putting%20Auction%20Theory%20to%20Work,%201996.pdf

Millward R (2005) Private and public enterprise in Europe: energy, telecommunications and transport 1830–1990. Cambridge University Press, Cambridge

Millward R (2008a) Business and the state. In: Jones G, Zeitlin J (eds) The Oxford handbook of business history. Oxford University Press, Oxford

Millward R (2008b) Private and public enterprise in Europe: energy, telecommunications and transport 1830–1990. Cambridge University Press, Cambridge

Millward R (2011) Public enterprise in the modern Western world: an historical analysis. Annals of Public and Cooperative Economics 82(4):375–398

Milne C (1998) Stages of universal service policy. Telecommunications Policy 22(9):775–780

Mortensen F (2008) Altmark, Article 106(2) and public service broadcasting. European State Aid Law Quarterly 7(2):239–249

Morton A (2011) The impact of European Union competition policy on public transport policy and provision in the UK. http://www.european-services-strategy.org.uk/news/2011/essu-launches-a-new-series-of-european-public/eu-public-transport-policy.pdf

Mossialos E, Dixon A (2002) Funding health care: an introduction. In: Mossialos E, Dixon A, Figueras J, Kutzin J (eds) Funding health care: options for Europe. European Observatory on Health Care Systems, 2002. http://www.euro.who.int/document/e74485.pdf?ua=1

Mueller M (1993) Universal service in telephone history: a reconstruction. Telecommunications Policy 17(5):352–369

Muller T (2009) Efficiency control in state aid and the power of member states to define SGEIs. European State Aid Law Quarterly 8(1):39–46

Naftel JM (1992) The natural death of a natural monopoly: competition in EC telecommunications after the telecommunications terminals judgment. Emory International Law Review 6(2):449–494

Naftel JM (1996) European Commission: telecommunications – universal services. Computer and Telecommunications Law Review 2(3):89–92

Nagy CI (2013) The metamorphoses of universal service in the European telecommunications and energy sector: a trans-sectoral perspective. German Law Journal 147(9):1731–1756

Napolitano G (2005) Towards a European legal order for services of general economic interest. European Public Law 11(4):565–581

Neergaard U (2009) Services of general economic interest: the nature of the beast. In: Krajewski M, Neergaard U, Van de Gronden J (eds) The changing legal framework for services of general interest in Europe: between competition and solidarity. T.M.C. Asser Press, The Hague

Neergaard U (2011) The commission's soft law in the area of services of general economic interest. In: Szyszczak E, Davies J, Andenæs M, Bekkedal T (eds) Developments in services of general interest. T.M.C. Asser Press, The Hague

Nenova MB (2007) The new concept of universal service in a digital networked communications environment. I/S: A Journal of Law and Policy for the Information Society 3(1):117–146

Nett L (1998) Auctions: an alternative approach to allocate universal service obligations. Telecommunications Policy 22(8):661–669

Nicolaides P (2003) Compensation for public service obligations: the floodgates of state aid? European Competition Law Review 24(11):561–573

Noaksson N (2005) Taking stock of the liberalization of public utilities: can structural reforms bring the Lisbon strategy back on track? European Trade Union Institute for Research, Education, Safety and Health, November 2005. https://www.epsu.org/sites/default/files/article/files/EPSU_Network_Industries_final_version_Nov05.pdf

Nomden K (1997) Reconciling liberalisation and public service obligations. EIPASCOPE 1997 (1):1–6

O'Leary S (2005) Solidarity and citizenship rights in the charter of fundamental rights of the European Union. In: De Búrca G (ed) EU Law and the welfare state: in search of solidarity. Oxford University Press, Oxford, pp 39–87

Obermann G, Hall D, Sak B (2005) Services of general interest in the internal market. http://www.europarl.europa.eu/RegData/etudes/etudes/join/2005/358357/IPOL-IMCO_ET(2005)358357_EN.pdf

Odudu O (2010) The public/private distinction in EU Internal Market Law. Revue trimestrielle de droit europeen 46(4):826–841

Odudu O (2011) Are state-owned health-care providers undertakings subject to competition law? European Competition Law Review 32(5):231–241

Oxera Consulting Ltd (2007) Funding universal service obligations in the postal sector. A study prepared for La Poste, De Post-La Poste, Hellenic Post, Poste Italiane, P&T Luxembourg, Correos, Magyar Posta, Cyprus Post, Poczta Polska. http://www.oxera.com/Oxera/media/Oxera/Funding-the-USO-in-the-postal-sector.pdf?ext=.pdf

Pappalardo A (1991) State measures and public undertakings: Article 90 of the EEC Treaty revisited. European Competition Law Review 12(1):29–39

Pescatore P (1986) Public and private aspects of European Community Competition Law. Fordham International Law Journal 10(3):373–419

Picard F (1998) Citizenship, fundamental rights, and public services. In: Freedland M, Sciarra S (eds) Public services and citizenship in European Law: public and labour law perspectives. Oxford University Press, Oxford

Prechal S (2008) Fundamental rights as limits to the liberalisation of service markets. In: Van de Gronden J (ed) The EU and WTO Law on services: limits to the realization of general interest policies within the services markets? Kluwer Law International, Alphen aan den Rijn

Prosser T (1986) Nationalised industries and public control. Basil Blackwell, Oxford & New York

Prosser T (2000) Public service law: privatization's unexpected offspring. Law and Contemporary Problems 63(4):63–82

Prosser T (2001) Regulating public enterprises. Public Law (Aut):505–526

Prosser T (2005) Competition law and public services: from single market to citizenship rights. European Public Law 11(4):543–563

Prosser T (2005) The limits of competition law: markets and public services. Oxford University Press, Oxford

Ranganathan K and Dey R (1996) Redirecting mail: postal sector reform. Private Sector Development Department of the World Bank, in Collaboration with Universal Postal Union, August. http://documents.worldbank.org/curated/en/1998/06/693346/redirecting-mail-postal-sector-reform

Rapp L (1996) Public service or universal service? Telecommunications Policy 20(6):391–397

Rawnsley D, Lazar N (1999) Managing the universal service obligation. In: Crew MA, Kleindorfer PR (eds) Emerging competition in postal and delivery services. Kluwer Academic Publishers, Boston, MA

Reay I (1997) The structure of postal markets. In: Crew MA, Kleindorfer PR (eds) Emerging competition in postal and delivery services. Kluwer Academic Publishers, Boston

Regan B (2008) Ushering universal service reform: politically feasible legislative principles. Common Law Conspectus 16(2):741–502

Reiss DR (2011) No innocents here: using litigation to fight against the costs of universal service in France. Creighton International and Comparative Law Journal 1(1):5–29

Reynolds-Feighan A (1995) European air transport public service obligations: a periodic review. Fiscal Studies 16(1):58–74

Robinson H (1953) Britain's post office: a history of development from the beginnings to the present day. Oxford University Press, Oxford

Rodger B (2008) Article 234 and competition law – an analysis. Wolters Kluwer. Alphen aan den Rijn

Rodrigues S (2009) Towards a general framework instrument related to SGEI? Political considerations and legal constraints. In: Krajewski M, Neergaard U (eds) The changing legal framework for services of general interest in Europe: between competition and solidarity. T.M. C. Asser Press, The Hague

Ross M (2000) Article 16 EC and service of general interest: from derogation to obligation. European Law Review 25(1):22–38

Ross M (2004) The Europeanization of public services supervision: harnessing competition and citizenship? Yearbook of European Law 23(1):303–319

Ross M (2007) Promoting solidarity: from public services to a European model of competition? Common Market Law Review 44(4):1057–1080

Ross M (2009a) A healthy approach to services of general economic interest? The BUPA judgment of the court of first instance. European Law Review 34(1):127–140

Ross M (2009b) The value of solidarity in European public services law. In: Krajewski M, Neergaard U, Van de Gronden J (eds) The changing legal framework for services of general interest in Europe: between competition and solidarity. T.M.C. Asser Press, The Hague, pp 81–99

Ross M (2010) Solidarity – a new constitutional paradigm for the EU? In: Ross M, Borgmann-Prebil Y (eds) Promoting solidarity in the European Union. Oxford University Press, Oxford

Rott P (2005) A new social contract law for public services? – consequences from regulation of services of general economic interest in the EC. European Review of Contract Law 1(3):323–345

Rott P (2007) Consumer and Services of general interest: is EC consumer law the future. Journal of Consumer Policy 30(1):49–60

Saltman RB, Figueras J (eds) (1997) European health care reform: analysis of current strategies. WHO Regional Publications, European Series, No. 72

Sauter W, Van de Gronden J (2011) State aid, services of general economic interest and universal service in healthcare. European Competition Law Review 32(12):615–620

Sauter W (1998) Universal service obligations and the emergence of citizens' rights in European telecommunications liberalization. In: Freedland M, Sciarra S (eds) Public services and citizenship in European law: public and labour law perspectives. Oxford University Press, Oxford, pp 117–143

Sauter W (1999) Competition law and industrial policy in the EU. Clarendon Press, Oxford

Sauter W (2008) Services of general economic interest and universal service in EU Law. European Law Review 33(2):167–202

Sauter W (2010) Services of general economic interest (SGEI) and universal service obligations (USO) as an EU Law framework for curative health care. In: Nickel R (ed) Conflict of laws and laws of conflict in Europe and beyond: patterns of supranational and transnational juridification. Intersentia Publishing, Antwerp

Sauter W (2011) Harmonisation in healthcare: the EU patients' rights directive

Sauter W (2012) The Altmark Package Mark II: new rules for state aid and the compensation of services of general economic interest. European Competition Law Review 33(7):307–313

Sauter W (2013a) Proportionality in EU law: a balancing act? Cambridge Yearbook of European Legal Studies 15:439–466

Sauter W (2013b) Proportionality in EU law: a balancing act? TILEC Discussion Paper No. 2013–003, 25 January 2013. http://ssrn.com/abstract=2208467

Sauter W (2013c) The impact of EU competition law on national healthcare systems. European Law Review 38(4):457–478

Sawhney H (1994) Universal service: prosaic motives and great ideals. Journal of Broadcasting & Electronic Media 38(4):375–396

Schweitzer H (2011) Service of general economic interest: European Law's impact on the role of markets and of member states. In Cremona M (ed) Market integration and public services in the European Union. Oxford University Press, Oxford

Schwintowski HP (2003) The common good, public subsistence and the functions of public undertakings in the European internal market. European Business Organisation Law Review 4 (3):353–382

Scott C (2000) Services of general interest in EC Law: matching values to regulatory technique in the public and privatised sectors. European Law Journal 6(4):310–325

Senden L (2004) Soft law in European community law. Hart Publishing, Oxford

Simmonds G (2003) Universal and public service obligations in Europe. Consumer representation in Europe policy and practice for utilities and network industries, Research Report 15. http://www.bath.ac.uk/management/cri/pubpdf/Research_Reports/15_Simmonds.pdf

Sinnaeve A (2003) State financing of public services: the court's dilemma in the Altmark case. European State Aid Law Quarterly 2(3):351–364

Slot PJ, Skudder A (2001) Common features of community law regulation in the network-bound sectors. Common Market Law Review 38(1):87–129

Slot VP, Hancher L (1990) Article 90. European Competition Law Review 11(1):35–39

Smith MP (2005) States of Liberalization: redefining the public sector in integrated Europe. State University of New York Press, Albany

Smith RC (2005) Public service broadcasting in the European Union: no longer simply a matter of domestic concern. Hong Kong Media Digest 3(9):0–13.

Sole D (2003) Services of general economic interest in the EU: a 50-year-battle between liberalization, deregulation and subsidiarity. European Journal of Law Reform 5(3–4):335–341

Somek A (2007) Solidarity decomposed: being and time in European citizenship. European Law Review 32(6):787–818

Soriano LM (2003) How proportionate should anti-competitive state intervention be? European Law Review 28(1):112–123

Steinfield CW, Bauer JM, Caby L (1993) Telecommunications in transition: policies, services and technologies in the European Community. SAGE Publications, Thousand Oaks

Stewart J, Walsh K (1992) Change in the management of public services. Public Administration 70 (4):499–518

Szyszczak E (2001) Public service provision in competitive markets. Yearbook of European Law 20(1):35–77

Szyszczak E (2007) The regulation of the state in competitive markets in the EU. Hart Publishing, Oxford

Szyszczak E (2009) Modernising healthcare: pilgrimage for the Holy Grail? In: Krajewski M, Neergaard U, Van de Gronden J (eds) The changing legal framework for services of general interest in Europe: between competition and solidarity. T.M.C. Asser Press, The Hague, pp 191–213

Szyszczak E (2011) Building a socioeconomic constitution: a fantastic object. Fordham International Law Journal 35(5):1364–1395

Tanzi V (1997) The changing role of the state in the economy: a historical perspective. IMF Working Paper, WP/97/114. www.imf.org/external/pubs/ft/wp/wp97114.pdf

Thatcher M (1999) The national politics of European Regulation: institutional reform in telecommunications. the 6th Biennial Conference of the European Union Studies Association, Pittsburgh June 1999. http://aei.pitt.edu/2401/1/002904_1.PDF

Tigchelaar N (2003) State aid to public broadcasting – Revisited. European State Aid Law Quarterly 2(2):169–182

Tosics N, Gaál N (2007), Public procurement and state aid control – the issue of economic advantage. Competition Policy Newsletter (3):15–18

Travers N (2003) Public service obligations and state aid: is all really clear after Altmark. European State Aid Law Quarterly 2(3):387–393

Van Cuilenburg J, McQuail D (2003) Media policy paradigm shifts: towards a new communications policy paradigm. European Journal of Communication 18(2):181–207

Van de Gronden JW (2008) Cross-border health care in the EU and the organisation of the national health care systems of the member states: the dynamics resulting from the European Court of Justice's decisions on free movement and competition law. Wisconsin International Law Journal 26(3):705–760

Van de Gronden JW (2009) Financing health care in EU law: do the European state aid rules write out an effective prescription for integrating competition law with health care? The Competition Law Review 6(1):5–29

Van De Velde DM (1999) Organisational forms and entrepreneurship in public transport: classifying organisational forms. Transport Policy 6(3):147–157

Van De Velde DM (2001) The evolution of organisational forms in European public transport. 7th Conference on Competition and Ownership in Land Passenger Transport, Molde (Norway), 25–28 June 2001). http://thredbo.econ.usyd.edu.au/downloads/thredbo7_papers/thredbo7-workshopE-Velde.pdf

Van De Velde DM (2008) A new regulation for the European public transport. Research in Transportation Economics 22(1):78–84

Van De Walle S (2008) What services are public? What aspects of performance are to be ranked? The case of "service of general interest". International Public Management Journal 11(3):256–274

Van Den Bossche AM, Coppieters S (1999) Service of general interest: a challenge for European economic integration. In: Meeusen W (ed) Economic policy in the European Union: current perspectives. Edward Elgar Publishing Ltd, Cheltenham

Van Der Horst M (2005) Postal liberalization in the EU: a small step in weights, a giant leap for the market. In: Crew MA, Kleindorfer PR (eds) Regulatory and economic challenges in the postal and delivery sector. Kluwer Academic Publishers, New York

Van Der Woude M (1991) State intervention: Article 90: competing for competence. European Law Review Supp (Competition Law Checklist):60–80

Verhoest P (2000) The myth of universal service: hermeneutic considerations and political recommendations. Media Culture & Society 22(5):595–610

Viegas JM (1999) Public transport in the sustainable urban transport policy package: taking an integral policy approach. Prepared for the ECMT/OECD Workshop on Implementing Strategies to Improve Public Transport for Sustainable Urban Travel, Athens, Greece, 3–4 June 1999. http://www.kas.de/upload/dokumente/megacities/sustainable_urban_transport.pdf

Vogel S (1998) Freer markets, more rules: regulatory reform in advanced industrial countries. Cornell University Press, New York

Von Danwitz T (2002) The new directive on the further liberalization of postal markets in Europe. In: Crew MA, Kleindorfer PR (eds) Postal and delivery services: delivering on competition. Springer, Boston

Walsh K (1995) Public services and market mechanisms: competition, contracting and the new public management. Palgrave Macmillan, London

West LS (1996) Deregulating telecommunications: the conflict between competition and universal service. DePaul Business Law Journal 9(1):159–188

WIK-Consult (2011) Universal postal service and competition: experience from Europe. Study for TNT Post UK. http://www.wik-consult.com/uploads/media/Universal_Postal_Service.pdf

Williams G (2005) European experience with direct subsidization of air services. Public Money and Management 25(3):155–161

Williams G, Pagliari R (2004) A comparative analysis of the application and use of public service obligations in air transport within the EU. Transport Policy 11(1):55–66

Winter C (1951) Parliamentary, ministerial, and judicial control of nationalized Industries in Great Britain. Law and Contemporary Problems 16(4):670–701

Winterstein A (1999) Nailing the jellyfish: social security and competition law. European Competition Law Review 20(6):324–333

Wu T (2007) A brief history of American telecommunications regulation. http://ssrn.com/abstract=965860

Yábar PC (2012) State aid in broadband infrastructures. Staff working paper, joint assistance to support projects in European regions. http://www.jaspersnetwork.org/download/attachments/4947983/State%20Aid%20Broadband_Guidelines.pdf?version=1&modificationDate=1366385314000&api=v2

Yergin D, Stanislaw J (1998) The commanding heights: the battle between government and the marketplace that is remaking the modern world. Simon & Schuster Ltd, New York

Young M (2005) The Future of universal service: does it have one? International Journal of Law and Information Technology 13(2):188–205

Zepos CJ (1992) Liberalizing the "sacred cows": telecommunications and postal services in the EC. Duke Journal of Comparative & International Law 3(1):203–234

Zevgolis NE (2012) Anti-competitive conduct from public or privileged enterprises: towards a per se abuse of dominant position? Applicability of the provision of TFEU Article by national competition authorities. European Competition Law Review 33(2):84–90

Index

L. Zhu, *Services of General Economic Interest in EU Competition Law*,
Legal Issues of Services of General Interest,
https://doi.org/10.1007/978-94-6265-387-0

The manufacturer's authorised representative in the EU is Springer Nature Customer Service Centre GmbH, Europaplatz 3, 69115 Heidelberg, Germany. If you have any concerns regarding our products, please contact ProductSafety@springernature.com

Printed and bound by CPI Group (UK) Ltd, Croydon, CR0 4YY
05/10/2026
02228120-0012